Race, Colonialism, and Social Transformation
in Latin America and the Caribbean

UNIVERSITY PRESS OF FLORIDA

Florida A&M University, Tallahassee
Florida Atlantic University, Boca Raton
Florida Gulf Coast University, Ft. Myers
Florida International University, Miami
Florida State University, Tallahassee
New College of Florida, Sarasota
University of Central Florida, Orlando
University of Florida, Gainesville
University of North Florida, Jacksonville
University of South Florida, Tampa
University of West Florida, Pensacola

Race, Colonialism, and Social Transformation in Latin America and the Caribbean

EDITED BY JEROME BRANCHE

University Press of Florida
Gainesville/Tallahassee/Tampa/Boca Raton
Pensacola/Orlando/Miami/Jacksonville/Ft. Myers/Sarasota

First cloth printing, 2008
First paperback printing, 2019

24 23 22 21 20 19   6 5 4 3 2 1

Library of Congress Cataloging-in-Publication Data
Race, colonialism, and social transformation in Latin America and the Caribbean/
edited by Jerome Branche.
p. cm.
Includes index.
ISBN 978-0-8130-3264-1 (cloth : alk. paper)
ISBN 978-0-8130-6423-9 (pbk.)
1. Latin America—Race relations. 2. Caribbean Area—Race relations. 3. National
characteristics, Latin American. 4. National characteristics, Caribbean. 5. Social
change—Latin America. 6. Social change—Caribbean Area. I. Branche, Jerome.
F1419.A1R35 2008
305.800989–dc22   2008025008

The University Press of Florida is the scholarly publishing agency for the State University System of Florida, comprising Florida A&M University, Florida Atlantic University,
Florida Gulf Coast University, Florida International University, Florida State University,
New College of Florida, University of Central Florida, University of Florida, University
of North Florida, University of South Florida, and University of West Florida.

University Press of Florida
2046 NE Waldo Road
Suite 2100
Gainesville, FL 32609
http://upress.ufl.edu

Contents

Illustrations

Acknowledgments

This volume represents the results of a collective effort. My first debt of gratitude therefore is to the contributors for offering the fruits of their intellectual labor and for responding so cordially to my own editorial requests and to those of the anonymous readers. No less deserving of thanks are the outside readers themselves for their patience in reading and rereading the manuscript and for their pointed and ultimately very helpful observations and recommendations. I thank also the editorial team at the University Press of Florida: Amy Gorelick in Acquisitions for accepting the initial proposal and for her patience as the challenges of working with ten contributors on three continents began to make themselves felt; the project editor, Jacqueline Kinghorn Brown, for shepherding the book from start to finish; and copy editors Christine Sweeney and Catherine-Nevil Parker for their assistance in working through the prose and the stylistic idiosyncrasies of a manuscript that included not only translations but also writers from disparate disciplinary backgrounds.

Introduction

JEROME BRANCHE

In a recent work on race and ethnicity in Latin America, Peter Wade alerted readers to a "deep-seated divide" in the study of blacks and Indians in the region and suggested that bringing both groups under the same theoretical perspective would highlight valuable contrasts and similarities between them (Wade 1997, 25). His recommendation is an important one, especially considering the foundational role of the idea of race in the theoretical and philosophical configurations of modernity, and more specifically, its deployment as a mechanism of social control over the formerly colonized populations of the Americas, Africa, and Asia (Winant 2001, Quijano 2000). To the degree that a recuperation of these similarities in particular might be articulated, they might profitably be harnessed in the service of a necessary counterdiscursive politics that would seek to unsettle the racial regimen produced by the duo of capitalism and coloniality and vindicate the essential humanity of its victims, whether at the level of the individual, the local community, or the state. If the region's racial taxonomy, as a product of and complement to the subjugation and enslavement of early colonialism, served as a temporal and material platform for naturalizing the inferiority of the two groups in Latin America, inexorably the elite *criollo/mestizo* project of *latinidad* elaborated in the postindependence, statist phase of the continent exacerbated their marginalization (Branche 2006, Mignolo 2005). Local assimilationist regimes of coloniality, reified under the stimulus of nineteenth-century scientific racism, would subsequently be reflected in the globalized racial hierarchy of the twentieth century and the precept of (first-, second-, and third-) worlding and north/south division.

It was Marx who famously pointed out the "untold suffering by Africans and American Indians" in the early acceleration of the capitalist engine under the colonialist impulse (quoted in Rodney 1982, 83). The apocalyptic moment of rupture, known as the *maafa* in Swahili and as the *pachacuti* in the Andean vernacular, marked the end of civilization as they knew it for the indigenous peoples of the Anahuac, Tawantinsuyu, Abya Yala, and of the wider geography of the newly minted "América."[1] The same fate befell the natives of West and East Africa and the interior areas of the continent because they could not escape the tentacles of the European slave traders and of subsequent colonial penetration and depredation. Part of the emerging world system of politico-racial dominance, the *maafa/pachacuti* has marked the colonial divide for the African and Amerindian worlds, and the unending crisis for its victimized millions simultaneously persuaded and coerced into a perspective that held their subordination as victims, to be natural and not naturalized, divinely ordained and not manmade. Indeed, the racialized regimen of coloniality, while *creating* a difference between the new categories of *negro* and *indio* in its variegated taxonomy, simultaneously *erased* that difference to the degree that it identified both groups as sources of labor and fodder for colonial production, and as inferior others under the white supremacist will to power.

The theoretical underpinnings of Walter Rodney's *How Europe Underdeveloped Africa* offer a supremely useful appreciation of this point in that they stress the idea of the *underdeveloped* (block, nation-state, individual) not as an ontological given, but as the result of a structured and calculated process of domination, exploitation, and victimization. Locating the source of underdevelopment in fifteenth-century colonialism, slavery, and emergent capitalism, Rodney emphasizes the dialectical relationship between the developed and the underdeveloped, and the interactive process that produced the two. Reflecting Bernal Díaz del Castillo's sense of amazement as the Spanish invaders gazed upon Tenochtitlán for the first time, Rodney recalls how the Dutch at Benin were also given pause as they first contemplated the ordered streets and buildings of the African city-state, indicating, further, that the intervening centuries between 1444 and 1884 would see genocidal depopulation, economic distortion and technological arrest, disintegration, and regression for Africa, even as the West marched onward to industrialization, material well-being for its citizenry, and ultimately nuclear superpotency. Rodney's postcolonial critique, an essay in early dependency theory, which stressed the abandonment and/or forced displacement of native industries and technologies in parts of Africa and India, and the rise of internal colonization and a local comprador class, was as pertinent for the African societies he cited as they are for other areas of the colonized world, Latin America included. With the ever more glaring contradictions arising from imperialism's current phase of globalization, its interventionism and the subsequent cost to human life and well being, such a perspective offers an invaluable prism for viewing the new peripheralization of the majority of the world's inhabitants (Amin 2004).

A recuperation of black and indigenous agency in the historico-cultural trajectory of Latin America, and from a transracial standpoint, flies in the face of the top down, conquer and divide paradigm upon which Occidentalist domination and the *criollo/mestizo* project of Latin America and Latin Americanism are premised. Emphasizing its transcultural, horizontalist content would make visible solidarian pathways to a politics of emancipation and social transformation in a way that still escapes, perhaps, much of the thinking that occupies itself with the historically necessary decolonial processes in avant-garde Latin Americanism. In this regard it is fair to say that the "Our America" precept, strategically articulated in the late nineteenth century by Cuba's José Martí as a term of difference vis-à-vis the U.S. hegemon and as part of a politics of broad national and regional inclusiveness, died a premature death, like its progenitor. Its more radical dimension, that which promised to fulfill the older egalitarian Enlightenment premises, fell prey to the racial conservatism and indecision of criollo nationalists of various stripes in the decades that followed, not least among whom figure such icons as Peru's José Mariátegui, Mexico's José Vasconcelos, and Brazil's Gilberto Freyre (see Laurence Prescott in this volume). In fact, it would not be until almost a century later, at the end of the nineteen hundreds, that new national constitutions would emerge, acknowledging the pluricultural and multiethnic make up of the region's populations and holding forth perspectives for the change for which the multiple social agents behind it, primarily the racial and social subalterns themselves, had striven.

To get back to the importance of the historical similarities mentioned by Wade above, it is by no means insignificant that some of the more emblematic moments of anticolonial insurgency were marked by black and Indian collaboration, even if the colonial racial regime that emerged was based on the divide and rule premise,[2] or if dominant discourse surrounding "the anticolonial" is located in the nineteenth-century independence movement and peopled with *criollo/mestizo* heroes and their deeds. As early as 1503, however, in the then colony of Hispaniola, escaped Africans, subsequently to be called maroons, supported an indigenous rebellion that shook the colonial confidence to the degree that Governor Nicolás Ovando would call for a cessation of imports of blacks. Scant decades later, in 1553, the insurgent Miguel would establish a short-lived settlement in the mountains near Barquisimeto in the Venezuelan Northeast, which sheltered both black escapees as well as Indians, confirming thereby an understudied transracial dimension to the intrinsic anticoloniality of the maroon initiative, which would repeat itself at various times and places in the continent. Similarly, in 1780, the insurgency of the Inca Tupac Amaru II in the Andes counted on the important contributions of black strategists and advisors, projecting a different sense of liberty, equality, and fraternity than that of the French revolution, which would follow shortly thereafter. An expanded history "from below" would therefore vindicate these moments when liberation was the common goal of subordinated Indians and blacks working together, and the past and present political trajectories instantiated by Afro-indigenous (*zambo*) groups such as Brazil's *mamelucos*, the Miskito of Nicaragua, or the Garífuna of Central America (see Whitten 2007). Correspondingly, discrete cultural productions of the twentieth century, such as *negrismo* and *indigenismo*, sanctioned by the *criollo/mestizo* state, even when not origi- nated by its agents, might recapture their implied or submerged political content and free them of their folkloric and exotic packaging.[3]

Afro-indigenous transcultural intercourse in Latin America is clearly not limited to its submerged political potentiality or to its most visible dimen- sion, the biological. It is readily evinced in the cultural, religious, and social life of the region, whether in Mesoamerica, Brazil, or the Andes, and in spite of the repeated royal edicts that sought to impose separate "republics" or of the racial hostilities generated by the colonial order. It was, for example, the mixture of African pharmacopoeia and pre-Colombian herbal medicines as well as ancestral Indian and African rubrics of divination that marked the trajectory of (San) Marín de Porras from healer to saint in seventeenth- century Lima. Similarly, in the wake of the depopulation of the central and southern Peruvian coast in the sixteenth century, and the corresponding decline in the cult to Pachacamac, the most important traditional deity of the Yunga Indians, the formerly enslaved Africans and their descendants took over as the primary preservers of the cult. The Señor de Pachacamilla, otherwise known as the Señor de los Milagros, or the Señor Negro, has now become a feature of the broader national patrimony and permanent evidence of horizontal transcultural movement in Peru.

The well-known instances of Afro-Creole influence in Andean religious dance and ritual are likewise enhanced by the singular phenomenon of the Qapaq Negro, performed in the Peruvian city of Chichenro among a mainly indigenous population, in which performers in chains and black body paint re-enact the drama of enslavement.[4] As a relatively unknown feature of Afro-diasporic cultural contact, Peruvian versions of "blackface" (the Negritos de Huanuco dance is a similar custom), differ diametrically from the aestheticized rejection of racial otherness that characterized the incorporation of blacks into the national imaginary of Renaissance Spain or the United States.[5]

One of the more remarkable episodes of indigenous and Afro-Creole symbiosis, however, is to be found in the Afro-Creole populations of the Bolivian province of Yungas. These Afro-Creoles speak Aymara and cultivate the coca leaf just as the surrounding indigenous populations do, even as they seek to preserve and rediscover their African cultural heritage.[6] The history of enslaved Africans in Bolivia's Potosí mines during the colonial period and their subsequent unpaid input as *pongos* (again like the Indians) in the feudal regimen in Bolivia that persisted into the twentieth century speak to an Afro-Indian commonality that reminds us that the extraction of labor was coloniality's primary motive force, and its raciological machinations a secondary, if equally turbulent, premise.[7]

The present volume, then, is a contribution to the construction of an alternative, emancipatory discursivity, which would probe—whether from an Afro-Creole perspective, an indigenous perspective, or an integrationist perspective that would combine the two points of view (José Rabasa's idea of plural-world dwelling seems a particularly fertile point of departure for an analysis of the Afro-indigenous dynamic)—the multiple registers offered by a horizontalist premise for the analysis of the region. It is organized around three interrelated concepts. The first part, "Coloniality as Legacy," explores some of colonialism's complex aftereffects, taking struggles in Uruguay, Haiti, Puerto Rico, and Brazil as its points of departure. In the second part, "Facets of the Insurgent," the focus is on the Zapatista rebellion in Mexico and the more recent ascendancy of Evo Morales's Movement towards Socialism (MAS) with all its underlying neo-indigenist content, to state power in Bolivia. The final part, "Signifying Subalterns," groups together noncanonical, counterinstitutional voices from Bolivia, the French Antilles, Colombia, and Ecuador, whose common objective is to unsettle the received knowledges that buttress(ed) colonial power, and by *their* use of the Word take one step more toward liberation.

The chapters themselves cover a wide epistemological and disciplinary spectrum. They derive from the Cultural Studies Symposium that has been held biennially at the University of Pittsburgh and hosted by the Department of Hispanic Languages and Literatures since 1998. More specifically, they have their origin in presentations at the meeting held in 2004. Accordingly, their common objective is contestatory vis-à-vis dominant Latin American narratives, as they advance new paradigms not only for reading, but also resolving the ubiquitous interlacing legacies of capital, coloniality, and race in the region, whether from the standpoint of pedagogy, philosophy, anthropology, sociology, history, or literary criticism.

Gustavo Verdesio's initial chapter recounts the burgeoning attempt to recover Amerindianness by several indigenous and indigenous-oriented organizations in Uruguay, and the confrontation of the mobile, "not-modern" Mbya-Guarani (to use a term by José Rabasa in this volume), with the geographical national boundaries of Uruguay, Argentina, and Brazil. Verdesio's discussion highlights the perennial (millennial) search by the Mbya-Guarani for the "Land without Evil," and his focus on their marginality invokes the larger North/South diasporic movement of the formerly colonized as they too seek a "better life" elsewhere, even as it raises the pertinent question as to the appropriateness of the modern state as a vehicle for human development in its widest sense. Carolle Charles's essay, which follows, offers an interesting counterpoint to Verdesio's study. The Mbya-Guarani may be regarded as "not belonging to" the states they traverse, and their corresponding liminality and diminution may be considered a distant legacy of the Encounter (they have now practically disappeared from Uruguay). In contrast, Haiti, the national state and homeland won by the blood, sweat, and tears of masses of formerly enslaved Africans, and the first nation in the hemisphere to declare universal rights of citizenship to all of its people, lives an unending limbo of underdevelopment, with a poverty index measured perhaps most graphically by the lengths taken by its citizens to escape the homeland to other regional or distant destinations. Haiti besides, provides the enigmatic example of black racial pride, won in its revolutionary war for independence, and of the corruption of racial pride, as Charles's discussion of the Duvalier dictatorship points out.

Kelvin Santiago-Valles's essay on the colonial nostalgia expressed by the Puerto Rican intellectual elite of the 1930s puts that particular discourse in a wider, global perspective. The nineteenth-century subtext of eugenics that fed *criollo/mestizo* nationalist discourse in Latin America at the turn of the century found an avenue not only in the social-science scholarship of the island, but more noticeably in Puerto Rican literature surrounding the black presence: its *poesía negrista*. The epistemic violence that characterized the genre stands in marked contrast to the declarations of the island's more liberal spokespersons who would minimize the importance of quotidian racial (white to black) interpellations, described in the words of one writer as of an "innocent game of children" (Blanco 1940, 4). If the "innocence" professed by *criollo/mestizo* writers on the interracial dynamic is evidence of the desensitization brought on by the regime of racialized domination, it is also evidence of the way in which such desensitization has been rendered invisible and stands in corresponding need of disarticulation and exposure. Part of this task is undertaken by Gislene Aparecida dos Santos as her chapter first of all speaks of racism in Brazil as a complex psychological process of self-induced "masking," whereby racists refuse to acknowledge the extent and prevalence of prejudice, and where even their victims often withdraw in denial from its specter. Her study of the attitudes of high school seniors toward affirmative action as a means of access to tertiary education highlights the identitarian ambivalence and doubt that characterizes Brazil's racial taxonomy. Significantly also, it underscores the traditional link between higher education, *criollo/mestizo* racial privilege, and politico-economic power.

In the second part of the book, José Rabasa offers an interesting twist on the Du Boisian notion of "double consciousness" in describing what he calls the multitemporal present of indigenous life forms in Mexico, as evinced in various groups' ability to accommodate their ancestral notions of temporality to the imposed Occidental cognitive and temporal mapping that came with colonialism. Rabasa offers two fascinating points of departure for this analysis. An indigenous post-invasion ability to "dwell in plural worlds" is first seen in the *tlacuilo* or mapmaker's double coding that is embedded in a map of Cholula from 1581, which allows a reading of the precolonial cityscape beyond and within the European-coded images that represent the geography of the (new) colonial city. He finds a similar sense of historical immanence in what he calls the "revolutionary spirituality" of the Las Abejas pacifist organization of Chiapas, Mexico, and in the declarations of the Zapatista National Liberation Army (EZLN). Testimonials from all three sources defy the narrow universalism of the Occidental colonizing mission, and through practical invocations of an ancestral indigenous outlook and discursivity they establish a doubleness or a sense of plural-world dwelling, which Rabasa sees as a source of political optimism, rather than of colonial contradiction and defeatism. Effectively it is the reinvoked presence of the past that has functioned in a powerful way in the Bolivian cycle of insurgency, leading to the election of its first indigenous president, which Denise Arnold's essay addresses. The practically unprecedented popular-ethnic protagonism of Bolivia's indigenous masses is certainly a watershed moment in the recent history of the country and indeed the region. The historical task of the Constituent Assembly that she discusses and the challenge of rearticulating the relationship between cartography, land tenure and the sources of politico-economic domination, and the assimilationism of recent *criollo-mestizo* policies of "multiculturality" or "interculturality" have made Bolivia the center of attention in the ongoing quest for social justice in Latin America.

If education for assimilation, the erasure of alterity, and the denial of literacy to the subjected populations were a political constant of coloniality, the recuperation of the Word and the vindication of the precolonial past turned out to be key features of postcolonial protest and critique in the twentieth century and into the present. In the final part of the book, various registers of the colonial grand narrative are directly and indirectly engaged. Marcia Stephenson documents the appropriation of the trope of nativism and savagery in this narrative by the Bolivian indigenous intellectual Fausto Reinaga, who was significantly influenced by the Afro-Caribbean rebel philosophy of Franz Fanon, to explain the quality of outrage that characterizes his writing as, with Reinaga's fellow Bolivian Roberto Choque Canqui, the past is made to yield the historical knowledge needed for empowerment in the present. Colonial historiographers, whose work documented and legitimized colonial expropriation, for example, are placed against living memory and popular oral history regarding the vexing question of land tenure and its recuperation.

In neighboring Ecuador and Colombia, the notion of "writing back" is equally charged as in the cases of the Colombian Manual Zapata Olivella, discussed by Laurence Prescott, and of the Ecuadorians Juan Montalvo and Juan Montaño Escobar, discussed by Michael Handelsman. Zapata Olivella, one of the few Afro-Hispanic creative writers to practice the genre of the essay, confronted the racial bias present in the reflections of his celebrated predecessors, more notably Argentina's Domingo Sarmiento and Mexico's José Vasconcelos, and by embracing and vindicating his own tri-ethnic heritage recast the discussion around identity and diversity in Latin America, underscoring at the same time the elitist tenor of *criollo/mestizo* versions of Latin Americanism and its ultimate complicity with racialized power. A similar trajectory is traced by the Afro-Ecuadorian journalists whom Handelsman studies. As with the present-day discourse of resistance in Bolivia, Montalvo's and Escobar's writings are also situated in a broader constituency inspired in the anticolonial movements of the 1960s and 1970s, and the civil rights struggle in the United States. Their references to Afro-diasporic elements of this struggle reaffirm the broader sense of continuity and solidarity evident in their work and complement their interest in anti-assimilationist ethno-education and social critique in Ecuador. Finally, Adlai Murdoch's chapter on the French Caribbean Overseas Departments of Martinique and Guadeloupe highlights the ongoing contradiction of center/periphery that underlies the presumptive commonality of territory and citizenship in this broader French community. This aspect of the Caribbean struggle for anticolonial difference in the context of the gross materiality of the globalized economy and of the islands' vulnerable economies inevitably affects the contours of the Franco-Antillean quest. It is what is responsible, perhaps, for the French Antillean focus on what one might call the "small view" vindication of the autochthonous, as seen in discussions around *antillanité*, as well as the "large view" poetics of relation, which acknowledge and embrace a broader version of human heterogeneity.

The volume, then, offers a wide spectrum of the varying legacies of colonialism in the region, and the challenges to emancipation and social transformation in an already globalized economic order. The juxtaposition of nomadic indigenous populations in the Southern Cone, the paralysis of Haiti, the region's first republic, the mutations of racial domination in Brazil, and the modernity/non-modernity of considerable sections of its inhabitants, only confirms the complex and discomfiting social inheritance of the past. In the current postdictatorial period, however, the collective mobilization that underlay Bolivia's challenge to neoliberalism must be regarded with optimism.

Finally, if the ubiquitous solemnization and observance of the Columbus quincentenary among the former colonial centers reprised the triumphalism of old, 1992 was also marked by a wave of wide and unprecedented critique, especially considering the spirit and letter of the *United Nations Draft Declaration on the Rights of Indigenous Peoples* that preceded it three years earlier.[8] Undoubtedly, the politics of agitation and contestation that followed, the coalition of international agencies with various national indigenous and Afro-descendant organizations in Latin America, the production of constitutional reforms that for the first time have recognized multiculturalism and pluri-ethnicity as fundamental principles of civil society, and initiatives such as affirmative action and the titling of ancestral indigenous and Afro-descendant lands in the region constitute a new vindicatory imaginary and praxis, with local, transethnic, and international implications. As a result, a term such as *reparaciones* (reparations), given renewed impetus as a result of the deliberations and resolutions of the conference against racism in Durban in 2001, might be taken, like the content and intent of the *United Nations Declaration on the Rights of Indigenous Peoples*, to encompass the healing of the multidimensional harms, both material and epistemic, inflicted upon the victims of coloniality. Active politicization of *reparaciones* might allow us to envision and effect the necessary changes relative to political participation, employment, administration of justice, education, housing, health care, and the right to the preservation of ethno-cultural values in the respective nation-states of the region.[9] It would propose, in other words, a radical racialization of democracy.

Notes

1. See Adorno 1987 for a discussion of *pachacuti*.

2. The role of armed black auxiliaries to the *conquistadores* (enslaved individuals themselves, assimilated initially into the Hispanic intruder from the standpoint of the indigenous peoples) was important in this regard (see Restall 2005). A corresponding deployment of Amerindians as "slave hunters" at varying times and places in the recuperation of black fugitives from slavery was an equally significant aspect of the colonial order.

3. See Moore 1997, for example.

4. See Celestino 2004 for a discussion of this phenomenon.

5. See Fra Molinero 1995 in this regard.

6. See Angola Maconde 2003 for a discussion of Afro-Creoles in Bolivia.

7. By referring to Afro-indigenous cultural symbiosis in Bolivia I by no means mean to deprive those of African descent of their cultural and political particularity, a distinct possibility that emerges from the "two Bolivias" (Indo-Hispanic) premise that is common in even some of the more progressive critical perspectives. Juan Angola Maconde, the president of Fundafro, the Afro-Bolivian Foundation, has observed not without some bitterness that "the Indigenous see us, but don't really appreciate our presence as part of the ethnic tapestry. It will take time before they really consider us a part of the Bolivian nation." Personal e-mail communication, December 28, 2005. On April 9, 2008, the Bolivian National Congress finally recognized Bolivia's *pueblo afrodescendiente* (people of African descent) within the context of the new multiethnic and pluricultural constitution.

8. The draft of the *United Nations Declaration on the Rights of Indigenous Peoples* was finally submitted on September 12, 2007, at the sixty-first session of the General Assembly, for adoption on November 1, 2007. See http://www.un.org/esa/socdev/unpfii/en/declaration.html.

9. See in this regard Antón Sánchez 2007; Ng' weno 2004; and the *United Nations Declaration on the Rights of Indigenous Peoples*.

Works Cited

Adorno, Rolena. 1987. "Notas sobre el estudio de los textos amerindios: El ejemplo del concepto de *Pachacuti*." *Discurso literario* 4.2: 367–75.

Amin, Samir. 2004. *The Liberal Virus: Permanent War and the Americanization of the World*. New York: Monthly Review Press.

Angola Maconde, Juan. 2003. *Raices de un pueblo: Cultura afroboliviana*. La Paz: Producciones Cima.

Antón Sánchez, John. 2007. "Afroecuatorianos: Reparaciones y acciones afirmativas." In *Afroreparaciones: Memorias de la esclavitud y justicia reparativa para negros, afrocolombianos y raizales*, ed. Claudia Mosquera et al., 155–82. Bogotá: Universidad Nacional de Colombia.

Blanco, Tomás. 1940. *El prejuicio racial en Puerto Rico*. San Juan: Editorial Biblioteca de Autores Puertorriqueños.

Branche, Jerome. 2006. *Colonialism and Race in Luso-Hispanic Literature*. Columbia: University of Missouri Press.

Celestino, Olinda. 2004. "Encuentro de los afrodescendientes e indígenas en las alturas andinas." In *Utopía para los excluidos: El multiculturalismo en Africa y América Latina*, ed. Jaime Arocha, 131–58. Bogotá: Facultad de ciencias humanas.

Fra Molinero, Baltasar. 1995. *La imagen de los negros en el teatro del Siglo de Oro*. Mexico City: Siglo Veintuno Editores.

Mignolo, Walter. 2005. *The Idea of Latin America*. Malden, Mass.: Blackwell Publishing.

Moore, Robin D. 1997. *Nationalizing Blackness: Afrocubanismo and Artistic Revolution in Havana, 1920–1940*. Pittsburgh: University of Pittsburgh Press.

Ng'weno, Bettina. 2004. "Autonomy, Self-governance, and the Status of Afro-Colombian Collective Territories." Paper read at the meeting of the Latin American Studies Association, Las Vegas, October.

Quijano, Aníbal. 2000. "Coloniality of Power, Eurocentrism, and Latin America." *Nepantla: Views from South* 1.3: 533–80.

Restall, Matthew. 2005. "Conquistadores negros: Africanos armados en la temprana hispanoamérica." In *Pautas de convivencia étnica en la América Latina colonial (Indios, negros, pardos y esclavos)*, ed. Juan Manuel de la Serna, 19–72. Mexico City: Universidad Nacional Autónoma de México.

Rodney, Walter. 1982. *How Europe Underdeveloped Africa*. Washington, D.C.: Howard University Press.

Wade, Peter. 1997. *Race and Ethnicity in Latin America*. Chicago: Pluto Press.

Whitten, Norman, Jr. 2007. "The Longue Durée of Racial Fixity and the Transformative Conjunctures of Racial Blending." *Journal of Latin American and Caribbean Anthropology* 12.2: 357–83.

Winant, Howard. 2001. *The World Is a Ghetto: Race and Democracy since World War II*. New York: Basic Books.

1

Coloniality as Legacy

1

From Meticulous Oblivion
to Unexpected Return

The Variable Fate of Indigenous People in the Uruguayan Imaginary
of the Nineteenth, Twentieth, and Twenty-First Centuries

GUSTAVO VERDESIO

Unlike other already extinct indigenous groups, the Charrua, who once inhabited what is currently modern-day Uruguay and part of the Argentine coastline, did not perish as a result of forced labor. There was no massive or exploitative agricultural development in the territory they occupied nor was there knowledge of any gold or silver mines at the time. Since they did not inhabit urban centers (unlike other, more prestigious and frequently studied Amerindians, for example, the Andean and Mesoamerican people), the Charrua did not live in concentrated circumstances nor fixed and determinate places, thanks to which they had very little contact with Europeans during the first two centuries of settlement by the latter. As a result, they were not very adversely affected by the new bacteria and viruses brought by the invaders. Their disappearance was the result of a series of actions that began as a great barbecue and ended as a betrayal.

In 1831, one of the first measures taken by the newly independent government of Uruguay was to ambush the few Charrua Indians who still inhabited the territory. Those very same Amerindians had been quite loyal to different leaders during various time periods throughout the long process that brought about what we now call "the independence" of the modern nation-state known as Uruguay. Among the leaders who were "friends of the Indians" was the charismatic Fructuoso Rivera, who at that time was president of the new Republic of Uruguay. Unfortunately, in the opinion of the *criollo* (native-born) elite, capitalism and the notion of private property were incompatible with the lifestyle of the Charrua, who moved freely about the territory in its entirety without requesting permission to set up camp or to remain wherever they pleased. For this reason, Rivera, the first constitutional president of the republic, organized an enormous outdoor picnic with the intention of inviting and then ambushing the Charrua. Once at the barbecue, the Charrua were urged to relinquish their weapons so they might more joyfully partake of the succulent, grilled meat in an atmosphere of peace and relaxation. When they got drunk, Rivera gave the order for his men to start freely and openly killing his guests. Immediately after that, the *criollo* establishment erased this event from memory, resolving to meticulously forget the prolonged massacre it had initiated—in reality a continued process of extermination that lasted for about one year.

Perhaps this tendency to forget an ignominious past can partly explain why neither the colonial period nor indigenous history has been the object of systematic or continuous analysis in Uruguay. After all, it is unpleasant to recall massacres perpetrated by one's ancestors. It is always simpler to try to effect pious and tranquilizing forgetfulness. What is certain, though, is that the debates that took place about the viability of Uruguay as a country among the intellectuals and politicians of the time, among men such as José Pedro Varela and Carlos María Ramírez, during the decade of Colonel Latorre's ascendancy (the 1870s), never included discussions about the Indians who remained in the territory (mostly Guaraní from other bordering countries, particularly Paraguay) after the extermination of the Charrua. In the aforementioned debates, Uruguay is imagined as a European and Western nation free of any indigenous contribution (or of any other non-Western influence, such as an African one).

It must be said of this other minority group, the Afro-Uruguayans, that it has been much harder to forget them, since they can still be found living within the republic's borders and enjoying Uruguayan citizenship, a label that seemingly establishes everyone's equality before the law in Uruguay but still permits and makes possible other kinds of socio-economic inequality, too. Demographic reports differ about the actual number of Afro-Uruguayans who currently live in the country, but it is safe to assume that they are somewhere between 2 percent and 6 percent of the total population. In any case, not being exterminated like the Charrua has not been enough to allow the citizens of these communities to develop their potential with regard to economic, social, and cultural equality, particularly when compared to the rest of the predominantly Europeanized population.

Ironically, the *candombe*, a musical form created and developed by the Afro-Uruguayan community has been adopted as a national musical genre. Over time (for reasons that are too complicated to address here) it has come to interpellate the rest of the Uruguayan population that was earlier described as being primarily of European origin. This interpellation has been very thorough and successful in that in the last few decades it has brought about a total appropriation of *candombe*. The following lines from a popular *candombe* song summarize this idea: "el candombe es de los negros/pero gozan los demás" (*candombe* belongs to black folks/but others enjoy it). The process by which this Afro-Uruguayan form was appropriated is mirrored in a recent but equally overwhelming tendency to appropriate indigenous traditions, or what people think they are—or were.

Let us return to the erratic itinerary of indigenous people in the Uruguayan imaginary. As previously mentioned, not only have those in the political elite ignored their presence or cultural legacy, but the situation in historiography is not much better. It is not an exaggeration to say that there is scarcely any serious academic work done on the indigenous past (more specifically the pre-Columbian era). Such has been the case up to at least a few decades ago and even those attempts lacked intellectual rigor. What I mean by this is that research about pre-Columbian Indians was (and still is for the most part) based fundamentally on prejudices inherited from a colonial past in which the only possible account of the facts and the only descriptions of the Indians were written by colonial chroniclers and those captains and soldiers who took pride in calling themselves "the conquistadors." The same can be said about Indians from the colonial period. Thus, it is not unusual that researchers simply reproduced, with almost no variation, the traces of indigenous images that those Spaniards left as their legacy.[1] Juan Manuel de la Sota, the first historian of the territory of Uruguay, in his book published in 1841, was an example of this practice. His image of the Indians reflects his acceptance of an account in which the Indians who received Juan Díaz de Solís, the discoverer of the region, in 1516, ate him (de la Sota [1841] 1965, 14). Yet this is really based on a myth whose origin is in the earliest chronicles and has enjoyed great success throughout history and is still popular today.[2] The systematic repetition of this narrative in primary schools has encouraged a large portion of the Uruguayan population to imagine this discovery scene as an anthropophagic episode that we cannot even confirm ever happened.[3] But the myth of anthropophagy is not the only tale that de la Sota takes from the colonial chroniclers. He also parrots other value judgments about the character of the region's Indians: he says they are cruel, barbarous, and ferocious (14). He accuses the Charrua, whom he calls "the Spartans of América," of cannibalism and of living in a barbaric state (24).

Sometimes the Indians seem to be seen as a part of nature, like a problematic element in the landscape. Francisco Bauzá, another historian, starts the introduction to his influential book with a depiction of the territory found by the discoverers as a "savage Indian stronghold" (1895, 3). The description that he offers of those inhabitants is well-known: they lived in rustic simplicity and were brave and austere (143); their language was as impoverished as their external appearance (146). Perhaps one of the most interesting aspects of Bauzá's book is that it is the first one in which a Uruguayan historian shows interest in the indigenous inhabitants of the territory before it was discovered by the first explorers. Unlike de la Sota, Bauzá mentions the Indians' mound-building culture, which he compares to those found in North America (131). Naturally, his main motivation for this comparison is the similarity between the mounds built in Uruguay and those found frequently in the United States. According to Bauzá, these architectural forms are evidence of a migration of the original mound builders (from North America) toward Central and South America (132). Thus, he believes these mound builders would have left their mark in Uruguay, too: evidence he believed was only recently being studied, in 1895, when his book was first published (133). The mounds of San Luis, in today's present Departamento of Soriano, cause him to conclude that the Indians who constructed those mounds were part of a much earlier and primitive civilization than the one the discoverers encountered upon their arrival (134).

This idea of representing the Indian mound builders as more primitive than the inhabitants the Spanish found at their initial time of contact is quite different from that generally found throughout the eighteenth and nineteenth centuries in the United States of America. In the United States, many writers considered the mound builders to be a superior race, a human group capable of producing a culture that, judging from other remaining material evidence, could be considered a precursor to (according to some) or a continuation of Western culture. According to Robert Silverberg, it is understandable that the settlers and their descendants rejected the idea of being the inhabitants of a land that had been populated by "naked wandering savages" (1986, 10). Notwithstanding, the westward movement of the settlers across the territory that is now the United States caused the settlers to discover a large number of earth-covered constructions hidden by abundant vegetation, which were interpreted as having been abandoned. For the settlers of the eighteenth and nineteenth centuries, those monuments became the raw material for the creation of myths about the land they ended up inhabiting and exploiting (10). The spectacular nature of some of those mounds caused them to suppose that the constructions had belonged to an extinct ethnic group, since in their Western view of the world the

Amerindians they knew were barbarous and unsophisticated and would have been incapable of erecting such impressive and complex structures as mounds, which require effort and the organization of labor (11). For many writers, this extinct or disappeared ethnic group (the term actually used by the writers is "race") could in no way have been of indigenous origin. On the contrary, this "race" must have been descendants of some Old World civilization such as the Phoenicians, Persians or Israelites, or of many others (5). In the opinion of Silverberg, this refusal to accept that the builders of these monumental structures at which the North American settlers so marveled were Amerindians could have been part of a campaign against Native Americans, who were considered obstacles to the development of Western civilization in North America (117). Roger G. Kennedy is another of those writers who explain the attitude of U.S. researchers who dealt with the subject of the mound builders as part of a Western civilizing or, if one prefers, civilizational project: "Hastily and unrepentantly, Jeffersonians and Jacksonians thrust the Indians aside by means that might be easier on the conscience if those who were displaced were thought to have neither history, art or religion worthy of the respect of the displacers" (1994, 223). In Uruguay in the 1880s, where the very same kind of archaeological work took place with regard to the territory's past and its inhabitants, this type of narrative was not necessary because of the prior elimination of the most populous and bothersome indigenous group in the interest of the nascent republic, as we saw earlier. The territory was already free of obstacles to the Western civilizing project.

In Uruguay of the late nineteenth century there were no proponents of this theory that the Uruguayan mounds (*cerritos*) should be ascribed an Old World origin. One of the period's most conspicuous writers, the aforementioned Bauzá, was not very impressed with the local *cerritos* builders, even to the point that he thought that the civilization of their builders had attained a level lower than that attributed to the Amerindians encountered during the colonial enterprise. One possible explanation that could shed some light on the differing interpretations and evaluations of the builders of the Uruguayan *cerritos* and the North American mound builders is that those mounds that so excited the imagination of the U.S. researchers were produced, above all, by cultures formerly known as the Adena and Hopewell, which according to Silverberg flourished between 800 BC and 500 AD (or 400 BC, according to others, such as Kennedy 1994, 15), and by an emerging Mississippian culture that produced prodigious architectural structures such as Cahokia (an urban center that was constructed starting in approximately the seventh century AD). These cultures of North American origin constructed enormous mounds and very complex and impressive embankments that were in some cases several kilometers long and sometimes reached great heights. In contrast, the Uruguayan *cerritos* look much more like North American structures built during the Archaic period (7000 BC to 1000 BC), which are much less spectacular (with the possible exception of archaeological sites such as Poverty Point in Louisiana) than those such as Cahokia that belong to the Mississippian tradition. North American mounds from the Archaic period did not inspire much enthusiasm among researchers (or the general public). Having been educated in a culture that, like the contemporaneous Uruguayan, one saw indigenous ruins from an evolutionary point of view, they judged only the complexity of the constructions and other material achievements, which prevented them from being able to understand these earth constructions as something that merited their attention or interest. (I would venture to say that this is still the case.)

What is certain is that not only politicians and historians but also practicing archaeologists of this incipient discipline knew to give a negative image to Indians who had inhabited the territory today known as Uruguay. José H. Figueira, an archaeologist (probably the first in Uruguay), said, "No one knows for certain about history prior to the Conquest," for which reason he had no choice but to do as Bauzá did, go back to the colonial chroniclers (1892, 14).

According to Figueira, the Charrua had no laws (1892, 22) and no religion, but they did have a vague notion about nature (25). They used their ideas, spiritual existence, and intellectual capacity almost exclusively to ensure their survival (28). They were also quite resistant to civilizing change, for which reason there were few changes in their lifestyle throughout the entire colonial period (33). "It was necessary to destroy them" to avoid their criminal acts (33). Yet, not only the Charrua appeared as barbarians in Figueira's text. Included in that category were all other indigenous groups who inhabited the north coast of the Río de la Plata. He presented them all as savages and as poor prospects for civilized life (43). This, according to the author, is a typical sign of racial inferiority (43).

This historical view of the Indian is in keeping with the image of a nation in which there was no room for cultures that could not adapt to European civilizing criteria. Institutions and disciplines (experts) worked to justify the territory upon which the nation was developing (Díaz-Andreu and Champion 1996, 3). The nation, then, was the basis and objective for all disciplinary research (3). In this manner, archaeology and the nation go hand in hand and it is at the moment in which the nation becomes consolidated that laws regulating the national patrimony and museum administration begin to appear (6).

One of the reasons the theme of the indigenous is taboo in the Uruguayan national narratives that appear in primary and secondary school texts is that the Indians who populated the territory at the time of the arrival of the Spanish were savagely exterminated, as previously mentioned. Since the crimes of one's ancestors are never one's favorite topic, the story of the extermination of the Amerindians known as the Charrua was avoided as much as possible by historians and educators, as well as by political leaders. This silence has not only left the Indians outside of the national narratives but also erased them from the Uruguayan imaginary for many years.

Thus, up until the 1980s, the image that had been constructed of the nation consisted of an immigrant society that had organized itself around egalitarian, or better yet, homogenizing social structures that had achieved the elimination of any element foreign to Western civilization. This is, in reality, Uruguay after the reforms implemented by José Battle y Ordóñez, who governed the country for two terms at the beginning of the twentieth century. His project was akin to that of a *criollo*-style welfare state, an attempt to forge a nation as a result of and by means of politics (Panizza 1990, 81).

That model country, a defender of democratic institutions, a lover of liberty and human rights, a devotee of *fútbol* (twice an Olympic champion and twice a world champion), and an enthusiast of spending (with its agropecuary economy but with consumer habits like those of an industrialized country), that Mesocratic, self-satisfied country became the victim of a dictatorship (1973) that seriously put into question the democratic precept upon which it was founded. According to Rosario Beisso and José Luis Castagnola, the breakdown of the democratic process produced social traumas at a national level, destroying the feeling of uneventful continuity that rituals tend to offer the societies that practice them (1987, 13). In the opinion of Carina Perelli, the military dictatorship produced a change in the Uruguayan social imaginary because it caused a questioning of the myths that preceded it (1986, 123).

That institutional rupture, the questioning of the propositions that regulated the Uruguayan social imaginary, brought about as a result the uncovering of an event that was usually forgotten: the existence of multiple collective memories (Perelli 1986, 127). It has become harder and harder to deny the multiplicity and fragmentation of the Uruguayan social imaginary (128). This has generated a series of anxieties that are reflected in the appearance of new attempts at constructing identities using nontraditional cultural resources for the new Uruguayan national narrative. As we saw earlier, those in the political class and practitioners of academic disciplines that developed in Uruguay in the second half of the nineteenth century, such as historiography and early archaeology, either ignored the Indians or represented them in a sufficiently pejorative manner so as to prevent even their consideration as an integral part of the national narrative. Nevertheless, after this institutional crisis, which lasted twelve years, there is now an appreciable attempt to recover the image of the Amerindian for these national narratives.

In his book *Artigas y su hijo el Caciquillo*, published in 1991, Carlos Maggi proposes a new explanation for why Uruguayans are different: the key, he says, is in their superior culture—a superior sociability, better ethics, a brotherly view of a community of equals—which the Charrua taught José Gervasio Artigas, the hero of national independence (Giorgi 2000, 47). The main thrust of Maggi's book is the idea that the revolution has roots in Artigas's contact with the Indians (Maggi 1991, 52).[4] In this text, Artigas is transformed into the best of all the Indians (52). This novelty (the Indianizing of none other than Artigas), which makes possible the enthusiastic integration of the indigenous into the national narrative, is possible, in part, because of the new intellectual climate that emerged in Uruguay at the end of the twentieth century. In this current climate, it is no longer taboo to search for the indigenous roots of the present. Instead, it has become something desirable, so much so that in many cases those who look for these indigenous roots end up with an idealized notion of the indigenous roots of the territory. This sort of idealization of the local Indians can be seen most prominently in the work of Danilo Antón, a contemporary author with good intentions but whose errors and idealized notions I have highlighted in another essay, "El retorno del indio olvidado" (The return of the forgotten Indian) (Verdesio 2000–2001).

The return of the Indian to the Uruguayan imaginary has come about at the discursive level, in the books of the aforementioned authors. But it can also be seen in two different types of actions: one, through the creation of various organizations for people of indigenous descent; the other, by the arrival of actual Indians (known as the Mbya-Guaraní) into Uruguay. In 1989, two organizations whose purpose it was to unite people interested in recovering the indigenous past and its traditions came on the scene: La

Asociación de Descendientes de la Nación Charrúa (ADENCH; the Association of the Descendants of the Charrua Nation) and la Asociación Indigenista del Uruguay (AIDU; the Indigenist Association of Uruguay). The objective of the latter organization is to assume the challenge of creating a totally inclusive American reality. The former sees the need to organize all descendants of the Charrua so they might show pride in belonging to this ethnic group (Basini 2001, 44). ADENCH's emphasis is the result of a meeting in which members of the society discussed biogenetic features or identifiers such as fingerprints, in the belief that fingerprints can reveal if someone has a Caucasian, African, or Amerindian origin (45). During the early days of the organization, focus was placed on another phenotypic feature—the Mongolian spot, a specific type of birthmark often found on people of Asian, Native American, black, or Hispanic origin. To appreciate the tenuous nature of the connection between the past and these self-declared descendants of the indigenous group massacred by Rivera, suffice it to say that a good number of people with an indigenous or Asian ancestor have a Mongolian Spot. This means that those members of the organization of Charrua descendants could well be descended from any other indigenous group, assuming that one accepts the infallibility of phenotypic evidence (which is very questionable).

To the ethical and symbolic virtues attributable to the attempt to recuperate the Charrua cultural heritage, I would like to oppose some of the disadvantages I see in the way they are carrying out this endeavor: for example, the total reduction of the many cultural differences of myriad indigenous groups that existed in the past to a group or an entity denominated the Charrua. Even if the overall group called Charrua is an important tool in the recovery of a sentiment, of something that was lacking in the current Uruguayan imaginary, it cannot explain historical fact and the many diverse cultural genealogies that developed in the territory. For example, it cannot explain the enormous demographic and cultural influence of the Guaraní, an element that is lost when we include the group in a wider category, the Charrua, despite the fact that the latter is just one of the Pampa groups that populated the territory that is today known as Uruguay. This is even more problematic when one considers that the Charrua, as has been well documented, were far fewer in number than the Guaraní (see González and Rodríguez Varese 1990; Padrón Favre 1996, 10; and Basini 2000, 14). Furthermore, Diego Bracco has shown recently (1998) that yet another large ethnic group totally absent from the national imaginary, because it has been forgotten by Uruguayan historiography, is the Guenoa or Minuan, who are generally, and erroneously,considered part of (or a faction of, as some experts on indigenous topics in Uruguay prefer to say) the macroethnic Charrua group. To conclude, the definition of race employed by ADENCH at that time was strongly dependent on phenotypic and genotypic features.

The founding of Integrador Nacional de los Descendientes de Indígenas Americanos (INDIA, National Integrator of Indigenous Descendants) in 1998 is the result of a self-evaluation by ADENCH ten years after its inception. It recognized its errors and felt compelled to group "all Indigenous descendants on a national scale, in an inclusive manner and without privileging any of them" (*Cartilla de fundación*, quoted in Basini 2001, 47). It is obvious that INDIA appears much more aware than ADENCH of the cultural diversity that existed in pre-Columbian and colonial times.

The other indigenous presence in Uruguay at the end of the twentieth century is the Mbya-Guaraní, a group whose current total population is just over 14,000, spread out among several countries in the following manner: 8,000 in Paraguay; 3,646 in Argentina; 2,640 in Brazil; and, 20 in Uruguay (Basini 2000, 2). They call themselves differently, the "jeguakáva tenonde porague'i, "which means 'the first chosen who attained feather adornments'" (Cadogan, cited in Basini 2001, 2). For centuries, this group has suffered changes to its lifestyle and culture due to its long pilgrimages throughout the territory of the aforementioned countries, which has caused them to confront a concept of space different from their own (Basini 2000, 2). The Myba-Guaraní have had to develop strategies to differentiate themselves and in that way guarantee their own survival as a group, as a defense against the bipolar logic (of either singling out or homogenizing indigenous groups) of those modern nation-states (2).

The problem that this group has created in the Uruguayan imaginary is understandable: a country that has constructed its identity without Amerindians is now faced with having to deal with the presence of indigenous people in its territory. If we add to this the fact that Uruguay is the only Latin American country that has no legislation with regard to indigenous peoples (Basini 2000, 3), it becomes clear that it is the Mbya-Guaraní who have real difficulties in Uruguay because they have decided to establish themselves there. This is compounded by the fact they do not define the territory by its borders nor see it as a possession but rather as a place in which to circulate (5). Of course, the nation-states in which they circulate, which espouse the notion that their territories are homogeneous and enduring for all the society included in them, do not understand this. These are the very nation-states that are now proposing exclusionary and confining interethnic relations with traditional societies. Not even the anthropologists or indigenists who supposedly support the Native peoples understand this (5). The Mbya-Guaraní claim, in contrast, their right to use appropriate ecological spaces for their agriculture and lifestyle. Yet, in doing so, they do not claim the whole of the territory but rather unrestricted movement through borders invented (because they are not natural) along the nation-states' boundaries (5).

The Mbya-Guaraní who have taken root in Uruguay have to renegotiate constantly their living space with the state, which for its part attempts to assign them space its own way. This constant negotiation has taken many forms (trips to see relatives who live in other nation-states, the creation of myths, adaptation to the ecosystem or terrain of the new place of residence, and so forth) and aims to resolve the epistemological limits the state imposes on them (Basini 2000, 8, passim). These aforementioned national borders are one of the most evident aspects of this conflict. They are an artificial yet tangible barrier the modern nation-state uses as an obstacle to the constant movement of the Mbya-Guaraní. Worse yet is that Western civilization is based in great measure upon legality, on a power and a normative system that requires individuals to behave as citizens. But in that legalistic system one is not a citizen unless one has an identity that is guaranteed by a state-issued document. The fact that the Mbya-Guaraní lack these documents (8) has caused them a series of difficulties for which they have had to find creative solutions. For example, in an interview with Basini a member of the Mbya-Guaraní group who lives in Uruguay told Basini that he had become friends with the border guards in order to be able to cross the border without serious problems. Today they have no need to use this kind of tactic because they have Uruguayan identity documents (called an "I.D. card for foreigners"), which facilitates their presence in the national territory and their frequent trips outside the national borders (9).

The case of these Native people can help us reflect on several topics that are relevant to current political thought and allow us to test the usefulness of certain categories elaborated by first world thinkers (or, if one prefers, those from primary capitalist countries). For example, I am thinking of Gilles Deleuze's and Felix Guattari's concept of the war machine from about two decades ago, in their book *One Thousand Plateaus* ([1980] 1987). In the chapter devoted to considering the possibility of a theory of nomadology, both men developed this category to be able to rethink the state and its others (or its opponents; or its excluded people, as we shall see) both historically and conceptually. Let us begin by considering the possible advantages to seeing the Mbya-Guaraní as a war machine or as nomads. The first thing that becomes obvious is that this group is not nomadic in the strictest sense. That is, while it is true that the Mbya-Guaraní move about, it is also the case that they establish themselves in a particular place for long periods of time and develop connections to the land that shelters them. This is not properly speaking territoriality in a modern or Western sense; it is also not, strictly speaking, a behavior typical of nomads.

Second, it is also obvious that these people do not contradict Deleuze's and Guattari's basic definition of a war machine: their existence predates the state ([1980] 1987, 351–52). In addition, that is, they manifest exteriority, like something that exists outside the state (354). Thus, from the point of view of the state, groups of this kind, who preexist and question by their very existence what we know as the state, can be seen as negativity. But, if one considers them from the point of view of exteriority they appear to be more like a part or incarnation of an alternative nature (354). If these indigenous groups that currently reside in Uruguay are not technically (or, in my view, in any way) nomadic they are most certainly itinerant and move about in such a way that it should be possible for them to avoid or get around the obstacles that the national boundaries of the region's nation-states present for them. It is possible, then, to say that they are opposed to this kind of modern and Western government. It is not that they oppose them in a negative sense (as a totally Western view of this phenomenon would want) but rather in a positive or constitutive way. Their very nature as Native peoples makes them not only anterior to the state but also predisposed to reject it. In other words, their own way of being as a people or a conglomeration of human beings, as societies with distinctive features, causes them to see the state as something to avoid (throughout their discussion of their theory of nomadology Deleuze and Guattari use a term whose English translation is "ward-off") because it is an obstacle to the development of cultural and social continuity of the Mbya-Guaraní people. In a language that today smacks a bit too much of evolutionism, despite the fact that the authors made a conscious and consistent effort to dismantle this Western-oriented cosmovision (see, for example, their carefully constructed arguments on page 430), Deleuze and Guattari say of these "primitive" societies (the quotes are mine) that their goal is to defend themselves from the state and (in fact even) try to keep one from forming (357).

It is in this sense that one might say the Mbya-Guaraní are a war machine: by their own nature, behavior, and existence in the world they are opposed to what we call the state. For this reason I have chosen to use this term freely and in a manner that is even a bit poetic and figurative but that is not in conflict with the way the actual creators of the expression used it in their study about the relationship between the state and other peoples or social formations opposed to it. In the Uruguayan case, it is evident that these indigenous people acted and continue to act as a threat, as a serious questioning of the principles that govern social life within the institutional framework delimited by the state. Their foreignness and exteriority are what constitute this threat. That foreignness is the result of at least two factors or characteristics: their mobility and their identity or self-definition or, as some anthropologists would prefer, their description of themselves as a group. (I am aware that my use of the preceding terms may have essentialist connotations, but I think they are sometimes useful nonetheless.)

Thus, it is not their supposed nomadism (we have already established that their behavior is not nomadic) or their capacity to initiate a state of war between themselves and the state—having never proposed this—that makes it possible for them to be seen or defined as a war machine. No. In this sense, the said Native group has not proposed using war as a weapon against the formation of the state. What might allow us to see this group as a war machine is its exteriority and rejection of the state, which are the elements that constitute its foreignness and threatening potential. In addition, I believe that the unpredictable movements of the Mbya-Guaraní and their refusal to accept dominant notions of territoriality in societies that have been organized on the assumption of the existence of a state also brings them closer to a notion of the war machine that I am freely employing.

Nevertheless, there is another side to this, a force oppositional to that of the cited war machine: the state's attempts to capture the groups that deny its existence or try to avoid it, through their incorporation into the rest of society (Deleuze and Guattari [1980] 1987, 355). In the Uruguayan case, the chosen form of incorporation was, without a doubt, the creation of identity documents and the ceding of land to the Indians. It is precisely at the moment that the state captures the war machine that it manifests its irreducibility (356): the Mbya-Guaraní defend themselves from the state by overcoming or confronting the limitations that the state places on the cultural and social practices that define their way of being Myba-Guaraní. In their search for the land with no evil, those Native people do not escape from the state in the sense that they seek to live outside their legal status or territory. Instead, they try to avoid or circumvent its normalizing attempts by means of a strategy that at first glance seems paradoxical: they violate the state's laws to be able to reside in their territory and to be able to continue with their search for the land with no evil, and they do this while still reproducing some of the distinctive features of what we might call their tradition or ancestral way of living. I believe this is a way one can explain how the violation of a state law that is imposed at the border takes place: the foreigner must enter the territory with a legal document in hand and these Native people have no such documentation. Despite this, they manage to enter by rather unorthodox means such as befriending the border guards, who then turn a blind eye. This is what makes possible the violation of a state law by the Mbya-Guaraní.

It appears that violation is necessary because the search for land with no evil, or of the Kechuita—or Jesuit (José Basini, personal communication, July 2001)—requires stopping in different places within an imagined territory that does not correspond to the state's notions of territoriality. The places they cover are subordinate to the paths outlined by them (as is the case with the nomads about which Deleuze and Guattari wrote) or, if one prefers, to the paths that create these coordinates (380). As we saw, for the Mbya-Guaraní the coordinates they cover are subordinate to a principal path: the one on which the search for the land without evil occurs. The trajectory of these people (who are not nomads but behave like a war machine, as I said earlier) distributes them in open spaces; that is, spaces that are not delimited by borders or other state markers (380). The Indians in question see the space they imagine, cover, cross, and exist in as not delimited by the notion of border. Yet, they cannot prove these demarcation lines do not exist either. That is why their strategies include first recognizing the existence of state law and, second, violating said law, all the while preserving their own view of the world around them. That way the Mbya-Guaraní make their territory increase in size, like nomads do (382), while simultaneously acknowledging that there are other people, and other powers, that see the territory in a different manner. More importantly, they recognize the ability of those people or powers to impose or force the question of territoriality, like it or not. So, when the state attempts to delineate or force a particular territoriality in order to eliminate exteriority (385, 386), it manages in some way to absorb (although not entirely) the itinerants who deny its concept and organization of the territory.

But the war machine is difficult to control because it operates in bands of small numbers of people, which gives them great mobility and flexibility. Thus, it is not always a powerful entity that can jeopardize the state's coercive power; a seemingly powerless entity can, if necessary, avoid the state and in that way undermine its efficiency or absolute nature. This rather modest and unspectacular war machine does not see war as its objective. Its objective is to occupy space (Deleuze and Guattari [1980] 1987, 417), that is, the space that this war machine conceives in a manner different from the state. Actual war only occurs when the war machine clashes with the state, which opposes the war machine's principal objective (417), which is, after all, its raison d'être. What we are dealing with here is a positive objective by a group that does not depend on the existence of the very state it does not need and even ignores until it comes into contact with it and perceives it as an obstacle to fulfilling its positive prime objective. Deleuze and Guattari re-iterate that the war machine's objective is not actually waging war but rather having the freedom to move about in an unrestricted or "smooth" space that is in opposition to or different from the space the state has organized and proposed (422). The reference to that "smooth" space implies that the jour-ney frequently changes direction because of its very nature or because of the variability of the objective that is pursued (478). This is precisely the case with the Amerindians under consideration: their negotiations with the state and concept of space serve for them to preserve their conceptualization of a "smooth" space that will allow them to continue journeying in keeping with their prime objective: the search for a land with no evil, despite the obstacle the borders present for them.[5]

The Mbya-Guaraní, understood as what Giorgio Agamben calls a form-of-life (that is, life that cannot be separated from its form), put their own existence as form-of-life into risk by acting the way they act—existence is what is at stake in the act of living itself, according to Agamben (2000, 3). Yet, the state's political power derives from the separation between the bare life (*nuda vita* in Agamben's original) and actual forms-of-life (2000, 4), that is, the context of incarnate life, which is inseparable from its form hence the conflict between this human group and the states through which it has to pass in pursuit of the land with no evil- that is, in pursuit of its positive objective.. This conflict can be seen as a relationship between bare life, citi-zens, and human beings (Agamben uses the term "man") who temporarily adorn or imbue it at its core with the issue of their rights. Because the state projects on to or sees bare life as citizenship or humanity, the Uruguayan state attempts to confer upon the Mbya-Guaraní rights by granting them documents that would allow them to become if not citizens at least legal inhabitants of the nation. With their arrival in a territory controlled by the Uruguayan state, they are just "nobodies" (Agamben used the term "qua-lunque," translated as "whatever" in the English version of his book, *The Coming Community*), since from the point of view of state law they had no identity. Thus, in the act of conferring upon them an identity, by giving them documents that recognize it, the state is concomitantly making them disappear as human beings while making them citizens (2000, 21). That is, the state causes them to lose their specificity as human beings (which they are not perceived as being by those who prior to giving them documents saw them as "nobodies") and confers upon them an identity as citizens or, at least, as foreigners or legal residents. In doing so, the state is engaging in a dehumanizing maneuver motivated by a legal system and worldview that seeks to divide and organize any war machine that has infiltrated or threatened its space.

According to Agamben, in today's world there will always be more and more human beings that are not representable within the framework of nation-states (2000, 21). The Mbya-Guaraní are just one more example, but their case is illustrative and deserves our attention because it reveals a possible limit to the Western concept of the nation-state and allows us to rethink the relationship between the powers that control our lives and whatever war machines might somewhere appear, which in turn tests or questions a model we see as natural. These Indians do not want to be Uruguayan (or Paraguayan, Brazilian, or Argentine, despite the fact they reside in the territories of these countries). On the contrary, the purpose of their movement through nation-states is to reaffirm their worldview and their lifestyle: they must transact with the states that are both obstacles and homes to them. In this sense, the Mbya-Guaraní share characteristics with Agamben's definition of refugees: they do not want to be citizens of the countries that offer them shelter, but they do not want to return to the place where they come from either (2000, 23). Their objective is, as we saw, to make possible and continue being who they believe they are.

There is one question that arises out of all of this: What comes out of these negotiations between the Indians and the state's legality? What do they gain or lose by them? There are probably no clear or definitive answers to these questions, but it does seem evident that they gain something. It would be important to see how high a price they are paying to gain those benefits or results. Something else that emerges from an analysis of this case is that the war machine's successful attempts to avoid or mock the state are both a confirmation of the existence of states, that they are alive and functional, and of their retention of a great deal of power not only over their citizens but also over all those who deal with the state's power, its legality and borders (contrary to those who think that globalization has undermined states' power). The presence of these Indians in Uruguay has been and should continue being a great reason for thinking about the effects national narratives have produced on the Uruguayan imaginary and about certain categories that allow us to consider the relationship between said groups and the state's status quo.

To summarize (although not necessarily by way of conclusion), we can see changes in the Uruguayan imaginary with regard to the topic of indigenous roots, as in the case of Uruguay's indigenous associations of the 1990s and in that of the Indians who have recently arrived in the territory. Those changes show us, on the one hand, a not so new tendency for *criollos* to appropriate (as the romantics did in the nineteenth century) indigenous elements for the construction of a new national narrative. On the other hand, though, these changes remind us that the appropriation of elements belonging to other cultures is not a *criollo* prerogative: the Indians, too, such as the Mbya-Guaraní, have appropriated Western elements in order to incorporate them into the survival strategies that, according to Basini, allow them to affirm their ethnic identity and avoid being stereotyped by the state (2001, 36).

In this last section, I would like to return to the issue of the knowledge that is produced about the Native peoples of the past (and present) in Uruguay today. We have seen the emergence of new writers from outside of expert disciplines or fields who want to represent them in an idealized manner and are generating a new series of images of Amerindians that are primarily products of their imagination. Concomitantly, archaeologists today are turning out a significant amount of information and theories about the mound builders of the eastern part of Uruguay (see Verdesio 2000, 2001a). The enormity of the changes they are proposing in the way we see the indigenous past is important and the result of a gaze very different from that of those experts at the end of the nineteenth century and the first three quarters of the twentieth. What I mean by this, without considering the epistemological and ethical problems that arise from archaeology as a discipline (see Verdesio 2001b for one of the numerous critiques), is that the gaze and attitude of today's archaeologists more thoroughly take into account the limits of the nation-state's narrative—as well as its Eurocentrism—which makes them much less colonizing of the indigenous past than those of their predecessors. Yet, although a blind belief in the scientific nature of archaeology is as dangerous as not having any of the information and knowledge produced by that discipline, what is true is that archaeology is one of the primary tools that is being used for the recovery of the indigenous past of contemporary Uruguay. Of course, we should also consider the memories and oral traditions of the Mbya-Guaraní who currently live in Uruguay, which doubtlessly constitute very valid forms of representing the indigenous past, too. But there are no oral traditions or memories referring to the ethnic groups (such as the Charrua and Guenoa) from what has been poorly conceived as "historical time" or those societies from the even more problematically denominated "prehistorical period" (such as the mound builders) of the territory—those memories have been lost for reasons that have already been discussed.[6] The only evidence we have of those indigenous groups are material vestiges of their activities.

I believe it is by means of an archaeology conscious of its limitations as a Western form of knowing that we will be better able to learn about a past that is totally unknown to us. Lamentably, the results of the most recent excavations are not as popular as other interesting yet less rigorous lucubrations by authors such as Maggi and Antón. In fact, it is their work (books that sometimes repeat myths or inaccurate facts) and not academic papers published in more recent specialized archaeology journals that have become the best-selling material favored by a public comprised mainly of primary and secondary school educators. Furthermore, it is easy to see why this would be the case given the long silence that has been maintained about topics of fundamental importance for the nation and also because of the absence of Native peoples from Uruguay since 1832. Yet, in my opinion, it is incumbent upon archaeologists to enter into public debate about the questionable, unfounded, or simplistic assertions about the past in those current bestsellers and about how expert knowledge was constructed in the past. It is not enough to produce archaeological research: said research must be made accessible for a non-expert public. If not, this knowledge will become the privilege of the chosen few while the vast majority of people will keep imagining the indigenous past through the inherited and conditioned lenses of the worst kind of colonialism. They will continue to treat and see the Indians in modern-day Uruguay in a manner marked by the nation's history, the state's apparatus of capture, and the production of images and concepts by the past's most traditional expert knowledges—which have always been at the service of the production and reproduction of the subalternity of indigenous groups and other subjects that are marginalized by modernity.

In Uruguay, a Europeanized country, different methods are being used to recover a cultural diversity that has been lost. This diversity has been systematically leveled and obliterated throughout the country's history. Yet, in the case of the indigenous mound builders, "level" is no longer a metaphor: many earth constructions have been leveled by bulldozers and other modern, Western machinery. Destroying those indigenous sites also levels the land and the material evidence of how the Amerindians modified nature. Lamentably, the means and strategies employed by most nonspecialized writers on the subject to counteract this leveling of the history of non-Western human acts in the territory have as many limitations as virtues, as we have seen. The same can be said for the attitude of traditional expert knowledges with regard to these issues—an attitude that, as in the case of archaeology, has only begun to change in the past two decades. These limitations do not apply only to writers or disciplinary experts on this topic. They are also most evident in the undifferentiating attitude of the Uruguayan state, in its paradoxical desire to divide and organize its territory but also level cultural differences without promoting social justice. This is from a state that had to issue special documents to assign identities, in a Western sense, to the Indians who came into its territory through the back door. In my opinion, all of these insufficient and unsatisfactory responses are part of a more generalized failure of civil society, which has proven itself to be lacking in fertile or effective strategies for dealing with the reappearance of the Indians in its territory and in its national imaginary, as well as on its cognitive horizon. Perhaps a rigorous study of the accumulating documentary evidence and of more recent archaeological excavations will allow us to get closer to this past in a manner less uncertain and, possibly, more respectful of differences. That might be the only way we will know when we are talking about the Charrua or the Guenoa or the mound builders. A greater understanding of the indigenous past might help us better comprehend the Indians who today live not only throughout the countries of Latin America but also in Uruguay, a country that constructed itself as a nation without Indians. In other words, it is by employing the expert knowledges that have traditionally excluded them from the national narrative that they might be given a place in it. This will allow us to understand a little better—and to rescue their cultural specificity by refusing to consider them as bare life— the indigenous peoples who populate today the Uruguayan territory.[7]

Notes

Translated by Kenya Dworkin.

1. See Verdesio 2001a for a study of three centuries of representations of Indians by chroniclers of the region.

2. See Verdesio 2001a for a study of the discursive history of the River Plate (chapter 1).

3. See Verdesio 1997 for a discussion regarding the verisimilitude of the myth of an-thropophagy in the discovery of the River Plate.

4. Artigas's interest in the indigenous people is a well-documented phenomenon. According to Renzo Pi Hugarte: "Fue el único caudillo de la independencia americana que reconoció como primordial la causa de los indios" (He was the only Caudillo from the Independence era who acknowledged the importance of the indigenous cause) (1993, 262). And as Luis Basini states, he was supported on more than one occasion by the Charruas as well as the Guaraní (2001, 4).

5. It should be noticed that they might not be only or simply seeking a land with no evil but following cognitive or imaginary maps that predate the processes of state forma-tion.

6. In societies in which indigenous people still live, it is absolutely necessary, also, to refer to the oral memory of people whose history we reconstruct without even consult-ing them. In the United States, in the framework of NAGPRA (a law passed in 1990 that legislates the repatriation and restitution of human remains and funeral objects associ-ated with Native Americans who can establish cultural affiliation with these remains), the oral tradition is accepted as proof of cultural linkage or affiliation. This means that the status of the memory of these subjects (the indigenous people) converted by science into objects of study, and science itself, has been placed today in a less asymmetrical rela-tionship than what it used to be. For a description of the legal framework being referred to, see Trope and Echo-Hawk 2000. For a brilliant justification of the use of indigenous oral tradition, including that of the remote past, see Echo-Hawk 2000.

7. The Mbya-Guaraní left Uruguay in April 2007 in their continued search for the land without evil.

Works Cited

Agamben, Giorgio. 1993. *The Coming Community*. Trans. Michael Hardt. Minneapolis: University of Minnesota Press.

———. 2000. *Means without End: Notes on Politics*. Trans. Vincenzo Binetti and Cesare Casarino. Minneapolis: University of Minnesota Press.

Antón, Danilo. [1994]. 1997. *Uruguaypirí*. Montevideo: Rosebud.

———. 1995. *Piriguazú: El gran hogar de los pueblos del sur*. Montevideo: Rosebud.

———. 1998. *El pueblo jaguar: Lucha y sobrevivencia de los charrúas a través del tiempo*. Montevideo: Piriguazú.

Basini, Luis. 2000. "Otra territorialidad, otras fronteras." Paper presented at the meeting of Social Anthropologists of Uruguay, Montevideo, Museo de Antropología, Decem-ber 24–25.

———. 2001. "Indios num pais sem índios: A estética do desaparecimiento." Unpublished manuscript.

Bauzá, Francisco. 1895. *Historia de la dominación española en el Uruguay*. 2 vols. Mon-tevideo: Barreiro y Ramos.

Beisso, Rosario, and José Luis Castagnola. 1987. "Identidades sociales y cultura política en el Uruguay: Discusión de una hipótesis." *Cuadernos del CLAEH* 12.44: 9–18.

Bracco, Diego. 1998. *Guenoas.* Montevideo: Ministerio de Educación y Cultura.

de la Sota, Juan Manuel. [1841]. 1965. *Historia del territorio Oriental del Uruguay.* Ed. Juan Pivel Devoto. 2 vols. Montevideo: Biblioteca Artigas.

Deleuze, Gilles, and Felix Guattari. [1980]. 1987. *One Thousand Plateaus: Capitalism and Schizofrenia.* Trans. Brian Massumi. Minneapolis: University of Minnesota Press.

Díaz-Andreu, Margarita, and Timothy Champion. 1996. "Nationalism and Archaeology in Europe: An Introduction." In *Nationalism and Archeology in Europe,* ed. Margarita Díaz-Andreu and Timothy Champion, 1–23. London: UCL Press.

Echo-Hawk, Roger C. 2000. "Ancient History in the New World: Integrating Oral Traditions and the Archaeological Record in Deep Time." *American Antiquity* 65.2: 267–90.

Figueira, José H. 1892. *Los primitivos habitantes del Urugua.* Montevideo: Dornaleche y Reyes.

———. 1957. "Contribución al estudio de los aborígenes del Uruguay: 'Los Charrúas' de Pedro Stagnero y 'Cerro de las Cuentas' por Mario Ísola." Montevideo.

———. 1958. *Una excursión arqueológica al Cerro Tupambay realizada en los comienzos de 1881.* Montevideo.

Giorgi, Alvaro de. 2000. "Transformaciones de la mitología nacional en el fin de siglo: Una lectura de *Artigas y su hijo el Caciquillo* de C. Maggi." *Anuario: Antropología social y cultural en el Uruguay* 1: 43–57.

González, Luis Rodolfo, and Susana Rodríguez Varese. 1990. *Guaraníes y paisanos: Nuestras raíces 3.* Montevideo: Nuestra Tierra.

Kennedy, Roger G. 1994. *Hidden Cities: The Discovery and Loss of Ancient North American Civilization.* New York: Penguin.

Maggi, Carlos. 1991. *Artigas y su hijo el Caciquillo: El mundo pensado desde el lejno norte o las 300 pruebas contra la historia en uso.* Montevideo: Fin de Siglo.

Padrón Fabre, Oscar. 1996. *Ocaso de un pueblo indio: Historia del éxodo guaraní-misionero al Uruguay.* Montevideo: Fin de Siglo.

Panizza, Francisco. 1990. *Uruguay: Batllismo y después; Pacheco, militares y tupamaros en la crisis del Uruguay batllista.* Montevideo: *Ediciones de Banda Oriental..*

Perelli, Carina. 1986. "La manipulación política de la memoria colectiva." In *De mitos y memorias políticas: La represión, el miedo y después . . . ,* ed. Carina Perelli and Juan Rial, 117–28. Montevideo: Ediciones de Banda Oriental.

Pi Hugarte, Renzo. 1993. *Los indios del Uruguay.* Madrid: Mapfre.

Silverberg, Robert. [1970] 1986. *The Mound Builders.* Athens: Ohio University Press.

Trope, Jack F., and Walter R. Echo-Hawk. 2000. "The Native American Graves Protection and Repatriation Act: Background and Legislative History." In *Repatriation Reader: Who Owns American Indian Remains?*, ed. Devon A. Mihesuah, 123–68. Lincoln: University of Nebraska Press.

Varela, José Pedro. 1965. "De nuestro estado actual y sus causas." In *El destino nacional y la universidad,* ed. José Pedro Varela and Carlos María Ramírez. Montevideo: Biblioteca Artigas.

Verdesio, Gustavo. 1997. "Las representaciones territoriales del Uruguay colonial: Hacia una hermenéutica pluritópica." *Revista de crítica literaria latinoamericana* 23.46: 135–61.

———. 2000. "Prehistoria de un imaginario: El territorio como escenario del drama de la diferencia." In *Uruguay: Imaginarios culturales*, ed. Mabel Moraña and Hugo Achurar, 11–36. Montevideo: Trilce.

———. 2000–2001. "El retorno del indio olvidado o los usos del pasado indígena en el imaginario uruguayo." *Revista canadiense de estudios hispánicos* 36.1–2: 633–60.

———. 2001a. *Forgotten Conquests: Rereading New World History from the Margins.* Philadelphia: Temple University Press.

———. 2001b. "Todo lo que es sólido se disuelve en la academia: Sobre los estudios coloniales, la teoría poscolonial, los estudios subalternos y la cultura material." *Revista de estudios hispánicos* 35: 633–60.

2

Coloring the Social Structure

Racial Politics during the Duvalierist Dictatorial Regime of 1957–87

CAROLLE CHARLES

Haiti, like most other Caribbean societies evolved after slavery into a so-cial structure characterized by the interconnection of socio-economic and socio-racial hierarchies. In Haiti, hierarchies of race and color (two distinct but interrelated terms), class, and gender are expressed in marked social inequalities. A paradox in the dynamic of race relations inherited with the Haitian Revolution and the end of the slave plantation economies is that patterns of racial identity are not exclusively shaped and conditioned pri-marily by race as they are in the United States. In all representations of the social structure, the realities of race, class, and at times ethnicity are so in-tertwined that race mediates class relations and class qualifies race relations. More importantly, such dynamics have led to the emergence of color as an important signifier that takes a life of its own as a marker of social differen-tiation and inequality. Color permeates all dimensions of social life and is consciously used as a political and ideological instrument for the acquisi-tion, maintenance, and/or reproduction of class position and privileges by different social groups.

In Haiti, racial meanings and racial relations do not necessarily inform all forms of labor and capital relations because the revolution allowed for the emergence of a ruling elite composed of blacks and mulattos. Nonethe-less, the continuing presence of hierarchy and cleavages along racial and color lines, the permanence of an ideology of color, and the pervasive effects of color meanings and stereotypes in social practices indicate that race and color remain significant in the dynamic of social relations and in the social structure of Haiti.

This chapter attempts to analyze the ways in which the Duvalierist state used an inherited color ideology and how racial politics become central to the exercise of power and to the creation of consent. As this chapter argues, with Duvalier, the categories of color/race and class took different mean-ings. A racial political project grounded in an ideology of black power or *noirisme*[1] informed policies and political practices. With the Duvalierist state, in particular under the regime of Duvalier senior, the race/color hierarchy became the only determinant of social inequalities; racial consciousness became the only form of consent and the black middle class was the only natural representation of the majority and of the masses.

Race/Color Dynamics in Haitian Social Structure

A first glance at contemporary Haiti conveys that the country's most important challenge is widespread poverty. Although this observation is accurate, there is evidence that class inequality is also compounded with the race/color hierarchy in the social and economic structure.[2] Studies that look at the ways in which race and color meanings shape social relations and social structure are scarce. In fact, race is never posited as an autonomous organizing principle of social relations. But as Hall notes, "The white eye is always outside the frame but sees and positions everything within it."[3]

For years, Haiti has occupied one of the lowest positions in the Human Development Index of the United Nations Development Program. In 2002 it ranked 153 out of 175 countries.[4] Such a position only reflects a more gloomy reality that has characterized life for the majority of the Haitian population for almost two hundred years of independence. Most Haitians live in abject poverty with an average annual per capita income of around $300. Most people have little access to basic necessities such as public education, health care, and potable water. Besides this economic deprivation, poor Haitians are also subject to political and social exclusion. That gloomy reality is also colored since 90 percent of the Haitian population is black.

A counterbalance to this extreme poverty is the concentration of wealth and privilege. In Haiti, income distribution is highly skewed and income inequality is dramatic. Less than 5 percent of the population receives more than 46 percent of the national income. Such a structured system of inequality also entails the centralization of decision-making activities in all spheres of life in the hands of a small elite of Creole whites of European and Arab descent, mulattos, and a small segment of blacks in decision-making positions. It also means the marginalization of rural areas to the benefit of the capital city, Port-au-Prince. Haitian society also displays, besides these class and color divisions, cleavages of language, religion, and culture, which separate the peasantry and the urban working poor from the urban elite (Charles 1995b; Fick 1984, Dupuy 1989; Hooper 1986; Foster and Valdman 1984).

The coloring of the social structure is evidenced in the ethnic and racial composition of different sectors of the economic and political ruling elite. For example, there are two sectors in the manufacturing and industrial sphere of economic activities. There is the import-substitution sector, producing mainly for the internal market, and the assembly-line industries, producing for export in free-trade zones. About 99 percent of these industries are concentrated in Port-au-Prince, where there are around 450 manufacturing enterprises (Delatour, Grunwald, and Voltaire 1984; Garrity 1981).[5] The differences between the export-oriented sector and the import-substitution sector are the result of two distinct processes. On the one hand, the import-substitution sector has emerged from an internal process of differentiation and diversification of the family firms originally involved only in the export of coffee. Since the late 1950s, merchant and export firms have invested in finance, in housing, and in industry. This sector is to a large extent controlled by the three most important coffee export firms—Brandt, Madsen, and Wiener—in addition to some other large families that are either mulatto or of European descent (the Acras, Coles, Berhmanns, Bigios, Mevs, Vorbes, and so forth). All of the members of this oligarchy are related directly or indirectly through informal networks and extended family ties (Labelle 1976, Girault 1984, Plummer 1988). A total of no more than fifteen family firms control this sector, producing textiles, beverages, shoes, metallurgic goods, and the like. On the other hand, the export-oriented sector has more to do with the restructuring of the world capitalist economy and in particular with the trend toward relocation of production to some peripheral areas of the world economy.

Within the black segment of the ruling elite, economic positions are also differentiated. Older strata comprise some important "notable families" of the provinces, who own large estates and employ wage labor and/or sharecroppers. Many are absentee landlords who are also engaged in commercial activities in Port-au-Prince or in the coastal cities in their regions. This group comprises no more than 2 percent of the rural population, but they live in the cities, maintaining provincial "status" on account of their close ties to the peasantry. Also, there is a group that includes those who manage estates on behalf of Haitian and foreign companies and various middlemen who buy from the peasants and sell to the coffee export houses controlled by mulatto and white Haitians. In total, they comprise about 5 percent of the rural population (Nicholls 1985, 29–30). During the mid-1970s, a few members of the black petty bourgeoisie or the middle class were able to enter the expanding manufacturing sector of off-shore production. Their particular ties to the Duvalierist state were crucial for their participation in production activities. However, most were unable to survive the downfall of the Duvalierist regime in 1986. The state constitutes also a site of control and power for a definite segment of the ruling elite. Historically, the Haitian state has been authoritarian but also an instrument of the accumulation of wealth (Pierre-Charles 1974; Hector 1972; Hurbon 1978, 1987; Trouillot 1987; Dupuy 1989).[6]

With the abolition of slavery and the formation of the nation, for the different factions of the ruling economic elite—and, since the U.S. occupation, for the black petty bourgeoisie—control of the state has become the means to serve the interests of "their" group. Control of the state thus favors and enhances the economic position of the faction of the ruling group in power. Control of the state provides opportunities for social promotion and is the basis for the development of clienteles. The Duvalierist regime would use racial politics in order to consolidate such control.[7]

The Dynamics of Race/Color and Class Politics

The use of racial politics is not a unique phenomenon of the Duvalierist regime. Racial politics has always been a salient feature in defining Haiti's position in the world and in informing power relations and struggles within Haiti. In 1789, on the eve of the revolution, the population of St. Domingue comprised of 400,000 slaves, 28,000 freedmen, the majority mulattos with a small percentage of blacks, and 40,000 white settlers. This three-tiered social structure, with its race and class hierarchies apparently well defined, was in fact more complex than it seemed. In spite of these (seemingly) fixed divisions, the socio-ethnic groups or ethno-classes were differentiated by their places in the economic structure, their socio-political status, their kinship networks, and the color of their skin.

Indeed, one of the most important features of St. Domingue as a slave-based colonial society was the transformation of its social structure and its racial dynamics. At the beginning a strict color line was in use in which racial categories and racial rankings grounded in a conception of purity of blood operated. Yet, what was even more important was the political status of the different social groups. In fact, being a slave was never defined and explained by one's racial status; it was more the conditions of coerced labor and the political status as a non-person that defined a slave as a lower-ranking subject. Thus, at the beginning there was no need to use race to justify a system in which naked violence was its hallmark. The status of the slave was never justified because of racial and color attributes. The emergence of a freed caste or class composed mainly of mixed race or mulattos would change the dynamics, shifting the racial divide from a racial hierarchy organized around dichotomist racial categories and forms of representation to one of a more complex race/color line differentiation informed by ancestry, appearance, political and legal status, education, and wealth. The color line became a new form of stratification measuring degrees of social status. It would not only modify the relationship and the position of whites vis-à-vis blacks but would also begin to shape the relationship among freedmen and freedwomen of different skin color. As soon as mulattos and blacks were able to become free, color became the signifier for distinction. In colonial St. Domingue, a mulatto slave could receive better treatment than a free black. Likewise, during the formation of the National Assembly in France in 1788, the delegation of propertied mulattoes identified themselves as people whose closeness to freedom was grounded in their property rights and, most importantly, in their ancestry (Barthelemy 1996, 236). Thereby, race/color could exist not simply as a biological construction but as a social construction based on social mobility, economic status, and descent. This clearly meant a shift from a dynamic of exclusion informed primarily by the conditions of coerced labor to one of caste status and class position with the intersection of phenotype, degree of assimilation, and closeness to whiteness with political status and ownership. With the Haitian Revolution, despite certain alterations in the social structure, the dynamic of the color divide remained.

The Haitian Revolution of 1791–1804 resulted in the demise of the white colonists and slaveholders and at the same time propelled important segments of free mulattos and blacks as the new emerging elite. Yet the revolution that led to the formation of the first black independent nation-state did not eliminate all the contradictions and divisions embedded in the colonial plantation society. The two new ruling groups, differentiated by race/color and class, inherited a society shaped by the relations of class, gender, and racial hierarchies as well as sharp regional and cultural divisions. Yet, at the same time, the revolution created a sense of racial pride that would become part of the processes of nationhood, of cultural nationalism, and of racial politics.

Confronted during the nineteenth century with systematic external aggression and international racist threats, both segments of the traditional ruling elite developed and claimed a common identity as members of a black nation. Haiti and the Haitian Revolution came to symbolize the dignity and pride of the black race. There are many Haitian proverbs and meta-phors, such as "Ti péyi, gran nasion" (small country but big nation), "Zafè nèg pa janm piti" (black projects are never simple), and "Dèyè monn gin monn" (behind mountains are other mountains), that clearly express this racial pride.[8]

In this process, the issue of race/color played a contradictory role. In fac-ing external aggression, racial politics of identity became the embodiment of nationalism and racial pride; internally race/color cleavages and politics were a source of conflict. Color, as Trouillot points out (1990), became the idiom of politics.

One of the first steps taken by the Haitian state was indeed to equate race and nation. Various articles of the Constitution not only defined Haiti as a black nation but also gave automatic access to citizenship to any nonwhite person who landed in Haiti. Likewise, no Europeans had the right to be-come citizens or to own property in the country. This also included Haitians of Arab descent. Such exclusion of certain groups from citizenship would end with the occupation by the United States in 1915–34, which would result in the rewriting of the Constitution.

The development of Western racist ideologies "à la Gobineau"[9] during the nineteenth century forced both segments of the ruling class to defend their common racial heritage as a nation and to present the Haitian state as the leader in the fight for racial equality in the world at large. By the end of the nineteenth century and the beginning of the twentieth, there was a vast movement to vindicate the race, which was expressed in various political and literary publications. Writers and politicians such as Antenor Firmin, with his book *L'Egalité des races humaines*, Louis Joseph Janvier in *La repub-lique d'Haiti et ses visiteurs*, and Hannibal Price in *De la rehabilitation de la race noire* were the most important defenders of the race. As Hannibal Price stated, "Haiti is a small country but a great nation, its history is a vindica-tion of the black race" (quoted in Hurbon 1978, 116). Moreover, defining the state as the embodiment of the race and nation allowed the two colored factions of the ruling bourgeoisie to become the exclusive social actors in all conflicts.

Struggles for control of the state by the two competing factions of the ruling elite were also expressed in terms of race and color. In fact, two sepa-ratist movements led by representatives of the two ethnic groups, the blacks and the mulattos, resulted in the formation of two distinct states: first in 1801 with Toussaint and Rigaud; then in 1807–20 with Christophe and Pétion.

During the nineteenth century, two political parties were created in order to control state power. Both reflected the racial and class divisions among the ruling elite. The two parties functioned on the basis of clienteles. Both used race and color politics as the most important element of their agenda. However, the recruitment and participation of members were determined more by class than by the alleged identification of phenotypes. One could find blacks and mulattos in both of these parties.[10]

For the black segment of the ruling class located particularly in the North and engaged primarily in agriculture, the claim to being the sole representative of the state and nation was based on numbers. Defining themselves as black and thus genetically closer to the masses, they claimed that the mulattos did not represent the majority of the population. Their argument not only confounded race and class, but also converted blackness into an essence. Moreover, the racial categorization hid the town and country divide and the cultural cleavages that separated the black faction of the bourgeoisie from the mass of peasants. What the black segment of the bourgeoisie called the "base" was a differentiated mass of free peasant farmers with small holdings, sharecroppers, and wageworkers with closer ties to a re-created African culture. The political translation of this ideological and cultural discourse was expressed in the motto of the National Party, "Power to the majority."

In contrast, the mulatto segment, which controlled trade and commerce and was concentrated in the West and the South, created the Liberal Party, whose motto was "Power to the fittest." The implicit (and at times explicit) assumption was that only mulattos were civilized. They had more experience as members of the propertied class during the colonial period and were thus best able to guarantee progress and democracy. The underlying assumption was that mulattos were closer to whites. And indeed, they sought to distance themselves from the "base," from the former black slave who had no access to power or to "civilization." However, this dominant segment of the ruling elite also claimed blackness as its racial heritage. Indeed, all mulatto intellectuals and/or politicians always proclaimed their black heritage. Thus the basis of their distinction, while primarily cultural, was partly racial.

A paradox is that both factions of the emerging ruling elite reproduced the same categories of exclusion and differentiation inherited from the colonial state. Indeed, the existence of these racial ideologies and racial practices did not prevent the dehumanization of the former black slave. The Haitian Revolution transformed the state into the most important landowner. Taxation of the newly formed peasantry, composed primarily of former slaves generated large revenues. The state also became the most important instrument of coercion and control for the emerging bourgeoisie. As during the period of slavery, both factions exercised class domination and racial oppression over the majority of the population. Many mulattos owned slaves or were in an exploitative relationship with slaves. Thus, practices of exclusion were part of the logic of their domination. Such was not the situation of most black generals who came to occupy the presidency. Yet, as they became part of the ruling elite, the black faction actively participated in these relations of domination and oppression. While claiming to be the real representative of the majority or the masses, the basis for their historical right to hold state power, they clearly despised these masses. Theoretically, "Power to the majority" aimed at the vindication of the race, but it also presumed redemption from evil, from the sins of slavery (Nicholls 1979, Hurbon 1987).[11] It also meant recognition of the fact that the black masses were different, if not inferior. Hence, their salvation was needed. Therefore only blacks with culture, civilization, and property could control the state and be equal to the mulattos.[12]

The Roots of Racial Politics under the Duvalierist Regime

Michel-Rolph Trouillot characterizes the nineteenth century in Haiti as a period of recurring crisis. Indeed beyond the continuous struggles for hegemonic control of state power between the two most important factions of the Haitian ruling class that emerged with the formation of the Haitian state, this crisis was often reflected in the question of the color line. To paraphrase Trouillot (1990, 83–84), there was a central imbalance in Haitian social life that took the form of a chronic political instability. The continuous battles among the many general-presidents in what a deceased Haitian historian, Roger Gaillard, named the "Republic of the Generals" turned out to be the hallmark of the many coups, exiles, and insurrections of political life in Haiti where peasants were used as soldiers in the fights between *caudillos*. Between 1804 and 1915, the year of the U.S. occupation, Haiti saw the succession of about 25 governments, many of them lasting less than one year and many exceeding the constitutionally permitted number of years. Among the presidents, only five were not career army officers and three of these were nominated honorary generals (Trouillot 1990). This crisis was also expressed in the introduction of some twenty new constitutions. Nonetheless, although these different governments could not prevent the political isolation of Haiti and the economic constraints imposed by powerful international forces, the Haitian ruling elite created a system whereby they could enrich themselves yet perpetuate dependency at the same time. This system implied the imposition of a regime of social apartheid and harsh and inhumane economic conditions on the majority of the population integrated primarily by the many strata of the peasantry and by the small segment of urban working poor. Up until the 1970s, the bulk of state revenues came from the taxation of peasants, who up to that period represented around 80 percent of the Haitian population. As Trouillot (1990, 61–62) again states, "The type of indirect taxation meant that injustice was built into the system." Moreover, the peasantry was as isolated on its pieces of land scattered in the mountainous areas of the country as was Haiti from the rest of the world. Although they were carrying the burden of the country's problems, the peasants were systematically denied education, health care, and decent housing. They had no access to land irrigation or to a credit system and their methods of cultivating were rudimentary. Their religious and cultural practices were ridiculed or repressed and their language ostracized in contrast to the French and Catholicism that symbolized civilization. In that general context, the government of Jean Pierre Boyer, a general of the revolutionary army who held power from 1818 to 1843, reunified the country in 1821 and also occupied the Dominican Republic during that same period, really consolidating the regime.

Meanwhile, Haiti had become the first site of experimentation of neocolonialism. Ostracized by the international community as punishment for its repudiation of slavery and the colonial system, Haiti was prevented from participating in the Panama Congress of 1825 despite its earlier support of the independence of Venezuela and Colombia. In 1825, France recognized its independence but on condition of a payment of indemnity. It was only during the 1840s that other European countries and the United States would follow. Moreover, in addition to the payment of indemnity French goods would also receive reduced customs tariffs. This was the beginning of a significant trend for foreign financial involvement. Haiti also became enmeshed in international debt with the borrowing of a foreign loan to pay its debt. By the 1870s French and German merchant houses had displaced the monopoly of the mulatto faction of the ruling elite in its control of the "bord de mer," that is, the international trade and commerce. In that vein, Boyer Bazelais, one of the most important mulatto leaders of the Liberal Party, was outraged with the Salomon government's decision to create the Banque Nationale with French capital. Bazelais denounced Salomon as the apostle of evil who had delivered the country to the whites. Yet, Salomon came into power under the banner of the National Party, the party of the blacks

(Nicholls 1979, 139). Nonetheless, from 1880 up to the occupation, most of the governments contracted with foreign powers for military supplies in order to defeat the various uprisings and rebellions led by their opponents. In addition to the French and the German commercial interests, a growing number of British and Syro-Lebanese merchants were also emerging. The presence of these foreigners led to frequent foreign interventions. As David Nicholls indicates, these foreign merchants resolved any problems that might arise between them and the Haitian state by appealing to their governments, which would send gunboats to extort compensation. On the eve of the U.S. occupation in 1908, Stenio Vincent, who became president of Haiti in 1930 and ruled until 1941, would lament that much of the cultural and economic life of the country was under foreign control (Nicholls 1979, 142).

The emergence of the United States as the dominant power in the Caribbean at the turn of the century with the outcome of the Spanish American War had important implications for Haiti. It meant the displacement of the Germans and the French and the entry of Haiti into the American sphere of influence. Racial policies of the United States would clearly favor the mulatto faction. The occupation also entailed the formation of a larger middle class composed primarily of blacks. From the ranks of that new class—which could consolidate itself only through the control of state power—arose such political figures as Duvalier. Differentiating itself from the traditional ruling groups, using color politics and a populist and/or technocratic ideology, this new class seized and controlled power from 1946 to its ouster in 1987.

In contrast to the patterns of capital penetration in Cuba or the Dominican Republic, the U.S. occupation of Haiti in 1915–34 did not bring with it any massive infusion of foreign capital. Yet, the penetration still created a crisis in both rural and urban areas. This had a profound impact on the process of class formation. The occupation also destroyed the historic compromise of alternate regimes between the two competing factions of the ruling elite. Moreover, U.S. representatives, as Hurbon (1987) argues, also manipulated racial conflicts inherited from the colonial period.

For the entire period of the occupation and up to the end of World War II, the politics of the occupying forces tended to reinforce the hegemony of the mulatto faction. All the governments of that period were integrated by or led by mulatto members (Dorsinville 1976, Paquin 1983, Plummer 1988, Dupuy 1989). These practices further exacerbated racial tensions because mulattos would hire only mulattos for public and military positions.[13]

Furthermore, the U.S. occupation created an imbalance in the rural areas because of the politics of centralization in what would become the Republic of Port-au-Prince. Prior to the occupation, there were many active regional city ports, many of which subsequently lost their economic importance. As a result, in many rural towns and villages, social agents, especially the speculators, the mid-scale landowners, professionals, and small merchants, ruined because of this imbalance, began to migrate to the cities, particularly Port-au-Prince. The majority of these people were black (Dorsinville 1976). What became more obvious to an educated yet dispossessed black petty bourgeoisie was that access to resources meant control of the state. Thus, the most urgent task was the formulation of a new agenda that would be presented first in the cultural movement of negritude, challenging the exclusionary practices of the traditional elite, using race and a populist discourse to create legitimacy for them.[14]

Opposition to the U.S. occupation of 1915–34 and its racialist practices tending to support the mulattos led to the emergence of an indigenous negritude cultural movement. In particular, with the publication in 1928 of Jean Price Mars's book *Ainsi Parla l'Oncle*, the Haitian negritude movement was also influenced by the pan-Africanism that had earlier emerged in Europe and praised a renewal of interest and pride in African heritage.[15]

Price Mars made an important sociological and cultural analysis of Haitian society, acknowledging the important contribution of the Haitian masses to Haitian culture and making the connection of Haitians to Africa. More importantly, Price Mars also criticized what he called the "bovarism" of the elite and their exclusivism. Price Mars demanded a better sharing of power between the mulattos and the blacks.

This was the most important statement about blackness since the Haitian Revolution, and it marked the beginning of the cultural nationalist movement known as Haitian negritude that soon would be translated in a political project of *noirisme*. The book would become an ideological tool and a framework for many members of the black petty bourgeoisie and of the black faction of the ruling elite among the petty bourgeoisie. Many indigenist cultural organizations of the 1920s and 1930s were influenced by the book's thesis, which posited a reexamination of elite practices that mimicked French and Western ethnocentrism. Duvalier and many members of his political party and of his government were active members of this movement. Moreover, Duvalier was a prominent member of the intellectual group Les Authentiques, which published historical studies and cultural essays. One of the studies was the analysis of class struggles in Haiti seen through the lenses of color and race (Nicholls 1985; Labelle 1976; Dorsinville 1980; Moise 1988).[16]

During the 1940s, Haiti experienced the transformation of the cultural movement, negritude, into a new political project of black power or *noirisme*, which led to the fall of the pro-mulatto government of Elie Lescot in 1946 and the elections of the noirist government of Dumarsais Estime, a member of the traditional black elite. Duvalier was a member of the cabinet of the Estime government. Three years later, a military coup would put a stop to the project. From 1949 until 1956, the military under the command of Eugene Magloire, a black who was an ally of the mulatto faction of the elite, would hold the reins of power.

The Nature of Duvalierist Racial Politics

Elected by universal suffrage in 1957, Francois Duvalier organized his campaign by promoting blackness and claiming to be the sole representative of the black power populist movement of 1946. Duvalier was a physician by training but also one of the most important members of negritude and *noirisme*.

The coming into power of Duvalier in 1957 would reenact and implement the racial project embodied in the ideology of *noirisme*. *Noirisme* as an ideology and practice of racial politics would consolidate with the Duvalierist state. Thus, a new conception of natural legitimacy to hold power emerged. It was a conception wherein the source of power became essentialized in the sheer physical presence of a black majority. It was a definition of power that called for a system of color quotas in state positions.

By claiming the legacy of 1946, the Duvalierist regime was able to inherit the political mantle of a segment of the black bourgeoisie and to get the support of many black intellectuals and lower level black army officers. The Duvalierist state would also share a vision and a political discourse of Haitian society as an unfinished revolution. For the Duvalierists, the majority of the Haitian people, the hinterland masses, which had been excluded from power since the foundation of the Haitian state, provided the basis for a populist discourse that centered on color distinction, and the Duvalierist state developed an agenda that included various issues that affected this majority of the population. Yet, race was defined as the most important determinant of social inequalities and the poor masses were referred to as "La Classe."

For the Duvalierist state, all of Haiti's problems were the result of the dominance and control of the economy by the mulattos. In order to eliminate such power, it was necessary to capture the state. Only representatives of the majority "race" had the legitimacy to control state power (Labelle 1976). In that vein, Duvalier successfully manipulated an inherited ideological and political culture, in which, race, nation, class, and state intersect and overlap. In the Duvalierist agenda the political manipulation of color was practiced, as evinced especially by the inclusion of many mulattos in the government, and for the first time in Haitian history a few Syro-Lebanese individuals.

The Duvalierist state pushed the racial discourse to its extreme. Under Duvalier race became class (Hurbon 1987). Likewise, the nation, rather than being a historical product, was conceived as a community of interests created biologically. One of the most important mottos of the Duvalier regime was illustrative: "I am the Flag and I am the Nation," claimed the man who also proclaimed himself father of the nation.[17] Duvalier reconceived the Haitian nation by completely redefining it in terms of race. In that perspective, mulattos were defined as "Haitians by accident" (Leslie Manigat 1975). They had no political legitimacy and should be removed from power and purged from the state apparatus (Dupuy 1989). With Duvalier, race, nation, and class became fetishized. Yet such self-proclaimed legitimacy did not prevent alliances with other dominant sectors that had been excluded from the political process. Indeed, in order to counter the dominance of the mulattos, the Duvalierist state included many members of the Lebanese community, as well as some mulattos who shared its view (Hector 1972; Pierre-Charles 1974; Nicholls 1979, 1985; Dupuy 1989). At the same time, as seen early in the presidential campaign of 1956, Duvalier would appeal to and exhort black politicians, the black middle class, and black landowners and speculators to oppose and reject candidates representing the mulatto bourgeoisie and supported by the foreign Catholic hierarchy.

In particular, two areas of state policies were even more reflective of such racial practices. They were the Haitianization of the Catholic clergy and the neutralization of the army. Up to the 1950s, the top hierarchy in the Catholic Church was white and foreign. One of the first repressive activities of the Duvalierist regime was the expulsion of many foreign white Catholic bishops and the closing of the seminary. At the same time, Duvalier nominated five Haitian bishops and renegotiated the Vatican agreement. Duvalier also acknowledged the popular religion of Vodoun as the authentic expression of the beliefs and values of the Haitian masses, defining it as a catalyst for national unity. For the Duvalierist state, Vodoun was a part of Haiti's African roots. It had played a crucial role in the war for independence. Only mulattos and the white Catholic clergy purportedly despised the popular Haitian belief system. Thus, Duvalier would integrate some black Catholic priests and Vodoun leaders in his government, offering them some important political positions. As such, religion had also become a code for racial politics. Likewise, in order to counterbalance the predominance of mulatto officers in the Haitian army, the Duvalierist regime began to promote an imposing group of under-officers that were mostly blacks and of poor middle-class rural background. To cover this massive introduction of blacks, two mulattos were named as chief of staff and as assistant chief of staff.

Duvalier ideologically exploited race, color, and religious issues. For him, the reaffirmation of black culture gave dignity to the people. Objectively, his government wanted to obtain a new equilibrium not only in the sharing of power but also in the forms of representation of a black heritage. The symbolic enactment of the ideology of *noirisme* was manifested in the changing of the flag of red and blue and its replacement to the red and black; the erection of a statue to the Unknown Maroon; the visit to Haiti by Haile Selassie, the Ethiopian head of state; and by paying homage to Martin Luther King.[18]

The political and ideological posturing was also accompanied by a personalization of power, and the first actions were to eliminate all real or perceived potential centers of opposition. Duvalier wanted to destroy the political power of any organized group, including political parties, trade unions, student associations, and business organizations. The first victims of the purges were the political opponents who rejected the results of the elections of 1957. While the mulatto candidate, Louis Dejoie, went into exile, the black middle-class opponents represented by the Jumelle brothers were assassinated. In a very macabre act, Duvalier seized the cadavers during their funerals. Many followers of Dejoie and Jumelle also went into exile. Because the two candidates had important ties to the ruling groups, a proportionate contingent of the exiles tended to be mulatto or very affluent blacks. Moreover, the first organized military resistance to the regime in 1958 and 1960 was led and integrated by many mulattos, some of whom were former high-ranking officers of the army. This led to the repression, including the killing, of many mulatto families, yet numerically the most important victims of the Duvalierist regime came from the working urban poor, the peasantry, and a large segment of the lower middle class.

In spite of the populist ideology, the racialist discourse, and the nationalist posture, the Duvalierist state really represented the political, economic, and cultural interests of the black middle class. The new black nationalist ideology had a double function. It legitimized the new political agents on the political scene and it became the ideology of power of that new group. Moreover, the economic policies of the regime were conservative. It never sought to alter the social structure. Once the Duvalierist state came into power, it defined as subversive and therefore subject to repression all ideologies and critics who questioned its legitimacy (Dupuy 1989).

Indeed, the coming to power of the Duvalierist regime in 1957 crystallized the efforts of the black faction of the middle class or petty bourgeoisie to secure state power in order to accumulate wealth. Yet, from its inception this effort had limits. The economic crisis, which had begun in the 1950s and which Duvalier had inherited, did not allow further economic expansion or mobility for many segments of the middle class, particularly those concentrated in the service and state sectors (Trouillot 1987, Jadotte 1977). These limits were clearly manifested by the overproduction of university graduates with no possibility of entering the labor force. Many of the democratic organizations, trade unions, student and professional associations, and cultural and political groups that emerged in the early 1960s and began to oppose the Duvalierist regime were a product of that crisis. For many members of these groups the only way to avoid more pauperization was to organize with the aim of seizing state power. This was part of the dynamic of the struggles of the 1960s that led to a systematic elimination of these politically organized groups during the 1960s and early 1970s.

The early 1960s saw the prohibition and dissolution of the trade unions and student associations. The repression also affected other sectors, with purges of the army and the expulsion of progressive elements in the church that were involved in education. At the same time, the government authorized the recruitment of professionals and graduate students for Africa. Thereafter, Haitians with expertise and skills in the fields of education, health, and administration began to migrate and form part of the personnel of the new African nation-states. Later, following the massive repression of the communist movement and the guerrilla strategy in 1969–70 under the leadership of the Unified Party of Haitian Communists (PUCH), a second wave of exiles, which really was part of a brain drain migration, came to Latin America and North America.

After the repression of 1968–69, many sectors of the mulatto elite came to terms with the Duvalierist regime, accepting its dominance. By then, for many who were living in Haiti or who returned after Duvalier's death in

1971, the Duvalierist regime was really defending and protecting their interests when faced by organized military opposition of some communist groups such as the PUCH. Although there were many mulatto militants in these groups, there was almost no outcry.

The manipulation of the race/color distinction as a central dimension in the exercise of power was also paradoxical, particularly after the death of Francois Duvalier. Although the main features of racial politics remained the hallmark of the regime, there was a new dynamic under Francois Duvalier's son, Jean-Claude Duvalier. By 1976 with the opening of the Haitian economy, and in particular after the marriage of Jean-Claude Duvalier to a mulatto woman in 1980, *noirisme* as a political project began to collapse, leading to a historical irony, this being that marriage allowed for the reappearance of the cult of *mulatrisme* and the consecration of mulattoness.

Conclusion

Although race/color cleavages are salient features of Haitian social structure, race has not become the mediating element in defining place in that structure. The valuation of race and its manifestation in color-shade differentiation has facilitated class mobility for some. With the Haitian Revolution and the creation of a new nation, the state became the embodiment of these struggles and at the same time a crucial signifier of the development of nationhood as well as the process of class formation and consolidation.

During the nineteenth century, the two political metaphors—"Power to the fittest" versus "Power to the majority"—clearly symbolized to a large degree these practices. "Power to the fittest" was the motto of the mulattos who thought that because of their closeness to whites they were better able to lead the country. The rationale behind the slogan "Power to the majority" had the same dynamic. Clearly race was also an important signifier in defining class position and political legitimacy. Because blacks were closer physically to the majority of the population, they should hold power. Moreover, for them, the category of "la Classe" became synonymous with race.

The political appropriation of the ideas and values of negritude by Duvalier led to the equation of class with race; in fact it was the redefinition of class through race. Therefrom, meanings of race and class became interchangeable. At times the use of both categories referred to the majority of the Haitian black population and to the peasantry in particular; yet at other times class or race indicated the black middle class. Nonetheless, the implementation of such political demagoguery was also accompanied by systematic repression of the population and by examples of corruption. Yet, at the end of the regime, the politics of color distinction that favored blacks was being replaced by the integration of more mulattos in positions of power in the regime. It was during the period of the Duvalier dictatorship that the most important flows of Haitian migration to North America occurred. Thus, the regime's populist and racial discourse could not resolve the structural and economic crisis facing important segments of the population.

The overthrow in 1986 of the thirty-year dictatorship of the Duvaliers opened a new democratic space into which new social agents could enter as new collective subjects. This was a real change in the political landscape since these new actors, who had been historically bypassed or manipulated, claimed direct participation in the political processes and demanded more inclusion. The time of Lavalas (flood), of "tout moun se moun" (we are all citizens), arrived with the emergence of a new fiery populist political leader, a former priest known as J. B. Aristide. Paradoxically the Lavalas movement was really a coalition integrated by many groups and individuals, including a few mulattos. Yet the movement (because it was composed of Christians, peasants, Marxists, and feminists among other groups) never used the idiom of color. To some extent, the experience under the Duvaliers, particularly during the last years of the regime, may have contributed to the relegation of the race/color issue to the rhetorical back burner. It was only with the emergence of a strong opposition to the second Aristide government in 2003 that the issues of color resurfaced. The government and some of its followers began a campaign against one of the most important opposition groups, the group of 84, led by two important members of the mulatto elite. However, a brother of one of the leaders had a very important political position in the Lavalas government. As in the past, the issue of the legitimacy of mulattos to govern was raised. However, this did not prevent the participation of a mulatto candidate in the elections of 2005. Nonetheless, the abysmal economic situation of the majority of Haitians, who happened to be black, in contrast to the obvious affluence of a relative minority of Haitians with a large percentage of mulattos in its ranks continues to show the interaction of class, race, and color as salient features of Haitian society, leaving open the potential for the resurgence of racial politics.

Notes

1. There is a difference between *noirisme* and negritude. The latter is an ideological and cultural standpoint regarding the contribution of Africa and of people of African descent to world civilization. Negritude also informs identity, both in individual and social terms, and is akin to the black power movement in the United States. To a certain extent, blackness is the closest English translation of negritude. In contrast, *noirisme*, while also being an ideology, does aim toward controlling state power. *Noirisme* is the political translation of negritude. For a more detailed analysis, see Hurbon 1987; Dépestre 1970, 1976; and Labelle 1976 among others.

2. See the works of Nicholls 1979, 1985 Labelle 1976; Plummer 1988; Paquin 1983; and Dupuy 1989.

3. Stuart Hall, "The White of Their Eyes," quoted in Howard 2001, 7.

4. The Human Development Index, published annually by the UN, ranks nations according to their citizens' quality of life rather than strictly by a nation's traditional economic figures. The criteria for calculating rankings include life expectancy, educational attainment, and adjusted real income.

5. For a detailed analysis of the assembly-line industry, see Stepick 1984; Delatour, Grunwald, and Voltaire 1984; and Garrity 1981.

6. On the nature of the Haitian state, see in particular Trouillot 1987, 1990; Hurbon 1978, 1987; Dorsinville 1976, 1986; Pierre-Charles 1974; Hector 1972, 1985.

7. On the authoritarian nature of the state, Dupuy writes that of the 23 presidents that Haiti had from 1804 to 1914, 20 were ex-generals, and of 24 governments in 111 years, 16 were overthrown by uprisings or coups d'etat (Dupuy 1989, 115); see also Moise 1988.

8. A literal translation of these proverbs is respectively: tiny country, great nation; Haitian matters are never small or simple; beyond mountains are more mountains.

9. As many scholars indicate, the development of what is defined as "scientific racist theories" took place during the nineteenth century in Western Europe. The publication in 1857 of Charles Darwin's *The Origin of Species* led to the acceptance of the theory of evolution and to the ideas of processes of differentiation and stratification among biological species and also of social institutions and civilization. Darwin's works would become the framework for the formulation of theories of social Darwinism by Herbert Spencer in order to explain social hierarchies and inequalities. Within that new paradigm, a series of race theories also developed. One of the authors was Joseph Arthur, the Comte de Gobineau, a French aristocrat who produced an early version of white supremacy with his book *An Essay on the Inequalities of the Human Race* (1853–55). The book was re-edited in 1884. Gobineau worked as a diplomat for France and thus was in contact with non-Europeans. He argued that race creates culture, that the distinctions between the races were natural, and that the white race was superior to the others. Gobineau's strong position against any form of racial mixing would be borrowed by Hitler and the Nazis. Many Haitian intellectuals and politicians would challenge Gobineau's ideas. For more detailed analyses of racial theories, see Gosset 1964, Charles Manigat 1975, Moise 1988, Howard 2001.

10. Many, like Nicholls (1985), have been mystified by the racial discourse of the Haitian elite groups. For Nicholls the divisions connected with color are one of the most important causes of the failure of the independence project. Nicholls argues that Haitian leaders could never resolve the contradictions between their racial pride, the basis of their alliance during their struggle for independence, and the color prejudice system inherited from the colonial past, which undermined the basis of that solidarity. Nicholls does bring new insights into that contradiction by looking at the distinction between race and color. He further comments that in the social history of Haiti, race and color had different roles and meanings. Race was a centripetal force while color was a centrifugal one. The distinction between race and color is vis-à-vis race, since all blacks and mulattos accepted the fact that they belonged to the African or black race. Biologically they share a common descent, yet they have denied the objective significance of this fact.

11. The sharing by both factions of the same racist ideologies and hierarchies prevailing in Western culture was manifested particularly in their ambiguity toward Africa. For both groups, to be civilized was to be European. Africans also had a civilization, yet they were a backward continent. In the 1840s that issue had become so explosive that the government had to issue a race relations act directed at immigration. The government wanted to receive new immigrants, but the mulattos demanded the exclusion of Africans, who would bring vices, laziness, idleness, ignorance, fetishism, and superstition into the country, though black Americans from the United States were welcome. For a more detailed account, see Plummer 1988; Nicholls 1985; Hurbon 1987.

12. In their struggles and also in the historical accounts of these struggles there is no mention of the foreign merchant groups who really controlled the import-export sector of the economy. Since the Haitian Constitution denied foreigners the right of citizenship, they were never considered nationals. This has important class and race implications. Although some of these white merchants had married mulatto women, all analyses of race and class in Haiti ignore them. This is a major limitation of this thesis. Any future study of Haitian race and class relations should take this segment of the population into account.

13. On the racial and class practices of these regimes, see Dépestre 1976 and Roger Dorsinville 1986, 1976.

14. Tinois (Gerald Brisson) in his analysis of the conditions leading to the development of racial politics, states: "Toutes les couches sociales à la campagne constituaient objectivement la poudre d'une explosion révolutionnaire sous la direction idéologique et politique de n'importe quelle classe ou force sociale active" (All the social sectors of the rural area objectively constituted a revolutionary powder keg that could be led politically and ideologically by any organized social class or any active social force) (Brisson 1976, 10).

15. The ideas of negritude as a cultural and ideological movement of the 1920s and 1930s that developed in Europe with Aimé Césaire, a poet from Martinique, and Léopold Sédar Senghor, a poet from Senegal and its future president, to cite but two, found solidarity in a common black identity in rejection of French colonial racism. Proponents

of negritude also believed in a shared black heritage among members of the African diaspora. These ideas of confirmation and affirmation of the significance of African culture were also part of the Harlem Renaissance movement in the United States.

16. There is a whole political school of thought that has analyzed the political history of Haiti as one of struggle between blacks and mulattos. The most important proponent of that thesis was Francois Duvalier.

17. There are many detailed historical accounts of the Duvalier regime. See, in particular, Rotberg 1971; Pierre-Charles 1974; Heinl and Heinl 1978; Hector 1972; and Diederich and Burt 1969. See also the analyses of Hurbon (1978, 1987); Dupuy (1989); Trouillot (1987); and Nicholls (1979, 1985), which give some significant insights.

18. Duvalier did not create the black and red flag. During the War of Independence, there were at least two flags representing the different groups. During the first year of national life, the two flags were alternatively used as symbols by different governments.

Works Cited

Barthelemy, Gerard. 1996. *Dans les Splendeurs d'un Apres-midi d'Histoire*. Port-au-Prince: Editions Henry Deschamps.

Brisson, Gerald (Tinois). 1976. "Fondements economiques de la situation revolutionnaire de 1946." In *Trente ans de pouvoir noir en Haiti*. Montréal: Collectif Paroles.

Charles, Carolle. 1994. "Sexual Politics and the Mediation of Race, Class, and Gender in Former Slave Plantation Economies: The Case of Haiti." In *The Social Construction of the Past: Representation as Power*, ed. Angela Gilliam and George Bond, 44–56. London: Routledge.

———. 1995a. "Gender and Politics in Contemporary Haiti: The Duvalierist State, Transnationalism, and the Emergence of a New Feminism (1980–1990)." *Feminist Studies* 21.1: 135–64.

———. 1995b. "Haitian Life in New York City." In *The Immigrant Left*, ed. Paul Buhle and Dan Georgakas, 289–301. Albany: State University of New York Press.

Delatour, Leslie, J. Grunwald, and K. Voltaire. 1984. "Offshore Assembly in Haiti." In *Haiti Today and Tomorrow: An Interdisciplinary Study*, ed. C. R. Foster and Albert. Valdman, 231–54. Lanham, Md.: University Press of America.

Dépestre, René. 1970. "Les Metamorphoses de la Negritude en Amerique." *Présence Africaine* 75.3: 19–33.

———. 1976. "La Révolution de 1946 est pour demain." In *Pouvoir Noir*, 57–95. Montréal: Collectif Paroles.

Diederich, Bernard, and Al Burt. 1969. *Papa Doc: The Truth about Haiti Today*. New York: McGraw-Hill Book Co.

Dorsinville, Roger. 1976. "1946 ou le délire opportuniste." In *Pouvoir Noir*, 35–57. Montréal: Collectif Paroles.

———. 1986. *Marche Arriere*. Montréal: Collectif Paroles.

Dupuy, Alex. 1989. *Haiti in the World Economy: Class, Race, and Underdevelopment since 1700*. Boulder, Colo.: Westview Press.

Fick, Carolyn. 1984. *The Making of Haiti: The Saint-Domingue Revolution from Below.* Knoxville: University of Tennessee Press.

Firmin, Antenor. 1885. *L'égalité des races humaines.* Paris: Libriarie Cotillon.

Foster, C. R., and Albert Valdman, eds. 1984. *Haiti Today and Tomorrow: An Interdisciplinary Study.* Lanham, Md.: University Press of America .

Garrity, Monica. 1981. "The Assembly Industries in Haiti: Causes and Effects." *Journal of Caribbean Studies* 2.1: 25–37.

Girault, Christian. 1984. "Commerce in the Haitian Economy." In *Haiti Today and Tomorrow: An Interdisciplinary Study,* ed. C. R. Foster and Albert Valdman, 173–80. Lanham, Md.: University Press of America.

Gosset, Thomas F. 1964. *Race: The History of an Idea in America.* New York: Schocken Books.

Hector, Cary. 1972. "Fascisme et sous-développement: Le cas d'Haiti." *Nouvelle Optique* 5: 39–72.

———. 1985. "Des Prises de démocratie dans la société civile (1975–1983)." *Collectif paroles* 32: 17–20.

Heinl, Robert, and Nancy Heinl. 1978. *Written in Blood: The Story of the Haitian People.* Boston: Houghton Mifflin Co.

Hooper, Michael S. 1986. *Duvalierism since Duvalier.* New York: National Coalition for Haitian Refugees and Americas Watch.

Howard, David. 2001. *Coloring the Nation: Race and Ethnicity in the Dominican Republic.* Oxford: Signals Books.

Hurbon, Laenec. 1978. *Culture et dictature en Haiti.* Paris: L'harmatan.

———. 1987. *Comprendre Haiti: Essai sur l'Etat, la Nation et la Culture.* Port-au-Prince: Editions H. Deschamps.

Jadotte, Harold. 1977. "Haitian Immigrants to Quebec." *Journal of Black Studies.* 7: 485-500.

Janvier, Louis J. 1882. *Les detracteurs de la race noire et de la république d'Haiti.* Paris: Marpon et Flammarion.

Labelle, M. 1976. *Ideologies de Couleur et Classes Sociales en Haiti.* Montréal: Presses Universitaires de Montréal.

Laguerre, Michel. 1989. *Voodoo and Politics.* New York: St. Martin's Press.

Manigat, Charles, et al. 1975. *Haiti, quel development?* Montreal: Collectif Paroles.

Manigat, Leslie. 1975. *Ethnicité, nationalisme et politique: Le cas d'Haïti.* New York: Editions Connaissance d'Haiti.

Moise, Claude. 1988. *Constitutions et luttes de pouvoir en Haiti.* Montréal: Cidihca.

Nicholls, David. 1979. *From Dessalines to Duvalier: Race, Colour and National Independence in Haiti.* Cambridge: Cambridge University Press.

———. 1985. *Haiti in Caribbean Context: Ethnicity, Economy, and Revolt.* Houndsville, Bassingstoke: Macmillan.

Paquin, Lyonel. 1983. *The Haitians: Class and Color Politics.* New York: Multi-Type.

Pierre-Charles, Gerard. 1974. *Radiographie d'une dictature.* Montréal: Nouvelle Optique.

Plummer, Brenda Gayle. 1988. *Haiti and the Great Powers, 1902–1915*. Baton Rouge: Louisiana State University Press.

Price Mars, Jean. 1928. *Ainsi Parla l'Oncle*. Paris: Imprimerie de Compiege.

Rotberg, Robert. 1971. *Haiti: The Politics of Squalor*. Boston: Houghton Mifflin and Co.

Stepick, Alex. 1984. "The Roots of Haitian Migration." In *Haiti Today and Tomorrow: An Interdisciplinary Study*, ed. C. R. Foster and Albert Valdman, 337–49. Lanham, Md.: University Press of America.

Trouillot, Michel-Rolph. 1987. *Les Racines historiques de L'état Duvaliérien*. Port-au-Prince: Editions Deschamps.

———. 1990. *Haiti State against Nation: The Origins and Legacy of Duvalierism*. New York: Monthly Review Press.

3

The Imagined Republic of Puerto Rican Populism in World-Historical Context

The Poetics of Plantation Fantasies and the Petit-Coloniality of *Criollo Blanchitude*, 1914–48

KELVIN SANTIAGO-VALLES

"Negro-themed" poetry (so-called *negrista* poetry or *poesía negroide*) was one of the principal literary expressions among the "native" intelligentsia in Puerto Rico during the collapse of British supremacy within the colonial-capitalist world-system[1] and the interwar period's global hegemonic interregnum. The infantilization of Afro-diasporic populations was one of the main traits of this *negrista* poetry of the *criollo* elites; the other was the need for the socio-cultural rebirth of "the nation." Both traits linked this poetic genre with narratives of racial democracy and the emerging populism of Puerto Rico from the late 1920s to the mid-1940s.

Contrary to mainstream literary history and received cultural-nationalist memory, this Negro-themed poetry was much less about Atlantic *négritude*, the New Negro, or *littérature indigène* (Price-Mars 1954; Locke 1968) than about a colonized variety of what Sylvia Wynter (1979) has called *blanchitude*. In the past thirty years a growing nucleus of scholarship has critically examined the racial/racist foundations of this poetic genre in the case of Puerto Rico.[2] For me, *poesía negroide* exemplified the Puerto Rican *blanquito*[3] variant of Aníbal Quijano's original concept of coloniality. For Quijano (2000, 537, 540–42, 552, 556–60), coloniality is the Eurocentric mode of intersubjectivity predicated on the colonial-capitalist world-system's racialized forms of labor control.

After the U.S. invasion of Puerto Rico in 1898 and by the early to mid-twentieth century, colonized *blanchitude* or *criollo* petit-coloniality meant reorganizing this local instance of the global-racial regime of the 1870s–1940s. Regarding Puerto Rico, such were the discursive mechanisms and socio-regulatory institutionalities whereby the displaced heirs and descendants of the Spanish colonizers on this island sought to renegotiate and maneuver their ambiguous and contradictory social position. On the one hand, these white-*criollo* owners of large properties and the new middle strata were *colonized* by U.S. capital and the colonialist bureaucracy of Europe and North America. On the other hand, the *criollo* elites were *colonizers* toward the inconclusively Puerto Rican descendants of nineteenth-century slaves, sharecroppers, and day laborers, now transformed into most of this island's peasants and wageworkers. For brevity's sake, this chapter's main focus is not on analyzing Negro-themed poetry but rather this genre's wider context to suggest how the panorama opened up by this literary form contributed toward the solution of colonized *blanchitude*'s crisis of representation during the interwar period.

By global-racial regime[4] I mean a particular kind of what Braudel (1972, 16–18) called a "social conjuncture" or "structure": namely, the trends of the last twenty to one hundred years or so within the racial *longue durée* of the last five hundred to eight hundred years (Winant 1994, 21) framing the architecture of world history itself and its patterns of change. Such is the historical specificity of the colonial-capitalist world-system's division of labor, which is akin to what Sylvia Wynter has called "the model of *physiognomic* difference" reconfigured in the sixteenth century and whose "*somatic* mode . . . would function from the early nineteenth century onwards as the *primary* 'totemic operator' of the principle of Sameness and Difference about which our present global and now purely secular order auto-regulates its socio-systemic hierarchies, including those of gender, class, sexual preference, culture . . ." (1990, 359, emphasis in the original).

At the epistemic level, these somaticized mental frameworks operate interwoven with biopolitical institutionalities constituting—*as natural*, in the final analysis—allegedly nonreproductive physiologies: global-racial regimes are inherently both "orders *of knowledge*" and "orders *of being*" (Wynter 2000) on a world scale.[5] It is possible to periodize a global-racial regime's phases and shifts to produce *a different* global-racial regime. This entails examining how new *physiognomized* knowledges and their corresponding *somaticized* forms of social regulation emerge, wrestle, and eventually prevail within and/or transform a global-racial regime's dominant mental frameworks and biopolitical institutionalities. Such a shift is precisely what occurred during the interwar period.

Conjuring Landscapes of Bestialization and Primitivism as "Local Color"

A number of overlapping and contested elements within island-based[6] narratives during this period reference the "race question," where matters of genre and canonicity were also relevant. But poetry seems to have concentrated the largest number of writings on the "race" topic, despite some of its early patrician detractors (de Diego Padró 1932a, 1932b; Miranda 1932; Miranda Archilla 1933). Hence, the *poesía negroide* written by learned white and near-white *criollos* such as Luis Palés Matos, and its content matter in general, very quickly became the modernist darling of both the bohemian avant garde and of established literary circles (including late romanticism and traditionalist folk-themes).

Although it was rare—though not impossible (for example, Ramírez 1930)—to find unreserved apologies for slavery within Euro-*criollo* elite literature as late as the 1930s, most mainstream "native"-cultured poetry tended to referentially embrace the "Negro element" by sentimentalizing slavery's inherently conflicting racial structures in general. Similar white-elite narratives of the late nineteenth century to the mid-twentieth from other plantation-based hegemonic cultures on both sides of the Atlantic, particularly in the Americas, corroborate the widespread character of this sentimentalization of slavery as local maneuvers constituting and transforming the dominant global-racial regime of the 1870s through the 1940s.[7] This is what I have called *plantation fantasies*: post-emancipation gnoseological-narrative machineries whose content converted slavery into love stories and family romances. Mary Louise Pratt has already indicated the seventeenth- and eighteenth-century, colonialist-racist antecedents of these Occidentalist maneuvers, where "romantic love rather than filial servitude or force guarantee the willful submission of the colonized. . . . In the transformation, a fundamental dimension of colonialism disappears, namely, the exploitation of labor. . . . It is, of course, characteristic of sentimental fiction to cast the political as erotic and to seek to resolve political uncertainties in the sphere of the family and reproduction" (1992, 97, 101). Sadiya Hartman described comparable stratagems in the antebellum South of the United States.: "Even the regime of production becomes naturalized as 'the rhythms of work,' as if slave labor were merely another extension of blacks' capacity for song and dance. The lure of the pastoral is in reconciling sentiment with the brute force of the racial-economic order. . . . The ruthless use of labor power and the extraction of profit are imagined as the consensual and rational exchange between owner and slave" (1997, 52–53).

As a literary cornerstone of the white-*criollo* cultural-nationalist landscape, one of the most common deployments of such plantation fantasies was the bestialization of the black and mulatto body in general and of the nonwhite woman in particular as telltale signs of their/our infantile primitivism. For example, around the time of the First World War, José P. H. Hernández wrote "Nigra sum, sed fermosa" (1966, 244). At first glance this piece gives the impression that the poetic persona is singing praises to a black woman . . . until one realizes that he is comparing her features to those of a wild, frenzied animal ("cabríos," "histéricos e indomables"). Such is also the case of Graciany Miranda Archilla's "A mi negra zamba" (1937, 65–66), where the affectionately crude and simple black woman-servant materializes as a Caribbean chimera, simultaneously metaphorized as a crab and a horse. This dark female monstrosity, with "las dos tenazas de sus dos mandíbulas" (the two pincers of its mandibles) merrily "galopa su trópico, martilla su paso" (gallops its tropic, making footprints like a hammer).

Another deceptively adulatory "inclusive" poem within this trend is Evaristo Ribera Chevremont's "Nuevo cantar de cantares" (n.d., 187, 190), published between 1924 and 1931. This is one of the most literal evocations of the feral [black-female] primitive: voiceless and lying prone among satins and pelts ("muda, tendida entre los rasos y las pieles"), once again gloriously untamed ("indomable, magnifica"), an insatiable beast ("cuando la bestia solicite el heno," "pantera"). Although this volume appears without a date of publication, it was already cited in Antonio S. Pedreira's (1932, 537) canon-constructing compilation *Bibliografía puertorriqueña*. Cabrera locates Ribera Chevremont as a major literary figure of the late 1920s who, after returning from Spain in 1924, brought with him the influences of the European avant-garde and influenced the *criollo* literary movements distinctive to that decade (279, 280).

In certain early verses by Palés Matos, "Esta noche he pasado" (written in 1921), the narrative voice anxiously projects this same kind of bestiality on to the facile somber screen of an entire black neighborhood. Here, croaking ebony frogs ("sapos negros croan") blur into the withdrawn, monkey-like dejection ("remota tristeza cuadrumana") of dark, filthy, decaying bodyscapes and landscapes ("un pueblo de negros . . . caserío inmundo, . . . andrajos y ruinas"), primeval and full of drunken hate and lust ("una pasión ardiente por los bravos alcoholes, el odio milenario . . . , y la insaciable lujuria de las toscas urgencias primitivas") (in Arce de Vázquez 1984a, 462–63).

Comparable visually evocative textual practices hark back to the eighteenth- and nineteenth-century deployments of the picturesque during earlier global-racial regimes (Meisel 1983, 3–13). This technical-visual approach to making sense of "nature" specifically focused on topographies and vistas but as a way of confirming the preconceived perspectives, desires, and descriptive vocabulary of the artist-technician (Batchen 1997, 69–80). The picturesque became a way of "looking for views of nature that looked like landscape pictures" and other narratively pictorial panoramas. Whenever "nature proved a little recalcitrant," it became necessary to mobilize "machines . . . to bring a more picturesque order to what was seen by the naked eye" (73). Originally linking together the quintessentially pictorial-narrative forms of the novel, theater, and pictures (including painting, print illustrations, and later photography), the picturesque soon came to encompass poetry, architecture, and music. In Latin America and the circum-Caribbean, the deployment of the picturesque encompassed the *costumbrista* and *indigenista* literature of the second half of the nineteenth century and the early part of the twentieth, as well as some modernist currents of the 1890s–1940s (including Atlantic *négritude*, the New Negro, and *littérature indigène*), signaling the emergent gnoseological elements that also would prevail during the new, postwar global-racial regime (1940s–1970s).

In early to mid-twentieth-century Puerto Rico, the evocatively visual imagery and pictorial content of *criollo blanchitude*'s Negro-themed poetry operated as the narrative machinery assisting this island's colonized elites in "bringing a more picturesque order" to a local and wider Caribbean "nature [that was proving to be] a little recalcitrant," thereby "providing a popular philosophical context within which larger questions of [cultural-national, aesthetic, and political] representation could be conceived and disputed" (Batchen 1997, 69). *Poesía negroide* in Puerto Rico thus became a conflicting epistemic amalgamation that both ruptured and drew from the visual travesties of social Darwinism and eugenics—for example, mass marketing, museums, traveling shows and tableaus, international exhibitions, caricatures, and other popular culture (Rydell 1984; Pieterse 1992, 64–235; Goings 1994)—and of their U.S. gunboat-diplomacy extensions into the Caribbean (J. Johnson 1980, 167, 169, 175 , 209; Santiago-Valles 1999). As it matured into racial-democracy narratives, this poetic genre tended to express more of a partial rupture than a continuation of the prevalent order of knowledge.

Negrista poetry replicated the very same "familiar" landscapes of "local color" and panoramas of strange "primitive exotica" validating the preconceived perspectives, desires, and descriptive vocabulary of the petit-coloniality of the *criollo* elite during the interwar social turbulence in Puerto Rico, in the rest of the Antilles, and in the rest of the world. Olga Ramírez de Nolla's poem "Año nuevo dandé" typifies the bucolic vistas that "dramatically resolved the tension between domination and intimacy by recourse to sentimental tropes of reciprocity, domesticity, and kinship" (Hartman 1997, 30). In this work the omniscient white-*criollo* character contemplates a cool night scene ("Hasta la noche fresca"), where an idyllic New Year's celebration in the slave's quarters ("La fiesta se derrama/En los altos barracones,/... De dulzor y de flama") is, in turn, calmly being viewed by blue-eyed masters ("Ojos azules miran/Filas de negras caras") (Ramírez de Nolla 1947, 64).

Such visual devices and colorful uses were alive and well in the better known works of Palés Matos, collected in *Tuntún de pasa y grifería* (1937 and 1950), as in the case of his "Elegía del Duque de la Mermelada." Within this piece, the contradictory results of the Haitian Revolution are quite literally parodied as the Frenchified affectations of—once again—barely tamed monkeys, whose prehensile toes long to climb up citadel spires ("a despecho de tus pies que desde botas ducales/te gritan—Babilongo, súbete por las cornisas del palacio"): clearly, the reader is being summoned to contemplate a historically but archetypally Caribbean terrain. Palés's poem "Lagarto Verde" pursues an identical anthropoid burlesque, where the white Puerto Rican consecrated man of letters once again parodies the black Haitian ruler/lesser primate ("Una monada/... aristócratas macacos/pasan armados de cocomacacos" [A cute little thing/... aristocratic macaques/pass armed with bludgeons]), who/which is, in turn, embodying a parody of the Versailles court ("solemnemente negros de nobleza" [solemnly Negroes of nobility]) (Palés Matos 1993; 135, see the critique in Zenón Cruz 1975, vol. 2, 131).

As in the already cited poems "Nigra sum, sed fermosa" by P. H. Hernández and "Nuevo cantar de cantares" by Evaristo Ribera Chevremont, in most *negrista* poetry too (Palés Matos included) the picturesque bestialization of nonwhites within modernist patrician poetics often surfaced in a highly sexualized manner. An exceptionally transparent case of such semiotic devices is the poem published in 1941 by Lauro Martínez, which is significantly titled "Orgía negra." The third stanza literally bursts with "local color," creating a direct homology between the roaring jungle ("Ruge la selva, tiembla el bongó"), the gyrating animalistic bodies of uncivilized blacks ("Negros con negras están bailando/... Sus movimientos y cabeceos/Son tan lascivos y tan eróticos"), and a leering—and phallic—snake, whose bestial compatibility with the Africans leads it to the point of feral sexual arousal ("Que una serpiente que los miraba/. . . Sintió de pronto gritar su sexo") (1941, 58–59).

Some of the more marginal poetical production of this period, namely, the work of nonwhite writers, invites pertinent comparisons insofar as it occasionally touched on the themes of bestialization and "race." The most representative example of such textual linkages is the poetry collection *Dinga y Mandinga* of 1942 by the consciously Afro-descended writer Fortunato Vizcarrondo, a mailman by occupation. "Baile cangrejero," as so much of his other work, is a parodic mixture of the quotidian (that is, strongly Africanized) vernacular of laboring poor Puerto Ricans of all races with the pseudo-vernacular of generic Hispanic-Antillean blacks and mulattos. Vizcarrondo vividly renders yet another scene of dancing Afro-diasporic bodies: this time it is a house party that includes monkey-faced women ("la negra cara e'mona"), cow-like aunts ("su tía y ej su suegra/. . .grande como una vaca"), and sweating black bodies ("Le corre po' lo' sobaco'/El sudó a Mateíta") (Vizcarrondo 1976, 3–5). The telling difference, however, lies in the politics of representation involved. In most of these other, nonwhite, noncanonical poetic practices the authorial voice is part of the scene being depicted. Vizcarrondo's narrative persona tends to include itself among—and at the same level as—the people he is speaking with and/or about whom he is speaking. Even the moments of brutal ridicule—and his work contains many—incorporated strong elements of Afro-descended *relajo* and *vacilón* (the Puerto Rican variant of jive humor), as well as of self-deprecation. Contrary to the *poesía negroide* of Euro-*criollo* modernists, Vizcarrondo's work tended to reduce to a minimum the distancing effects of racial voyeurism.

Yet other common and related themes surfaced within *blanquito*-lyrical plantation fantasies during the early twentieth century. This literary genre additionally included or summoned the "Negro element" within the mainstream cultural nationalist terrain via the (hyper)sexualization of nonwhite female bodyscapes, primarily focusing on the latter's hips and buttocks. Such literary devices trivialized—or even erased—the eroticized brutality culturally underpinning the era of slavery in Puerto Rico (Roy-Féquière 1993; Santiago-Valles 1998, 1999; Jiménez-Muñoz 1998; C. Williams 2000). Such artifices percolate throughout certain unpublished verses by Francisco Negroni Mattei written circa 1933–35 where, similar to the bestialization motif, the (pre)dominant theme in one of the poems was the anxious, yet "civilized" voyeurism of the white-*criollo* narrative voice. Here the corresponding reinscription of nonwhite, fictive, female corporality surfaced again as primitive sensuality ("Baila la negra al son/con el vientre desnudo/y las nalgas redondas"), bringing such subjects closer to Nature ("se mueven/ con firme oleaje") (quoted in Lluch Mora 1961, 293–94).

(Hyper)sexualization is even more evident in a poem published in 1948 by Julio Enrique Iguina significantly titled "¡Carimba! ¡Caramba!," a play of words that literally translates as "How *about that* branding iron!" Here the poetic persona manages to suture seamlessly together—with a grotesque attempt at humor—a fascination with the female slave's hips ("Real negra viendo de anca desbordada") and slavery's branding of black flesh ("candente hierrito/Que un marcador blandía sospechoso/. . . cuando fué sellada"), while depicting the entire scene in ostensibly comical tones—as indicated by the diminutive form of several of the more striking words used by the author ("hierrito," "Fuego africano bien concentradito," "Subiósele el tufito") [little iron, well-concentrated African fire, her odor rose up to meet him] (Iguina 1948, 248). Similar to the sexualized pastorals during legal slavery, "within this [sensual] economy, the bound black body, permanently affixed in its place, engenders pleasure" insofar as these narrative forms "restaged the seizure and possession of the black body for the [white] other's use and enjoyment" (Hartman 1997, 31–32). This sort of epistemic violence and lyrical "restaging of seizure and possession" probably reached an all-time low with Ribera Chevremont's famous poem of 1946, "La negra muele su grano" (C. Williams 2000, 133–34), whose seventh stanza leaves little room for misinterpretation:

Es su alegría salvaje
cuando lo blanco la llena,
cuando es el blanco que toma
su ardiente masa de negra.

(It is savage bliss to her
when the white man fills her
when it is the white man who takes
her ardent black mass.)

(Ribera Chevremont 1957, 177)

Most of the characteristically marginalized poetic work of nonwhite authors during this period tended to recast (and re-member) slavery and its aftermath in a much different light: that is, hardly as a humorous topic. The partial exception is the work of Fortunato Vizcarrondo, who wrote several partly satirical poems referencing slavery, as in "La mulata" (curiously dedicated to the predominantly serious and solemn poet, Carmen María Colón Pellot), "Blanca y negro," and "El español y la negra," in his collection of 1942, *Dinga y Mandinga* (1976, 56–57, 62, 63–64). But even in these examples Vizcarrondo's poetic voice is still the self-parodying, jive-humored, and razor-sharp ironic timbre of the trickster.

For most of these other(ed) writers, slavery quite literally referenced a completely different landscape and an altogether opposite (and, hence, oppositional) historical memory: namely, crude brutality. Such was the case of the anger and outrage marshaled at the beginning of the poem "Indiana," written by the black politician and journalist Luis Felipe Dessús (1916, 59). There, indignantly ("Rabia y fuego le dejaron"), the narrative voice fuses together African bondage with the sixteenth-century enslavement of the indigenous population of the Caribbean ("indio y africano/. . . las cadenas/ Que a mis razas humillaron" [Indian and African/. . . the chains/which humiliated my races]). Similarly grim visions appear in the poem *La Perla* by the journalist and dark mulatto politician Tomás Carrión Maduro (1927, 9), whose poetic persona evokes the greed of the slave trade ("En codicioso tráfico, mercaban"). The third example attesting to the barbarities of the Middle Passage ("con mano de hierro/. . . los barcos negreros") was "Canto a la raza mulata," written by the school teacher and mulatto author Carmen María Colón Pellot (1938, 23). Even the usually humorous Fortunato Vizcarrondo, in "Lamento de esclavo," musters heavy pathos and sardonic irony, where the lyrically onomatopoeic Caribbean-Spanish patois (re)presents the grievances of an old, infirm slave being beaten to death by the overseer driving him to work in the cane fields (1976, 73).

The more mainstream *criollo* plantation fantasies, in contrast, evoked the days of slavery in much more Arcadian terms. The *blanquito/a* nostalgia narratives incarnating the local equivalent of what in the United States are called mammy figures were among the more common renderings of these plantation fantasies. Here the older black or dark mulatto woman is integrated within the cultural nationalist landscape of *criollo blanchitude* via the racial/racist mirage of the loving domestic and/or nursemaid (slave, emancipated, or freeborn) depicted as the paragon of devotion and selfless service (C. Williams 2000, 126–27). This bodyscape deployment of plantation fantasies dovetailed with the local populist uses of the later, official racial-democracy narratives. Such resonance was partly corroborated by the fact that some of these specific poems were reprinted as literary and cultural exemplars within an anthology aimed at "native" students in Puerto Rico's public high schools (Gómez Tejera 1958). This anthology was published by the postwar, formally populist, colonial administration's explicitly *dirigista* and socially disciplinary Departamento de Instrucción (often misleadingly translated as "Department of Education").

However, imagery of this sort was not limited to the domain of poetry. There is no shortage of prose regarding the trope of the "selflessly devoted" and "loyal" black nanny or servant—slave and nonslave—among patrician literary production during the entire first half of the twentieth century. Such is the case of the "Lupe" and "Baquiné" chapters of Luis Palés Matos's unfinished autobiographical novel *Litoral*, serialized in *El Mundo* in 1947 (in Arce de Vázquez 1984b, 67–68, 85–92), as well as María Cadilla de Martínez's *Hitos de raza* (1945, 49–53) and Pepita Caballero Balseiro's "Dedicatoria" to her novel *Bajo el vuelo de los alcatraces* (1956). Critiques of this trope and some of its uses already exist, including Roy-Féquière (1993, 173–76, 195–96), Santiago-Valles (1998), and C. Williams (2000, 117–21, 126–29).

The number of semi-autobiographical poems, under the often recurring designation of "La negra que me crió," offers a paradigmatic example of these seemingly lifelike socio-racial utopias. One such work was written at the turn of the century by Félix Matos Bernier; in it the slave-nanny is not sold but handed down to the white-*criollo* child as part of his birthright ("La negra que me crió/nunca la vendió mi abuelo"). The "native" patrician child in turn inherits her spiritual goodness ("Ella su ejemplo me dió/porque era buena y decente"), enabling her to transcend bondage and death through the living example of the Euro-Caribbean boy turned honorable man ("libre y honrada murió/y aún vive gloriosamente/porque vivo yo") (in Morales 1981, 35). This widespread theme achieved canonical stature in the case of the brother of Luis Palés Matos—Vicente—who has another autobiographical poem within this subgenre, also titled "La negra que me crió." Written during the interwar period, and with practically indistinguishable family-romance motifs, this poem focused on the black nursemaid's ample bosom ("y el gordo seno que me daba") (Gómez Tejera 1958, 97).

Such was also the case of Ramírez de Nolla's (1947, 59–60) "Tonga Bembé," wherein the suffering of the Middle Passage is transcended ("Piensa . . ./en el calvario de su viaje") as the fictive mammy joyfully cradles and nurses the snow-white baby in her coal-black arms (". . . en la nueva/felicidad del hijo blanco en/su regazo," "fruta de nieve de blanca mujer/. . . Mi leche africana le doy a este ser"). Hartman's incisive critique of the slave era's version of such tropes once again comes to mind: "Thus, the brutality and antagonisms of slavery are obscured in favor of enchanting reciprocity. The pastoral renders the state of domination as an ideal of care, duty, familial obligation, gratitude, and humanity" (1997, 53).

Melodramatic reveries about interracial relations were also implicitly or candidly sexualized in additional and no less hackneyed ways. In the poem "Angustia" from the 1930s, the narrative persona of the "native," white patrician author Clara Lair (a.k.a. Mercedes Negrón Muñoz) anxiously avoids the dark-skinned street man ("hombre de la esquina, . . . moreno"). The latter figure luridly eyes her (white) breasts (". . . que mira a mi seno/que masculla entre dientes una frase lasciva"), even as she feels aroused by his lecherous glances ("que encendiera en mi cuerpo su mirada lasciva") (Lair 1937, 38). Likewise, in "Puertos del Caribe," Ribera Chevremont portrays yet another white-*criollo* character consumed by erotically charged "local color." The *blanquito* in question nervously stares at—and aches for—Africoid flesh, this time in the form of sun-browned women with wide-hipped cadences ("Muchachas de ancho ritmo/de talles en meneo") (Ribera Chevremont 1971, 58–59). In "Arrabales" this same author's poetic voice dis-covers identical textual landscapes and sexual topographies in the island's slums and their dilapidated movie houses ("Arrabales de cines mal cuidados"). This sexually charged landscape is populated by "crude dances" and "African rhythms" ("crudos bailes de africanos ritmos") that "inflamed the hips" ("Que inflaman las caderas") (1951, 23).

However, it was again Palés Matos who most effectively branded this motif (of "naturally" sensual black and mulatto bodies) into the memory of the elite *criollos* and their literary expressions. Palés practically—and magisterially—copyrighted the formula for including the "Negro element" within the neo-foundational ways of narrating the nation. One of his best-known poems, "Majestad negra," is perhaps the quintessential example of how these plantation fantasies and petit-coloniality's politics-of-the-gaze were being recast. As we will see below, such portrayals lyrically—as well as literally—embodied alternate solutions to the locally dominant elites' crisis of representation during the interwar years, exemplifying Puerto Rico's contributions toward the interwar shift in the global-racial regime of the 1870s through the 1940s. This poem has been characterized, then and to this day (for example, Ortíz 1935; Marzán 1995, 42, 93, 109), as one of the premier odes to the alleged majesty of the black and/or dark mulatto woman of the Caribbean ("la Reina avanza"). The specific focus is on her thighs and posterior ("Culipandeando," "meneos cachondos"), which metamorphose into the grinding mechanisms of a sugar mill ("prieto trapiche de sensual zafra/

el caderamen, masa con masa") (Palés Matos 1993, 114–15). What usually gets overlooked—albeit, not by everyone (for example, Zenón Cruz 1975, vol. 2, 101–3; Roy-Féquière 1993, 216–19; Branche 1999; C. Williams 2000, 53–54, 56)—is how in these verses the allegedly majestic object of desire is reduced to her constitutive body parts as Palés's poetic voice textually slices and dices this generic black and/or dark mulatto woman.

Such a preeminently emblematic poem was not only extensively re-printed (in Puerto Rico, Cuba, Colombia, and Venezuela) between 1934 and 1936 before it was officially anthologized in 1937 (López Baralt 1997, 138). The prominence and representative nature of "Majestad negra" is also illustrated by the poem having been performed in 1938 as part of the colonial *Escuela del Aire* radio programs. These radio performances sponsored by the Departamento de Instrucción were aimed at "combating illiteracy, providing information about social and economic problems, and offering musical and theatrical entertainment." "Majestad negra" also became part of the repertoire of González Marín and Eusebia Cosme in their much touted and widely acclaimed recitals of Negro-themed poetry performed in Puerto Rico and in Spain between 1934 and 1938 (López Baralt 1997, 133, 137–45).

For much canonical literary criticism of the past four decades, Palés Matos was "merely" approaching "the Negro," "Africa," and "Africans" with "the nostalgia with which a civilized man sees beings who live closer to nature" (Vientós Gastón 1959, 7–8) due to the "profound and radical disappoint-ment of Man" with "the sophistry which has civilized him" and his "constant preoccupation with returning to what is essential, basic, rudimentary, pri-mordial" (Agrait 1959, 39). The petit-coloniality reinforced by such neo-pa-trician paternalism and racialized infantilization evokes (presciently or not) the grand coloniality of European liberalism (for example, Sartre) parodied by Fanon (1967, 132). The modernism of Palés exemplified how the Occi-dentalist imaginary of *criollo blanchitude* was but the local Puerto Rican in-stance of the ascendant patterns of intelligibility within the world-historical shifts in the prevailing global-racial regime throughout the interwar period. Within this context, "the Negro," specifically the Negro's laboring-poor ma-jority (as with other "lesser races" and "subject peoples," like "the Indian"), was a space or landscape—and a stage—of racial childhood. This stage was the phase Europeans, European Americans, Euro-Caribbean modernists, and even some elites, both *mestizo* and those descended from Africans, could turn to for aesthetico-spiritual and national-cultural revitalization, identity boundary maintenance, and/or self-discovery.

In contrast and according to Díaz Quiñones, what Palés Matos does in

Tuntún de pasa y grifería is recuperate and mobilize "blackness" for two overlapping reasons. On the one hand, *lo negro* is the "important element of Antillean culture" that Palés allegedly wants to explain and defend, thereby "reconstructing that society in his poetry." On the other hand and for the Palés of Díaz Quiñones (1982, 85), "blackness" is a cultural-political catalyst enabling this necessary Antillean rebirth and reinvention due to the differentiating characteristics of "the Negro" vis-à-vis both Spain and the United States. What could be missing from the latter interpretation is how exactly the "Tronco" ([tree] trunk) and "Rama" ([tree] limb) segments of *Tuntún de pasa y grifería* (for example, poems such as "Kalahari" and "Pueblo negro") recast and re-presented "Africa," "Africans," and "blackness" (including the diaspora). All three overlapping categories materialize as a pre-text for the poet's journey into "his" interior being/child/origins as the displaced referents of this Antillean selfhood and as fascinating outlandish curiosities for Occidentalist voyeurism and/or desire, as well as for Western and Westernized introspection and critique (Roy-Féquière 1993, 212–13).

The Interwar Shifts in the Global-Racial Regime and Puerto Rico's Crisis of Representation in the 1930s

Racialized infantilization and socio-cultural rebirth linked *poesía negroide* and racial-democracy narratives with the emerging populism, both semiotic and juridico-political, of Puerto Rico (early 1930s to mid-1940s), which partially included leading Nacionalistas. Of course, there were the increasingly dated patrician narratives à la Pedreira (1934) and the more contradictory *blanchitude* of literary figures such as Emilio S. Belaval (1977, 41–42, 56, 59, 85, 94–95). The latter two exemplified the local instances of the older, global episteme of social Darwinism and eugenics, which was in crisis during the interwar period due to the challenges of both the subaltern and elite *criollo* sectors.

However contradictory, Palés's *negrista* poetry was a key component of this interrogation of social Darwinism and eugenics because it included *lo negro*; unlike that of its predecessors and detractors, his *poesía negroide* included "Africanity" within the grand narrative of Puerto Ricanness. Even so, this socio-racial Other was incorporated only as a subordinate, immature, domesticated, exoticized, and distanced component within the shifting imaginary of the cultural nationalism of whites and near-white *criollos*. Within the topography of Palés's Negro-themed poetry, *lo negro* was abstracted right out of the very Antillean culture—and right out of the very nation—of which it was supposed to be such an "important element." It is in this sense that *poesía negroide*, racial-democracy writings, and their corollary populist discourses in Puerto Rico helped constitute the new techniques of signification (the order of knowledge) that would coalesce into one aspect of the postwar global-racial regime, in addition to its bio-political components and hierarchy of forces (its order of being). Such an articulation between "the local" and "the global" is itself illustrated by how these very same Puerto Rican textual practices were partly responding to the effects of the interwar planetary hegemonic breakdown and tensions, including Caribbean-wide anti-systemic challenges.

The First World War resulted in the United States and Germany (and their respective allies) vying against each other over who was going to oc-cupy the vacuum left by the final collapse of British hegemony. Neverthe-less, the end of the European War also brought about wide-ranging strata-gems implemented by global capital to address the downward phase in the systemic cycle of accumulation in the interwar period. The latter included massive lay-offs, work speed-ups, sharp drops in income levels, and rural expulsions, all of which hit peripheral populations the hardest (Arrighi 1994, 270–95). As in previous centuries, numerous resistance movements erupted when subaltern and laboring-poor sectors across the globe stepped into the breach in the structural integrity of the colonial-capitalist world-system. But certain global-capitalist factions were also contesting the declining episteme of social Darwinism and eugenics, which was in crisis, by proposing new, elite racial-signification practices and bio-political institutionalities, as we will see below.

Some of the most significant mass struggles between the two world wars were spearheaded by racially depreciated populations under direct colonial domination in Asia, Africa, North America (Padmore 1931, 78–103; Crum-mey 1986, 311–22, 333–50; Walton 1986, 49–51, 116–19, 123; Aldrich 1996, 269–72), and the British West Indies during 1914–20 and the 1930s. The Caribbean revolts asymmetrically overlapped with militant trade-union-ism, nationalist activism, Garveyism, rastafari, pan-Africanism, and anti-imperialist rebellions on both sides of the Atlantic (C. James 1969; Martin 1973, 1974; Campbell 1987, 69–92; W. James 1998, 122–257; Bolland 2001, 212–378). Comparable hostilities broke out during 1914–39 in those coun-tries in the Caribbean Basin that were under direct U.S. military occupation: Haiti, the Dominican Republic, Nicaragua, El Salvador, and Cuba (Farber 1974, 28–51; Alvarez Soliz 1982; Langley 2002, 111–220).

Strikes across Puerto Rico during 1915–21 and again in 1928–34 and

1938–39, especially in the cane fields and the dockyards, became another regional component of this worldwide wave of social turmoil (Silvestrini 1979, 55–72; Silvestrini 1980, 61–64, 69–70, 75–80; Quintero Rivera and García 1982, 106–13, 118–20). These strikes were part of a wider social unrest associated with material life and subaltern illegalities in Puerto Rico stretching into the 1940s (Bary 1923, 26, 28–29; Enamorado Cuesta 1929, 75–76; Roosevelt 1930, Clark 1930, 465, 565). Local journalists and social reformers tended to identify this disorder as implicitly (and sometimes explicitly) with blacks and mulattos (for example, del Valle Atiles 1919, 7, 10–11; Rosario 1933, 11, 54–55; González Prieto 1939, 60). These discursive uses underpinned the "public opinion" of the *criollo* elites on how *lo negro* was being read at this time, supplementing the tropes of patrician and bohemian *negrista* poetry. Yet the racialization of this largely urban and/or coastal social unrest also stemmed from the high concentrations of blacks and mulattos in the coastal areas with most of the island's seaports and sugar-cane plantations. This connection heightened in the Great Depression when many Puerto Ricans of color migrated from the central highlands to coastal towns and cities during 1935–40 (Zelinsky 1949, 215). Although by 1940 Afro-descended males were only 22 percent of the entire labor force in the island, they constituted 30 percent of the sugar-cane workers and 44 percent of the longshoremen and stevedores (USBC 1941, 61, 63).

In the case of overseas colonial and neo-colonial contexts, the core governments and/or their comprador client-states responded in two ways to this global anti-systemic wave, worldwide hegemonic breakdown, and downward economic phase. On the one hand, there was brutal (racialized) repression, corroborating the persistence of coercion as a definitive and continuing feature of the older episteme of social Darwinism and eugenics that was in crisis. Yet the continuing saliency of force likewise confirmed coercion as constitutive of the new semiotic and bio-political elements that would transform the reigning global-racial regime. In terms of regulating racially depreciated populations, this included massacres and pogroms in British India (1919), the United States (1917–21), French-ruled Syria-Lebanon (1925), U.S.-occupied Nicaragua (1926–27), colonial Puerto Rico (1937), and the neo-colonial Dominican Republic (1937) (Megee 1965; Pérez Marchand 1972; Draper 1981; Rabbath 1982; García 1983; Shapiro 1988, 115–18, 145–57, 181–84).

On the other hand and between the two world wars, an emergent hierarchy of economic, cultural, and administrative forces began transforming the global-racial regime via measures that included, among other things, the limited introduction of "native" legislative authority, import-tariff reforms, and/or local industrialization programs in British India (1919–35), French Algeria (1928), other French colonies in Africa and Asia (1936–38), the British West Indies (1938–45), and many of Britain's African colonies (1939–45) (Tomlinson 1979; Aldrich 1996, 118–19, 214; Bush 1999, 263–65); in the United States, the New Deal's judicial reorganization paved the way for postwar formal and legal desegregation (Sitkoff 1978, McMahon 2003). Similar economic and administrative permutations transpired at this same time within the formally independent regions of the world-system's periphery, in how the local elites administered and socially controlled laboring populations—particularly their racially subordinate populations. Examples include the partial import-substitution-based economic programs, social reforms, and/or related populist socio-economic measures of the 1920s–40s in Mexico, Ecuador, Brazil, Argentina, and, to a certain extent, even the Dominican Republic (Germani 1973; Murmis and Pontantiero 1974; Weffort 1976, 71–75; Betances 1995, 100–107).

The cultural, civico-juridical, and socio-economic reforms unfolding in Puerto Rico from the end of the First World War to the mid-1940s are yet another example of the bio-political and institutional aspects that characterized the nascent global-racial regime. First of all and by the interwar years, the split between *criollo blanchitude*'s "high culture" and the "lowlier" knowledges of Afro-descended groups and other subaltern sectors became a distinction between "higher" college careers (for example, professional writers college instructors, lawyers, physicians, pharmacists, and engineers) and the "lower" professions (for example, teachers and registered nurses) (Osuna 1949, 532–54, 586–90; Benner 1965). Although this shift hardly erased the elitist-racist two-tiered system of the professions, it did expand the access of plebeian sectors to higher education, even as it maintained the relative privileges of the white and near-white *criollo* patricians. Colonial(ist) personnel from the United States also expanded the material conditions for the vociferous Hispanophilia of Puerto Rico's foundational elite and its cultural nationalism, literary renovation, and institution building. Josephine W. Holt (a professor at the University of Puerto Rico's Spanish Summer School for U.S. students) and particularly Thomas E. Benner (the first chancellor of the newly augmented Río Piedras campus of the University of Puerto Rico during 1924–29) were instrumental in establishing the Departmento de Estudios Hispánicos in close cooperation with the Ateneo and in recruiting to this department many other top intellectuals from Spain. Naming as its director Federico de Onís (then a professor at Columbia University), the new department followed the model of Madrid's Centro de Estudios Históricos, which several of these Spanish scholars belonged to. Holt and Benner also played an important part in creating the Instituto de Literatura Puertorriqueña, while Benner himself invited to the University of Puerto Rico leading Latin American politico-literary figures. Foremost among such visits was the commencement address and lecture series in 1926 by José Vasconcelos, the world-renowned Mexican educator-cum-*arielista* and—at that time—an *indigenista* icon and *mestizaje* champion (Vasconcelos n.d., viii–ix, xv–xxiii, xxviii–xxxii; Benner 1965, 55–56, 64, 74, 81–97; Cabrera 1969, 280–84; Roy-Féquière 1993, 23–27).

Second, U.S. colonialism acquiesced to the partially successful demands of patrician *criollos*, enabling *blanquito* sectors to expand significantly their role in running the affairs of the colony by swelling all the ranks of the colonial(ist) executive and legislative bureaucracies in Puerto Rico (1917–45). There was even a marked accretion of high-ranking "native" bureaucrats at the federal levels of the colonial civil service (Mathews 1960, 23). Finally and similar to France and England, the U.S. government too partially extended specific features of its early Keynesian social reforms to the Puerto Rican colony from the mid-1930s to the mid-1940s and for comparable reasons. This eventually entailed unevenly raising the consumption capacities of particular sectors of the "native" population and revitalizing local industrial output, while neutralizing the elevated levels of social unrest via the Puerto Rico Emergency Relief Administration, the Plan Chardón, the Puerto Rico Reconstruction Administration, the inclusion of the island within certain federal minimum wage legislation, a very limited land reform, and the creation of state-owned light industries (Perloff 1950, 37–39, 60, 83–84, 136–47; Edel 1962, 38, 52–53, 55–57; Lewis 1963, 124–87).

In any case, the 1910s–40s and particularly the 1930s also coincided with the *criollo* elites' crisis of representation. The upsurge of restless landless peasants and destitute small-property owners—uneasily associated with the Unionista party and (after 1931) its Liberal successor—overlapped with growing unrest protagonized by coastal and/or urban laborers historically identified as the Socialista party's rank and file. As we already saw, this local discord in turn mirrored the revolts and bloody repression spanning the Caribbean Basin and the broader Atlantic during the 1930s. From the perspective of most "native" patricians, this turbulent panorama was further complicated in the 1930s by two additional events.

On the one hand and beginning in the late 1920s, a minority fraction of this "native" elite's constituents—particularly their younger progeny now in the urban "higher" professions—began revamping the old Nacionalista party (established in 1922), closing ranks with extremely pauperized small-property holders and landless peasants (Ferrao 1990, 90, 92–94, 141–42). Before long the new Nacionalista party jettisoned its earlier moderate stance of "home rule" or independence "in friendship with the U.S."—that is, the stance still favored by the cultural-nationalist wing of the Unionistas, later the Liberales. Under the singular leadership of the mulatto lawyer and fiery orator Pedro Albizu Campos, throughout the 1930s the Nacionalistas adopted a platform couched in *arielista* terms that was aggressively opposed to U.S. corporations (see, for example,: Rivera Matos 1930; Albizu Campos 1934a, 1934b, 1935, and 1972, 194, 198–99, 206, 211, 217). Soon the party adopted a strong populist conviction (Albizu Campos 1930, 1934a, 1972) and sporadic displays of armed direct action. On the other hand, the Socialista party, which was based in the trade unions, co-captured the reins of the colonial legislature (1932–40) in an electoral front (La Coalición) that was opposed to the cultural-nationalists. This electoral victory was only made possible under the direction the Socialists' fellow coalition partners, namely the local political representatives of the U.S. sugar companies, the Partido Republicano leadership, which advocated a program of "industrial peace" (Silvestrini 1979).

This was one way in which the bifurcation between the "higher" and "lower" professions and the corresponding bifurcation of "native" *belles lettres* reflected and reinforced elite white-*criollo* anxieties and tensions over the upheavals and incertitude disrupting Puerto Rico during the inter-war period. Most of these patricians were unaware that the Socialistas and their trade-union federation were morally bankrupt in the eyes of many rank-and-file laborers. Examples of this bankruptcy include the wildcat general strike of 1933–34 (when the cane workers sought and received Nacionalista support and direction) and the massive dockyard strike of 1938. Likewise, this white-*criollo* minority could not initially ascertain whether or not Puerto Rico's dispossessed rural majorities (who so far had backed the Unionistas/Liberales) would eventually turn to the more militant Nacionalistas. For the majority of genteel Euro-*criollos* their dream of "home rule"—or even of eventual, moderate independence—was melting into air. The imagined republic of *criollo blanchitude* was being shattered not only by Coalición legislators and colonial officials, who now included a handful of black and dark mulatto bureaucrats. These genteel patriotic aspirations were disrupted and challenged by Nacionalista rabble-rousing provocations led by the putative *hispanismo* of a mulatto firebrand such as Albizu Campos.

Such was the crisis of representation among the island's locally dominant sectors during the 1930s. The social unrest of this decade confirmed
the worst fears of the Hispanophile Unionista/Liberal elites, who could no
longer take for granted their erstwhile social base of destitute peasants and
landless workers as subaltern illegalities increasingly echoed the growing
Caribbean and Latin American instability. For their part, the Republicano
bourgeois leadership could no longer guarantee the Socialista bureaucrats'
ability to rein in the even more disorderly urban protests and the militancy
of coastal laborers. All the major, "native," political high commands (along
with their big-business- and/or middle-class supporters) had ended up
further alienating their laboring-poor electorate. An important piece was
missing from the island's political puzzle: most *blanquito* circles could not
fathom the socio-racial content of the "labor"-"land" questions.

Yet, through fits and starts, a variegated politico-cultural alternative was
on the rise, pointing toward several populist solutions to Puerto Rico's version of what in Latin America has been called an "unstable equilibrium
among the dominant groups" (Weffort 1976, 95). This alternate vision came
from certain déclassé urban professionals among the heirs to declining coffee fortunes and small to medium sugar estates, such as Tomás Blanco, Vicente Geigel Polanco, and, especially Luis Muñoz Marín. This vision overlapped contradictorily with certain top Nacionalista proposals, whether
from high-born white-*criollos* (for example, Antonio J. Colorado) or nonwhite and near-white elements of laboring-poor background (for example,
Albizu Campos and Clemente Soto Vélez). The textual practices of this
amalgamated fraction of the "native" intelligentsia foresaw that this island's
laboring-poor masses—particularly in terms of socio-racial discourses—
were a pivotal social force to be mobilized to create a "state of compromise"
(Brandão Lopes 1966, 102; Weffort 1976, 96) between the local elites administering the colony's government.

Such proposals were part and parcel of Latin America's populist-inflected
racial-democracy texts, including the burgeoning *indigenista* sectors whose
unfolding helped establish what soon would become the postwar global-
racial regime's order of knowledge, in part due to the rise to prominence of
its constitutive elements between the two world wars. Luis Villoro's comments about interwar Mexico could easily have applied to Puerto Rico,
the rest of the Caribbean, and Latin America: the goals of this generation's
politico-cultural program were "social nationalism, the pursuit of a culture
of one's own, the betterment of the masses through the conscious actions
of a popular state, the salvation of the indigenous peasant" and/or other

nonwhite masses, plus "the construction of a more equitable society" (1995, 66). Eduardo Devés Valdés's remarks about Gabriela Mistral during this period also come to mind: "The subject of racial mixture, of *indigenismo*, and, to a lesser extent, of African heritage, cannot be separated from the land question and of agrarian claims" (2000, 118). Comparable contributing elements to the interwar crisis of the global-racial regime comprised those arguing—for example, Jacques Roumain, Normil Sylvain, Jean Price-Mars, Georges Petit, and Carl Brouard, particularly those grouped in L'Union Patriotique—that true Haitian culture was not a mere European transplant but a unique French-African amalgamation where the *créole*-speaking peasantry was vital (Nicholls 1996, 149–64).

In Puerto Rico this type of conciliatory writing tended to suppress socio-racial contradictions, as compared to those writers who saw a "biological civil war" spreading across the island (Pedreira 1934, 24–30). Instead, those advocating racial democracy—whether from above (Blanco, Palés) or from below (Albizu Campos)—argued that what in fact predominated was an extensive racial-cultural mixture and a concomitant "leveling effect" linked to the overwhelming Hispanization of the entire population.[8] Race-class divisions were perceived to have been mostly surpassed, despite certain residual, benign prejudice among white-*criollos*, an inferiority complex among Afro-descended individuals, and/or the absence of any "real" and "true" racism, a classification solely reserved for the U.S. South.[9]

This was how Negro-themed poetry, in particular of the Palés variety, became integral to Puerto Rico's elite racial-democracy standpoints, emerging as a local instance of the advancing modes of intelligibility that would comprise the postwar global-racial regime. These narratives too placed a greater emphasis on cultural-behavioral factors ("Hispanization" regardless of race), rather than on the physical elements ("biological civil war"). It is true that certain aspects of racial-democracy discourses asymmetrically predate the last phase of global liberalism (1873–1915), as in the literature informed by Western and Westernized abolitionism and social reform. But advocates of racial democracy actually flourished in Latin America and the Caribbean as a response to the worldwide labor strife and subaltern resistance during and between the twentieth century's two world wars. The order of knowledge that these new perspectives confronted globally were the then predominant social Darwinism (1876–1900) and its successors, which were in favor of "hard" eugenics (1901–45) (Gould 1981, 73–233; Stepan 1991, 96–97; Baker 1998, 26–98). In Puerto Rico social Darwinism and/or "hard" eugenics had a number of eminent partisans between the 1890s and the 1930s, including Manuel Zeno Gandía (1975, 24), Manuel Fernández Juncos (Carroll 1899, 245–48), José de Diego (1901), Francisco del Valle Atiles (1913, 1914a, 1914b), and Antonio Pedreira (1934). Albeit chronologically—and, at times, conceptually—overlapping with social Darwinism and eugenics during the 1890s through 1945, the rising "ethnicity theories" and "race-relations" interpretations represented the Western critique of the ruling episteme. From this other, divergent standpoint, cultural (not biological) factors were understood as the principal explanatory component behind the existence of racial-ethnic differentiation (Cox 1970; Stepan 1982, 140–69; Barkan 1992; Baker 1998, 101–87; Jacobson 1998, 99–109).

This crucial shift spanned the decades between British hegemony's *belle époque* and the triumph of the "American century" at the end of the Second World War. At that time, these Western "ethnicity theories," "race relations" studies, and new natural science analyses were imbricated with the Latin American, Caribbean, and African American literature, political tracts, social science investigations, and natural science studies espousing *mestizaje*, *négritude*, and/or *indigenismo*. But in varying degrees such perspectives still subscribed to some form of European culture as the ultimate depository of modernity and progress.[10]

At that time, extensive exchanges occurred among various elements within the Latin American, Caribbean, and/or Afro-diasporic advocates of racial democracy and ethnic roots. In Puerto Rico, as was previously mentioned, in 1926 the University of Puerto Rico sponsored a tour by Vasconcelos, who also met with top Nacionalista leaders, especially Albizu Campos, given Vasconcelos's (n.d., xxiv–xxv, 18–21, 70–108) expressed interest in Puerto Rico's racial-ethnic mixture vis-à-vis the rest of the Americas. In turn, Albizu's visit to Haiti the following year was received by, and involved contacts with, part of the leadership of Price-Mars's L'Union Patriotique (*El Mundo* 1927). Parallel links included Fernando Ortiz's essays on Palés's *poesía negroide* and on the *bomba* genre of Afro-diasporic Puerto Rican music (Ortíz 1935, 1953). Similarly, Tomás Blanco premiered his famous essay on racial prejudice in Puerto Rico, not in this island, but in Cuba. Blanco presented his essay in 1937 at the Institución Hispano-Cubana de Cultura, a forum organized by Fernando Ortíz. Not coincidentally, Blanco's essay saw its first publication in 1938, again not in Puerto Rico, but in a Cuban journal also inspired by Ortíz: *Estudios Afrocubanos* (Blanco 1938; 1942, 1).

Conclusions

Such was the world-historical juncture in which Negro-themed poetry in Puerto Rico was embraced and mobilized by key elements of the island's intelligentsia. This poetic genre was the literary equivalent of the racial democracy writings and social science scholarship, as well as of the populist rhetoric conveyed by the rising stars of public oratory (Albizu Campos) and of the political campaign circuit (Muñoz Marín). The maximum exponent of this genre, Palés Matos, had foreseen these very same possibilities regarding the black-mulatto-African poetic subject matter in an interview with Angela Negrón Muñoz in 1932 in *El Mundo* (see Arce de Vázquez 1984b: 297-302).

Like the racial democracy literati, the social science essayists, and the populist elite politicians, for Palés Caribbean poetic practices pursuing cultural-national legitimacy needed to remain among "the people." The latter's indisputable nonwhite racial markers were no less authentic ("passions," "vital rhythm"), their corporeal topography no less racialized: "people" here meant "the basic adaptation between race and landscape" (in Arce de Vázquez 1984b, 298–99). Therein exists the profuse blurring between physical environment and bodyscapes within his *poesía negroide*—with all the modernist odes to primitivism this implied, ultimately reducing persons to their natural surroundings and instincts. Identical to social scientists and populist politicians, Palés argued that the *negrista* poet transformed, reshaped, distilled, and purified this social element, "stylizing it," "taking away its heaviness and quotidian characteristics." The poet's expert knowledge and learned craft masterfully accomplished this transformation "through graceful irony and selection." It is this appropriately transfigured yet still infantilized vitality that would enable the (re)birth of the "new race" of the (Hispanic) Antilles, apparently no longer Spanish (in Arce de Vázquez 1984b, 298–99).

The 1938–45 Muñocista *caudillos* surpassed the Albizuista chieftains (despite the latter's much more militant anti-imperialism) insofar as the Muñocistas garnered the means to organize Puerto Rico's laboring-poor masses as the key social force electorally mobilized to create the desired "state of compromise" between locally dominant classes. At this level, the Muñocistas also went beyond most of the racial democracy essayists who, like the Nacionalista top leadership, had also argued for the leveling effects of widespread racial mixture and a complicated Hispanization that allegedly had suppressed all fundamental socio-racial conflicts. It is precisely at this level where the textual practices of Palés Matos were much closer to those of Muñoz Marín than to those of Albizu Campos. For Palés, cultural nationalism had to "intermingle" with "the fertility, the strength, and the vigor" (in Arce de Vázquez 1984b, 299, 300) of the Afro-descended populations (disproportionately the laboring poor). Such "intermingling," under white-*criollo* command, would enable the spiritual-psychological renewal of Puerto Rico. For Palés and his politico-literary cohort, *this* was the road to the cultural and political (re)birth of the "new race" of the (Hispanic) Antilles in the midst of an increasingly stormy and volatile Caribbean region and Atlantic world.

Notes

1. This terminological modification draws on Aníbal Quijano's argument that the capitalist world-system, from its origins to the present day, is *inherently colonial* due to the racialized character of its global division of labor (Velarde 1991; Quijano 1997, 2000). Of course, the world-historical links between global capitalism and colonialism—which for much of their existence have been based on chattel slavery and racism (past and present)—had previously been pointed out by Du Bois ([1915] 1995, 48–49, 52), as well as by E. Williams (1966), Oliver C. Cox (1970, 322, 330–45), and Cedric Robinson (2000, 9–10, 16–21, 24–27, 103–20, 125–30, 199–203).

2. See Zenón Cruz 1974–1975; Jackson 1976, 42–45; Jackson 1988; L. Johnson 1977; Wynter 1977; Roy-Féquière 1993; Santiago-Valles 1998; Jiménez-Muñoz 1998; Branche 1999; Rivera Casellas 1999; C. Williams 2000, 53–56, 60–63, 86–89.

3. *Blanquito/a* was the derisive term used by most of Puerto Rico's population—since at least the late nineteenth century—to refer to the *criollo* white and near-white propertied and highly educated classes.

4. For a different conception and usage of this term, see Holden 1995, Jacobson 1998, Holt 2000.

5. On this particular point, I disagree with Quijano (2000, 533–34), who mostly understands "race" in mainly instrumentalist-ideational terms: a "mental category," "an idea," "a codification" justifying the colonial domination and exploitation of labor in the periphery (see also Quijano and Wallerstein 1992, 551).

6. Although the writings of Puerto Ricans in the United States *did* address the issue of "race" (e.g., Arturo Schomburg, Bernardo Vega, Jesús Colón, Pura Belpré, Ramón A. Martínez, and others), for reasons of time and space I am not going to examine that literary production in this essay.

7. See Matheus 1938; Lopes 1989; Summer 1993, 114–37, 153–54, 160–61, 181–82, 199–202, 364–65; Kutzinski 1993; Sharpley-Whiting 1999; Ruíz 2003.

8. See, for example, Albizu Campos 1934b; 1935; 1972, 195–96, 211–12; Geigel Polanco 1936.

9. See, for example, Rosario and Carrión 1939, 51–87; Blanco 1942, 10–11, 14–17, 20–23, 31–35, 60, 63–65; Albizu Campos 1972, 213–14.

10. In the rest of Latin America, the Caribbean, and/or the African diaspora at this time, such scholarship and writing encompassed that of Rubén Darío (1950; 1953), José Martí (1959; 1980, 11, 15, 17, 26), Manuel González Prada (1924), Andrés Molina Enríquez (1981), Manuel Gamio (1960), Ricardo Rojas (1924), José Carlos Mariátegui (1969), José Vasconcelos (n.d.; 1948), W. E. B. Du Bois ([1915] 1995; 1984), Alain Locke (1968), Arthur H. Fauset (1927), Zora Neale Hurston (1930; 1931), Ellen Irene Diggs (1971; see also Baker 1998, 166), Claude McKay (1973), Jean Price-Mars (1954), Fernando Ortíz (1973), Emilia Bernal (1937), Manuel del Cabral (1935; 1943), Mário de Andrade (1935), Ciro Alegría (1971), Edgar Roquette-Pinto (1978), Artur Ramos (1935), Gilberto Freyre (1978), St. Clair Drake and Horace R. Clayton (1945), and E. Franklin Frazier (1939). See also Stepan (1991, 145–51, 160–69); Summer (1993, 162–63, 364–65, 367–68); Arroyo (2003); Duno Gottberg (2003, 45–155), and Jacques Roumain (1995; see also Nicholls 1996, 160, 163).

Works Cited

Agrait, Gustavo. 1959. "Una posible explicación del ciclo negro de la poesía de Palés." *Revista del Instituto de Cultura Puertorriqueña* 2.3: 39–41.

Albizu Campos, Pedro. 1930. "Comentarios del Presidente del Partido Nacionalista al margen del informe rendido por el Instituto Brookings." *El Mundo*, May 29: 3, 5.

———. 1934a. La esclavitud azucarera" El Mundo, January 19: 2,19.

———. 1934b "Correspondencia sobre la Bandera de la Raza." *El Mundo*, May 30: 2, 10, 12.

———. 1935. "Concepto de la raza." *La Palabra*, October 19: 7.

———. 1972. "Discurso del 'Día de La Raza' [Oct. 12, 1933]." In *La conciencia nacional puertorriqueña*, ed. Manuel Maldonado Denis, 191–218. Mexico City: Siglo XXI Editores.

Aldrich, Robert. 1996. *Greater France: A History of French Overseas Expansion*. London: Macmillan.

Alvarez Soliz, Antonio. 1982. *El Salvador: La larga marcha de un pueblo, 1932–82*. Madrid: Editorial Revolución.

Arce de Vázquez, Margot, ed. 1984a. *Luis Palés Matos: Obras, 1914–1959*. Vol. 1, *Poesía*. Río Piedras: Editorial de la Universidad de Puerto Rico.

———. 1984b. *Luis Palés Matos: Obras, 1914–1959*. Vol. 2, *Prosa*. Río Piedras: Editorial de la Universidad de Puerto Rico.

Arrighi, Giovanni. 1994. *The Long Twentieth Century*. London: Verso.

Arroyo, Josianna. 2003. *Travestismos culturales*. Pittsburgh: Instituto Internacional de Literatura Iberoamericana.

Baker, Lee D. 1998. *From Savage to Negro*. Berkeley: University of California Press.

Barkan, Elazar. 1992. *The Retreat of Scientific Racism*. Cambridge: Cambridge University Press.

Bary, Helen V. 1923. *Child Welfare in the Insular Possessions of the United States, Part I: Porto Rico*. Washington, D.C.: U.S. Child Welfare Bureau, Government Printing Office.

Batchen, Gregory. 1997. *Burning with Desire*. Cambridge, Mass.: MIT Press.

Belaval, Emilio S. 1977. *Problemas de la cultura puertorriqueña*. Río Piedras: Editorial Cultural.

Benner, Thomas E. 1965. *Five Years of Foundation Building: The University of Puerto Rico, 1924–1929*. Río Piedras: University of Puerto Rico Press.

Bernal, Emilia. 1937. *La raza negra en Cuba*. Santiago de Chile: Prensas de la Universidad de Chile.

Betances, Emelio. 1995. *State and Society in the Dominican Republic*. Boulder, Colo.: Westview Press.

Blanco, Tomás. 1938. "El prejuicio racial en Puerto Rico." *Estudios Afrocubanos* 2.1: 19–39.

———. 1942. *El prejuicio racial en Puerto Rico*. San Juan: Editorial Biblioteca de Autores Puertorriqueños.

Bolland, O. Nigel. 2001. *The Politics of Labour in the Caribbean*. Princeton, N.J.: Markus Wiener Publications.

Branche, Jerome. 1999. "Negrismo: Hibridez cultural, autoridad y la cuestión de la nación." *Revista Iberoamericana* 61.188–89 (July-December): 483–504.

Brandão Lopes, Juárez Rubens. 1966. *Desenvolvimento e mudanza social*. São Paulo: Edit. Mimeo.

Braudel, Fernand. 1972. "History and the Social Sciences." In *Economy and Society in Early Modern Europe: Essays from the Annales*, ed. Peter Burke, 11–42. New York: Harper and Row.

Bush, Barbara. 1999. *Imperialism, Race, and Resistance: Africa and Britain, 1919–1945*. London: Routledge.

Caballero Balseiro, Pepita. 1956. "Dedicatoria." In *Bajo el vuelo de los alcatraces: Novela ochocentista*, ed. Pepita Caballero Balseiro. Madrid: Ediciones Ensayos.

Cabrera, Manrique. 1969. *Historia de la literatura puertorriqueña*. Río Piedras: Editorial Cultural.

Cadilla de Martínez, María. 1945. *Hitos de raza*. San Juan: Imprenta Venezuela.

Campbell, Horace. 1987. *Rasta and Resistance*. Trenton, N.J.: Africa World Press.

Carrión Maduro, Tomás. 1927. *La perla*. Ponce: Tipografía El Aguila.

Carroll, Henry K. 1899. *Report on the Island of Porto Rico*. Washington, D.C.: Government Printing Office.

Clark, Victor, ed. 1930. *Porto Rico and Its Problems*. Washington, D.C.: Brookings Institution.

Colón Pellot, Carmen María. 1938. *Ambar mulato (ritmos)*. Arecibo: n.p.

Cox, Oliver C. 1970. *Caste, Class, and Race*. New York: Monthly Review Press.

Crummey, Donald, ed. 1986. *Banditry, Rebellion, and Social Protest in Africa*. London: James Currey.

Darío, Rubén. 1950. "Rojo y Negro." In *Obras completas*. Vol. 2, *Semblanzas*, 91–94. Madrid: Ediciones Castilla, Afrodisio Aguado, S.A.

———. 1953. "Canto a la Argentina." In *Obras completas*. Vol. 5, *Poesía*, 1083–1117. Madrid: Ediciones Castilla, Afrodisio Aguado, S.A..

De Andrade, Mário. 1935. *O Aleijadinho e Álvares de Azevedo: Ensaio*. Rio de Janeiro: N.p. (typewritten original).

De Diego , José. 1901. *Apuntes sobre la delincuencia y la penalidad*. N.p.: Tipografía "La Correspondencia."

De Diego Padró, José1932a. "Antillanismo, criollismo, negroidismo." *El Mundo*, November 19.

———. 1932b. "Tropicalismo, occidentalismo, sentido de la cultura." *El Mundo*, December 18.

Del Cabral, Manuel. 1935. *Doce poemas negros*. Santiago: Tipografía femenina.

———. 1943. *Trópico negro*. Buenos Aires: Editorial Sopena.

Del Valle Atiles, Francisco. 1913. "Puerto Rico ante la eugénica." In *Conferencias dominicales dadas en la Biblioteca Insular de Puerto Rico (desde marzo 9 a mayo 25 de 1913)*, 9–21. San Juan: Bureau of Supplies, Printing, and Transportation.

———. 1914a. "Eugenesis: La base más firme de nuestro progreso." In *Conferencias dominicales dadas en la Biblioteca Insular de Puerto Rico (desde octubre 12, 1913 hasta abril 19, 1914)*, 56–84. San Juan: Bureau of Supplies, Printing, and Transportation.

———. 1914b. "La contribución higienista al futuro de Puerto Rico." In *Conferencias dominicales dadas en la Biblioteca Insular de Puerto Rico (desde octubre 12, 1913 hasta abril 19, 1914)*, 228–37. San Juan: Bureau of Supplies, Printing, and Transportation.

———. 1919. *Un estudio de 168 casos de prostitución: contribución al examen del problema del comercio carnal en Puerto Rico*. San Juan: Tipografía El Compás.

Dessús, Luis Felipe. 1916. *Flores y balas (estados de alma)*. Guayama: Tipografía Unión Guayamesa.

Devés Valdés, Eduardo. 2000. *Del Ariel de Rodó a la CEPAL (1900–1950)*. Santiago: Editorial Biblios/Centro de Investigaciones Diego Barros Arana.

Díaz Quiñones, Arcadio. 1982. *El almuerzo en la hierba*. Río Piedras: Ediciones Huracán.

Diggs, Ellen Irene. 1971. "Attitudes Toward Color in South America." *Negro History Bulletin* 34.5: 107–8.

Drake, St. Clair, and Horace R. Clayton. 1945. *Black Metropolis: A Study of Negro Life in a Northern City*. New York: Harcourt, Brace.

Draper, Alfred. 1981. *Amritsar: The Massacre That Ended the Raj*. Delhi: Macmillan, India, Ltd.

Du Bois, W. E. B. [1915]. 1995. "The Negro Problems." *W. E. B. Du Bois: A Reader*, ed. David Levering Lewis, 48–53. New York: Henry Holt and Company.

———. 1984. *Dusk at Dawn*. New Brunswick, N.J.: Transaction Books.

Duno Gottberg, Luis. 2003. *Solventando las diferencias*. Madrid: Iberoamericana.

Edel, Matthew. 1962. "Land Reform in Puerto Rico—Part I." *Caribbean Studies* (October): 26–60.

El Mundo. 1927. "Albizu Campos estuvo algunas horas en Puerto Príncipe, Haiti. Allí se relacionó con los líderes del nacionalismo haitiano." *El Mundo,* October 1: 17.

Enamorado Cuesta, José. 1929. *Porto Rico, Past and Present.* New York: Eureka Print Co.

Fanon, Frantz. 1967. *Black Skin, White Masks.* New York: Grove Press.

Farber, Samuel. 1974. *Revolution and Reaction in Cuba, 1933–1960.* Middletown, Conn.: Wesleyan University Press.

Fauset, Arthur H. 1927. *For Freedom.* Philadelphia: Franklin Publishing and Supply.

Ferrao, Luis Angel. 1990. *Pedro Albizu Campos y el nacionalismo puertorriqueño.* Río Piedras: Editorial Cultural.

Frazier, E. Franklin. 1939. *The Negro Family in the United States.* Chicago: University of Chicago Press.

Freyre, Gilberto. 1978. *Casa-grande and senzala.* Rio de Janeiro: J. Olympio.

Gamio, Manuel. 1960. *Forjando patria.* Mexico City: Editorial Porrúa.

García, Juan Manuel. 1983. *La matanza de los haitianos, 1937.* Santo Domingo: Editorial Alfa y Omega.

Geigel Polanco, Vicente. 1936. "La nacionalidad puertorriqueña." *Ateneo puertorriqueño* 2.2: 87–93.

Germani, Gino, ed. 1973. *Populismo y contradicciones de clase en Latinoamérica.* Mexico City: Ediciones Era, Serie Popular.

Goings, Kenneth. 1994. *Mammy and Uncle Mose.* Bloomington: Indiana University Press.

Gómez Tejera, Carmen, ed. 1958. *Poesía puertorriqueña para la escuela secundaria.* Hato Rey: Departamento de Instrucción Pública.

González Prada, Manuel. 1924. "Nuestros indios." In *Horas de lucha,* ed. Manuel González Prada, 331–38. Callao: Tipografía "Lux."

González Prieto, Ada María. 1939. "A Study of One-Hundred Twenty-Four Dependent Children in Puerto Rico (1935–1938)." M.A. thesis, Catholic University of America.

Gould, Stephen Jay. 1981. *The Mismeasure of Man.* New York: W. W. Norton.

Hartman, Sadiya. 1997. *Scenes of Subjection.* New York: Oxford University Press.

Hernández, José P. H. 1966. *Obras completas.* San Juan: Instituto de Cultura Puertorriqueña.

Holden, Matthew. 1995. *The Changing Racial Regime.* New Brunswick, N.J.: Transaction Publishers.

Holt, Thomas C. 2000. *The Problem of Race in the 21st Century.* Cambridge, Mass.: Harvard University Press.

Hurston, Zora Neale. 1930. "Dance Songs and Tales from the Bahamas." *Journal of American Folk-Lore* 43: 294–312.

———. 1931. "Hoodoo in America." *Journal of American Folk-Lore* 44: 317–417.

Iguina, Julio Enrique. 1948. *Con lira y guitarra.* Santurce: Imprenta Soltero.

Jackson, Richard. 1976. *The Black Image in Latin American Literature.* Albuquerque: University of New Mexico Press.

———. 1988. *Black Literature and Humanism in Latin America.* Athens: University of Georgia Press.

Jacobson, Matthew Frye. 1998. *Whiteness of Another Color*. Cambridge, Mass.: Harvard University Press.

James, C. L. R. 1969. *A History of Pan-African Revolt*. Washington, D.C.: Drum and Spear Press.

James, Winston. 1998. *Holding Aloft the Banner of Ethiopia*. London: Verso.

Jiménez-Muñoz, Gladys. 1998. "Carmen María Colón Pellot: On 'Womanhood' and 'Race' in Puerto Rico during the Interwar Period." Paper presented at the 21st International Congress of the Latin American Studies Association, Chicago, September 24–26. A slightly revised version of this paper was published in *New Centennial Review* 3.3 (Fall 2003): 71–92.

Johnson, John J. 1980. *Latin America in Caricature*. Austin: University of Texas Press.

Johnson, Lemuel. 1977. "*El Tema Negro*: The Nature of Primitivism in the Poetry of Luis Palés Matos." In *Blacks in Hispanic Literature: Critical Essays*, ed. Miriam DaCosta, 123–36. Port Washington, N.Y.: Kennikat Press.

Kutzinski, Vera. 1993. *Sugar's Secrets*. Charlottesville: University Press of Virginia.

Lair, Clara. 1937. *Aras de cristal*. San Juan: Biblioteca de Autores Puertorriqueños.

Langley, Lester. 2002. *The Banana Wars*. Wilmington, Del.: Scholarly Resources.

Lewis, Gordon K. 1963. *Puerto Rico: Freedom and Power in the Caribbean*. New York: Monthly Review.

Lluch Mora, Francisco. 1961. "Francisco Negroni Mattei, vida y obra." M.A. thesis, University of Puerto Rico, Río Piedras.

Locke, Alain, ed. 1968. *The New Negro*. New York: Atheneum.

Lopes, Francisco Caetano, Jr. 1989. "*Bom-Crioulo*: Between Love and Death." In *Proceedings of The Black Image in Latin American Culture Conference*, ed. Elba Birmingham-Pokorny, 230–40. Slippery Rock, Pa.: Slippery Rock University.

López Baralt, Mercedes. 1997. *El barco en la botella: La poesía de Luis Palés Matos*. San Juan: Editorial Plaza Mayor.

Mariátegui, José Carlos. 1969. *Siete ensayos de interpretación de la realidad peruana*. Lima: Amauta.

Martí, José. 1959. *La cuestión racial*. La Habana: Editorial Lex.

———. 1980. *Nuestra América*. Buenos Aires: Ediciones Losada.

Martin, Tony. 1973. "Revolutionary Upheaval in Trinidad, 1919: Views from British and American Sources." *Journal of Negro History* 58.3 (July): 313–26.

———. 1974. *Race First*. Westport, Conn.: Greenwood Press.

Martínez, Lauro. 1941. *Sentires*. San Juan: Imprenta Rosario.

Marzán, Julio. 1995. *The Numinous Site: The Poetry of Luis Palés Matos*. Madison, N.J.: Fairleigh Dickinson University Press.

Matheus, John F. 1938. "African Footprints in Hispanic-American Literature." *Journal of Negro History* 22.3 (July): 265–89.

Mathews, Thomas. 1960. *Puerto Rican Politics and the New Deal*. Gainesville: University of Florida Press.

McKay, Claude. 1973. "An Open Letter to George Lansbury: A Black Man Replies," "Birthright," and "The Negro in the Future of American Democracy." In *The Passion* of Claude McKay: Selected Poetry and Prose, 1912–1948, ed. Wayne F. Cooper, 54-57, 73-76, 280–82. New York: Schocken Books.

McMahon, Kevin. 2003. *Reconsidering Roosevelt on Race: How the Presidency Paved the Road to Brown*. Chicago: University of Chicago Press.

Megee, Vernon. 1965. "The Genesis of Air Support in Guerrilla Operations." *United States Naval Institute Proceedings* 91 (June): 49–57.

Meisel, Martin. 1983. *Realizations: Narrative, Pictorial, and Theatrical Arts in Nineteenth-Century England*. Princeton, N.J.: Princeton University Press.

Miranda, Luis Antonio. 1932. "El llamado arte negro no tiene vinculación con Puerto Rico." *El Mundo*, November 26, 6.

Miranda Archilla, Graciany. 1933. "La broma de una poesía prieta en Puerto Rico." *Alma Latina* (February): 5, 43.

———. 1937. *Sí de mi tierra: Poemas nuevos*. Puerto Rico, n.p.

Molina Enríquez, Andrés. 1981. *Los grandes problemas nacionales*. Mexico City: Ediciones ERA.

Morales, Jorge Luis. 1981. *Poesía afroantillana y negrista*. Río Piedras: Editorial de la Universidad de Puerto Rico.

Murmis, Miguel, and Juan Carlos Pontantiero. 1974. *Estudios sobre los orígenes del peronismo*. Buenos Aires: Siglo XXI Editores.

Nicholls, David. 1996. *From Dessalines to Duvalier*. New Brunswick, N.J.: Rutgers University Press.

Ortíz, Fernando. 1935. "Los últimos versos mulatos." *Revista Bimestre Cubana* 36.2: 327–28.

———. 1953. "La 'bomba' en Puerto Rico." *Asomante* 9.2: 8–12.

———. 1973. *Contrapunteo cubano del tabaco y el azucar*. Barcelona: Editorial Ariel.

Osuna, Juan José. 1949. *A History of Education in Puerto Rico*. Río Piedras: University of Puerto Rico Press.

Padmore, Roger. 1931. *The Life and Struggles of Negro Toilers*. Hollywood: Sun Dance Press.

Palés Matos, Luis. 1993. *Tuntún de pasa y grifería*. San Juan: Instituto de Cultura Puertorriqueña/Editorial de la Universidad de Puerto Rico.

Pedreira, Antonio S. 1932. *Bibliografía puertorriqueña (1493–1930)*. Madrid: Editorial Hernando.

———. 1934. *Insularismo*. Madrid: Tipografía Artística.

Pérez Marchand, Rafael V. 1972. *Reminiscencia histórica de la Masacre de Ponce*. San Lorenzo: Partido Nacionalista de Puerto Rico.

Perloff, Harvey. 1950. *Puerto Rico's Economic Future: A Study of Planned Development*. Chicago: University of Chicago Press.

Pieterse, Jan Neverdeen. 1992. *White on Black*. New Haven, Conn.: Yale University Press.

Pratt, Mary Louise. 1992. *Imperial Eyes*. New York: Routledge.

Price-Mars, Jean. 1954. *Ainsi parla loncle*. New York: Parapsychology Foundation.

Quijano, Aníbal. 1997. "Colonialidad del poder, cultura y conocimiento en América Latina." *Anuario Mariateguiano* 9: 113–22.

————. 2000. "Coloniality of Power, Eurocentrism, and Latin America." *Nepantla* 1.3: 533–80.

Quijano, Aníbal, and Immanuel Wallerstein. 1992. "Americanity as a Concept, or the Americas in the Modern World-System." *International Social Science Journal* 134: 549–57.

Quintero Rivera, Angel, and Gervasio García. 1982. *Desafío y solidaridad*. Río Piedras: Ediciones Huracán.

Rabbath, Edmond. 1982. "L'Insurrection syrienne de 1925–1927." *Revue historique* 267.2: 405–47.

Ramírez, Rafael. 1930. "El bando del General Prim." *Indice* 1.12: 188–90.

Ramírez de Nolla, Olga. 1947. *Cauce hondo*. San Juan: Imprenta Venezuela.

Ramos, Artur. 1935. *Guerra e relação de raça*. N.p.: Departamento União Nacional dos Estudos.

Ribera Chevremont, Evaristo. N.d. *El templo de los albastros*. Madrid: Ediciones Ambos Mundos.

————. 1951. *Creación*. San Juan: Imprenta Venezuela.

————. 1957. *Antología poética (1924–1950)*. San Juan: Universidad de Puerto Rico.

————. 1971. *Canto de mi tierra*. Río Piedras: Editorial Universitaria.

Rivera Casellas, Zaira O. 1999. "Cuerpo y raza: El ciclo de la identidad negra en la literatura puertorriqueña." *Revista Iberoamericana* 61.188–89 (July-December): 633–48.

Rivera Matos, Manuel. 1930. "'Aquí se dilucidará cuales son los planes y actitud de Estados Unidos hacia los pueblos de nuestra raza,' dijo Albizu Campos en el banquete en su honor." *El Mundo*, March 19: 6.

Robinson, Cedric. 2000. *Black Marxism*. Chapel Hill: University of North Carolina Press.

Rojas, Ricardo. 1924. *Euroindia*. Buenos Aires: Librería de Juan Roldán.

Roosevelt, Theodore, Jr. 1930. "Children of Famine." *Review of Reviews* 81.1 (January): 73.

Roquette-Pinto, Edgar. 1978. *Ensaios de antropología brasileira*. Rio de Janeiro: Editora Nacional.

Rosario, José C. 1933. *A Study of Illegitimacy and Dependent Children in Puerto Rico*. San Juan: Imprenta Venezuela.

Rosario, José C., and Justina Carrión. 1937. "Rebusca sociológica: Una comunidad rural en la zona cañera." *University of Puerto Rico Summer School Review* 15.5: 4–14.

————. 1939. "Problemas sociales: El negro: Haití—Estados Unidos—Puerto Rico." *Boletín de la Universidad de Puerto Rico* 10.2 (December): 1–165.

Roumain, Jacques. 1995. *When the Tom-Tom Beats: Selected Poetry and Prose*. Trans. Joanne Fungaroli and Ronald Sauer. Washington D.C.: Azul Editions.

Roy-Féquière, Magali. 1993. "Race, Gender, and the 'Generación del Treinta': Toward a Deciphering of Puerto Rican National Identity Discourse." Ph.D. diss., Stanford University.

Ruíz, Blamidir. 2003. "Incorporaciones y exclusiones al proyecto de nación: El negro y el indio en la narrativa decimonónica venezolana." *Revista Iberoamericana* 69.205 (October-December): 883–94.

Rydell, Robert. 1984. *All the World's a Fair.* Chicago: University of Chicago Press.

Santiago-Valles, Kelvin. 1998. "The Mark of Colonial Difference in 'Porto Rico' during the Early Twentieth Century: Writing 'Race' and Racialized Writing in the Shadow of the War of 1898." Paper presented at the 1998 Faculty Research Seminar "Legacies of 1898," Obermann Center for Advanced Studies, University of Iowa, Iowa City, June 15–July 2.

———. 1999. "'Still Longing for de Old Plantation': The Visual Parodies and Racial National Imaginary of U.S. Overseas Expansionism, 1898–1903." *American Studies International* 37.3 (October): 18–43.

Shapiro, Herbert. 1988. *White Violence and Black Response.* Amherst: University of Massachusetts Press.

Sharpley-Whiting, T. Denean. 1999. *Black Venus.* Durham, N.C.: Duke University Press.

Silvestrini, Blanca. 1979. *Los trabajadores puertorriqueños y el Partido Socialista, 1932–1940.* Río Piedras: Editorial Universitaria.

———. 1980. *Violencia y criminalidad en Puerto Rico, 1898–1973.* Río Piedras: Editorial Universitaria.

Sitkoff, Harvard. 1978. *A New Deal for Blacks.* New York: Oxford University Press.

Stepan, Nancy Leys. 1982. *The Idea of Race in Science.* London: Macmillan Press, Ltd.

———. 1991. *The Hour of Eugenics.* Ithaca, N.Y.: Cornell University Press.

Summer, Doris. 1993. *Foundational Fictions.* Berkeley: University of California Press.

Sylvain, Normil. 1927. "Un rêve de Georges Sylvain." *Le Revue Indegène* (July): 5.

Tomlinson, Brian R. 1979. *The Political Economy of the Raj, 1914–1947.* London: Macmillan.

U.S. Bureau of the Census. 1941. *Sixteenth Census of the United States: Puerto Rico.* Bulletin no.3, *Occupation and Other Characteristics.* Washington, D.C: GPO.

Vasconcelos, José. n.d. *Indología.* Barcelona: Agencia mundial de librería.

———. 1948. *La raza cósmica.* Mexico City: Colección Austral, Espasa-Calpe.

Velarde, Nora. 1991. "Entrevista a Aníbal Quijano: La modernidad y América nacen el mismo día." *Boletín Illa* 10 (January): 42–57.

Vientós Gastón, Nilita. 1959. "Dedicación y homenaje." *Asomante* 15.3: 7–8.

Villoro, Luis. 1995. *En México, entre libros.* México City: El Colegio Nacional/FCE.

Vizcarrondo, Fortunato. 1976. *Dinga y Mandinga.* San Juan: Instituto de Cultura Puertorriqueña.

Walton, John. 1986. *Reluctant Rebels.* New York: Columbia University Press.

Weffort, Francisco C. 1976. "Clases sociales y desarrollo social (Contribución al estudio del populismo)." In *Populismo, marginalización y dependencia,* ed. Francisco C. Weffort and Aníbal Quijano, 17–169. 2nd ed. Ciudad Universitaria, Costa Rica: Editorial Universitaria Centroamericana.

Williams, Claudette. 2000. *Charcoal and Cinnamon: The Politics of Color in Spanish Caribbean Literature.* Gainesville: University Press of Florida.

Williams, Eric. 1966. *Capitalism and Slavery.* New York: Capricorn Books.

Winant, Howard. 1994. *Racial Conditions.* Minneapolis: University of Minnesota Press.

Wynter, Sylvia. 1977. "The Eye of the Other: Images of the Black in Spanish Literature." In

Blacks in Hispanic Literature: Critical Essays, ed. Miriam DaCosta, 8–19. Port Washington, N.Y.: Kennikat Press.

——. 1979. "Sambos and Minstrels." *Social Text* 1 (Summer): 149–56.

——. 1990. "Afterword: Beyond Miranda's Meanings: Un/silencing the 'Demonic Ground' of Caliban's 'Woman.'" In *Out of Kumbla: Caribbean Women and Literature*, ed. Carole Boyce-Davies and Elaine Fido, 354–72. Trenton, N.J.: Africa World Press.

——. 2000. "Unsettling the Coloniality of Being/Power/Truth/Freedom: Towards the Human, After *Man*, Its Over-Representation—An Argument." Paper presented at the 3rd Annual Conference of the Coloniality Working Group, entitled "Unsettling the Coloniality of Power." State University of New York at Binghamton, April 27–29. A slightly revised version of this paper was published in *New Centennial Review* 3.3 (Fall 2003): 257–337.

Zelinsky, Wilbur. 1949. "III: The Negro Population Geography of Cuba and Puerto Rico." *Journal of Negro History* 34.2 (April): 208–21.

Zeno Gandía, Manuel. 1975. *La charca.* San Juan: Instituto de Cultura Puertorriqueña.

Zenón Cruz, Isabelo. 1974–75. *Narciso descubre su trasero.* 2 vols. Humacao: Editorial Furidi.

4

Racism and Its Masks in Brazil

On Racism and the Idea of Harmony

GISLENE APARECIDA DOS SANTOS

A recent book by Guimarães and Huntley on racism in Brazil bears a rather suggestive title—*Tirando a máscara* (Removing the mask). Why should studying racism, understanding it, and appreciating its dynamics, vicissitudes, framework, and strategies imply removing a mask, suggesting thereby that there was something hidden that the mask kept one from seeing? Guimarães's and Huntley's title invites us to look beyond that which wants to be seen, to reveal the truth about what is really there—the falseness of Brazil's racial democracy. The removal of the mask implies a different way of seeing, so that we are not carried away by an illusion and can seek out the true nature and essence of things and not their mere appearance.[1]

Seeing Brazilian racism as a masked phenomenon means taking it not merely as an amalgamation of facts and opinions, because the latter are covered over. The covering over prevents us from understanding how Brazilian society really works. We are better off understanding that we are simultaneously attracted to and distracted by these strategies and ideas that constitute the covering over and thus act in a racist manner without realizing it, precisely because we have put on the racist mask. It is also important to appreciate that we have a terrible fear of seeing our unmasked selves and flee from this realization in the same way that mortals averted their eyes in order to avoid gazing on the countenance of the mythical Medusa. Such a gaze would reveal us to ourselves: we would see ourselves as racists. That is why the mask cannot be removed. One either accepts being petrified by the reality of racism or flees from it in terror. To understand this is to understand the way the mask of racism covers the face of many Brazilians. But realizing that we are wearing masks and are being racist by denying it would be a transformative experience.

One way to better appreciate this fear would be to start by looking at a current myth in Brazil (one of many, like the myth of racial democracy, for instance): it is the myth of Brazil as an earthly paradise, a Garden of Eden.

It is in the interest of many to maintain this illusion of Brazil as a paradise, a kingdom of delights, in which all its citizens and residents live and prosper effortlessly and eternally, free of pain and suffering, and enjoy a kind of life that other peoples can only attain through great effort. The modern Brazilian philosopher Marilena Chaui has described the idea of a Brazilian paradise in terms of a foundational myth. She reminds us that "a foundational myth is one that always finds ways of expressing itself, [through] new languages, new values, and ideas, so that the more it seems to be something else, the more it is a repetition of itself" (2000, 9). She goes on to explain that said myth expresses itself through the invisible nature of social inequality in Brazilian society and through its authoritarianism:

> Because it preserves the vestiges of colonial slave society, or what some scholars call manorial culture, Brazilian society is marked by a hierarchical structuring of social space . . . social and interpersonal relations within this structure are always realized as a relationship between a superior, who has authority, and an inferior, who obeys. Difference and asymmetry are always transformed into inequalities that reinforce this uneven power relationship. *The "other" is never seen as a subject or as a subject with rights: he or she is never seen as having subjectivity or alterity.*
>
> Social divisions are naturalized in an inequality based on natural inferiority (in the case of women, workers, blacks, native people, immigrants, and the elderly), and differences, also naturalized, are presented sometimes as a deflection from norms (in the case of ethnic or gender differences), sometimes as a sexual perversion or freakishness (in the case of homosexuals, for example). This process of naturalization, which is key to the historical genesis of inequality and difference, allows the naturalization of all kinds of visible and invisible forms of violence because they are not perceived [by Brazilians themselves] as violence. (2000, 89–90 my emphasis)

This inability to acknowledge or see authoritarianism, inequalities, injustices, and violence is due to the continuous camouflage permitted by the paradise myth. Its propagation makes it impossible to see that Brazil is not a paradise, that each instance of violence, discrimination, and inequality calls into question its claims and the idea that Brazil is a tropical country blessed by God, free of wars, and full of nature's bounty.

Even the ways in which racism manifests itself bears this out. In Brazil it is acceptable to speak of something called "cordial" racism. The idea that the practice of racism can be "cordial" leads us to believe that even the most violent form of discrimination could manifest itself in a gentler manner in Brazil than in other parts of the globe. Meanwhile, this false cordiality allows discriminatory behavior to extend even beyond the limits of the public sphere and into the private lives of blacks and whites, their relationships of love and hate, of desire and rejection. Effectively, it is in the realm of the private and the personal that we find the most telling manifestations of discrimination and the "cordial" demarcation of spaces in Brazilian society.

Racism in Brazil is based on the representation of black people as exotic and sensually attractive to "us" or exotically violent and frightening to "us." Brazilian society, additionally, has created many strategies to alienate blacks from their own image, culture, and bodies, and to see humanity, rationality, and intelligence as peculiarly white attributes. This results in the creation of extremely difficult conditions of psychological survival for blacks because what is produced is an ambiguous gray area between behavior that is considered racist, violent, and discriminatory and behavior that is considered not to be so racist, violent, or discriminatory, as if it were possible to establish some quantity of discriminatory and disrespectful experiences, insults, and aggressions that one would endure without being affected negatively. This gray area, which is defined not only by laws or facts but rather by individuals in their personal evaluation and interpretation of events and never admitted by them as examples of discrimination, is what allows racism to flourish. That is to say that to the institutional structures of racism, which prevent blacks from sharing political and economic power, we should add the actions of ordinary people who practice discrimination on an everyday basis. One facet of the phenomenon cannot survive without the other. Racist structures need the support of individual action every day. In conjunction they allow events to be seen dubiously as instances of "quasi-violence" and "quasi-discrimination."

It seems impossible for people who have been shaped by this idea of the existence of a nationally "cordial" character, of national harmony, to agree openly to live at the same time with horror, violence, and racism. It seems impossible, but it is not, and even if it were, it is still alleged that the situation is not as serious as all that. According to this gray area, it seems that black and poor people should be able to put up with much more aggression than whites and the well off. Furthermore, they should also not feel attacked, violated, or suffer any pain.[2]

This discriminatory dynamic, as mentioned, is sustained by the fact that racism in Brazilian society operates by creating people who cannot discern its very existence; they cannot recognize it because they cannot admit they are part of it. Not only does the discriminator not see that he is discriminating; the victim cannot see himself as a victim of discrimination either. In fact, he also cannot see how he helps support discriminatory structures or rhetoric. Brazil is a society in which recognition is blocked, in which its citizens cannot see, hence the idea of the mask and the need for its removal. When one wears a mask one does not show one's real face; neither can others see one. The only thing that shows is the mask and the image of a harmonious society. Consequently, recognizing and denouncing racism in Brazil is therefore seen as a threat against an imagined peace and order that in reality do not exist. That is why it is necessary to show that the idea of harmony is the bedrock and keystone of the paradise myth. Even when it is admitted that discrimination exists here in Brazil, as pointed out before, it is held to be not that serious.

Of course, losing this false sense of harmony would plunge us into the deepest of chaos; it would mean our total disintegration as a society. This idea is confirmed in the way that the protests of certain groups from within civil society (the landless, rural workers, machinists, homeless people, professors, and members of diverse black movements) are understood as disorderly events that inflame the public to turn against them. Their protests are seen as a threat to the peaceful nature of Brazilian society.[3]

Whether it is taken as alienation or as an ideological tool of the dominant class or how one group's use of power can be reproduced in microspaces, what is revealed is that the idea of harmony (of our paradise) is ritualistically reiterated in our daily lives as often as is necessary. We are the agents for the perpetuation of racism. That is why rather than removing our masks one by one, it would be better for us to see ourselves with them on and ask ourselves what they (we) actually represent.

Masking in the Brazilian Educational System

It is not difficult to see the presence of this discourse of harmony and masking, for example, in two specific areas in the field of Brazilian education that are closely interconnected. The first is the way in which knowledge created by blacks is received in universities and the academy. For universities and academics, black ways of knowing are perceived firstly as folkloric and only rarely as instances of "high culture," and secondly as "emotional expressions" but rarely as pure knowledge.

On a recent research visit to London I experienced this phenomenon firsthand. During a tour of a museum a tour guide explained to us why a particular piece (which contained a black character) had been preserved by the museum. Whether a self-portrait or a commissioned painting (it was of the Jamaican poet Francis Williams), it had been preserved by the museum as part of an exhibition of eighteenth-century furniture and placed in that section accordingly. But the painting of the man and his particular story mattered little. The works of art relating to black people, she said, were dispersed throughout the museum according to how they fit into white cultural themes. A coin with a black face could therefore be found in the numismatics section, a few images of blacks in the section for sacred art (in a Nativity scene for example), but there was nothing to help a researcher seeking the black artistic presence in a consistent, organized manner. That would require a search of the entire museum. Alternatively, in the ethnographic museum one would find all such representations of Africana culture. The works of blacks are not to be found among "serious" art, in other words, except in a marginal way.

The way in which academic knowledge is produced about blacks in Brazil is also an example of this. It is therefore not uncommon to find in academic discussions or thesis defenses that perspectives that do not conform to Eurocentric paradigms are disqualified and considered to be lacking in objectivity or deemed un-academic. Research on issues concerning blacks has been centered through the years in the field of anthropology, with a corresponding exotic framing, or in history courses with a focus on slavery. Even in these subject areas, which are disproportionately attended by black students—vis-à-vis such majors as medicine, engineering, and technology—prevailing Eurocentric prejudices are brought to bear on their performance.

These issues are intimately linked to discussion about affirmative action in Brazilian universities. There are myriad arguments against the adoption of quotas for blacks. They range from the accusation that quotas are an infringement on the autonomy of universities to the supposed lack of knowledge and intellectual competence of students who would register through quotas while not possessing the intellectual wherewithal or training or the financial background for university study. Even so, such arguments prevent another conversation from taking place; that conversation would acknowledge the injustice that for centuries has been perpetrated against the black population and recognize that Afro-Brazilians can contribute significantly to the creation of academic knowledge. Statistical studies done by agencies of the federal government between 1992 and 2001 show that a large number

Brazil: Rate of illiteracy (in population 25 years old or older), 1999

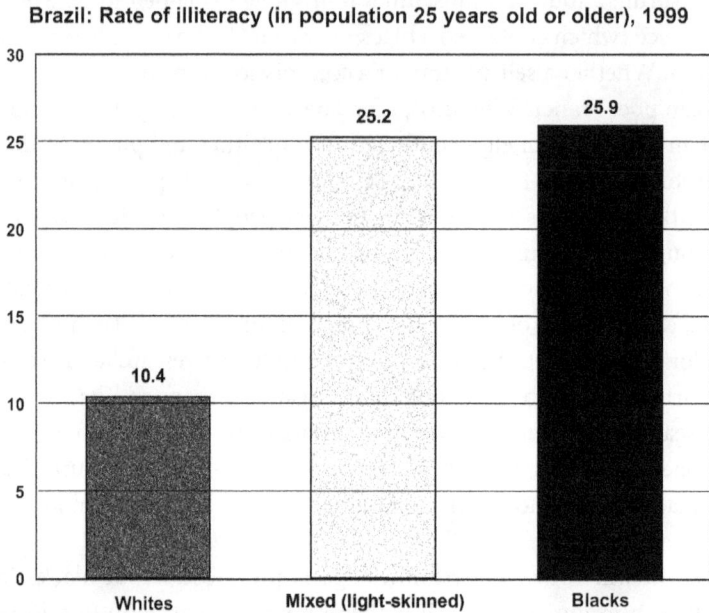

Figure 4.1

of blacks come from the poorest sectors of the population and that they have been gradually excluded from the educational system. The illiteracy rate and the gap between blacks and whites in Brazil, in fact, are both on the rise (fig. 4.1).[4] These studies on blacks and whites reveal exclusion of blacks primarily from the highest levels of formal education. (figs. 4.2 and 4.3).

Despite the fact that this data, showing a minimal presence of blacks in the sector of highest educational attainment, has been provided by officials at governmental population and economic agencies, there seems to be a general refusal to accept the urgent need for compensatory policies to gradually lessen the inequality. The obvious conclusion is that denial of access is a means of perpetuating the exclusion of blacks from the formal system of education. This denial of access to higher education in Brazil simply results in exclusion from the spheres of power, since the contest for influence and power is premised upon knowledge of the world that is acquired through academia, and the majority of the people in the country's spheres of influence come from its universities. (Lula is the only president to have come out of the working class.) It also means being relegated to the worst jobs and the lowest salaries, if not to unemployment or underemployment as fig. 4.4 shows. Additionally, it means being denied the formal sphere's general ideas and knowledge of its own reality and of the reality that will be produced for

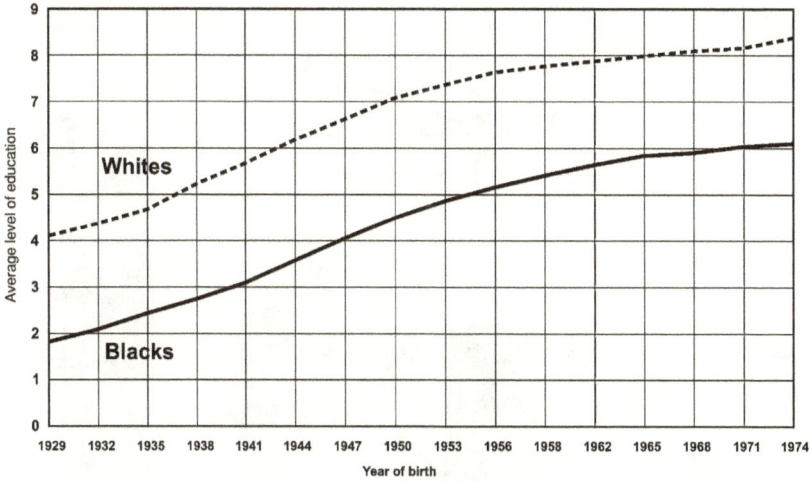

Brazil: Average level of education, cohorts, and color

Whites

Blacks

Average level of education

Year of birth

Source: Pesquisa Nacional por Amostragem de Domicílios (PNDA) 1999.

Figure 4.2

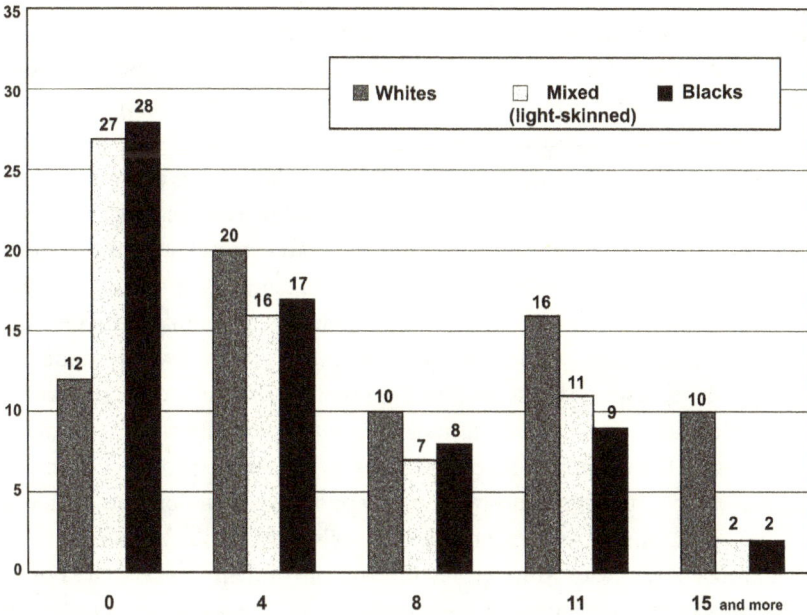

Brazil: Percentage of adults with *x* years of education, 1999

Whites   Mixed (light-skinned)   Blacks

Figure 4.3

Brazil: Percentage of unemployment by gender and color, 1999

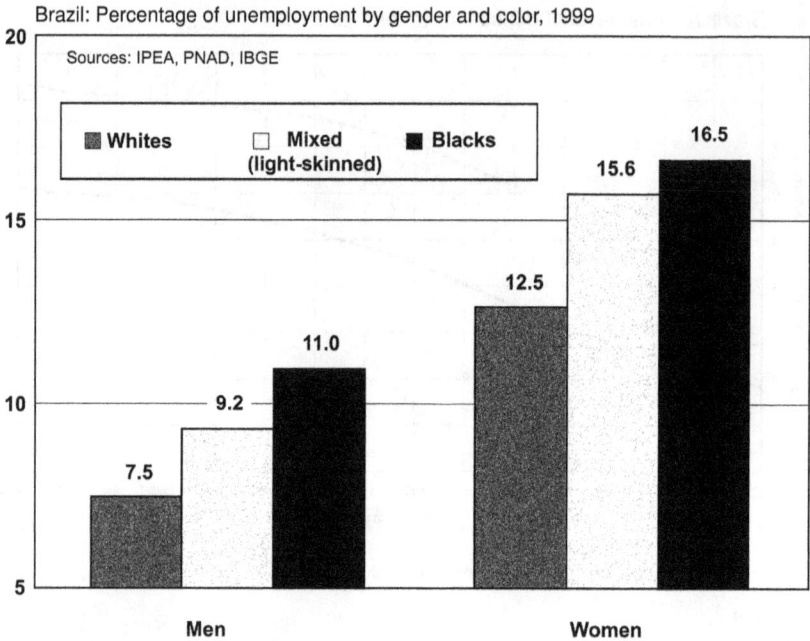

Figure 4.4

the nonblack population, even when the object of that knowledge generated was blacks themselves. The few students who manage to break through the barrier of racism and remain in school at the primary and secondary school levels, or who register for tertiary education, are caught up in a real battle of psychological resistance: "For the black university student class-related stress actually equals racial stress" (Carvalho 2002, 96). It is a stress that increases in response to the subtle institutionalized racism that has been built into the actual structures of colleges and that often causes students to drop out, as Carvalho observes: "What we find are students abandoning their classrooms, an inability to adapt, misunderstandings, 'chilly' climate, and psychosomatic reactions that are common among black university students, e.g., speaking in whispers, silence, embarrassment, frequent dyslexia, excessive irritability . . . a set of symptoms that result in difficulty with classes and, finally, with the dropping of courses. Meanwhile, white professors remain indifferent; or if they become aware of any particular situation, they lack the analytical training to examine the specific crisis of that black student" (93).

In most of the cases white professors, in spite of their intellectual knowledge, seem to be unaware that there is discrimination against blacks inside the classroom and that this discrimination affects the performance of blacks in many ways. This could simply be the result of a denial of racism on the part of the professors themselves, or it could be due to academia's unwillingness to acknowledge black points of view and the personal histories of blacks when it comes to race relations in Brazil. In all this, the adoption of quotas continues to be seen with suspicion, confirming the premise that the field of education is one of the most powerful bastions of racism in Brazil today.

A common argument put forward by opponents of affirmative action is that since blacks are not properly prepared for tertiary education, universities would be jeopardizing their interests by admitting students ill-prepared for the completion of their chosen majors. These opponents also point to the unfairness of adopting compensatory policies for only one specific group, stressing in addition that it is impossible to decide who is black and who is not black given that Brazil is such a highly mixed country in terms of race. This pretense at ignorance overlooks the fact of what the sociologist Oracy Nogueira (1998) has called "brand prejudice." According to Nogueira, a kind of "brand prejudice" or "brand discrimination" is what takes place in Brazil (1998). Here blacks are not discriminated against by the principle of hypodescent or the one-drop rule, but by their appearance and skin color. It means that "lighter skin provides more privileges," even if an individual has many blacks in his or her family tree. The stigma of Afro-descendence is not triggered if dark skin is not evident, though dark skin is very common in Brazil.

Brazilian Youth and Racial Quota Policies

In spite of elite resistance, there are currently two important bills under discussion in Brazil to determine public policy concerning racial equality: PL73/199 to establish racial quotas in public universities and PL3.198/2000, called the "Racial equality statute." (In practice, many public universities have, since 2004, initiated a trial period of quotas.) The proponents of these bills believe that the inclusion of a greater number of blacks in higher education would gradually contribute toward the lessening of the socio-racial gap since it would provide better conditions for the insertion of blacks into the job market.

Interviews with high school students regarding the proposals for affirmative action allowed me to see the emotional impact that constant exposure to cordial racism had on them. In 2006 I conducted thirty-five interviews with students in their final year of high school in Sao Paulo's east end and south end ghettos on their perception of the question of racial quotas.[5] They were presented with IBGE (Brazilian Institute for Geography and Statistics) criteria for racial classification (white, black, light-skinned [*pardo*], indigenous, and yellow) and asked to self-identify according to their skin color. Afterward, all the interviewees in all the schools were asked questions regarding the themes of identity, quota policies, racial inequality, and the elimination of racial inequality.

It turned out that the majority of the interviewees self-identified as *pardo* or light-skinned and a goodly percentage as black. They also described the Brazilian population as mainly light-skinned. Even with the IBGE criteria for classification in mind, they opted for their own definitions, which were respected in reporting this exercise (in place of Negro [*preto*] they preferred the term "black" and introduced the category *mestizo* in addition to light-skinned).

It was also noted that each group tended to describe the country's racial characteristics in accordance with how they saw themselves as individuals. Accordingly, the majority of the black students said that the Brazilian population was mainly black, and the majority of the light-skinned ones said that the population was mainly light-skinned. Those that self-identified as *mestizo* or mixed described the Brazilian population as mixed, and the groups that saw themselves as white and yellow likewise saw the majority of the Brazilian population in terms of their own categories.[6] The reason for studying youngsters who were in the last year of public high school was that they were thought to be the group most directly interested in having public policies entitling them to free passes into the universities and colleges (figs. 4.5 and 4.6).

In general the interviewees validate and reinforce the precept that the Brazilian population comprises a mixture of races and colors. They also affirm that this mixture is to be found also in their own families. A Brazilian, for the majority of these young students, "could be a mixture of everything, he's a *mestizo*. You are not likely to find a Brazilian of one single color, not even blacks themselves are only of one color," as one student asserted.

While the students think of the Brazilian population as mainly mulatto or mixed race (fig. 4.7), they also think that there are inequalities in Brazil related to "race" and "color" (fig. 4.8). As their statements indicate, they perceive that there is prejudice against blacks and that it is shown by the stereotypes built up toward this group: "If you were walking on a dark street and you see someone coming right behind you, if it were a white person, you wouldn't worry. But, if it were a black, you would probably think that person

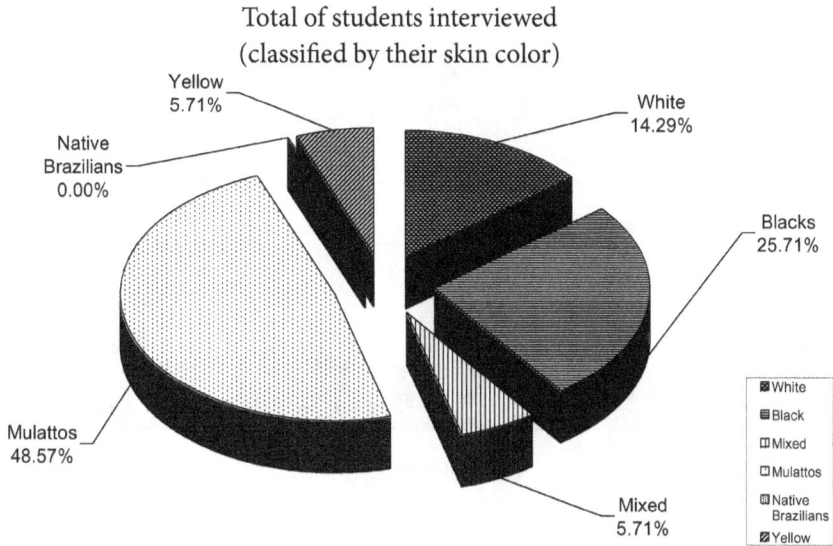

Total of students interviewed
(classified by their skin color)

Yellow 5.71%
Native Brazilians 0.00%
White 14.29%
Blacks 25.71%
Mulattos 48.57%
Mixed 5.71%

White
Black
Mixed
Mulattos
Native Brazilians
Yellow

Figure 4.5

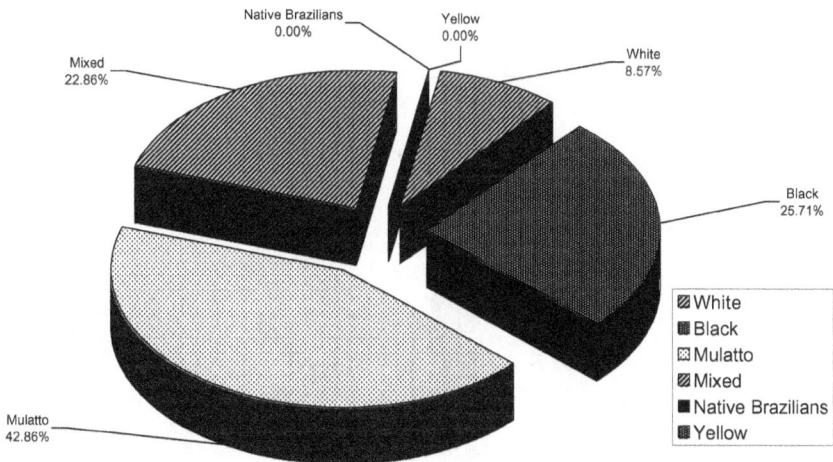

How students identified the majority of the Brazilian population, by race

Native Brazilians 0.00%
Yellow 0.00%
White 8.57%
Mixed 22.86%
Black 25.71%
Mulatto 42.86%

White
Black
Mulatto
Mixed
Native Brazilians
Yellow

Figure 4.6

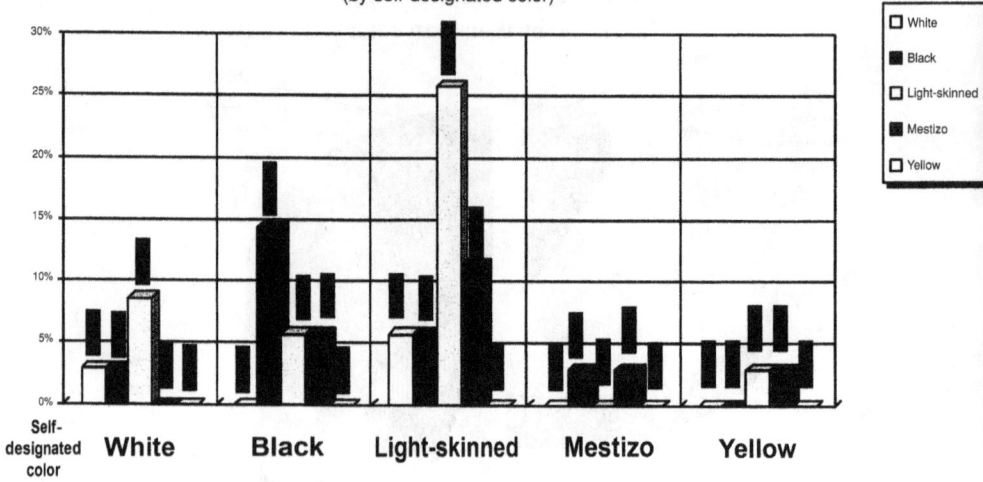

How students identified the Brazilian population by majority
(by self-designated color)

Legend: White, Black, Light-skinned, Mestizo, Yellow

Self-designated color: White, Black, Light-skinned, Mestizo, Yellow

Figure 4.7

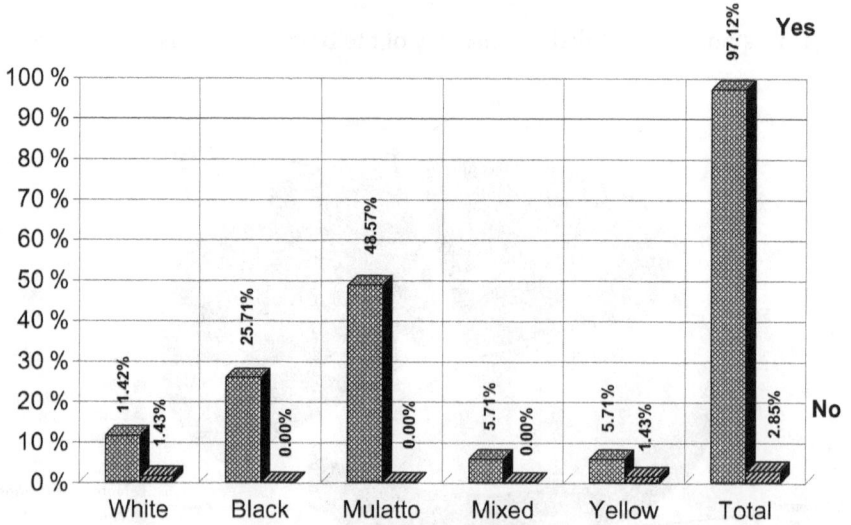

Students who thought inequalities are generated by race/color

	White	Black	Mulatto	Mixed	Yellow	Total
Yes	11.42%	25.71%	48.57%	5.71%	5.71%	97.12%
No	1.43%	0.00%	0.00%	0.00%	1.43%	2.85%

Figure 4.8

Students' opinions of quotas

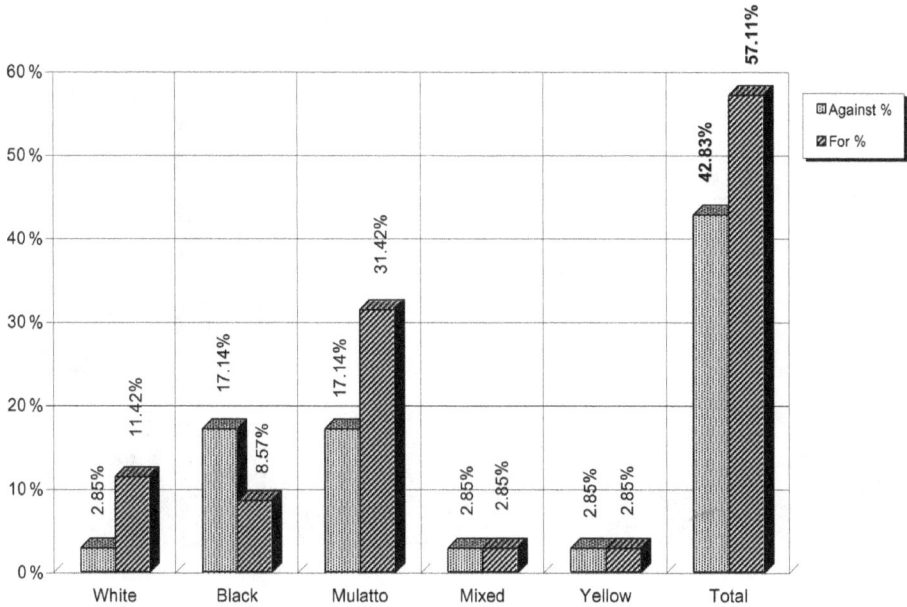

Figure 4.9

would rob you"; "Whites have more privileges. If a person sees a black in an imported car, 'he's a thief,' a white, 'he's a businessman.'" Discrimination is easy to allege because it is so prevalent: "You apply for a job and don't get it, regardless of what explanations they give, I think it's because of color." Humiliation and pain are noticed: "Many white people and mulattos think they are better than blacks and put them down"; "Blacks suffer more"; "Blacks have more problems." One might have expected, bearing all of this in mind, that there might be full support for racial quotas, but the interviews did not bear this out.

The following graphs present data for or against quotas (fig. 4.9); what the students thought of quotas as a tool for overcoming inequality (fig. 4.10); and whether or not they would use them for getting into college (fig. 4.11). Although many students indicated that they thought that quotas would contribute toward overcoming racial inequality (74.2 percent of the entire sample thought so; 70.5 percent of the group that self-identified as mulatto and 88.8 percent of the group that self-identified as black), some of the interviewees were against the implementation of quotas (42.8 percent of the entire sample; 35.2 percent of the mulattos and 66.6 percent of the blacks).

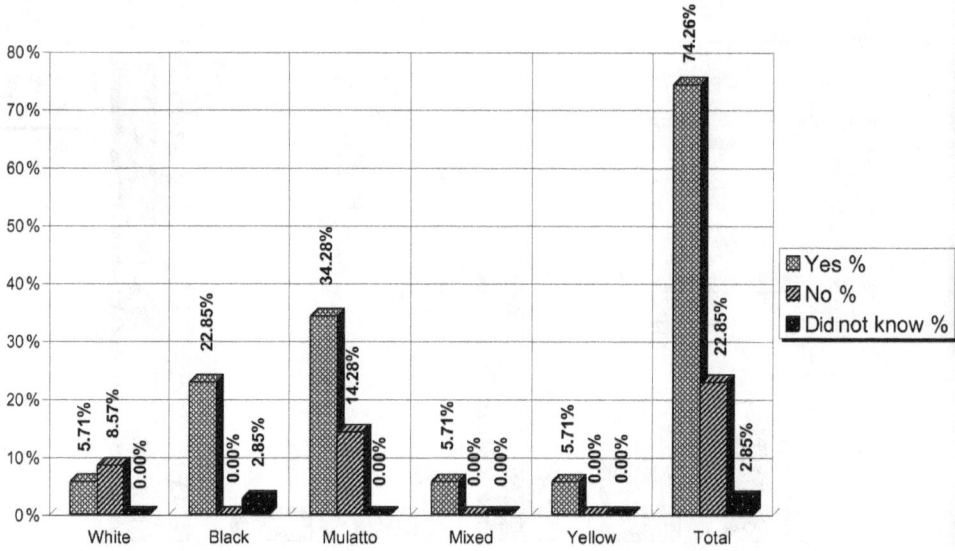

Students who thought that quotas could contribute to
suppression of inequalities by race/color

Figure 4.10

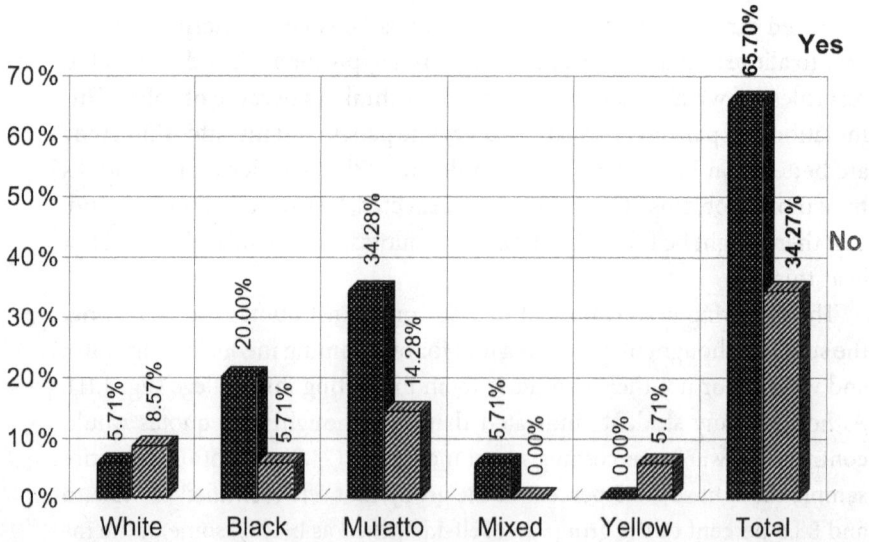

Students who would use quota criteria to enter the university

Figure 4.11

Students acquainted with affirmative action
policies and the quota system

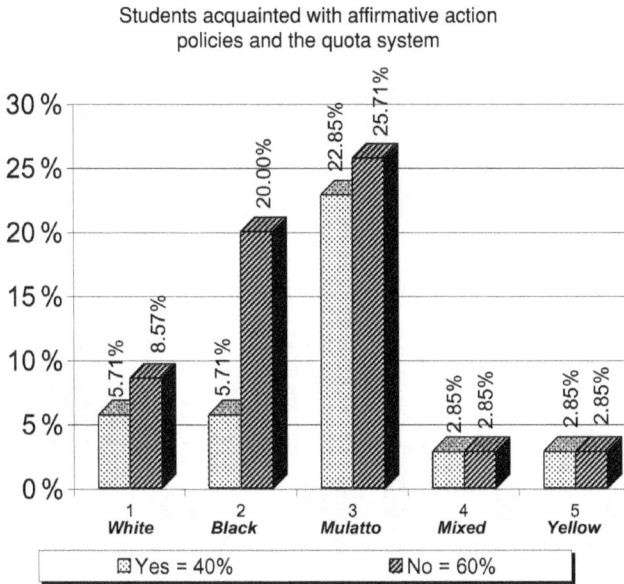

Figure 4.12

Of the self-declared mulattos, 64.7 percent support quotas, but not the majority of self-declared blacks (only 35.2 percent were in favor). This data
seems to indicate unfamiliarity with affirmative action and the quota policy.
Sixty per cent of the sample admitted that they did not know about quota
policies or about affirmative action (52.9 percent of mulattos; 77.7 percent
of blacks). Many of them did not readily associate quota policies as a means
of access to the university through such criteria as phenotype, genotype, or
self-identification. Whereas 60 percent of the interviewees declared at the
beginning of the interview that they did not know about quota policies, in
the end, after having been shown criteria used for entry to university, 68.5
percent declared that they had discussed the questions raised during the
interview. Racism, prejudice, quotas, and affirmative action turned out to
be topics already talked about among friends and relatives or at school (figs.
4.12, 4.13).

The data also reveals that some of the students believe that quota policies
may imply some sort of discrimination or reflect negatively on the intrinsic
merits of their beneficiaries (an argument raised by 43 percent of those who
were against quotas). Notwithstanding this and in spite of declaring themselves against it, the majority of the interviewees stated that they would use

Students who had discussed questions raised

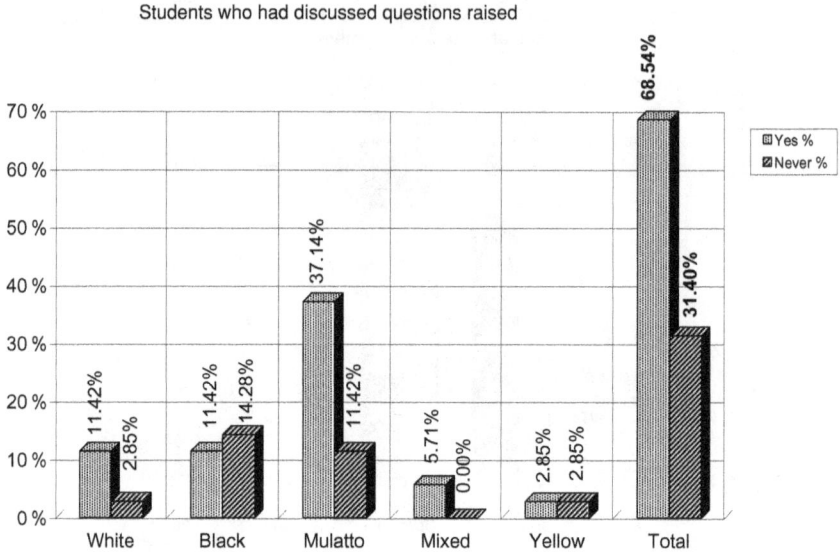

Figure 4.13

a racial criterion to gain access to the university. Of the criteria available (phenotype, genotype, and self-identification), the majority opted for self-identification (in the general sample and also in the groups of *pardos* and blacks).

The arguments they presented indicate that they would use whatever criterion they thought would be least harmful, though they would refrain from fully endorsing any of them. Some stated that they would use quotas and the associated criteria since these might be the only means of getting into college. This is indicated in some of the arguments they put forward:

> "For me this business of setting aside places for blacks and Indians is prejudice, because we are all equal. Everyone studies, everybody learns. Phenotype is not a good criterion, ancestry is a better one."
>
> "Using phenotype as a criterion discriminates too much. I believe ancestry is very wrong, because it is not the same for everyone. I feel that self-identification is best."
>
> "Phenotype is okay. I don't think they should use ancestry; anyone can enter the university without needing to use color and not because their foreparents were white or black. I think self-definition is best."

"It's all racism I feel. All racism because everything should be equal because we are all people. I don't even agree with self-identification, but I would use it."

"I don't agree with it. I don't believe that someone should get into school because he belongs to one race or another. I don't believe in phenotype either. Self-definition is a bit better, it's the person himself who should say who he is."

"It should be on the basis of the person's ability and not his color; phenotype is a joke, ability is what matters. Self-definition is best."

"It is the only way we have to get into college, just doing the test is not enough. Sometimes you have to try those other ways; show a side of yourself that you don't usually show. You want to get through on merit, but you don't get a chance. I say, if I get a chance through the quota system I'll take it."

"I think the ancestry business is good because I know I have blacks in my family, but how am I to know how much of it is in me? How do you measure that? I believe phenotype is wrong. Self-definition is more valid, although I think all three are wrong."

"I would use ancestry if I were a descendant. That would be best for me because it would be a way of proving that even being white or light-skinned I had black blood."

"It's a good resource, but it would be good if everyone studied and only depended on that to get into college. It's good for those who want to make it and are afraid. But I wouldn't use it."

One can see on the basis of these statements how opinions vary among black students over the use of a civil right and whether or not it is even appropriate to use it. What is most intriguing here is that at the same time that students were saying that quotas were useful in overcoming race and color inequality, and that they would use a racial criterion to get into college, they were also saying that they were against quotas and that quotas in principle were wrong.

This shows racism in Brazil in its most cruel dimension, when black youth are doubtful over whether or not they should use a right that they have and which was the result of a social victory. Their doubt is a function of the ideology according to which those who enter the university by way of racial quotas are held to be less capable and less intelligent and ultimately less worthy than those who opt for the open system of access. Subsequently, many young blacks do not use this right and do not go to college. The use

Students who chose as the best criterion phenotype, ancestry, or
self-definition, or who didn't agree with any of the criteria

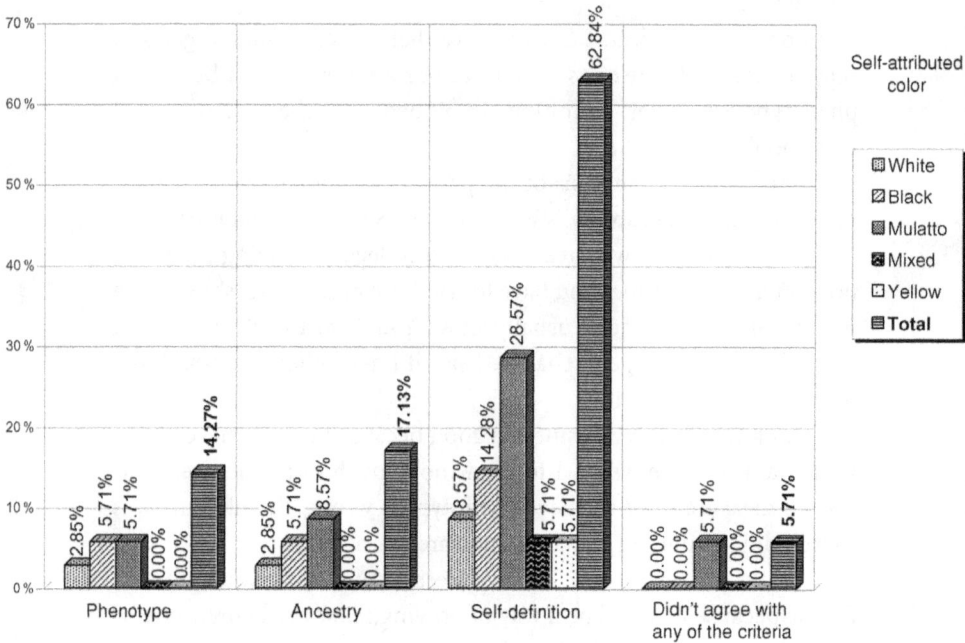

Figure 4.14

of a right (accessing a college education through the quota system) thus
becomes the equivalent of a punishment, that is, a way of bringing greater
prejudice upon themselves beyond what they already experience on a daily
basis.

It is to be noted that the idea that blacks have an inferior knowledge
base and that they should be tested more stringently appears in these circumstances as a means of creating more symbolic barriers to college access
for young blacks. We therefore see a difficulty in making public policy for
Brazilians work since the denial of racism and the masking of its forms of
operation make it hard even for blacks themselves to realize that they are
acting in ways that the racist society wants them to act. Because of racism's
mask even those who enter college through the quota system are made to
feel ashamed, and this feeling of shame is itself a symptom of defeat (fig.
4.14).

Creating Networks and Widening the Horizons of Desire

The quota system, as public policy, guarantees access to college, but it cannot prevent the prejudice that befalls blacks and quota students. Neither can it prevent new forms of stigma from being immediately created against those who benefit from it. Therefore many students in the struggle against discrimination create special protective mechanisms through networking and through the construction of markers of black group identity (the use of braids, natural hair styles, dress, and the adoption of peculiarly black ethnic forms of behavior). One aspect of the resulting networking strategies and cooperativeness put in place by quota students has precisely to do with their visiting high schools in marginal areas to explain that quotas are a legal entitlement and that using them does not imply that their beneficiaries are intellectually inferior to other students who don't need or use them. In this way they work against the transformation of a public policy entitlement into its opposite, that is, an opportunity for further discrimination.

However, there are many high school students who never even think of college as a possibility. The gap between their objective reality and all that college implies is so great that they cannot conceive of it as a possible goal. Wanderley Guilherme dos Santos's study of Brazilian society proposes that to understand why some groups, particularly those in adverse circumstances, encounter difficulties in upward mobility we need to take into consideration their relative need as a fundamental variable. "The distress of relative need, as against absolute need, appears precisely in the interstices that expand and contract between what one has and what one wishes to have, between daily reality and the horizons of desire" (2006, 131). The author explains that the feeling of relative deprivation is "the result of a perception of need, relative to those who don't have needs, needs that ought not to exist or which can be fulfilled. . . . The inequalities implied by relative deprivation can, in principle, be understood and explained, and also in principle, disappear. Whether correctly or not, individuals identify the relative social space they occupy and on that basis establish the particular social rung they want to get to, provided they acquire the means to get there" (148).

Dos Santos analyzes the logic behind the thinking of the poor to explain their lack of participation. By way of a complex analysis that takes such factors as income, consumption, and desire into consideration, he proposes that the level of relative need increases (that is, the expectations relative to material acquisition) to the degree that it becomes obvious that it was possible in the past to acquire some things in the short term. This leads to the belief that more will be available in the near future, thereby raising expectations and the sense of relative need. In other words, I have X, which is little, but I can have Y, which would be good, and W, which would be even better.

However, if it is not evident that there is a great gap between what one has and what one might achieve, or if there is no reason to believe that it might be possible to reduce this gap or that the resources might be acquired for this, the sense of relative need no longer functions as a point of departure for collective mobilization. Dos Santos shows how in Brazil the gap between desire and possibility is so great and the gap between relative deprivation and absolute need is so close that the poor don't harbor any desires because they, in fact, have no possibility of change before them.

> Taking into consideration, besides, the respective concentration of income and of people, at the higher and lower extremes, it makes sense for the size of relative deprivation to be so reduced. There may be paralyzing envy, but none of the poor ever imagine that they will ever get anywhere near the top. It is the horizon of the possible, which contains progress and mobility, that propels relative need. On this basis a qualification might be made of the Toqueville hypothesis. According to the hypothesis, it would be enough for change in the direction of accumulation to begin, within an economically stagnant population, for there to be an explosion in the process of rising expectations and a prolongation of the period of relative need. Perhaps not. Perhaps change needs to surpass certain limits of social sensibility for the deprivation gap to be perceived. On this side of the dividing line, the horizon of desire is still too weak for a precarious marginal change to be interpreted as a catalyst for future demands.
>
> It is quite probable that poverty is not the only stimulus for escaping poverty, but that also the level of this poverty is responsible for the demarcation of that particular limit of social sensibility, short of which any relative movement is insufficient to modify the type, the quantity, and the intensity of expectations, which, in the final analysis, lends dynamism to relative deprivation. Short of this limit, possibly the fear of falling back or simple deterioration is greater than what might be expected through taking the risk of organizing and making demands. In that case, why dream? (Dos Santos 2006, 174)

The poorest elements of the population, those who have no hope for improvement in the sense that they recognize the price of failure (of becoming even worse off), acknowledge the absence of possibilities for upward mobility and, with no way out, accept their situation in order to avoid a worse fate. When the Brazilian elite disseminates information that leads young blacks to believe that to be a quota student is to be inferior, it makes the possibilities for overcoming the socio-economic gap even more remote and their domination even more practicable. The predictable and desired result is that they stay out of college. This is why the network of students who work at fostering black identity and the idea of valuing the rights acquired through the work of social movements is a fundamental aspect of the consolidation of these same rights. Their work is a means of upturning racist ideology and the masking of racism in Brazil.

Conclusion

My research data reveals that the idea of Brazilian race mixture and of harmonious relations among all of its people is very powerful and efficient because it has a real material basis. It is a fact that Brazil is a country with much racial mixture, one in which there is great variety in skin color. This race mixture does not necessarily mean, however, an absence of racial discrimination. This was borne out in a study by Robin Sheriff (2001), which highlighted the innumerable labels used by residents of the Morro do Sangue Bom neighborhood to refer to their own skin color and to that of their neighbors.

Sheriff reports that he quickly learned what all Brazilians already know: when one speaks of color and race in Brazil, people's "way of speaking," their location, and the particular speaker matter more for understanding what it is they are trying to communicate than what one assumes the semantic-referential content of their words to be. He concludes, "During my research in the community, I also learned that some people make a distinction between what they thought was the 'real color' of the person and the words that are conventionally used to speak of the color of a particular person. When I asked a young lady what was her color, she laughed and said, 'People call me white, but I'm not really. I'm, I don't know, light-skinned?' Similarly, a man told me that his wife was white. Then he laughed and added, 'She isn't really, but people say so'" (Sheriff 2001, 221). The same thing occurred with the high school students I interviewed:

"I think I am [a] yellow [Asian] woman because I am not white, but I am not black either. I'm yellowish. When I was younger I thought I was white. Everybody used to say I was white."

"Because of my family I consider myself to be a black woman. Most of the people in my family have dark skin. I'm a bit more mixed because my mother is white and so on. I always considered myself to be mixed, light-skinned."

"I am light-skinned; it says so on my birth certificate: light brown color. I don't say that I'm white because for me that has to do with two things; clear eyes, clear hair. So I'm light brown. People used to joke with me saying I was yellow. But I've always been light-skinned. I never had those ideas of being white, I am sort of darker, I always considered myself to be light- skinned."

"I think I am light-skinned, because for me white means blonde people, and darker people are brown, so I consider myself light-skinned."

"I am white. I have black ancestry, but I consider myself white because of my color. I always thought of myself as white."

These responses show just how important this question is in Brazilian society, the care that is taken in describing the details of each person's appearance and skin tone, and mainly individual's furtiveness regarding the importance of each detail. It also reveals the sense of fantasy present in people's speech as Sheriff pointed out—referring to someone as brown to avoid saying black, for example. "Some of my interviewees defined the term 'brown' in purely subjective terms, as someone who was 'neither black nor white,' but, in truth, these same people in conversations referred to very dark-skinned relatives as *brown* [morenos]. As one woman said: 'Brown is used so as not to say black, they say brown to not offend'" (Sheriff 2001, 225).

Statistics reveal, as I have shown, that the importance of race can be clearly seen through the lack of access of blacks to educational institutions and through dropout rates. Blacks are absent from schools but overrepresented among the poorest and the underemployed. Even so, the question about who is black in Brazil persists. Blacks are the poorest of the poor, those excluded from formal education, the ones who are most likely to have the worst jobs.

What is evident is that these constant questions about who is black, about racial or ethnic identity, about Brazilian identity, and the purportedly racially mixed nature of the population have often served to obfuscate or camouflage the reality of exclusion and the exploitation of social, ethnic, or racial groups in Brazil. It is as though with every step forward that we try to make we constantly have to go back to the initial questions of who are blacks, who are whites, who defines the color of Brazilians before we can actually defend any sort of social justice and rights for those suffering from discrimination. This constant movement back and forth hampers progress toward eventual social rights for blacks and seems to be a perverse strategy aimed at keeping political and economic power among those who have it.

As to the question about who is black in Brazil and our search for genetic or aesthetic criteria to answer the question, what becomes clear is that in real life blacks who go unnoticed by those who have the power to pose and reformulate the question are the very ones who are unemployed, under-employed, and outside the educational system. For that reason, one might rightly enquire as to who is interested in research about Brazilian national identity. Who stands to gain today from a debate on miscegenation?

Our respective emphases apart, I would like to draw a parallel between the ideas I am presenting and an article by Renato Janine Ribeiro in which he discusses the invention of a new society, of a new democracy in which human relations would be considered without being subordinated to a search for identity or an ontology. His conclusion is that

> it is not necessary to answer the question of national identity to re-
> spond to the question of action. I even believe that subordinating the
> question of action to the one of national identity was a mistake that
> has affected history and political initiative, making it depend on an
> ontology of what it is to be Brazilian. Liberating our political action
> and unblocking our policies for emancipation does not first require
> a prior knowledge of who we are. On the contrary, political action
> would be more effective if we lessened our need for a particular iden-
> tity. If in order to act we need to be a certain way, our actions will
> always repeat or reflect already consecrated models. Our ideal will
> never go beyond just imitating "truly existing" democracies. This is
> not enough. In reality, our creativity could be quite fruitful precisely
> because of our lack of a fixed identity, that is, because of our freedom.
> (Ribeiro 2002, 174)

If we take into consideration that in some form or another the debate about Brazilian national identity has always brought up the issue of national har-mony, the existence of a peaceful and orderly population, and national miscegenation, we would see that this generalizing, universalist, and closed discussion is not what is of interest to blacks, poor people, or others who are excluded. This form of argumentation almost always overlooks the changing nature of constructed identities, whether as projects or as acts of resistance put in motion by different social and ethnic groups, despite or contrary to the legitimate identities of the dominant classes who hold on their idea of a racially mixed nation when it suits them only to establish later color lines to identify darker people and favor lighter-skinned people.

For their part, Brazilian universities often help in covering up this discussion while they concomitantly refuse to acknowledge the absence of black students or even teachers from their classrooms, as if nothing were wrong, and as if they, the very intellectuals who helped create the idea of the existence of a Brazilian racial democracy and a harmonious and heavenly country, now had absolutely nothing to do but sit back and wait for things to work in their favor. They are wearing the mask of racism; they are afraid to look at their real faces; they are afraid to acknowledge exactly how complicit they are in the practice of exclusion. In that way, they multiply the number of masks that cover up their false knowledge about what would be best for blacks while at the same time they refuse to look at themselves.

Notes

1. In this essay I return to a discussion I raised in *Mulher negra, homen branco* (Black woman, white man), in which I show how the mask of racism affects interracial romantic relationships in Brazil and discuss, from a different standpoint, the reasons for wearing the Medusa mask. Funding for research in this essay was provided by the Foundation for Research Support of the State of Sao Paulo (FAPESP). I am indebted to the graduate students Maria Leticia Puglisi Munhoz and Vera de Almeida Parasmo, and to Jerome Branche for help with the translation of this paper into English.

2. In Brazil blacks are always assumed to be stronger and more resistant to pain, suffering, violation, and violence than whites. In his analysis of stories of torture, Sergio Adorno reveals that when political and social violence is perpetrated against the poor and/or black population there is a denial of it ever having happened. The difficulty of proving acts of violence against blacks is the result of a constant amelioration, as if it were only quasi-violence, quasi-discrimination. Perhaps this fact is one more factor in helping us understand why it is so difficult to punish someone for a racist crime in Brazil. Violence against blacks and poor people is tolerated and minimized because they are seen as "quasi-citizens," whose rights are "quasi-respected," so that they are "quasi-equal" to the rest of the country's citizens. The way in which Brazilian anti-racism laws are considered and applied, with the subjective elements involved, reveals this fact. See Silva 2000 and Racusen 2002.

3. In Brazil the idea of chaos that is associated with citizens' movements seems to be unchanging. Right after the abolition of slavery, the associations of slaves, freedmen, slave descendants, and abolitionists, for example, were criminalized and portrayed as il-

legal movements whose objective was to transform Brazil into another Haiti. This might be the source of the fear that most white people in Brazil have, even today.

4. All graphs and tables presented in this text have as their source reports prepared by the Institutos de Pesquisas Econômicas Aplicadas (Institutes of Applied Economic Research, or IPEA), an organ of the federal government of Brazil. There is more information available about racial and socio-economic inequality on IPEA graphs, tables, and reports at http://www.ipea.gov.br.

5. Roseli Figueiredo Martins, Leon Santos Padial, and Kledir Henrique Salgado contributed in carrying out this research. Roseli Figueiredo and Henrique Salgado were responsible for the field research and collection of data herein presented.

6. See the website of the Prefeitura Municipal de São Paulo, http://www.prefeitura. sp.gov.br/juventude.

Works Cited

Adorno, Sérgio. 1996. "Violência e racismo: Discriminação no acesso à justiça penal." In *Raça e Diversidade*, ed. Lilia Schwartz and Renato S. Queiroz, 255–75. São Paulo: Edusp.

Bardin, L. 1979. *Análise de conteúdo.* Lisboa: Edições 70.

Carvalho, José Jorge. 2002. "Exclusão racial na universidade brasileira: Um caso de ação negativa." In *O Negro na Universidade*, ed. Delcele Queiroz, 79–99. Salvador: Novos Toques.

Chaui, Marilena. 2000. *Brasil: Mito fundador e sociedade autoritária.* São Paulo: Perseu Abramo.

Dos Santos, Gislene Aparecida, 2004. *Mulher negra, homem branco: Um breve estudo do feminino negro.* Rio de Janeiro: Pallas.

Dos Santos, Wanderley Guilherme. 2006. *Horizonte do desejo: Instabilidade, fracasso coletivo e inércia social.* Rio de Janeiro: FGV.

Guimarães, Antonio Sérgio, and Lynn Huntley, eds. 2000. *Tirando a máscara: Ensaios sobre o racismo no Brasil.* São Paulo: Paz e Terra.

Nogueira, Oracy. 1998. *Preconceito de Marca: As relacoes raciais em Itapetinga.* São Paulo: Edusp.

Racusen, Seth. 2002. "Race, Nation, and Justice: Punishing Prejudice in a Racial Democracy (Brazil)." *Ethnos Brasil: Cultura, Sociedade* 1: 63–82.

Ribeiro, Renato Janine. 2002. "Brasil: Entre a identidade vazia e a construção do novo." In *Estudos sobre ética*, ed. Gislene dos Santos and Divino Silva, 155–75. São Paulo: Casa do Psicólogo.

Sheriff, Robin. 2001. "Como os senhores chamavam os escravos: Discursos sobre cor, raça e racismo num motto carioca." In *Raça como retórica*, ed. Y. Maggie and C. B. Rezende, 213–37. Rio de Janeiro: Civilização Brasileira.

Silva, Hédio, Jr. 2000. "Do racismo legal ao princípio da ação afirmativa: A lei como obstáculo e como instrumento dos direitos e interesses do povo negro." In *Tirando a máscara: Ensaios sobre o racismo no Brasil*, ed. Antonio Sérgio Guimarães and Lynn Huntley, 359–87. São Paulo: Paz e Terra.

2

Facets of the Insurgent

5

Revolutionary Spiritualities in Chiapas Today

Immanent History and the Comparative Frame
in Subaltern Studies

JOSÉ RABASA

This chapter traces some of the signature concepts of the Zapatista insurrection of 1994 and the pacifism of Las Abejas back to native colonial pictorial articulations of the possibility of dwelling in a plurality of worlds, of the possibility of being modern and not-modern without incurring a contradiction. I prefer the notion of the "not-modern" to the "premodern" in that the latter carries a built-in teleology that posits modernity as a historical necessity. It has been argued that the Spanish invasion of the Americas in the sixteenth century should be considered as the beginning of modernity; we should take care not to define indigenous forms of life under colonial power as one more instance of the modern, but rather as life forms with their own periodicity. In this regard, the juxtaposition of Mesoamerican, colonial, and modern texts in this essay seeks to reproduce the sense of a multi-temporal present that characterizes the native colonial pictorial maps and histories, the Zapatista communiqués, and even Antonio Gramsci's understanding of historical immanence. I first draw from the map of Cholula in the *Relación Geográfica* of 1581 an example and a definition of immanent history, and finally I close with the question of revolutionary spiritualities in Chiapas today. If native hybrid pictorial and alphabetical texts from central Mexico lend themselves to an initial articulation of historical immanence and plural-world dwelling, these colonial texts also give historical depth to the mural "Vida y sueño de la cañada Perla" and the photographic testimonio of Las Abejas that I examine at the end of the essay. My critique of Gramsci's conception of subaltern studies enables me not only to document further what I mean by immanent history, but also to lay out strategies for curtailing the constitution of a transcendental concept or institution that would subordinate immanence to an exterior source of meaning.

Cartographic Specters or the Immanence of Memory

In the map of Cholula from 1581 (fig. 5.1), we can trace the indigenous production of artifacts for Spanish bureaucrats that comprised at least two
codes. While we know the identity of the *corregidor*, Gabriel Rojas, who
provided the verbal responses to the questionnaire of the *Relaciones Geográficas*, which included a question requesting a pictorial representation of the
locations, the *tlacuilo* (the native painter) who drew the map of Cholula
remains unknown. For the most part the painting of maps was delegated
to the *tlacuilo*, but as we will see further down Rojas's written information
proves invaluable for tracing the double register the *tlacuilo* deploys in the
map of Cholula. On the one hand, the townscape of Cholula would satisfy
the *Relaciones Geográficas*'s request of pictorial representations. On the other
hand, the *tlacuilo*, the native painter, inscribed the signs that would enable
readers to recognize precolonial structures and meanings beyond the colonial order signified by the gridiron pattern of streets, the use of alphabetical
writing, and the massive buildings occupying the center of the town.[1] The
tlacuilo displays an ability to use European cartographic systems of representation, but the map also contains indigenous pictographic forms. Under
close examination, the map manifests that the Spanish pictorial vocabulary
is used as signifiers rather than the signifieds usually associated with the
meanings conveyed by grids, perspective, and landscape in chorographic
maps and townscapes. These forms do not convey the corresponding realities of street patterns, the realistic depictions of cities, and the topography
of the surroundings, but rather the system of representation itself. That is
not to say that buildings and temples represented in the map did not have
a corresponding reality, but that beyond these structures we find an immanent historical layer that becomes manifest when we juxtapose a map
of precolonial Cholula (fig. 5.2) from the *Historia Tolteca-Chichimeca* (ca.
1545–65).[2] As in the case of the *tlacuilo* who drafted the map of Cholula, the
"authors" of the *Historia Tolteca-Chichimeca* remain anonymous, the latter
having been produced independently of Spanish authorities and intended
mainly for use within the community of Quautinchan. In both cases we
must assume a collective "author" rather than an individual *tlacuilo* working
independently. Even when the map of Cholula was produced at the request
of the *corregidor* Rojas, we can imagine the *tlacuilo* consulting the elders of
Cholula, and, as such, tracing the past under the ruins that remain legible in
spite of the erasure inflicted by the colonial city. The juxtaposition of the two
maps, which constitute places of memory for the collective remembrance of

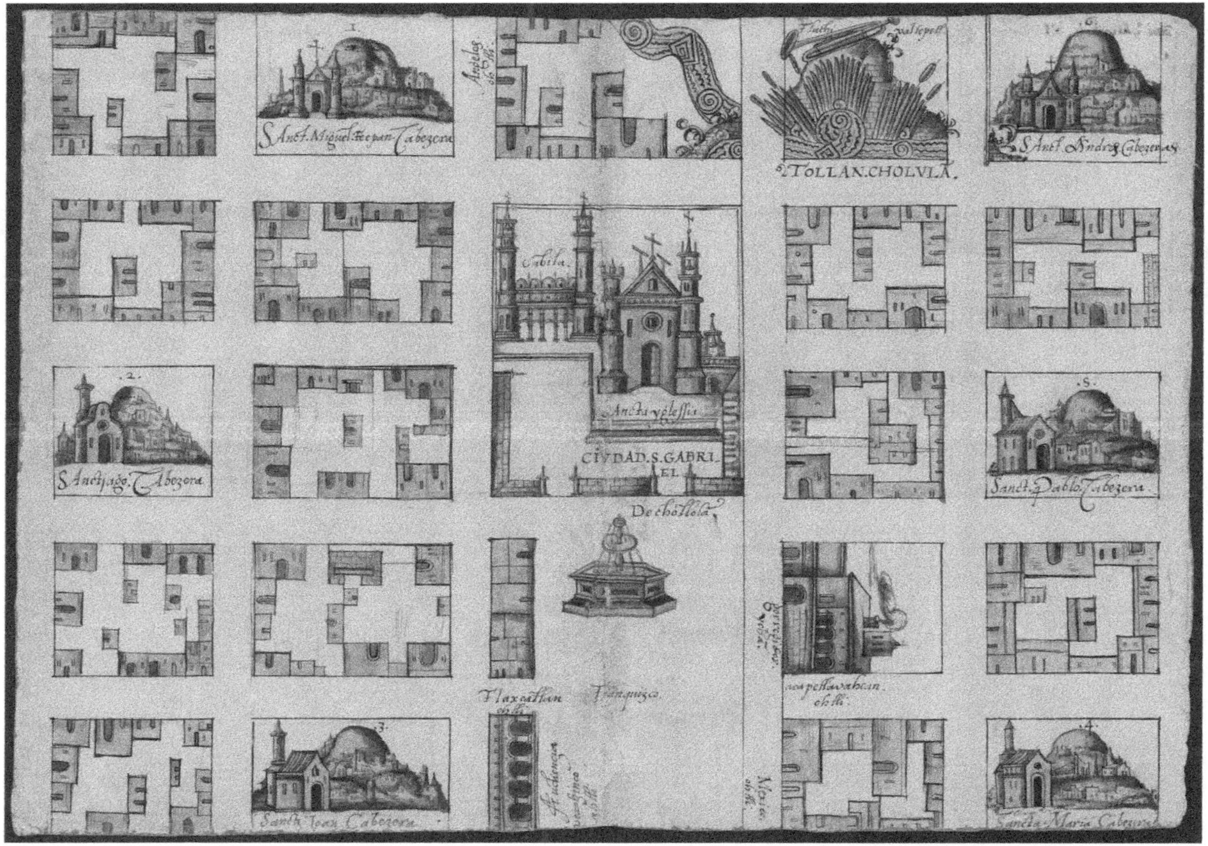

Figure 5.1. Map of Cholula (1581). Courtesy of the Nettie Benson Latin American Collection, University of Texas Libraries, University of Texas at Austin.

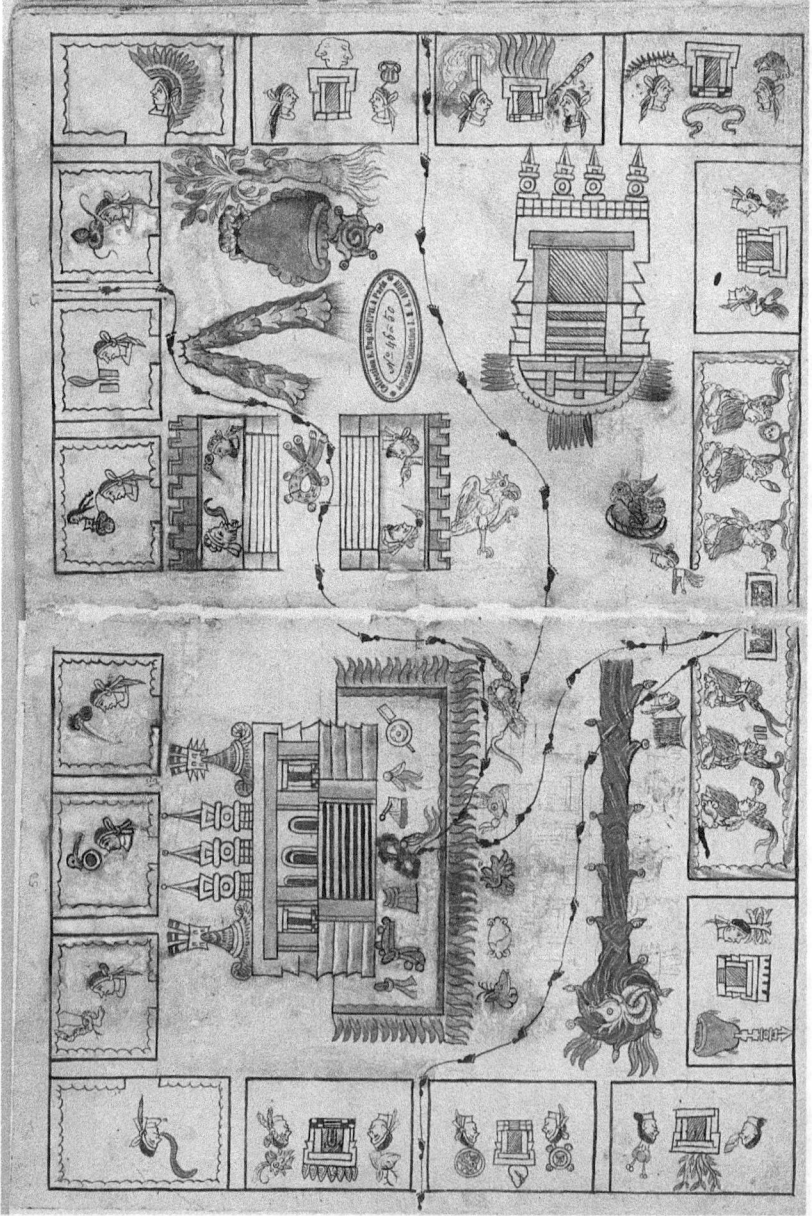

the ancient past, reveals a palimpsest in which under the new Cholula one can trace the continuation of the ancient Mesoamerican past in the Indian colonial present. Thus, the map of Cholula provides a frontispiece for the question of immanent history that I elaborate in this essay.

The first thing one notices is the conjunction of at least two codes operating on the surface of the map (fig. 5.1). We find a body of water represented by a traditional glyph in the central square on the top and the inclusion of glyphs that write the name of Tollan, a combination of *tolin* (rush, reed) and *-tlan* (a relational word that means next to, among). The juxtaposition of the sign of water (*atl*) and a hill (*tepetl*) is a conventional form of writing *altepetl*, the term for the precolonial polity that included a conglomerate of *calpulli* (from *calli* [house] and *-pul*, a suffix that denotes large), the most basic social unit, often translated as big house or neighborhood. In this case it names Tollan Cholula and thereby establishes the connection of the city with the ancient civilization of the Toltecs, who abandoned Tollan in the ninth century. Separated by the trumpet is the term *tlachiualtepetl*, which combines *tlachiualli* (something made, artificial) and *tepetl* (mountain), the name of the main precolonial temple in Cholula. The pyramid consists of a series of layers that correspond to different historical moments and form a hill in their superimposition. The trumpet, which in Nahuatl is called *tepuzquilistli*, a combination of *tepuztli* (metal) and *quiquiztli* (conch), invokes the blowing of the conch in precolonial times to congregate the community around the temple. According to Gabriel de Rojas, the *corregidor*—a bureaucrat charged with administering tributaries of the crown—the missionaries found "muchos caracoles marinos con que los indios antiguamente tañían en lugar de trompetas" (many snails that Indians played instead of trumpets) when the missionaries inquired about the two occasions on which lightning destroyed the large cross that was constructed on top of *tlachiualtepetl* to neutralize the forces of Chiconauh Quiahuitl (*chiconauh* [seven] and *quiahuitl* [rain]), the deity to whom the ancient temples was dedicated (Acuña 1985, 143).[3] The trumpet fulfills this function now under Christianity. The Franciscan monastery of Saint Gabriel and the chapel to the side in the central part of the map have replaced a precolonial temple; as well there are six churches next to hills in the squares surrounding the map. These churches correspond to the sites of six *calpulli* that the map identifies as *cabeceras*. Each of these *calpulli* had a temple that is now symbolized by a hill, but Cholula was flat with the exception of two smaller mounts next to the *tlachiualtepetl*, the artificial hill.

Serge Gruzinski sees in this recurrent hill different perspectives from which the *tlachiualtepetl* could be perceived from the different neighborhood (2002, 139). If this is the case, the representation of the hill, always on the right-hand side, is not very realistic. The painter obviously could have placed the hill in locations that would correspond to the positions of the churches with respect to the *tlachiualtepetl*. In the same fashion that the *tlachiualtepetl* has been reduced to a mount, the hills on the different neighborhoods could be seen as conveying the political autonomy of the *calpulli*, which in precolonial times had a particular temple. We can read behind the churches the presence of the old temples, a continuation of the past in the present that the citizens of Cholula could not have failed to recognize. Indeed, Gabriel de Rojas confirms this when he writes, "Y estos ídolos tenían, también, unos cerrillos menores hechos a mano a modo del sobredicho, con su ermita en lo alto, llamada *teucalli*, que quiere decir 'casa de dios'" (And these idols also had handmade small hills according to the mode explained above, with its hermitage on top, called *teucalli*, which means "house of god") (Acuña 1985, 132). Further down, Rojas adds, "Y aun hay hoy, por toda la ciudad, reliquias de otros muchos menores que, con los edificios de las casas, [se] han ido gastando, como lo hace hoy de los que hay" (And even today, there are relics all over the city of other less important ones, that with the structures of the houses, they have been decaying, as it occurs today with those still standing) (132). The temples and their hills have been destroyed and the debris has been used for the construction of the new city. Note that for Rojas the debris is not just material remains, but relics that haunt the city with a memory of old. Moreover, the debris from the old temples and houses coexists with the ruins of the chapel's dome, which collapsed on the night that followed the celebration of its completion: "Que fue milagro que Dios obró en que cayese de noche, que, de ser asi el día antes, hiciera un estrago notable, por haber más de mil personas dentro. Estas ruinas se han quedado así porque, como los indios van en disminución, no la tornan a edificar" (That it was a miracle by God that it collapsed at night, that, if it had been the day before, it would have a notable devastation, since there were more than one thousand people inside. These ruins remain as such, because the Indians become increasingly fewer, they do not rebuild it) (144–45). In the map of Cholula, the elaborate dome of the chapel, on the left of the convent of San Gabriel, figures intact. The map simulates an organized town built on a geometric grid, but archaeological digs have demonstrated that the depiction of the grid stands for the new Spanish order rather than for an accurate representation of the city blocks. The scenographic realistic repre-

sentation of the hills and the churches of the neighborhood, a highly symbolic gesture, alternate with orthographic schematic depictions of buildings
within the blocks. Thus the *tlacuilo* displays his mastery of Spanish codes in
his juxtaposition, in his citing of orthographic and scenographic systems of
representation.

For Gruzinski, the map resembles a Necker cube that shifts backgrounds,
alternating between a hollow cube and a solid one. He also speaks of a *mestizo* mind to characterize the genius of the *tlacuilo*'s production of cultural
artifacts that deploy elements from different cultures for an end not contemplated by the supervising authorities. As such, the mixture of the precolonial
and the colonial alternate in the dominance of one of the components that
ultimately makes it very hard to distinguish the Indianization of Christianity from the Christianization of the precolonial (2002, 140–41). Thus, the
discreetness of the European and the Indian life forms would disappear
into a *mestizo* mind. For Barbara Mundy, this is an instance of double consciousness, a terms she derives from W. E. B. Du Bois, though she fails to
mention the African American scholar: "In this respect they [Indian maps]
show us the double-consciousness of the colonized artist: working to satisfy
an immediate local audience and laboring with a set of expectations about
the colonizers; this artistic double-consciousness marks a much larger set
of images from the New World" (1996, 215–16). If the mere fact of using
European systems of representation and categories makes the artist colonized, then the fact that I am writing here in English and within an U.S.
academic context would also make me and you who reads this colonized. I
am contaminating you, if you were not already, by the mere fact that you are
following me. There may certainly be a conflict between the two demands
of speaking to the community and responding to the colonial instructions,
but there is no reason why the *tlacuilo* could not have perceived himself as
mastering the codes of European cartography while at the same time knowing that there is more to the townscape than mere European institutions. He
may have experienced a conflict between Christian and Indian spirituality,
but this would be a result of the imposition by missionaries and lay officials,
not one that the *tlacuilo* would have necessarily internalized. The internalization of the conflict is in fact the end of the ideological warfare conducted
by the colonial order, which should not imply that the internalization of
incompatibility would need to be a natural consequence of the evangeliza-
tion. Indians expressing perplexity over the need to abandon their gods in
order to embrace Christianity is at least as notorious in missionary literature
as the friars' lamentations that for the Indians the Christian God was one

more god that could coexist with the rest. To my mind, the coexistence of multiple systems of representation conveys a capacity to dwell in a plurality of worlds without incurring contradiction. Plural-world dwelling would not necessarily imply a struggle between two consciousnesses as manifest in Mundy's definition of double-consciousness or the blending of two life forms into one as in Gruzinski's notion of *mestizaje*, but would rather imply the ability to participate in at least two discreet worlds without incurring contradiction. The *tlacuilo* displays knowledge of Western forms but also of local practices;, as in the case of the Necker cube, in the blink of an eye one finds a Nahuatl world signified.

Subalternized indigenous subjects developed the ability to dwell in more than one world because colonial orders demanded that Indians recognize the authority of and subject themselves to Spanish institutions. The colonial order constituted itself as the only true world whether under the axis of Christianity or of modern science. In order to protect the integrity of their worlds, indigenous subjects systematically excluded others from learning about and dwelling in their culture. The *tlacuilo* who drafted the map of Cholula was expected to produce a townscape that would follow the principles of European map making. One finds a double coding on the surface of the map that did not seem to have posed a threat to the *corregidor* Rojas. Although Rojas consulted Indians, he does not give us their names. To all appearances Rojas was a *nahuatlato* (speaker and interpreter of Nahuatl) who translated all the information provided by the Indian informants.

Let's now juxtapose a map from the *Historia Tolteca-Chichimeca*, a hybrid text that uses both the alphabet and pictorial representation and was produced outside the supervision of Spanish authorities. The fact that the *tlacuilo* used both the alphabet and pictography does not make this text less indigenous, as if one would lose one's Indianness by the mere fact of riding horses, weaving with wool, or using the pen to write letters. Nothing remains pure in the aftermath of the European invasion. The *Historia Tolteca-Chichimeca* provides a pictographic history and an alphabetical transcription of an oral performance of the stories associated with the paintings. This map underlies the map of Cholula of 1581 as in a palimpsest that manifests the ghostly continuity of the precolonial order in the colonial map. It provides a key for understanding the background of the map of Cholula as indigenous. I understand by *background* the philosophical concept that stands for the absolute presupposition from which and against which one makes sense of life forms.[4] Here I have been arguing for multiple absolute presuppositions that remain discreet though never pure in plural-world dwelling.

The existence of discreet worlds does not imply that one cannot make sense, *exappropriate*, and transform life forms belonging to another world with its own absolute presuppositions. I derive the term *exappropriation* from Derrida: "What is a stake here, and it obeys another 'logic,' is rather a 'choice' between multiple configurations of mastery without mastery (what I have proposed to call 'exappropriation'). But it also takes the phenomenal form of a war, a conflictual tension between multiple forces of appropriation, between multiple strategies of control" (Derrida and Stiegler 2002, 37). This process of deploying and making sense with life forms belonging to another culture would not exclude the possibility of also understanding those forms in terms of their own background. The ability to switch backgrounds might enable someone to describe the rules of or the contradictions in the social and cultural practices of another culture. The example of the anthropologist who isolates the rules of a culture comes to mind, but we must also observe colonial spaces in which Indians saw through the social, cultural, and religious forms practiced by Spaniards. In fact, indigenous people under colonial regimes have an advantage over the anthropologist in that Indians are required to understand and make themselves familiar with European institutions. Spanish lay officials and missionaries often expressed dismay and persecuted and repressed Indians who showed them contradictions in their most valued doctrinal beliefs and evangelical practices.[5]

In the map of Cholula of 1581 the indigenous background coexists with a Spanish background that defines space in terms of European forms of representation and urban landscape. The European life forms function not only as signifieds but also as signifiers that now constitute a vocabulary that the *tlacuilo* has invented to represent European objects from within an indigenous conception of the world. The correspondence of the map of Cholula with the structure that supposedly existed centuries before the arrival of the Spaniards reveals that the new map constitutes a palimpsest for those who could trace the old in the terms of an indigenous background. In addition to the *tlachiualtepetl* (the artificial hill), the map invites the reader to locate the institutions that made up "yn uel ytzontecon mochiuhtica yn toltecayolt" (the true head of the essentially tolteca): "Tlachihualtepetl ycatcan, Atlyayauhcan, Xochatlauhtli ypilcayan, Quetzaltotl ycacan, Iztaquautli ytlaquayan, Iztaczollin ynemomoxouayan, Calmecac, Ecoztlan, Temmatlac, Apechtli yyonocan y Couatl ypilhuacan" (Kirchhof et al. 1976, 181). With the exception of the *tlachiualtepetl* (the artificial mountain) and the *calmecac* (the school), the other institutions listed defy translation. The *tlacuilo*, or at least the recorded verbal performance of the map, speaks in the present tense: "uel nican monezcaycuiloua yn imaltepeuh yn iuh yyollo quimatico yn tachtouan yn tocolhuan auh tel yn axcan zan iuh catqui yn imauh yn intepeuh yn tolteca calmecactlaca" (here is painted the figure of the town; thus it is; thus our great-grandfathers and grandfathers came to know it; and notwithstanding today also as such it is the pueblo [*auh, tepeuh,* or *altepetl*] of the Tolteca, the Calmecactlaca) (180–81). The *Historia Tolteca-Chichimeca* speaks of the coming to be of Cholula in exclusively Indian spiritual terms, "yn zan ipaltzinco yn ipalnemoani, yn tlalticpaque" (only with the power of that by means of which we live, the possessor of the earth) (180). There is no mention of a Christian deity or an attempt to demonize these manifestations of the creative force. By underscoring the present, the world witnessed by the ancient great-grandparents remains accessible even after the havoc brought about by the Spanish invasion.

The *tlacuilo* of the map of Cholula conceived at least in part an audience that participated in the indigenous background of the *Historia Tolteca-Chichimeca.* Those native informants that provided the *corregidor* Rojas with information about precolonial Cholula would have unfailingly recognized the indigenous past on the surface of the depicted colonial present. Rojas quite laconically states, "Y aun hay hoy, por toda la ciudad, reliquias" (and even today, there are relics all over the city) (Acuña, 143). In the map of Cholula, the *tlacuilo* conveys her mastery of several codes and the ability to include at least two radically different readings. Beyond comparison and translation, the map of Cholula invites us to shift backgrounds. Thus, the *tlacuilo* manifests her capacity to dwell in multiple worlds. Moreover, the mastery of Spanish forms then and modern discourses today need not entail getting caught on the rails of the dialectic bound to hegemonizing and homogeneizing discourses.

The *Historia Tolteca-Chichimeca* also illustrates the fascination native scribes had with the alphabet as a technology for the recording of voice. The record of voice by means of the alphabet obviously embalms, some would say kills, orality, but by the same token it gives place to a site for the resurrection of the dead. Indian alphabetical texts, at least those recording speech and song, like the *Historia Tolteca-Chichimeca,* were not intended to be read in private but rather to be subjected to an oral performance, much like in the pictorial codices of the precolonial period. Note the opening remarks that invite the elders to sit and listen to the performance of the alphabetical and pictorial text:

chacui—chini tanquehue xihuiqui notlatzin ximotlali ypan ycpalli—
    chitao

chacui qieaha tanquehe xihualmohuica ximotlali
chacui tachi—tanquehue—xihuiqui nocoltzin ximotlali
chontana dios tachi—ma Dios mitzmohuquili nocoltzin
chini yn chay—tihimaxoconmit notlatzin tepitzin
chontana chana Dios ma Dios mitzmohuiquili tlatouane

(*chacui—chini tanquehue* come my uncle sit down on the chair—*chitao
chacui qieaha tanquehe* come sit down
chacui tachi—tanquehue—my grandfather, come sit down
chontana dios tachi—my grandfather, may God take you
chini yn chay—may you drink my uncle a little bit
chontana chana Dios Oh ruler may God take you)

(Kirchhof et al. 1976, 131)

This is a bilingual text that juxtaposes Popoloca and Nahuatl. I have underlined the Popoloca. This opening statement most likely dates from the early eighteenth century. By invoking the elders to sit and drink this brief text testifies to a performance almost two hundred years after its production. Several interpretations have been given for the inclusion of a Popoloca version of the Nahuatl. Michael Swanton has argued that this is a ritual text, though he does not fully explain the function bilingualism would have played in the ritual (Swanton 2001). A simpler explanation would be that Popoloca speakers attended, and that it merely reflects an invitation. What remains beyond doubt is that it signals the collective participation in the ritual that recalls the origins and foundation of Quautinchan. We know the document remained in the community up to 1718, when it became part of the Lorenzo Boturini collection. Today it is housed in the Bilbiothèque nationale de France. Since it remained in the community for two hundred years we may argue that the *Historia Tolteca-Chichimeca* was produced for internal consumption rather than for arguing a case in Spanish courts. We must also assume that the production of the verbal and the pictorial document involved the whole community and that alphabetical writing was soon to be understood as a record of voice, of a particular voicing of a pictorial text that could be brought back, enhanced, relived in future generations. Ghosts particularly haunt writing as a record of voice.

These two maps are products of immanent history that is constituted in the speech of the communities. This space of immanence makes worlds through native languages and backgrounds that often coexist with Euro-American backgrounds. The community may master the Western codes, stop being subalterns according to a Gramscian definition, but without necessarily subjecting the meaning and significance of their discursive practices to a transcendental principle or institution.

The Comparative Frame of Subaltern Studies

One can open just about any page in Gramsci and find a vocabulary of progress and historical development that establishes a teleology for comparative purposes. Gramsci's terms include historical places, emergence, conditions of transformations, levels of development, degrees of homogeneity, forms of political consciousness, historical maturity, and so on. There is a vanguardism in his call for subaltern studies, if this is what Gramsci would have called his studies of dominance and subordination. Vanguardism is perhaps nowhere more clearly articulated than when he appraises Henri de Man and Lenin indirectly in a note on Machiavelli from 1930: "He (De Man) demonstrated the need to study and develop [elaborare] the elements of popular psychology, historically and not sociologically, actively (i.e., in order to transform them, by educating them, into a modern mentality) and descriptively as he [Maeterlinck] does. But this need was at least implicit (perhaps even explicitly stated), in the doctrine of Ilitch [Lenin]—something of which De Man is entirely ignorant" (Gramsci 1986, 810; 1971, 197).

Gramsci goes on to distinguish "scholars who argue that spontaneity is the immanent and objective 'method' of the historical process, and political adventurers who argue for it as a 'political' method" (1986, 810; 1971, 197). Whereas the former betrays a mistaken conception, the latter entails the desire to replace a given leadership by a different one. I don't quite understand what Gramsci means by the mistaken conception of "the immanent and objective method" (though I suspect he is alluding to Lenin's negative conception of sponteneity in *What Is to Be Done?*); nevertheless, I will derive from these passages a concept of historical immanence that should shed further light on the colonial texts we have examined above and the discussion of insurgency in Chiapas today. Under Gramsci's formulation subalterns may know spontaneously the causes of their oppression and the need to organize politically (that is, they contain the rudimentary elements of conscious leadership, of discipline), but only modern theory will give them a full understanding and guarantee that their force is not misdirected by reactionary groups. Gramsci makes room for knowledge through a popular conception of the world, "what is unimaginatively called 'instinct,' although it too is in fact a primitive and elementary historical acquisition," but he advocates for "a reciprocal 'reduction' so to speak," claiming that "a passage from one to the other and vice versa must be possible" (1986, 811; 1971, 199). Although Gramsci here lays out the indispensable unity between "spontaneity" and "conscious leadership," which constitutes "the real political action of subaltern classes, in so far as this is mass politics and not merely an adventure by groups claiming to represent the masses" (1986, 811; 1971, 198, 198), the comparative frame of subaltern studies ultimately defines the project as one in which subordinated groups must be educated so that they may overcome their subalternity.[6] Elsewhere, Gramsci does make allowance for processes that seem to be understood by the subaltern classes directly, but then he adds that this understanding implies that it is no longer a subaltern class "or at least is demonstrably on the way to emerging from its subordinate position" (1986, 829; 1971, 202). Has there ever has been an absolute state of subalternity, that is, one that ignores its subordinate condition and lacks any form of significant resistance? In other words, aren't all subalterns always already "on the way to emerging from their subordinate position"? Gramsci's premise is that elementary forms of consciousness must be translated into a theoretical language and that in the process of putting it into practice, theory will override the elementary forms. In fact, even if modern theory builds from the spontaneous knowledge of subalterns, it will in the end constitute itself as the source of truth and parameter for defining errors, such as the "mistake" of the immanent method. The new prince in its embodiment in the party transcends the everyday practices, languages, and articulations of alternate worlds. But the party and modern theory in general must also translate their articulations into a language that would make sense in terms of the forces of immanent history.

Gramsci remains exceptionally lucid with respect to issues of spontaneity and his call to attend the particular forms of thought that inform social movements and revolutionary process. These forms most often clash with modern knowledge; nevertheless, he considers that they must be translated into theoretical language. If there is a dialectic between these two forms of life, the telos undoubtedly points to the homogenization of thought in modern science and the party, to the "homogeneous politico-economic historical bloc, without internal contradictions" (1986, 767; 1971, 168).

The concept of the subaltern as conceived by Gramsci bears a comparative frame that defines the dissolution of subalternity in forms of consciousness that make possible the organization of political blocs that can bring about a revolution, even if he makes allowances for spontaneity or immanent forces. In its most refined form, the teleological impulse in the comparative frame of subaltern studies constitutes its model of interpretation and evaluation as an end. The present from which we write, the hindsight of how history evolved, cannot but be privileged in comparative studies. If comparisons are unavoidable, I would recommend limiting them to artifacts and forms of thought that share a background. The issue here is whether history reads in the singular. Inevitably we will compare singular vis-à-vis multiple historical horizons. Questions of beginnings also come into play in comparative historical processes: for example, the dating of modernity in the Enlightenment vis-à-vis the dating in 1492. What is at stake in building a narrative using these two moments? Lest we forget that the constitution of a beginning, of a zero point constitutive of historical narrative, is a choice the historian makes to tell a story, rather than an onto-historical claim, the stories we tell should make sense in terms of the immanent forces manifest at any given moment. World historical narratives that locate key moments in world history around European-global moments (whether these moments may involve 1492, the French Revolution, or the Industrial Revolution does not make a difference) subordinate the significance of immanent history by positing a transcendental narrative. Thus, world-system models undermine the periodization of indigenous histories that cannot be reduced to mere reactions to global formations even when conceived as resistance. These models make Eurocentric conceptions of history and the world all but inevitable. We may seek to debunk the European hubris by documenting how non-Europeans contributed, anticipated, and inaugurated life forms that tend to be identified as solely products of Europe. This is a just project and must be done, but we may end up with an even more hegemonic system of thought in that the dominant would now include as the natural way of seeing and understanding the world the true knowledge that all mankind has contributed to the making of modernity, rather than a predominantly Western epistemological regime that historically has and continues to subordinate all not-modern forms of life. The irony of those who make the modern the only existing world (an undeniable fact if defined as the shared temporality that makes all cultures contemporary) resides in the inherent practice of modern thought to define correctness and error in terms of advanced and backward life forms. For instance, a culture that believes in the agency of the "gods" might be as modern as any other coeval cultural formation, but it could nevertheless be relegated to a mistaken conception of history by the most "advanced" modern ideas. Modernity, in its race toward progress, is comparativist through and through, hence teleological in its characterization of the not so modern. Given that the comparative frame of subaltern studies also entails the notion that subalternity is a relational concept, we could very well end up speaking of subalterns as comprising a marginalized middle class consisting of slighted intellectuals, ineffectual political activists, political prisoners, and a broad panoply of modern types. Rather than speaking of the modern and the premodern, I have been using the concept of the not-modern to understand a whole series of life forms that are impermeable to the teleology that constitutes the *pre-* of the modern. The definition of indigenous knowledges as premodern is primarily the result of exclusionary practices that confine indigenous epistemes to the realm of superstitions, folklore, magic, and so on, which keep us from understanding indigenous life forms in their positivity. Given the inherent logic of subordination in discourses of modernity that constitute the premodern and structurally determine the anti-modern, the not-modern offers the possibility that one may practice the most modern without letting it encroach on the not-modern. Nativist and revivalist movements may conceive of themselves as not-modern but not necessarily as anti-modern. A most common rebuttal to not-modern is that subalterns also want to be modern and desire modern technology, and so forth. Of course they do, but there are subalterns who do not find a contradiction between desiring, acquiring, and mastering modern life forms and continuing to practice forms of life that have nothing to do with modernity, that, in fact, modernity often finds incompatible. But this epistemic violence that defines modernity in exclusionary terms need not be internalized.

From a Gramscian perspective, the ability to understand and articulate historico-political conditions of oppression is already a sign that one no longer is a subaltern. The question, however, is whether the language one uses to articulate these conditions must correspond to Euro-American theory, hence all nativistic discourses would signal a condition of subalternity. This makes sense in terms of the practicality of nativistic forms in circles such as the IMF or the World Bank, in that these institutions will dismiss any claims that do not meet the standards of their discourse. Does that mean that a social group must abandon nativistic and revivalist discourses or that they must understand these discourses as subaltern forms given the privileged position of science? Wouldn't this logic imply a colonialist impulse that in subordinating forms of discourse inflicts epistemic violence? These questions signal the dead-ends of the comparative frame in subaltern studies.[7]

Now, the comparative frame of subaltern studies may lose its grip if we consider the possibility that subalterns, say Amerindians under colonial rule—a colonial condition that by the way does not end with the Wars of

Independence in the nineteenth century but continues up to the present—may dwell in more than one world without comparing them and thereby without enduring the internalization of modernist hubris.

Revolutionary Spirituality in Las Abejas and the Zapatistas

I will now examine two instances of revolutionary spirituality in Chiapas today in which one can trace the work of immanent history. The first example is the mural "Vida y sueños de la cañada Perla" (fig. 5.3), which exemplifies the warrior mysticism expressed in the murals of the Zapatista bases that lend support to the Zapatista Army of National Liberation (EZLN).[8] This mural includes Emiliano Zapata, the leader of the Southern Armies of the Revolution of 1910, riding his horse and holding a rifle, and Ricardo Flores Magón, the anarcho-communist theoretician of the Mexican revolution of 1910, who is also armed with a cartridge belt. Both are identified with slogans. A passage from Flores Magón's last article in *Regeneración*, the organ of the Partido Liberal, illustrates his call to action: "Para lucha actividad, actividad, actividad es lo que reclama el momento" (for the struggle, activity, activity, activity, is what the moment demands). Observe the word "libertad" spinning on his left hand. Zapata's *paliacate*, his scarf, bears the inscription "La tierra es de quien la trabaja." Zapata's takeovers of the haciendas in the state of Morelos, a brilliant instance of Gramsci's immanent history, have their match in Flores Magón's theorization of direct action. As in the case of the map of Cholula, we find multiple backgrounds for interpreting the mural. One can at once provide a reading that places the emphasis on a long anarcho-communist tradition and the program of the rural peasantry led by Zapata. The reference to Zapata, I would argue, makes manifest an immanent history of indigenous peoples' demands of land and of sovereignty over their territories. Zapata also merges with the precolonial figure of Votán, the "the guardian and heart of the people." Zapatista spirituality invokes a nativistic tradition that often juxtaposes Zapata and Quetzalcoatl in murals in the Zapatista bases. Here we find a reference to the two Quetzalcoatl that correspond to the diurnal and nocturnal passage of Venus: The legendary Zapata dressed in white that appears on the horizon riding his horse and the clandestine Zapatistas on the mountains that guard Taniperla. Jan De Vos has traced these two Quetzalcoatl to a communiqué by Marcos from December 1994 (2002, 376–90). In response to Marcos's question about the relationship between Zapata and the gods Votán and Ikal, Old Man Antonio responds:

El tal Zapata se apareció acá en las montañas. No se nació, dicen. Se apareció así nomás. Dicen que es el Ik'al y el Votán que hasta acá vinieron a parar en su largo camino y que, para no espantar a las gentes, se hicieron uno sólo. Porque ya de mucho andar juntos el Ik'al y el Votán aprendieron que era lo mismo y que podían hacerse uno sólo en el día y en la noche y cuando se llegaron hasta acá se hicieron uno y se pusieron de nombre Zapata y dijo el Zapata que hasta aquí había llegado y acá iba a encontrar la respuesta de a dónde lleva el largo camino y dijo que en veces sería luz y en veces oscuridad, pero que era el mismo, el Votán Zapata y el Ik'al Zapata, el Zapata blanco y el Zapata negro, y que eran los dos el mismo camino para los hombres y las mujeres verdaderos (That Zapata appeared here in the mountains. He wasn't born, they say. He just appeared just like that. They say he is Ik'al and Votán, who came all the way over here in their long journey, and so as not to frighten good people, they became one. Because after being together for so long Ik'al and Votán learned that they were the same and could become Zapata. And Zapata said he had finally learned where the long road went and that at times it would be light and times darkness but that he was the same, Votán Zapata and Ik'al Zapata, the white Zapata and the black Zapata. They were both the same road for the true men and women). (December 13, 1994)[9]

Note that in Codex Borgianus and in Codex Vaticanus B, two precolonial religious codices, we find representations of a black Quetzalcoatl linked at the waist to a white Mictlantecutli, "the lord of death." These opposites, as well as the white and black Ik'al and Votán, need not have the positive and negative meanings commonly associated with these colors in the West; actually, one can read elements of one god in the other.[10] This is, in fact, the gist of Old Man Antonio's story. As Ik'al and Votán merge into one in Zapata, Old Man Antonio in his conversation with Marcos brings together a millenarian memory for the articulation of a revolutionary conception of history and the world, one grounded in the precolonial and espousing a multi-temporal sense of the present. Other nativistic motifs in the mural include the figure of Mother Earth, as embodied in the large woman on the left side of the mural, and the birds, which a new age reading might interpret as a sign of a native colorful view of the world, but a more historically informed reading would identify with *quautli*, with eagle warriors descending to the earth as Zapatista forces. Mother Earth stands as the beginning, as a point of departure, as emblematic of the place women should have in Mayan communities

Figure 5.3. "Vida y sueños de la cañada Perla," comunidad de Taniperla, Chiapas (1998). Printed with the authorization of the Junta de Buen Gobierno el Camino del Futuro. Caracol de Resistencia hacia un Nuevo Amanecer.

and the important role they play in the Zapatista insurrection. At the other end of the ideological spectrum, the telecommunications tower conveys the use and mastery of Western technology. Even though the dominant spirituality is nativistic, the mural includes a temple committed to ecumenism, to countering the violence that banishes non-Catholic members from their communities and the terrorism of paramilitary groups associated with the Presbyterian Church that murder Zapatista sympathizers. The mission of ecumenical dialogue neutralizes religious warfare and condemns the explanation of massacres in terms of religious conflicts. In Taniperla, there is room for Protestants, Catholics, nativists, and atheists, if we are to take seriously the figure of Ricardo Flores Magón as an ancestor, as a revenant that together with Zapata infuses life into the community.

One of the most distinctive traits of the Zapatista insurrection has been the respect *mestizo* leadership has shown for the life forms of indigenous communities. Indeed, there has been a concerted effort to avoid all forms of vanguardism. Subcomandante Marcos has played an important role as a spokesperson of the EZLN, but his position has been of *sub*-comandante at the service and orders of the Indian-led Comité Clandestino Revolucionario Indígena, Comandancia General, which, in turn, always acts on the consensus of the communities. There is an undeniable theorization on the part of Marcos and other comandantes such as Tacho, David, and Azevedo, and even more importantly by the women Zapatistas such as the comandantes Esther, Ramona, and Trinidad, to mention just some names. It is beyond the scope of this essay to go in any detail into the question of gender in the Zapatista insurrection,[11] but the organization of the movement, the articulation of programs, and the definition of autonomies have been informed by indigenous thought. In the mural a man and woman carry proposals worked out in the separate assemblies and meet at the door of the Casa Municipal, which the sign on top in Tzeltal identifies as *Sna yu'un ateletic yu'un comonaletic* (House of the authorities of the communities). The woman wears traditional Tzeltal dress. The decisions at the meeting will define the practices of the everyday life of the communities, will be articulated in Tzeltal, and will retain their roots in millennial communal practices. Marcos has brilliantly articulated the link between historical immanence and constituent power in "Chiapas: La Treceava Estela (primera parte)," the series of seven communiqués that announced the creation of the Juntas de Buen Gobierno, the *caracoles*:

> Durante varias horas, estos seres de corazón moreno han trazado, con sus ideas, un gran caracol. Partiendo de lo internacional, su mirada y su pensamiento ha ido, adentrando, pasando sucesivamente por lo nacional, lo regional y lo local, hasta llegar a lo que ellos llaman "El Votán." "El guardian y corazón del pueblo," los pueblos zapatistas. Asi desde la curva más externa del caracol se piensan palabras como "globalización," "guerra de dominación," "resistencia," "economía," "ciudad," "campo," "situación política," y otras que el borrador va eliminando después de la pregunta de rigor "¿Está claro o hay pregunta?" Al final del camino de fuera hacia dentro, en el centro del caracol, sólo quedan unas siglas: "EZLN." Después hay propuestas y se dibujan, en el pensamiento y el corazón ventanas y puertas que sólo ellos ven (entre otras cosas, porque aún no existen). La palabra dispar y dispersa empieza a hacer camino común y colectivo. Alguien pregunta "¿Hay acuerdo?" "Hay," responde afirmando la voz colectiva. De nuevo se traza el caracol, pero ahora en camino inverso, de dentro hacia fuera. El borrador sigue también el camino inverso hasta que solo queda, llenando el viejo pizarrón, una frase que para muchos es delirio, pero que para estos hombres y mujeres es una razón de lucha: "un mundo donde quepan muchos mundos." Más despuesito, una decisión se toma (Over several hours, these beings with a brown heart have traced, with their ideas, a gigantic snail. Starting from the international, their sight and thought have gone deeper, successively passing by the national, the regional and local, until reaching what they call "El Votán, El Guardián y corazón del pueblo," the Zapatista peoples. Thus from the most external curve of the snail they think such words as "globalization," "war of domination," "resistance," "economy," "city," "country," "political situation," and others that the eraser eliminates after the essential question "Is it clear or is there another question?"

At the end of the path from the outside to the inside, in the center of the snail, only the abbreviation "EZLN" remains. Afterward there are propositions and windows and doors are drawn that only they see [among other things, because they don't exist yet]. The unequal and disperse word begins to make its common and collective path. Someone asks "Is there agreement?" "There is" responds in the affirmative the collective voice. Again, the snail is traced, but now in the inverse direction, from within to without. The eraser also follows the inverse path until there only remains, filling the old blackboard, a phrase that for many is delirium, but that for these men and women is a reason to struggle: "a world in which many worlds fit." A bit later, a decision is taken). (Marcos 2003)

The movement inward and outward within the *caracol* establishes that the reflection on categories and social projects will be in indigenous terms. I read in the call for "un mundo donde quepan muchos mundos" a felicitous expression of the plural-world dwelling that I have identified in the map of Cholula and other colonial pictorial codices. This sense of a plurality of worlds has little to do with the liberal multiculturalism that global corporations espouse in their promotion of a homogenous, albeit multiracial, profile of the employees and the world to which they cater. The call for "un mundo donde quepan muchos mundos" constitutes a statement about globalization that underscores the possibility of multiple socio-economic, political, and cultural worlds. In the world of the "multicultural" corporations, there is no room for autonomous Indian peoples debating and arriving at consensus on the use and benefits to be derived from the natural resources in their territories.[12] Nor is there room for spiritual revolutions that neutralize the exappropriation and commercialization of indigenous life forms. Earlier on, Marcos reminds us that the *caracol* represented the ancients' understanding of knowledge as entering the heart. And as in the case of the *caracoles* of Cholula that convoked the people, the *caracol* now fulfills the promise of bringing the community together so that "la palabra fuera de uno a otro y naciera el acuerdo" (the word would go from one to another and gave birth to agreement). This politics of consensus underlies the gathering of men and women at the Casa Municipal, at the *Sna yu'un ateletic yu'un comonaletic*, represented in the mural of Taniperla.

This takes me to the second example of revolutionary spirituality: the Tsotsil pacifist organization Las Abejas and its commitment to Christianity. I find particularly interesting the group's use of writing and more particularly of photography in the production of a *testimonio* of the massacre of Acteal on December 22, 1997, when several dozen armed paramilitaries organized by the army and the state police murdered forty-five members of Las Abejas, the majority women, elders, and children, while they prayed. The testimonio, . . . *Esta es nuestra palabra* . . . , includes photographs by Jutta Meier- Weidenbach and Claudia Ituarte, an (unsigned) introduction by Pablo Romo, then the director of the Centro de Derecho Humanos "Fray Bartolomé de las Casas," and a short text by Elena Poniatowska. In this case, immanent history corresponds to an indigenous Christianity that informed the emergence of this association, which is committed to pacifism, in 1992, two years before the Zapatista uprising. As in the case of the Zapatistas, with whom Las Abejas sympathizes, though it does not share their call to arms, Las Abejas organized to fight the corruption of native officials associated with the PRI, then the official state party, and more generally with the forces of globalization that are destroying native communities in Chiapas. I do not have the space to provide a history of the organization.[13] Let me just point out that the group is committed to radical pacifism, perhaps nowhere better expressed than in Pedro Valtierra's photograph of a Tsotsil woman physically resisting the army's entrance to the refugee camp of Xoyep. This image has circulated all over the world, drawing the attention of pacifist organizations such as the Christian Peacemaker Teams. Members of Las Abejas know the power of photography but also the logic of exappropriation that haunts the circulation of images. Thus, they converse with the most radical pacifists for the invention of new forms of action.

The production of the verbal testimony involved a process in which human rights workers from the Centro de Derechos Humanos "Fray Bartolomé de las Casas" recorded *testimonios* in Tsotsil and the simultaneous translation into Spanish by a bilingual member of the community. The *frayba* (as sympathizers know the center) then transcribed the translation into a computer file. Having read the *testimonios* before spending time in Acteal, I had the impression that the *testimonios* were by speakers who had difficulties expressing their ideas in Spanish. The *frayba* made the concerted effort to remain faithful to the language of the translator to the extent that the expressions of the translators were intelligible. The translations were edited not only with an eye for intelligibility but also for producing short statements often punctuated by ellipses. This editing further fragments the flow of speech implicit in the alphabetical transcription and even in the audio recording of voice. During my visit in the summer of 2003, the community of Las Abejas was involved in producing a series of *testimonios* to be presented at the Interamerica Human Rights Court. For this dossier, Las Abejas first recorded the *testimonios* in Tsotsil, then transcribed them into an alphabetical text, and finally translated and typed the Spanish version into a computer file.

On this occasion, they were assisted by a group of students from a Je-suit high school (Instituto Lux of León, Guanajuato) who were doing their social service in Acteal. Members from the community met and discussed how much to alter the Spanish version. Under the advice of the *frayba*, they decided that the transcriptions should remain faithful to the literal transla-tions of the bilingual Tsotsiles. The *frayba* warned the high school students against polishing the language because the text could be subjected to a "per-itaje antropológico," to an anthropological evaluation. At first, I thought the issue of producing a text that "sounded" Tsotsil was an odd way of proving authenticity. My immediate suggestion was to submit the tapes and written transcription to the anthropologist doing the arbitration. I have come to realize that the presentation of a document that even in Spanish carries the force of Tsotsil rhetoric and poetics not only testifies to authenticity and to an indigenous production, but forces those involved in the court to recog-nize Tsotsil signifiers as legitimate. Here we find an instance in which the exappropriation of Spanish in the process of translation, a step that really didn't need the high school students, since the bilingual translators were proficient in Spanish, would have rendered the document proper at the ex-pense of Tsotsil life forms.

If the verbal testimonies describe the massacre in detail, the photography never documents the physical effects. As a technology, photography has the capability of producing incontrovertible evidence of torture and murder. The photographers working with the community chose to capture the peo-ple in mourning and the abjection poverty and displacement had brought to their lives. We find instances in which the subjects interact with the pho-tographer with the intent of addressing us, the observers. There is a clear understanding of what photography does and how it is consumed. In some instance the subjects note the presence of the photographer but choose not to acknowledge her presence. I am particularly impressed by Jutta Meier-Weindeback's photograph that captures an old woman holding a dry piece of tortilla and staring at the photographer and us (fig. 5.4). The other two women ignore the presence of Meier-Weindeback rather than interact with her. The old woman conveys the suffering due to the lack of food. The piece of tortilla could stand for the centrality of maize in Mayan civilization, but also for the sacred host that brings grace and solidifies the commitment of

Las Abejas to pacifism. In colonial times, the use of tortillas as wafers was so common that is was the term used when speaking of the sacrament. Take, for example, the following passage from an *Exercicio quotidiano* that was found among the papers of the Nahua historian from Chalco, don Domingo de San Antón Muñón Chimalpahin Quauhtlehuantzin (1593–1621): "Auh in ihquac yuh quimihtalhui yn totecuiyo Jesu Christo: niman oconmocuilli yn tlaxcalli, auh quinmomaquillitzino yn Apostolome. quimihtalhui, Jnin na-mechmaca ca nonatcayotzin yn amopampa temac tlaçaloz" (And when our Lord Jesus Christ had thus spoken, then He took tortillas and gave them to the apostles. He said: This that I give you is My body, which because of you is to be betrayed into others' hands) (Anderson and Shroeder 1997, 172–73). *Tlaxcalli* (tortilla) stands as the most obvious "bread" that Jesus would have broken among the Apostles and the most natural signifier for the host, the Eucharistic wafer. When speaking of the host, contemporary Tzatzil uses *cuxul waj* (bread or *tortilla viva*) or *sh'ul waj* (*santa tortilla*). It is a common practice among the Abejas to end a fast by passing around a dry piece of tor-tilla with a sprinkle of salt. Jutta Meier-Weidenbach, however, has reminded me that the three women could only have been fasting out of extreme hun-ger. We should not read too much into this image. But the symbolism that exceeds the immediate intentions of the photographer would in this case lead us to relate the dry tostada with the host, and the practice of breaking a fast as an act of communion. Moreover, we could extend the metaphor of the tostada and the host to the photograph itself in as much as it consti-tutes a vehicle for the spirits. One cannot but associate these three women belonging to different generations with the three Marys of the passion. In tracing this Indianization of the host, we should avoid a facile celebration of how Indians appropriate Christianity to meet their non-Christian spiri-tual needs and beliefs. I say facile because such tracing tends to underesti-mate how essential to Christianity is the appropriation of Christian truth as one's own. Appropriation also plays into a logic in which property and propriety inflect each other. As it were, one becomes proper in participating in a regime of property. Derrida's concept of exappropriation reminds us that the logic of appropriation involves a two-way street, which is fraught with struggles over truth and symbolism. The old woman of the photograph knows that her image will be consumed and exappropriated in spaces out of her control. These could include a human rights discourse that would pity her condition without recognizing the force of her pacifist convictions or, by the same token, the theoretical dismissal of the testimonial power of her image on the grounds that human rights discourses undermine the agency

Figure 5.4. *Esta es nuestra palabra . . .* (1998). Courtesy of Jutta Meier-Weidenbach.

of Las Abejas by emphasizing their victimization. Moreover, she knows that the aesthetic power of photography could depoliticize her image. By these comments, I would not want to take away the immediacy and truthfulness of her immediate interaction with the photographer in which, as Meier-Weidenbach conveyed to me, "she was 'saying' something like 'look at me and tell my story.'" In facing the photographer, in looking back at us, and in holding the dry tortilla she seems to ask us to acknowledge her awareness of how her image will inevitably be exappropriated.

Observe how proper is her attire, considering that she is living in a muddy refugee camp under a shelter made of plastic sheets set up to protect herself from the torrential rains of the season. She understands well the power of photography to transform her image into an icon of Christian pacifist resistance. She seems to be aware of the fact that the photographic image anticipates her death but also that spectrality indwells the photographic experience. The notion that Indians fear photography turns into a cliché once we understand that photography *does hold the power* to fragment life and thus to remind us of our mortality. After the work of Benjamin, Barthes, Cadava, and Derrida, it has become a commonplace in the West to associate photography with death and phantoms. It should not surprise us that Indians would perceive the power of photography to capture death as time passed but also as hosting revenants. The tomb of those murdered in Acteal displays the photographs of all the victims. It is a space for recollecting the semblance of the dead, but also a reminder that their deaths were not in vain and that on the celebration of the massacre every month on the twenty-second they are brought back to dwell once more among the living. The revenant of all revenants, the sacrifice of Christ and his return in the Eucharist, which now includes those massacred as witnesses to the truth, is embodied in the dry tortilla held by the old woman.

Not unlike writing, which embalms voice, photography embalms life and temporality. Thus, photography also becomes the site for the return of ghosts. In this regard, we can speak of photography and writing as technologies for countering colonialism. The photographs produce signifiers of mourning rather than records of fact. In this respect they are closer to pictographic writing that did not represent objects realistically but prompted verbal performances that told stories not bound to a mere description of the pictographs. The spoken word bore the responsibility of communicating the horrors in their very detail. Consider the following words of terror:

Las balas cruzaban las cabezas de los niños y los agresores decían *eso sí, eso sí*! Se sentían aliviados; ellos pensaron que todos habíamos muertos. (The bullets crossed the heads of the children and the aggressors said *do it, do it*! They felt relieved because they thought we were all dead.)
Catalina Jiménez Luna
Acteal

Bueno, cuando pasó dos o tres días de la matanza de allá de Acteal, entonces ahí contó mi papá y dice que esta viendo qué está pasando, "yo les eché cuchillo y machete a las que están embarazadas," dijo. Le dijo a mi mamá. Yo lo escuché, lo que dijo mi papá. (Three days after the massacre in Acteal, then my father told the story and said that he was seeing what happened, "I used my machete against those who were pregnant," he said. He told my mother. I heard what my father said.)
Juan Javier Ruíz Perez, thirteen years old

Canolal

(Centro de Derechos Humanos "Fray Bartolomé de las Casas" 1998, 58, 73)

Let me now juxtapose a passage from the *Historia de Tlatelolco* (1528), arguably the first alphabetically scripted history in Nahuatl: "Auh yn otlica omitl

xaxamantoc tzontli momoyauhtoc calli tzontlapouhtoc calli chichiliuhtoc/
Ocuilti moyatlaminaotlica Auh yn caltech hahalacatoc quatlextli" (And on
the roads lay shattered bones and scattered hair; the houses were unroofed,
red [with blood]; worms crawled in and out the noses; and the walls of the
houses were slippery with brains) (Lockhart 1993, 313 n. 31). We do not
have the pictorial version, but we can ascertain from extant pictographic
codices that the details were not represented in as realistic a form as the
verbal account. One may say that the reason the photographic component
of . . . *Esta es nuestra palabra* . . . does not include images of the mutilated
corpses is because the photographers were not allowed in Acteal until the
bodies had already been sent to Tuxtla Gutierrez, the capital of the state of
Chiapas, in an attempt to cover up the massacre. But the contrast between
Jutta Meier-Weindeback's and Claudia Ituarte's photographs in . . . *Esta es
nuestra palabra* . . . , and José Angel Rodríguez's (brilliant) photograph of
a group of people holding handkerchiefs on their faces to avoid breathing
the stench of the cadavers and observing a putrefied partial leg on a coffin
bearing a tag on one of the toes could not be more striking (Rodríguez 2002,
65). Meier-Weindeback and Ituarte avoid capturing this sort of images out
of respect but, perhaps, also because of their understanding of photography
as a place for mourning rather than as a record of morbid curiosity.

In the case of Las Abejas, we find an indigenous organization that has
learned to use the codes of human rights organizations and international
courts while retaining a sense of its community and its project in terms
of an immanent history. Competency in Western forms of discourse and
the ability to produce documents for international courts does not entail
an abandonment of the group's forms of life. The members of Las Abejas
are no longer subalterns—or at least are on their way to end their subalternity—according to Gramsci's definition, but they prove resistant to the
forces of comparison that would lead to the subordination of their language
and culture within a teleology that privileges the West as an unsurpassable
background.

In reading colonial and contemporary pictorial and verbal texts, I have
traced elements of a long memory that entails modes of historical immanence and diverse backgrounds that define the *absolute presuppositions from
and against which* Indians made and continue to make sense of the world.
The map of Cholula suggests that the *tlacuilo* who painted it used a map
from the *Historia Tolteca-Chichimeca* as a prototype. But we also saw that
the verbal component of the *Historia* conveyed a history in which the ancient past of the elders was told as part of an evanescent present of the per-

formance in spite of the havoc brought about by the Spanish invasion. This temporality suggests that the essence of the Toltecs, the *toltecayotl*, retained its actuality, even if under clandestinity. This long memory, this immanent history, constitutes the background of the *tlacuilo* charged with painting the map of Cholula. In the case of the Zapatistas and Las Abejas, we found the coexistence of the precolonial past and the most modern forms of communication. Ancient dual representations of the ancient gods come into play with Zapata, and a piece of tortilla could at once signify millenarian associations of maize with life-giving forces and the Christian host. If I defined two forms of spirituality it was not to oppose them but to signal two forms of revolutionary activity that in the end might not turn out to be that different: there is a pacifist element to the Zapatistas and a radical militancy to Las Abejas.

But, why Gramsci? I would simply say that Gramsci enabled me to conceive of historical immanence precisely by elaborating a critique of the need he found for a transcendental principle or institution, that is, modern theory and the party. By refusing to lend credence to such a demand I have created one more palimpsest, one more juxtaposition of texts in which the past and the present coexist immanently without any appeal to transcendence. It is not a question of opposing immanence and transcendence but of refusing to subordinate meaning and history to an external principle. Already in Gramsci historical immanence and modern theory feed into each other. Notwithstanding the privilege he gives to the "most modern theory," one could recognize in Gramsci an effort to reflect on the popular and the subaltern in ways that would not dismiss the place of historical immanence in revolutionary processes. We should not expect him to have articulated what has only very recently, in the past ten years or so, become the signature of the Zapatista movement and the EZLN. Marcos's description of the *caracol* suggests a process in which theory (as well as all those other words Marcos mentions in his communiqué, for example, "globalization," "war of domination," "resistance," "economy," "city," "country," "political situation") becomes meaningful only as a result of the process that leads to the heart of the *caracol*, to the EZLN, to the innermost core in which theoretical terms are exappropriated for the creation of new spaces; in turn, the process outward culminates with the proposal for "un mundo donde quepan muchos mundos" (a world in which many fit). This proposal for a world in which many worlds coexist without incurring contradiction, if my analysis is correct, corresponds to the articulations of plural-world dwelling in the map of Cholula and other native pictorial maps and histories in which one can trace

not only the coexistence of many worlds, but also the expression of perplexity with respect to the enforcement of one world, one history, and one creed
by missionaries and lay officials. Spanish imperialism and universal evan-
gelization summoned all peoples on earth into a single universal history
wherein an iron-fisted logic defined the spectral past and its immanence as
without history, at once a lack and an outside in which apostasy threatened
the colonial order. Today, insurgency opens spaces—creates an outside of
the state and its institutions—for the invention of new political practices.

Notes

1. There is a large literature on the *Relaciones Geográficas*, but to my knowledge, Barbara Mundy's *The Mapping of New Spain* (1996) provides the most exhaustive and detailed study of the maps. Serge Gruzinzki (2002) provides a most interesting reading of
the Map of Cholula in *The Mestizo Mind*. I have benefited greatly from both Mundy and
Grusinski. In the appropriate places, I have indicated my differences with Mundy's and
Gruzinski's readings.

2. It is worthwhile reminding readers of the demographic collapse in central Mexico
during the sixteenth century. As Mundy points out, "At the time of the conquest, Cholula
held one of the larger populations outside the Valley of Mexico, holding about 100,000
inhabitants within about eleven or twelve square kilometers; at the time the *Relación
Geográfica* was made, Cholula had perhaps 9,000 people" (Mundy 1996, 127). Mundy
bases her numbers on Cortés's description of the Cholula in the Second Letter and the
estimates of twentieth-century geographers and demographers (Gerhard 1986, 117; Peterson 1987, 71).

3. In his introduction, René Acuña (1985, 124) identifies Gabriel de Rojas as an *er-
asmista* who manifested a highly critical consciousness when he undermined the
missionaries' speculation on the mysteries behind the lightning strikes that destroyed
the crosses: "Y, quien considera bien la naturaleza de los rayos, y que en esta ciudad y
comarca de ordinario caen muchos, no tendrá a milagro (como algunos historiadores
quieren) el haber derribado dos veces aquella cruz, por estar, como está dicho, mas alta
que los altos edificios de la ciudad [en] cuarenta varas" (And whoever considers well
the nature of lightning, and that in this city and region there are ordinarily many, will
not have for a miracle [as some historians want] that the said cross was destroyed twice,
because it stands forty *varas* above the tallest buildings of the city) (143). A *vara* is a unit
of measurement equal to .83 meters. As Acuña points out in a footnote, the reference was
most similar to Motolinía's manipulation of the Indians in *Memoriales*: "Confundiamos
a los indios, diciéndoles que por aquellas idolatrías enviaba dios sus rayos" (We confounded the Indians, telling them that God sent the lightning because of their idolatries)
(143). Whether it is in response to a pious association of the lightning strikes with God's
wrath or an equally Erasmian-like rational manipulation of fear, Rojas could have also
reflected the Indians' incredulity for such an explanation. After all, Indians had observed

the phenomenon of lightning for millennia and given their construction of large temples could have very well experienced the connection between height and lightning.

4. I am here borrowing Ankersmit's definition of background in *History and Tropology* (1994). I have also benefited from John Searle's discussion of "background abilities" in *The Construction of Social Reality* (1995). As Searle points out, "background abilities" imply knowledge of basic rules but not that one's actions can be explained as following rules consciously. He provides the example of the baseball player who follows the rules she learned early in her life in the choices she makes but does not actively bring to consciousness. We may extend Searle's point and say that one is never fully conscious of the absolute presuppositions *from which* and *against which* we make sense of the world.

5. I have examined these questions in a detailed reading of a page from Codex Telleriano-Remensis (Rabasa 1998).

6. For an elaborate critique of the comparative frame in subaltern studies, see Rabasa 2005a.

7. Note the language of the following passages on folklore and teaching in which Gramsci subjects historical immanence to a transcendental source of meaning: "Folklore should instead be studied as a 'conception of the world and life' implicit to a large extent in determinate (in time and space) strata of society and in opposition (also for the most part implicit, mechanical and objective) to 'official' conceptions of the world (or in a broader sense, the conceptions of the cultural parts of historically determinate societies) that have succeeded one another in historical process. This conception of the world is not elaborated and systematic because, by definition the people (the sum total of the instrumental and subaltern classes of every form of society that has so far existed) cannot possess conceptions which are elaborated, systematic and politically organized and centralized in their, albeit contradictory, development." "For the teacher, then, to know 'folklore' means to know what other conceptions of the world and of life are actually active in the intellectual and moral formation of young people, in order to uproot them and replace them with conceptions which are deemed to be superior" (1985, 189, 191).

8. I can only briefly dwell on this mural from the community of Taniperla. For a detailed reading, see Rabasa 2003. In that article I juxtapose the revolutionary ideals of Emiliano Zapata and Antonio Negri. For an English version, see Murphy and Mustapha 2005.

9. The communiqués by Marcos and other members of the EZLN have been posted on http://www.ezln.org/. In this case only the English version appears. For a Spanish version, see Marcos 1994.

10. See plates 75 and 76 of Codex Vaticanus B (1993) and plates 56 and 73 of Codex Borgianus (1993).

11. The literature on the role of women in the Zapatista insurrection is enormous. I have found useful Carlsen 1999; Eber and Kovic 2003; Millán 1996, 1997; Ortiz 2001; M. Rabasa 2004; Rovira 1997; and Vrijea 2000.

12. The struggles of the indigenous in Chiapas have less to do with seeking the recognition of their rights by the state than with the recognition of their right to autonomous regions in which they will conduct their affairs according to their normative systems, the

"usos y costumbres" in governmental documents. It is not the recognition of the rationality of their normative systems but of the right to determine their legality and justice internally. Carlos Montemayor's closing statement at the 2004 Latin American Cultural Studies Conference offers a most comprehensive and brilliant articulation of the history of the indigenous normative systems and colonialist impulse in the governmental use of the term "usos y costumbres." For a discussion of the processes of autonomization in Chiapas, see Rabasa 2003 and 2005b.

13. To my knowledge, the most thorough study of Las Abejas is Tavanti 2003. The members of Las Abejas practice a form of Christianity known as *teología india* (Indian theology), an inter-American movement that seeks to recognize the spirituality of millenarian indigenous religious practices as compatible with Christianity. Its leadership includes Samuel Ruiz, a former bishop of San Cristóbal de las Casas. Whereas liberation theology promoted a form of Christianity that emphasized the commitment of the Catholic Church to social causes of the poor, *teología india* insists on the need to consider ethnicity and language. For several publications of conference proceedings, see *Teología India* (1991) and *Teología India Mayense* (1993).

Works Cited

Acuña, René, ed. 1985. *Relaciones Geográficas del siglo XVI: Tlaxcala*. Vol. 2. Mexico City: UNAM.

Ankersmit, F. R. 1994. *History and Tropology: The Rise and Fall of Metaphor*. Berkeley: University of California Press.

Anderson, Arthur J. O., and Susan Schroeder. 1997. *Codex Chimalpahin*. Vol. 2. Norman: University of Oklahoma Press.

Beverley, John. 1999. *Subalternity and Representation: Arguments in Cultural Theory*. Durham, N.C.: Duke University Press.

Carlsen, Laura. 1999. "Las mujeres indígenas en el movimiento social." *Revista Chiapas* 8. http://www33.brinkster.com/revistachiapas/No8/ch8.htm.

Centro de Derechos Humanos "Fray Bartolomé de las Casas." 1998. . . . *Esta es nuestra palabra*. . . . San Cristóbal de las Casas: Centro de Derechos Humanos "Fray Bartolomé de las Casas."

Chakrabarty, Dipesh. 2000. *Provincializing Europe: Postcolonial Thought and Historical Difference*. Princeton, N.J.: Princeton University Press.

Codex Borgianus. 1993. *Los tiempos del cielo y de la oscuridad: Oraculos y liturgia; Libro explicativo del llamado Códice Borgia* . Introduction and explanation by Ferdinand Anders, Maarten Jansen, and Luis Reyes García. Madrid: Sociedad Estatal Quinto Centenario; Graz, Austria: ADEVA; Mexico City: Fondo de Cultura Económica.

Codex Vaticanus B. 1993. *Manual del Adivino: Libro explicativo del llamado Códice Vaticano B*. Introduction and explanation by Ferdinand Anders and Maarten Jansen. Madrid: Sociedad Estatal Quinto Centenario; Graz: ADEVA; Mexico City: Fondo de Cultura Económica.

Cortés, Hernán. 1963. *Cartas y documentos*. Mexico City: Porrúa.

———. 1971. *Letters from Mexico*. Trans. Anthony Pagden. New York: Grossman.

Derrida, Jacques, and Bernard Stiegler. 2002. *Echographies of Television*. Trans. Jennifer Bajorek. Cambridge: Polity Press.

De Vos, Jan. 2002. *Una tierra para sembrar sueños: Historia reciente de la Selva Lacandona, 1950–2000*. Mexico City: Fondo de Cultura Económica.

Eber, Christine, and Christine Kovic, eds. 2003. *Women in Chiapas: Making History in Times of Struggle and Hope*. New York: Routledge.

Gerhard, Peter. 1986. *Geografía Histórica de la Nueva España 1519–1821*. Trans. Stella Mastrangelo. Mexico City: UNAM.

Gramsci, Antonio. 1971. *Selections from the Prison Notebooks*. Ed. and trans. Quintin Hoare and Geoffrey Nowell Smith. New York: International Publishers.

———. 1985. *Selections from Cultural Writings*. Trans. William Boelhower. Cambridge, Mass.: Harvard University Press, 1985.

———. 1986. *Scriti politici*. Ed. Paolo Spriano. Rome: Editori Reuniti.

———. 1995. *The Southern Question*. Trans. Pasquale Verdicchio. West Lafayette, Ind.: Bordighera, Inc.

Gruzinski, Serge. 2002. *The Mestizo Mind: The Intellectual Dynamics of Colonization and Globalization*. Trans. Deke Dusinberre. New York: Routledge.

Guha, Ranajit. 1983. *Elementary Aspects of Peasant Insurgency*. Delhi: Oxford University Press.

Guha, Ranajit, and Gayatri Chakravorty Spivak, eds. 1988. *Selected Subaltern Studies*. New York: Oxford University Press.

Kirchhof, Paul, Lina Odema Güemes, and Luis Reyes Garcia, eds. 1976. *Historia Tolteca-Chichimeca*. Mexico City: INAH-SEP.

Lockhart, James. 1993. *We People Here: Nahuatl Accounts of the Conquest of Mexico*. Berkeley: University of California Press.

Marcos, Subcomandante. 1994. "Carta de Cartas." In *La palabra de los armados de verdad y fuego*. Vol. 3, *Entrevistas, cartas, y comunicados (18 de julio al 31 de diciembre de 1994)*. Mexico City: Editorial Fuenteovejuna. English version at http://www.ezln.org/.

———. 2003. "La treceava estela. Primera parte: Un caracol." http://www.nodo50.org/pchiapas/chiapas/documentos/calenda/chiapas.htm.

Millán, Márgara. 1996. "Las zapatistas del fin del milenio: Hacia políticas de autorepresentación de las mujeres indígenas." *Chiapas* 3. http://www.revistachiapas.org/No3/ch3millan.html.

———. 1997. "Chiapas y sus mujeres indígenas: De su diversidad y resistencia." *Chiapas* 4. http://membres.lycos.fr/revistachiapas/No4/ch4millan.html.

Montemayor, Carlos. 2004. "Reformas constitucionales y juntas de buen gobierno: Realidad social y ficción juridical." Closing remarks at the 4th International Conference in Latin American Cultural Studies, University of Pittsburgh, March 18–20.

Mundy, Barbara. 1996. *The Mapping of New Spain: Indigenous Cartography and the Maps of the Relaciones Geográficas*. Chicago: University of Chicago Press.

Murphy, Timothy, and Abdul Mustapha, eds. 2005. *The Philosophy of Antonio Negri: Resistance in Practice*. London: Pluto Press.

Ortiz, Teresa. 2001. *Never again a World without Us: Voices of Mayan Women in Chiapas, Mexico*. Washington, D.C.: Epica.

Peterson, David A. 1987. "The Real Cholula." *Notas mesoamericanas* 10: 71–117.

Rabasa, José. 1998. "Franciscans and Dominicans under the Gaze of Tlacuilo: Plural-World Dwelling in an Indian Pictorial Codex." *Morrison Inaugural Lecture Series* 14. Berkeley: University of California, Doe Library.

———. 2003. "Negri por Zapata: El poder constituyente y los límites de la autonomía." *Revista Chiapas* 15. http://www.ezln.org/revistachiapas-pres.html———. 2005a. "The Comparative Frame in Subaltern Studies." In "The Subaltern and the Popular," ed. Swati Chattopadhyay and Bhaskar Sarkar, special issue, *Journal of Postcolonial Studies* 8.4: 365–80.

———. 2005b. "Negri by Zapata: Constituent Power and the Limits of Autonomy." In *The Philosophy of Antonio Negri: Resistance in Practice*, ed. Timothy Murphy and Abdul Mustapha, 163–204. London: Pluto Press.

Rabasa, José, C. Javier Sanjinés, and Robert Carr, eds. 1996. "Subaltern Studies in the Americas." Special issue, *Dispositio/n* 46.

Rabasa, Magali. 2004. "New Social Movements: New Testimonio; Latin American Women and the Negotiation of Identity in Representation." B.A. honors thesis, University of Oregon.

Rodríguez, Ileana, ed. 2001. *The Latin American Subaltern Studies Reader*. Durham, N.C.: Duke University Press.

Rodríguez, José Angel. 2002. *Lok'tavanej, cazador de imágenes*. N.p.: La Casa de las Imágenes/Conaculta-Fonca.

Rovira, Guiomar. 1997. *Mujeres de maíz*. Mexico City: Biblioteca Era.

Searle, John R. 1995. *The Construction of Social Reality*. New York: Free Press.

Swanton, Michael. 2001. "El texto popoloca de la *Historia Tolteca-Chichimeca*." *Relaciones* 86.22: 114–29.

Tavanti, Marco. 2003. *Las Abejas: Pacifist Resistance and Syncretic Identities in a Globalizing Chiapas*. New York: Routledge.

Teología India. 1991. *Teología India: Primer encuentro taller latinoamericano*. Mexico City: Cenami; Quito: Abya-Yala.

Teología India Mayense. 1993. *Teología India Mayense: Memorias, experiencias, y reflexiones de encuentros teológicos regionales*. Mexico City: Cenami; Quito: Abya-Yala.

Vrijea, María Jaidopulu. 2000. "Las mujeres indígenas como sujetos políticos." http://www.revistachiapas.org/No9/ch9jaidopulu.html.

6

New Cartographies of the Bolivian State in the Context of the Constituent Assembly, 2006–2007

DENISE Y. ARNOLD

Introduction

Speaking of postcolonial studies, John Beverley, in *Subalternity and Representation* (1999), warns us against examining culture alone, since this ignores the relations of power, and above all the potentially antagonistic relations between the people and the state. As an alternative, he asks us to redefine, from a subaltern perspective, the limits of postcolonial theory, and from there the political theory of the state. Beverley finds this sense of subalternity in those territories where the power of domination is greater than hegemony, for example (and he cites Guha) in the periphery "where the Nation has never fully taken hold." However, subalternity functions just as well, as the Aymara sociologist Félix Patzi Paco has pointed out (2002), in the very pinnacles of power of countries such as Bolivia, whose leaders feared, until the government of Evo Morales, to defy the world hegemonies under which they work.

In this chapter, I wish to examine both senses of subalternity in the present situation of political change in Bolivia. Basically, I shall compare the predominant *mestizo-criollo* perspective of previous governments, such as that of Gonzalo Sánchez de Lozada, of 1994, with its gamut of constructions to define the nation in terms of the assimilation of indigenous peoples within the subaltern framework of "multiculturality" and its derivative "interculturality"[1] to the more indigenous-oriented models under discussion in the Constituent Assembly of 2006–7.

In this new political conjunture, the former framework of coloniality has been questioned, and new proposals concerning the state and the nation itself are being raised. This radical questioning comes from many more factions than the so-called popular classes. It derives from the processes of change that are the direct result of seven popular uprisings from 2000 to 2005. The first, as the War of the Ayllus (January 2000), was still limited to the rural periphery. Then came the Water War (2000) in the very center of Cochabamba, followed by the month-long Siege of La Paz under the command of the Aymara "Mallku" Felipe Quispe (2000). These were followed by the War on Coca (2002), the Tax-Rise War (February 2003), and then, the most intense of all, the Gas War (October 2003), with its repercussions in May to June of 2005 (the demand of the full nationalization of gas), when the whole country came to a standstill.

John Beverley has been severe in his critique of the limitations of such subaltern movements to challenge the status quo, and of their lack of real proposals for change. But in a country such as Bolivia, it is just as important to be aware that such challenges are founded in the unequal politics of the state regarding the distribution of riches, education, health care, roads, and so on, which cannot be changed overnight. In addition, many of the proposed alternatives in the past have been systematically silenced (if not simply assimilated) by what Patzi Paco and others call state "ethnophagy."

Given this ongoing context of massive uprisings, we academics working in the country are compelled to rethink our professional positions. Beverly encourages us to transcend subaltern challenges in order to put into motion real proposals of change. This presents a challenge, especially when our professional training is directed toward *descriptions* of reality, and not necessarily toward the theoretical and practical apparatus necessary for documenting and then generating this change. Félix Patzi Paco (2004) expresses the historical roots of this professional dilemma when he points out how, in the times of Plato, Greek thought was expressed in *two* complementary views: one that considered reality just as it is, and another that was dedicated more to "eroticism," in the sense of *imagining* new possibilities. He suggests that the "triumph" of positivism in the social sciences in the nineteenth century annulled this latter tendency toward the imagination, which it considered as just ideology or speculation. From then on, empirical observations of the world would justify and legitimize society "just as it is" and be considered academically superior to any other possibility of transforming the world. Only Marxist praxis would still allow the possibility of acting with the intention of reforming and changing reality.

Given these challenges, in practical terms we now face questions: How might we overcome the negation of subaltern politics (or even of deconstructionism) to attain a politics of affirmation? How might we begin a political project to redefine the state, a new state that would avoid the subalternization of the great majority of the population? To do this, we must also redefine power, and in positive rather than negative terms.

An Anthropology of the Bolivian State

First let us examine the morphology of the existing *mestizo-criollo* model of the Bolivian state and its limitations. The traditional definitions of a state include *three* key elements: its territory, its population, and its structure of power or government in the sense of the political relations between those who govern and those who are governed.

According to Costas Arduz, a Bolivian writer, a medical doctor, and a member of many years standing with the Electoral Court, the state is "a society organized juridically, which has a given population established in a given territory, and with an organization subject to a juridical normativity that covers public, political, constitutional and administrative rights" (2003, 93). However, this description, which is expressed in predominantly passive terms, still lacks any dynamic and operative sense of the relation territory-population-government, that is to say a teleology of development driven by human initiative. One alternative here would be to rethink "territory" as the physical element that depends for its development on the actions of its governors. Likewise, "population" would be the human element that also depends on the direct action of those that govern the country for its development (or the postponement of such). In synthesis, territory and population, in their projection and development, depend on the direct action of those who govern.[2]

From this perspective, many of the shortcomings in political decisions made until now at a state level are due to *those that govern* and not to the *apparatus of government* as such. This would suggest that many of the failures of this governing element can be found in the governmental apparatus of power, and in its administration, which together seem to constitute the Achilles heel of Bolivian political reality. This lack of a dynamic apparatus for administering state organisms is also dependent on the fact that Bolivia, from its very creation, never had a political objective as a sovereign state. Thus, any new democratic model would have to define these new goals and objectives.

Such monolithic definitions of the present state also ignore many of its historical precedents. In reality, the historical occupation by various indigenous nations (and federations of these indigenous nations) of the territory that is now Bolivia is well documented (see Bouysse-Cassagne 1987, Platt

1987, among others). Moreover, this part of the southern Andes was not conquered through making treaties between states. Rather, the founding of the colony depended on the juridical conditions of the *Requerimiento*, a document of potential conquest and the submission of the enemy drawn up by the Spanish crown and read aloud before battle. This was followed by a period of agreement between *two* parallel republics: the República Española and the República de los Indios, both under the protection of the Spanish crown. Finally in 1825, with independence from Spain, the Bolivian Republic was established on the basis of the juridical document *Uti possidetis jure*, which many argue covered up a series of absences of consultations with the preexisting República de Indios, now converted juridically into "indigenous" populations.

Recent reports to the United Nations by Erika Daes (1999) and Miguel Martínez Cobo (1999) regarding the occupation of territory, and those by lawyers versed in the theme (Barros 2003), underline these past absences as one of the main causes of present inequalities, the uncertainty of indigenous peoples, and even the endemic corruption in many Latin American countries, which continually attempts to disguise the lack of justice in territorial distribution since the colonial period. In reality, then, Bolivia, far from being a monolithic territory, is a series of administrative and political incompatibilities centered in disputed territories.

Various studies, including those by geographers, have indicated some of the reasons for these incompatibilities. For example, Dory et al. (2000) identify the colonial inheritance, above all the conformation of the *intendencias* after 1776, as well as the slowness of the processes of exploration, cataloging, and appropriation of Bolivian territory, and a constant political instability. Even in the case of attempts at making plans, they underline the absence of scientific competence and the inertia of reality. They also criticized the lack of a national territorial ordering plan, and the fact that existing attempts were in the hands of bilateral aid. These same organizations still dominate the cartography of the Bolivian state today.

But a major part of the problem in the Bolivian Andes goes much deeper than the colonial *intendencias* to what Silvia Rivera and others have termed "history and long-term memory," in the sense of a historical awareness that a series of state decisions concerning Bolivian territory had not considered sufficiently the preexisting territorial needs of the great majority of the population. These kinds of practices also go in the face of the set of laws, standards, and recommendations, at the national and international levels, that relate to the question of indigenous territories. These norms tend to accept and validate the existence of the territories of these peoples if they can show appropriate proof of their occupation "from times immemorial" and if they prove their occupation in terms of the use and management of land and other territorial resources, and the produce of these lands. In this context, it is urgent to make more compatible the state and communal perspectives regarding the notions of territory, the "subject" of that territory, the modes of government that rule in that territory, and the laws that are applied there. At the same time, this whole field of juridical struggle for territories has to be resituated within the framework of the "life worlds" that develop there. In this case, we would have to go beyond the technical-bureaucratic discourse of mapping the "limits" between territories in order to understand the regional territorial dynamics that unite cultures in common.

Let us now focus on each of the *three* components of the state in turn: territory, population, and the structure of government, in the sense of the political relations between those who govern and those who are governed.

New Cartographies of the Bolivian State, 1994–2001, in a "Pluri-Multi" Context

As many have pointed out, the National Revolution of 1952 was based on many of the same founding concepts as those of the Bolivian nation-state in 1825, that is to say within the framework of cultural and linguistic homogeneity that accorded with a dominant *mestizo-criollo* ethnic model. With the introduction of a neoliberal political model from 1985 onward, this situation changed slightly. Now, a number of alternative cartographies of the nation-state have resorted to the framework of what has come to be known as "pluri-multi" as the most appropriate political reconfiguration of the pluralism and diversity in the country.

This occurred in the context of a wide demand for the greater decentralization of government. In Latin America, from the 1980s and 1990s onward, a series of modifications in state organization, which sought to decentralize a set of political functions, especially at the municipal level, were put into motion (García Linera 2003a, 169). Here, "multiculturality" began to function at the municipal level, while it was still absent at the higher levels of the state apparatus. As a part of these reforms, from 1994 onward, under the government of Gonzalo Sánchez de Lozada, a set of laws destined to resolve some of these problems of territorial incompatibility were passed. However, the framing of these laws was still in the hands of the *mestizo-criollo* elite, and there was little real consultation with the indigenous populations whose territories they were to affect. As a result, these laws generated yet another series of superimposed territorial configurations in which indigenous territories had to participate simultaneously. These new laws emerged from the legal framework established with the promulgation of a new Bolivian Constitution, on August 12, 1994, which initiated a new stage in Bolivian juridical planning that now recognized, on paper at least, the multiethnic diversity and pluri-culturality of the country, and the indigenous populations in its interior. Taking on board the question of self-definition, juridical planning also had to recognize from then on the terminological difference between the "indigenous" populations of the lowlands, and the "original" (*originario*) populations of the highlands, names derived originally from the dominant fiscal categories that had operated over the centuries. In this context, new citizens' rights were to be held by indigenous peoples in the highlands and lowlands, as well as the rural peasant communities in both settings. These were to recognize their status as distinctive collectivities in a framework of consolidation, at once unitary and plural (Calla Ortega 2000). From now on, these collectivities were to be recognized as subjects of the law and as legal entities in and of themselves, although in a limited way.

In practice, however, the legal recognition of these collectivities was to pass through a series of juridical obstacles, in which the prior territorial divisions of the republic (departments, provinces, subprovinces, and cantons) would not cede their status or vitality.[3] The first territorial formulation within the framework of the new Constitution was the passing of the Law of Popular Participation, in 1994, which proposed the territorial division of the country into municipalities subdivided into municipal districts (that now included the municipal indigenous districts), as well as the possibility of the wider grouping of municipalities into "mancommunities." The second was the Land Law (INRA) of 1996, which instituted a new application of the Agrarian Reform, and which proposed a territorial division for land entitlement as Native Community Lands (Tierras Comunitarias de Origen [TCO], a colonial term now reworked) or simply Communal Lands (Tierras Comunales [TC]). The third was the Law of Administrative Decentralization, and fourth the Law of Municipalities of 1999, which concerned municipal management in practice.

According to Ricardo Calla Ortega (2000), these laws responded to centuries of demands, claims, petitions, and even preparatory juridical formulations presented to the state by indigenous and peasant movements, both in the highlands and lowlands of Bolivia, within the context of a discriminatory colonial and republican ordering that was insensitive and contrary to the needs for juridical security of these populations. But in reality, there was still little attempt on the part of the state to make the new territorial framework of the Law of Popular Participation compatible with indigenous territories.

In practice, the Law of Popular Participation began to *municipalize* the country, just as the Law of Administrative Decentralization began to *departmentalize* it, and the INRA Land Law *divide it up* into Native Community Lands or TCOs. Moreover, each law looked to a different set of authorities to implement these processes. For example, the Law of Popular Participation designated autonomy for the task of dividing the country into districts in the hands of the new municipal mayors or *alcaldes* (and the *sub-alcaldes*), while the Law of Administrative Decentralization left this autonomy in the hands of the government prefects, and the INRA law left the TCOs in the hands of indigenous authorities. All of this was to happen outside the framework of a national plan for territorial ordering, so in practice the operative plans, whether at a national, departmental, or municipal level, were little more than names. Besides which, as Dory et al. point out (2000), these plans were drawn up in the usual framework of an anticipatory politics and planning that simply sought funding, and not as a reaction to the criteria already established.

The resulting exclusion of indigenous territories from state maps in the 1990s was all the more surprising considering the collaboration by international organizations in those same years to support civil initiatives to understand indigenous territorial conformations and to draft alternative maps, many of them in the hands of the Bolivian sociologist Ricardo Calla Ortega. These maps could have come into operation with the promulgation of the new Law of Popular Participation, but they did not.

For example, the "Mapa preliminar de Ayllus y Comunidades rurales en el Departamento de Potosí (Fines del Siglo XX)" (Preliminary map of the *ayllus* and rural communities in Potosí department [at the end of twentieth century]), directed by Ricardo Calla Ortega and financed by the Dutch Technical Cooperation Mission and the FAO Project/Holland/CDF (1994), is a sketch of the *ayllus* and communities in the region based on some academic and technical studies from the 1980s, although many had been drawn up at random and without being formally published (see figs. 6.1 and 6.2). This map initiated a series of new territorial proposals, which delineated not only departmental and provincial boundaries but also those of the *ayllus*. It

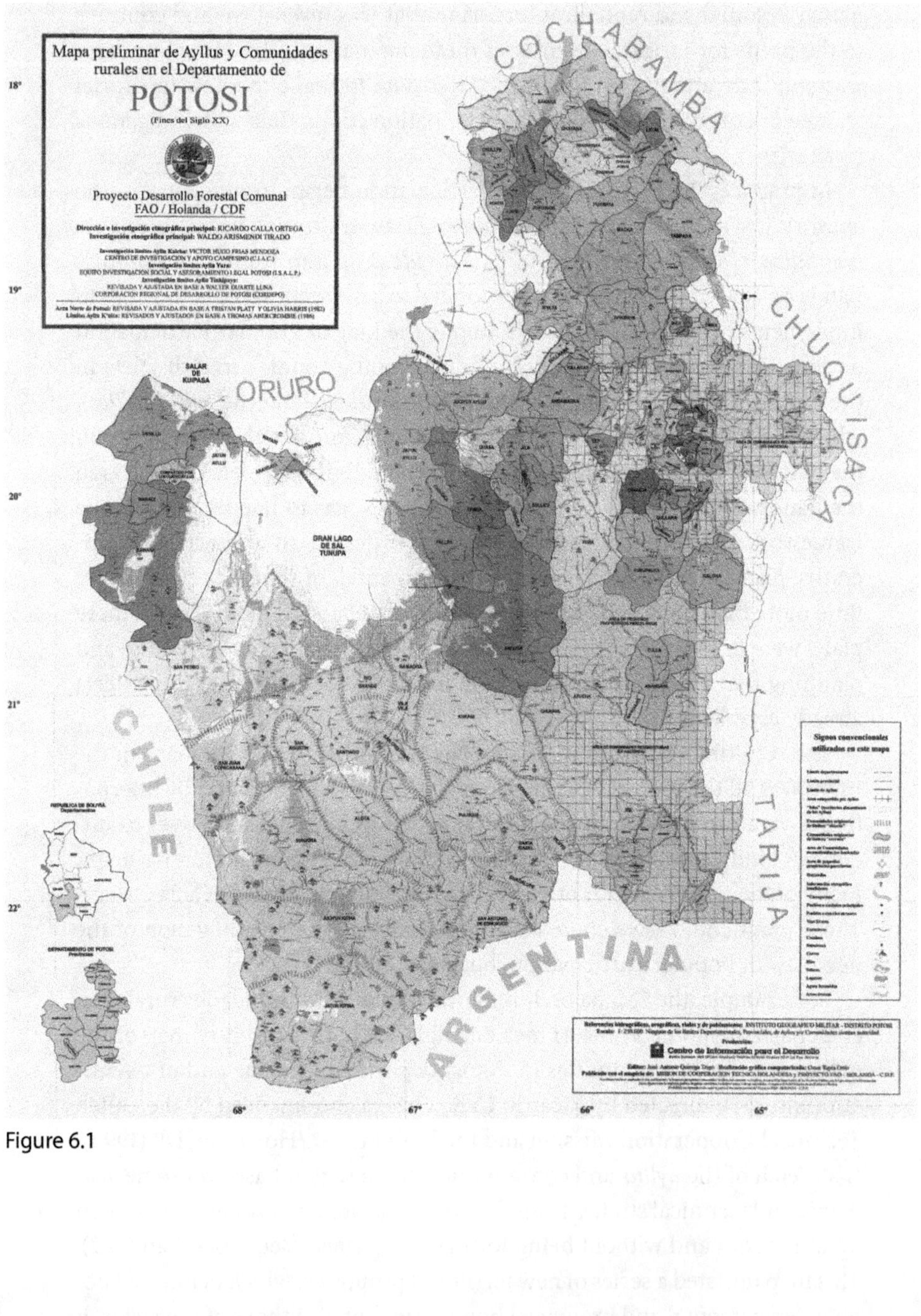
Mapa preliminar de Ayllus y Comunidades rurales en el Departamento de
POTOSI
(Fines del Siglo XX)
Proyecto Desarrollo Forestal Comunal
FAO / Holanda / CDF
COCHABAMBA
CHUQUISACA
ORURO
CHILE
ARGENTINA
TARIJA
GRAN LAGO DE SAL TUNUPA
SALAR DE KUIPASA
Signos convencionales utilizados en este mapa
Centro de Información para el Desarrollo
18°
19°
20°
21°
22°
68°
67°
66°
65°

Figure 6.1

Figure 6.2. Detail of the "Mapa preliminar."

also initiated a period of recuperating the Andean terminology (in Aymara and Quechua) for the toponyms of the *ayllus* and communities, although the spelling adopted to write these terms leaves much to be desired.

Notwithstanding, the "Preliminary map" does recognize the complexity of Andean territorial organization, characterized by the so-called islands or archipelagos. The recognition of this complexity made the cartographic process more difficult. Above all, the mapping of the typical discontinuous territories of some *ayllus* had to extend beyond the immediate *ayllu* borders in order to include related "islands" scattered throughout the whole region. One disadvantage of this map was that it limited the political and administrative organization of the *ayllus* to their minor territorial levels without going into the greater study of the larger territorial units of which they were a part.

Figure 6.3. Preliminary map of *ayllus* and ethnic identities, Chayanta Province (end of the twentieth century).

In the following years, there were other attempts of this kind. In 1993, the Polytechnic Institute of Tomás Katari (IPTK), located in Ocurí in Northern Potosí, together with the Engineering Center of Regional Economic and Social Projects (CIPRES), produced a "Map of Chayanta Province" (under the direction of Catherine Francis). Then, in 1996, they produced a "Preliminary map of the ayllus and ethnic identities in Chayanta Province (at the end of the twentieth century)" (see fig. 6.3). This political map also went a step further than the previous studies. Besides giving the boundaries of departments, provinces, and cantons, the map recognized those of the *ayllus* and the colonial *cabildos*, or councils, as well as the hierarchical division of some *ayllus* into major and minor units, and the fragmentation of others. This map also indicated some of the boundaries that were in constant conflict. But again, there was a haphazard spelling of the Aymara and Quechua place names.

As part of the initiatives taken by the Program for Campesino Self-Development (PAC), Potosí, to extend its knowledge of the territories in the region and the real situation of its populace within the framework of the institutional reforms since 1994, the "Atlas of Chayanta *ayllus*, vol. 1, the Highland territories" was produced by Mendoza, Flores, and Letourneux (see fig. 6.4). This ethno-cartographic research goes much further in its attempt to understand and reproduce graphically the territorial complexity of the nine *ayllus* of Chayanta, and it uses great care in toponym orthography, the result of teams of regional speakers of native languages and of a strategy of participatory work between academics, traditional authorities, community members (*comunarios*), and state institutions.

Apart from the cartography itself, the atlas also includes an analysis of regional history, linguistic and territorial dynamics, and the social and economic organization of the *ayllus*, with a study of the different production zones. The territorial dynamics also include an analysis of the articulation between the ethnic economy and markets in the region, and between the political-administrative organization of the republic and of the peasant unions (*sindicatos*) and *ayllus* themselves.

The *Atlas de los ayllus de Norte de Potosí, territorio de los antiguos charka* (Atlas of the *ayllus* of North Potosí, the territory of the former Charkas) (Mendoza and Patzi G. 1997), this time under the auspices of the European Commission's delegation to Bolivia and PAC-C, develops these participative techniques further. It contains a set of maps and analyses of each territorial unit, intercalated with details of their populations, cultures, languages, and territorial and political dynamics.

These conflicting attitudes between the state and civil society to cartographic layout and content continued. In 2003, the Danish development agency DANIDA financed another map of the *ayllus*, this time of the department of La Paz (including the provinces of Pando and Ingavi), and once again in the hands of Ricardo Calla Ortega. This map was produced in the context of an intense institutional rivalry over the demand for an immense Native Community Land (the TCO of Pakajaqi) between the World Bank and the National Council of Ayllus and Markas of Qullasuyo (CONAMAQ), an indigenous organization, and its advisers.

Evidently, there were deeper issues at stake in these institutional clashes. One of these was how to implement programs of rural development in Bolivia, while another was how to carry out the administration of the recon-

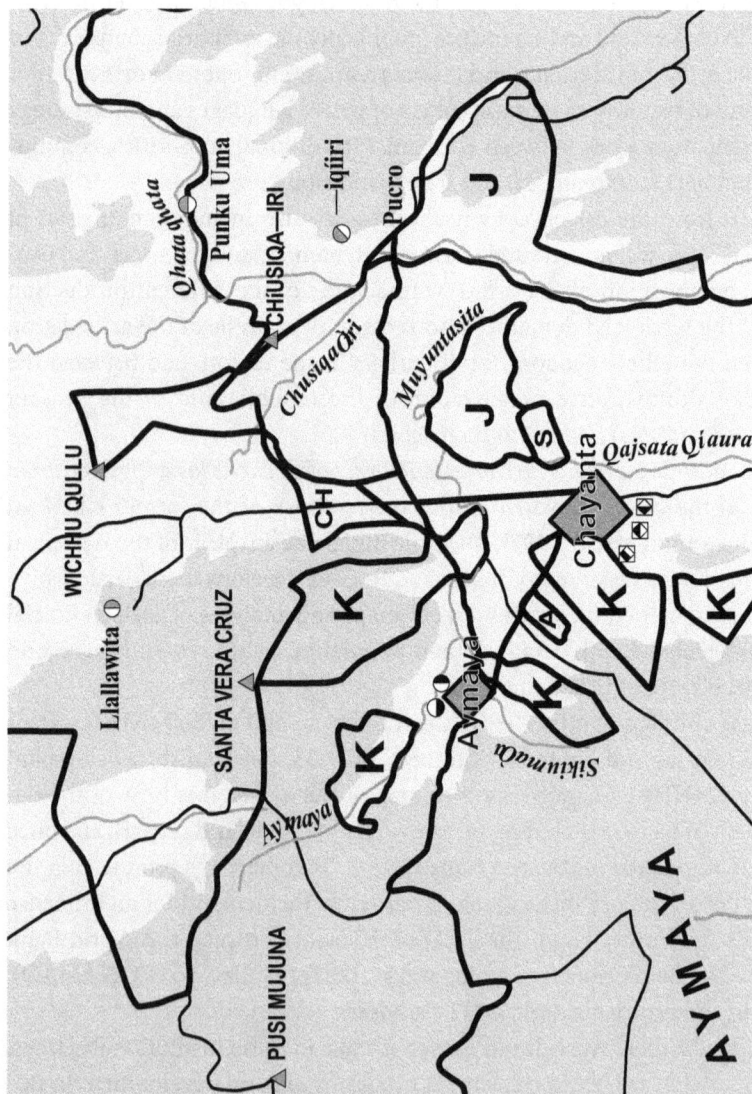

Figure 6.4. Atlas of the *ayllus* of Chayanta, vol. 1, Suni territories (1994).

CH Chullpa **S** Sikuya **A** Aymaya **J** Jukumani **K** Kharacha Isla territorial

stituted indigenous territories. The inertia of the *mestizo-criollo* state apparatus, despite the passing of the new laws, was to thwart both initiatives.

The New Municipalities of 1994 and the Continuing Conflicts over Territories

So, on the very eve of the Popular Participation Law (1994), the Bolivian state
continued its own map work, through the Military Geographical Institute
(IGM), of the usual departmental, provincial, and cantonal boundaries in
the dominant *mestizo-criollo* republican model of political and administrative divisions. The Law of Popular Participation simply followed this official
trend, in which indigenous territories, at least in the highlands, were once
again ignored in the new state program for defining municipal districts.
Instead, the proponents of the law turned to the divisions of the republican
provinces, called "sections," as the most appropriate territorial framework
for the new municipalities.

As García Linera points out (2003a, 171), every process of decentralization is a way of reconfiguring the organization of the state into smaller
spaces in which certain volumes of state and bureaucratic capital are redis-
tributed. In societies that have gone through repeated processes of cultural
homogenization, this territorial reconfiguration into municipalities or regions permits a certain degree of socio-economic autonomy without major
problems. However, in complex pluri-cultural and multinational societies
such as Bolivia, the deconcentration of state capital should have recognized
a communal basis as the governing principle for the reorganization of these
elements of the state (171–72). In this way, cultural identity could have been
the point of reference for the constitution of the public subject of political
decentralization, and as a consequence, the territorial dimension of such
deconcentration would have depended on the geographical situation of this
cultural subject. But this would have required a much more elaborate process of national and subnational state engineering (172).

In practice, the disputes in the municipal sphere over available resources
resulted, in many instances, in a reinvention of local or provincial ethnic
identities within these new territorial limits (for example in Northern Potosí
and Oruro). There, the various preexisting social collectivities had to invent
new strategies and competencies in order to get access to the additional
resources, recognition, prestige, and political influence in play (cf. García
Linera 2003a, 170–71). Sometimes this resulted in open conflict between

neighboring municipalities. This happened, for example, in the region of the War of the Ayllus of the year 2000 (Arnold and Yapita 2003a).

In practice then, even though Bolivia had been characterized in 1994, at the highest level, as a "multicultural, multicivilizational, and multisocietal" society, the debate over decentralization was approached from one side only, from a homogenizing, *mestizo-criollo*, Spanish-speaking, and individualistic cultural model. Even when the theme of multiculturality has been present, it has been reduced to the municipal level instead of being considered as the basis for the redistribution of the whole gamut of political power. Looking back at these political decisions made during the 1990s, the question arises: Would it not have been better in the long run to have resorted to the preexisting indigenous territorial units as the basis for decision making?

Let us return to the matter of the alternative maps drawn during this same period. These civil initiatives, sometimes backed in part by organs of the state, included in their cartography both the republican political-administrative divisions of the country and also the divisions into *ayllus* and other units prior to the conformation of the republic. These other divisions (such as the *cabildos* with their colonial origins) still operate in the political, economic, and ceremonial organization of the *ayllus*, and above all in the segmentary structure of their social organization, which still has a direct relevance in the customs of occupation, management, and spatial organization of rural Andean indigenous populations and territories (cf. Calla Ortega 2000). In this context, another question arises: In the Andean region, what level of the indigenous social segmentary organization should be titled as Native Community Lands or TCOs—the major or the minor units?

With reference to the highland indigenous territories, the greatest level of political inclusion nowadays tends to be the moieties (or *saya*), while the *ayllu* exists at an intermediate level, followed by the political units called *cabildos*, and finally, at a minor level, the communities themselves. However, in the colonial past, Spanish administrations recognized in their treaties and other documents the indigenous "nation" above all these other levels, with a certain sense of autonomy within its historical meaning as a kind of a fatherland (*patria*), state (*estado*), or kingdom (*reino*), under the protection of the Spanish crown. In the Andean region, the legal recognition by the crown of the two republics (the Hispanic and the Indian) ensured the continuity of this legal autonomy (Fernández 2000). However, in contemporary practice, the issues of organization and hierarchy have become much more blurred. In the context of the Law of Popular Participation, the state, for political reasons, preferred to recognize the smaller *ayllu* and community units, rather than the larger ones. But even then, as Calla Ortega (2000) points out, there were important operative questions that the state should have been taking into account. For example, in practice, the legal processing of six minor *ayllus* as Native Community Lands (TCOs) costs much more than processing just one major *ayllu* as the larger political unit in question. Here, the state might have been expected to show some guidance in advising indigenous peoples as to which level would be more appropriate to declare as a Native Community Land. But all of this demanded a new understanding of national territorial layout and a historical reflection on the juridical nature of "indigenous peoples": whether these in fact refer to the major or minor political and population units. The impacts of these decisions often have binding ramifications, for example in the makeup and conformation of the new indigenous municipal districts, and municipal and institutional planning in the region, so much is at stake.

With the gradual integration of more organizations of the state into the same sphere of activity, there was a divergence of state approaches concerning these operational criteria. The process of territorial reordering, under the charge of the departmental prefects, opted for a more operative cartography focused on development, in which priority was given to soil analysis and its potentialities, rather than defining the indigenous territorial and political units that should have been managing and developing the resources in their domain. All of this operates within the macro framework of the Plans of Soil Use (PLUS) developed by international organizations as plans of territorial ordering conceived in terms of technical knowledge of regional resources, instead of in terms of preexisting indigenous territories.

In 1999 another atlas was produced under the auspices of the National Institute of Statistics (INE), the Ministry of Sustainable Development and Planning (MDSP), and the Swiss Agency for Development and Cooperation (COSUDE). Typically, the *Atlas estadístico de municipios* (Statistical atlas of municipalities), which is often called *Bolivia: Un mundo de potencialidades* (Bolivia: A world of potential), sought to contribute to the implementation of the Law of Popular Participation by strengthening municipal development programs. However, the way in which this *Atlas* organizes statistical information, national and provincial maps, and the studies of the developmental potential in these municipalities curiously ignores the territorial conformation of the indigenous nations under their jurisdiction (Instituto Nacional de Estadística 1999).

Instead, in its sixteen different kinds of map (political, physical, hydrographic, isohyet, and so forth), the *Atlas* restricts its analysis of indigenous territories to the conformation of Native Community Lands or TCOs in the lowlands (following the INRA Land Law) and omits mention of any municipal indigenous districts, OTB, or *ayllus* in the highlands. The only exception is the description of the new regional "mancommunities" (as groups of municipalities) as the most suitable units for rural development, above all for regional tourism and production, given that there were so many problems trying to access the funds of the Law of Popular Participation for this purpose. There is said to have been an internal debate in the World Bank concerning the unsuitability of the Popular Participation Law for the purposes of rural development, and finally agreement was made to transfer these competences to the sphere of international aid. In this sense, Bolivia as a "world of potentiality" for the National Institute of Statistics, or the internationally defined Plans of Soil Use, depends more on the policies and methodologies of rural development than on the participation of social actors living in their own territories and managing their own resources as "life worlds."

As a result, as Calla Ortega (2000) points out, until now the Bolivian state has inadvertently put into motion *two* processes of decentralization, which had been insufficiently articulated. On the one hand, the municipality-centered decentralization process, initiated within the framework of the Law of Popular Participation, had forged ahead with the legal conformation of OTBs (municipalities and municipal indigenous districts). On the other hand, the INRA Land Law had put into motion the land-titling of Native Community Lands (TCOs), on the macro level as well as the intermediate and micro levels, within the framework of an indigenist territory-centered decentralization. Meanwhile, as a third option, the conformation of municipal groupings into larger mancommunities was thought to be the most suitable way toward regional development.

For Calla Ortega, the decentralized municipality option, in and of itself, is a complex system of government that includes under its jurisdiction a territorial configuration, populations, resources, and the ideal of "participative planning." The second option, that of the decentralized indigenous territorial regime, also includes a complex system of authorities, a territorial setting, a population (or populations), natural resources, and ideally the "collective management of territories." What concerned him was that the increasing empowerment of indigenous authority systems in Bolivia into real systems of authority with local and supra-local power (even trans-provincial and trans-departmental power), with a "quasi-legal" status, is happening without a due consideration of the structural placement of such systems within the state apparatus. In reality, these systems of indigenous authority still exist outside of, and often in positions of tension and confrontation with, the central, subcentral, or decentralized governmental organic structures of the Bolivian state.

Another aspect in play in this struggle over conflicting operative levels of municipal authority was the access to and the manner of administrating the co-tributary resources of Popular Participation, a head tax that totals about U.S.$21 per person annually.[4] With the change in government in 1999, and the greater penetration of the traditional political parties into all levels of the country's political and administrative apparatus, the question became:, Who was going to administer the state's resources, and how?

One solution that emerged was what some called "ILDIS thinking" after the Latin American Institute for Social Research, a German-financed research institute with an interest in Bolivian territorial planning (García et al. 2002). The ILDIS-type solution to the emerging set of problems at the municipal level was to develop the intermediate state level between the central governmental apparatus and the municipalities into a so-called *meso* level, rather like the federal governments of Germany, but again the preexisting indigenous territories were ignored.[5]

The Former Patterns of State Administration of Majority Indigenous Populations

A similar set of monolithic preconceptions is evident when we examine how the *mestizo-criollo* state administered the various populations that occupy national territories, above all the large indigenous populations. To date, demographic studies in Bolivia are carried out under a North American theoretical slant that influences the policies of electoral geography and their institutionalization in the National Electoral Court, as well as the demographic and population policies institutionalized in the National Institute of Statistics (INE). Underlying these different institutional positions is the notion of individualized citizenship as the basic unit of the nation, and, in spite of the social demands to rethink citizenship in terms of "pluri-multi," this model still holds. An alternative solution here would be "differential citizenship," explored by various authors (Taylor 1992, Young 1999, Kymlicka 1996, Baumann 2001, and others), which grants full political rights when you belong to a particular ethno-cultural or national community within the wider state.

Under this dominating theoretical stance, there is little institutional interest in identifying demographically the different regions and subregions of the country, with their own socio-cultural characteristics. Likewise, there is still a notorious absence of public policies concerning linguistics, education, and health matters, which could apply these regional distinctions in developing differential policies, say in regional curricula, regional production plans, regional administration, or regional epidemiological study institutes. Only the differences between urban and rural areas are underscored, regarding poverty for example.

The same occurs in the obtaining of data regarding the populations of Bolivia, and the maps of their whereabouts. The work always proceeds from top to bottom (there is no obtaining data from the grass roots up), and it is generally full of confusions about terminology and rife with discrepancies in calculations, even in the national census. For example, in studies of indigenous populations there is a generalized confusion about the question of languages and cultures. Moreover, a marked *telos* tends to counterpoint languages in expansion with languages in danger of extinction, weak languages with strong languages, and so on. As Silverstein has pointed out (1998, 414), it is precisely this kind of numerical data that permits the classification of "dominant" and "minority" languages within an economic conceptualization directed at markets and with a political agenda. Besides this, in no example to date have linguistic and cultural maps been made to coincide with the linguistic territories and populations of the indigenous nations of the country; they are still done in terms of current *mestizo-criollo* republican political and administrative divisions.

The same happens with production. Nowhere can you find reliable data concerning the productive hectares of a given region, or what is produced, or the quantity of what is produced. And in all of this, there is a notable absence of a common teleology, whether of the national or regional identities and objectives.

The Social Movements of January 2000–June 2005 and "Pluri-Multi" Revisited

This generalized absence of concerted state policies for resolving the many matters at the heart of the crisis that Bolivia was facing have given rise, since the year 2000, to what Luis Tapia calls "underground" movements, and what Felipe Quispe calls the confrontation of the "two Bolivias," reiterating the expression of Fausto Reinaga, the Indianist intellectual. "The two Bolivias" in question are the "Bolivia of European extraction" and the "Indian Bolivia" (Patzi Paco, 2003, 220).

These various social movements expressed the different facets of Bolivian society: on one occasion a popular stance, on another occasion a *campesino* or indigenous one, even a middle-class one, according to the region, cause, demand, and sphere of action. The beginning of this new cycle of uprisings all over the country was the War of the Ayllus, principally between the Qaqachakas and Jukumanis (in January 2000). The actions and consequences of this indigenous confrontation revealed vital flaws at the heart of the state apparatus. This was followed by the Water War in Cochabamba (in the same year), followed by another water battle in El Alto of La Paz in 2004, endless marches by teachers and retired folk, the Tax-rise War in La Paz (in February 2003), and finally the Gas War, principally in El Alto of La Paz (in October 2003), which was to erupt again in May to June 2005 when the whole country came to a standstill to cries for the full nationalization of gas. These social movements changed the political imagination and the very scale of social demands in the country. Immediately at issue were the mechanisms for the administration of resources in determined territories, but the heart of the matter was the nature of political sovereignty. Above all, in the Gas War, the constantly heard phrase was "the people (*el pueblo*) want this."

During these new junctures, the political culture of the country was to undergo a short-lived but radical change. New configurations of "left" and "right" crystallized out along the political axis. The unexpected political rise of the Movimiento al Socialismo (MAS) of the coca growers, led by Evo Morales, was to define the new leftist space, while the racial division of the country between Collas (mainly Aymaras in the highlands) and Cambas (led by the elites of Santa Cruz in the lowlands) was to give rise to a new right-wing configuration with fascist leanings (Patzi Paco, 2003, 272–74).

In the more indigenist tendency, the political party of the "Mallku" Felipe Quispe, called the Movimiento Indio Pachakuti (MIP), held sway between the pragmatics of the traditional political parties and a romanticism toward *lo andino*. In this new play of political positioning, Felipe Quispe reinterpreted the blocking of roads, a common tactic of the *campesino* movement since the 1950s, according to the Andean rural metaphors of "sowing the roads with stones," organized according to a "plan of fleas" (*plan pulga*) or "lightning blockades" (*bloqueo relámpago*). Ample publicity was given to the fact that the blockades were organized according to the traditional Andean system of rotating turns or lists.

In the light of these new tendencies, the traditional political parties (MNR, ADN, MIR), which were unable to respond with convincing policies, were to cede space to the new social and identity movements with their more immediate demands. A new form of government, based on civic and grass-roots organizations— the FEJUVES or Federations of Neighborhood Associations in El Alto, the trade unions and guilds, the OTBs and *ayllus* to give a few examples—was to replace the system of political parties in the country, but only for a short time.

Some commentators (Prada 1997, García Linera 2001) on these new alliances remarked on their lack of a conventional leadership and reflected on the fact that these movements seemed to embody the rise of the new leaderless "multitude" described in the book *Empire* (Hardt and Negri 2000). Others, for example Patzi Paco (2003), saw in this juncture a contemporary recovery of a previously submerged "long-term memory," which had re-emerged to vindicate the historical struggles and demands of Tupaq Katari in the eighteenth century and Zárate Willka in the nineteenth century for regional autonomies with their own indigenous governments.

In this emerging context, Patzi Paco criticized the former neoliberal proposals for a multiethnic and pluri-cultural nation as simply giving in to the present *mestizo-criollo* state, a "negotiated inclusion" that requests through decrees and through Parliament "that a space be made for the Indians" (1999, 67; cited in Spedding 2003, 103). As is well known, this kind of liberal "multiculturalism" has always been uncomfortable, both for the political left and for indigenous movements.

The constant fear of both groups is that multiculturalism, particularly of the North American school, has the purpose of relegating the cultures of the periphery to the hegemony of the center. In the juridical sense, too, at an international level, many official documents drawn up in the legal framework of "multiculturalism" have referred to "linguistic groups" or "cultural groups" (rather than "linguistic communities"), thereby using definitions that really describe the situations of diaspora, migration, or polyethnicism simply to accommodate minority groups within the territories occupied historically by other majority groups (see also Kymlicka 1996). In this sense, the term "multicultural" can be used purposely to thwart the sovereign status of indigenous nations. Many argue that this is precisely the function of the official use of this term in educational reforms throughout Latin America.

In reaction to this trend elsewhere, groups such as the Cree in Canada have rejected the use of multiculturality in an educational setting, as it implies their lesser status as a sovereign nation (Arnold and Yapita 2003b, 57).

Contesting this notion of multiculturalism, Félix Patzi Paco holds that in the case of societies that have been invaded and subalternized, such as the Aymara or Quechua in Bolivia, and moreover where these groups form the national majority, the use of the term "multicultural" is part of a continuing colonizing attempt to identify pockets of indigenous territories within the nation-state when these are just the fragments produced by the colonial process of dismemberment. From Patzi Paco's point of view, indigenous populations are dispersed all over the national territory, including in the cities, where they now constitute the different social classes of Bolivian society (Patzi Paco 2004, 138).

According to his argument, officialism, backed by the anthropological theory of cultural relativism, has developed a complex strategy of assimilation (what Díaz Polanco [1996] calls "ethnophagy"), in which the state, appealing to an indigenist stance, recognizes certain indigenous practices (generally the cultural and symbolic ones of language, culture, and "*usos y costumbres*," what Patzi Paco calls "surroundings" or "*entorno*"), while at the same time imposing over and above them other liberal values considered universal (Patzi Paco 2004, 165). For Patzi Paco, this is the version of indigenist politics that is expressed in the packages of liberal multiculturalism. He goes a step further to put into the same bag those who defend the pluralism of "pluri-multi" with those who back the present demands for indigenous autonomies (141).

In his attempt to redefine the values of Andean cultures rather than Hispanic ones as the universal norm, Patzi Paco resorts to the "clash of civilizations" argument. There, he sees Quechuas and Aymaras as having built another civilization (even in their periods of clandestinity and subalternity), one that defies the West and that has emerged with greater resilience in the social movements of the 1990s to vindicate its cultures and ways of life (141–42). For Patzi Paco, then, "indigeneity" is the recognition of an alternative universe of meaning. In comparison, the "pluri-multi" proposal of the same period is simply a liberal and reformist answer to an uncomfortable political juncture. The problem for him is that the "pluri-multi" approach does not even include indigenous culture in a real policy of articulation with the state, where, for example, Spanish speakers would also learn Aymara, and in which certain indigenous practices could even emerge as universal values (142). The "pluri-multi" tendency only accommodates itself to a persistent coloniality in which "race" and "ethnicity" are the organizing principles.

Here, the distinction that Patzi Paco draws between "system" and "surroundings" is useful, as it illustrates the way in which the neoliberal model allows the incorporation into state policies of some of the universal criteria of an intercultural and bilingual educational program, even the recognition of "usage and customs" in the legislative sense, but without changing the administrative system or the underlying political and economic systems. All this is quite different from a political atmosphere in which the detailed study of regional linguistic history would serve as the baseline for regional linguistic planning procedures under the control of indigenous nations for their own territories.

Even so, the present demands for regional autonomies, even of those who defend the "pluri-multi" idea, do have historical antecedents of long standing. For example, the current demand for an Aymara nation that emerged with renewed vigor in the year 2000 with the uprising led by Felipe Quispe (and backed by the Jach'ak'achi Manifesto) has historical antecedents in a similar attempt to reconstitute Qullasuyu at the founding of the Bolivian Republic. This demand was reiterated during the self-determination movement led by Zárate Willka in the Federal War of 1899, then in another led by Manuel Chachawayna in the 1920s, and again in the proposals for a "Republic of Nations called Kollasuyo" (which included all of Bolivia) by Nina Quispe in the 1930s. These demands were followed by a call for an Aymara Republic by Laureano Machaqa in 1956, and a similar call in 1973 in the Manifiesto de Tiwanaku, in which Xavier Albó participated (see Ticona 2003, 13–15). Later on, this same idea gathered strength and greater coherence with the Red Offensive of the Tupaqkatarista Ayllus and the Indianist Movement of the 1980s, which was led by Felipe Quispe, the "Mallku," through the Tupac Katari Guerrilla Army (EGTK) (Patzi Paco 2002, 71). With the resurgence of the policies of the "Mallku" Felipe Quispe in the year 2000, the renewed demand for an Aymara nation was to identify its ceremonial center as Tiwanaku (and its administrative center as the modern Achakachi) (Patzi Paco 2002, 69; Arnold and Yapita 2005). Later on, as we shall see, Aymara nationalism was to compete with the Camba nationalism of the Santa Cruz region for the major stake in any alternative model of Bolivian government.

How did Félix Patzi Paco propose to go beyond the notion of regional autonomies and toward more fundamental changes in regional policies? For

Patzi Paco, if multiculturalism is simply "disguised assimilation and its political means is submission" (2002, 112–17), then any solution must define a
different notion of sovereignty. Here, he contrasts *two* kinds of political representation. In representative party democracy (which he terms "liberal"),
the citizen relegates the power of decision making by delegating it to a small
group of representatives, which then monopolizes the conduct of public
affairs. Patzi Paco contrasts this concept to that of Andean "sovereignty,"
exemplified in grass-roots communal organizations and which is rotational,
collective, and with the participation of all (2002, 127; summed up in Spedding 2003, 103).

   In his book *Sistema comunal* (2004), Patzi Paco develops this idea into
a political platform, which totally rejects the ideas of the founding fathers
of representative democracy (Kant, Locke, and Adam Smith) for their fundamentally bourgeois interests, as well as the failure of the liberal political
system to respond to any preexisting indigenous reality. For Patzi Paco, a
real change demands transformations not only in the superficial milieu of
regional languages and cultures, or the control and administration of regional resources (the crux of the autonomy proposals), but rather in the
whole political and economic apparatus in the very heart of the neoliberal
and *mestizo-criollo* state.

   However, this kind of play of oppositions between political models, much
practiced among the Comuna group of which Patzi Paco was a member,
tends to postulate models of the ideal type (in a Weberian sense) rather than
describe reality.[6] Likewise, García Linera, another member of the Comuna
group, spoke about the "trade union form," the "multitude form," and the
"community form," in a pure conceptual sense, relating them to the excep-
tional revolutionary events of the last few years but not to everyday rural daily life (2001, 54–79). So neither of these intellectuals was known for
practical suggestions. And there was still the question of how this proposed
transformation might come about in practice, and which would be the conceptual frameworks on which the new state policies might be based.

   In practice, Patzi Paco became the minister of education in 2006, when
Álvaro García Linera became vice president of the new government of MAS
under Evo Morales. Here, real events rapidly overtook the ideal models
constructed by these intellectuals in the lead-up to the election of MAS
in December 2005. In the case of Patzi Paco, his year in office saw few real
changes in educational policy, and his conflictive ideas tended rather to stall
change by way of his constant battles with the church and the teachers. For
his part, faced with reality, García Linera began to speak more about the

Soviet model of "democratic centralism" as a way of controlling change in the *mestizo-criollo* state apparatus, rather than his former discourse in favor of indigenous solutions.

Toward a New Kind of State: The Bolivian Constituent Assembly of 2006–2007

The popular proposal in October 2003 for a Constituent Assembly, as a way of changing once and for all the apparatus of the former *mestizo-criollo* state, was unanimous, although it occurred in an atmosphere of real desperation. As the Aymara historian Esteban Ticona recounts, "The *pueblo* arrived at the entrance of the governmental palace but couldn't enter" because "their power structures are so different from ours" (personal communication). At that point, the participants in the uprising realized that the very structures of the state had to be changed before they could take power. The most viable way to do so seemed to be via a Constituent Assembly.

The origins of this renewed demand for a Constituent Assembly had their roots in the social demands of the Bolivian lowlands rather than the highlands, formulated in the long march of 1990 for land and territory, led by CIDOB, an indigenous organization. This same demand was taken up again by the Coordinadora del Agua during the Water War in Cochabamba, in April 2000. And another mention of the Constituent Assembly to receive massive publicity was a call for profound constitutional reforms by the rebel judge Alberto Costas Obregón in the context of the general elections of 2001, when his political party participated for the first time. Gradually this demand became disseminated throughout the indigenous movement, first through the various movements of the lowlands with another march in the year 2002 (the "indigenous march" in which the people requested a Constituent Assembly, although neither the demands nor the negotiations were clear). Another march in the same year, demanding a Constituent Assembly, was headed by the *campesinos* of Potosí and organized by entities affiliated with the highland indigenous organization CONAMAQ. This demand was to be reiterated in another march by the same organization from Oruro to La Paz in the following year, 2003, as one of a series of events that led up to the general uprising of October.

In this new juncture, one of the main issues was how the various demands for reforms to the state, from these grass-roots social and identity movements, would be implemented through a Constituent Assembly. Some of the juridical criteria for doing so had already been declared. But other questions then arose: How could the new forms of social heterogeneity be institutionalized while avoiding a clash between a multinational civil society and a monolithic state? Likewise, how could the "position of a popular subject" that divided political space into two antagonistic blocks, the *pueblo* and the elites, be avoided? More specifically, how could the demands of liberal multiculturalism for equal opportunities, according to the legal category of the subject and the principle of individual rights, be rethought in the new heterogenous context? And finally, how could liberal multiculturalism be superceded and the conceptual and cultural basis for a new collective subject begin to be articulated?

Certain tendencies in the existing literature answered some of these questions. For example, Paalo Virno contrasts the unitary and homogenous modern subject with the idea of "the *pueblo*" or the "multitude." Moreover, this idea of the "*pueblo* multitude" as a political and cultural expression of the egalitarian imaginary is already inherent (up to a point) in multicultural heterogeneity. It could also be argued that the *pueblo* is also "essentially multicultural" when seen from the idea of "strategic essentialism" developed by Gayatri Spivak (1990) and Stuart Hall (1996). García Linera's (2003b) own definition of "identity" as a relational, dialogic, contingent product of the work of resignifying the symbolic order of collectivities goes in the same direction. In this sense, multiculturalism is a necessary aspect rather than a contingent aspect of the identity of the *pueblo*, and something internal to a united *pueblo* when this is opposed to a constitutive exterior. What exactly is the nature of this constitutive exterior? Some would argue that this "exterior" is constructed precisely according to the "logic of acculturation" of capitalist modernity and its law of values to be incompatible with both the redistributive claims of class or the politics of multicultural identity.

One solution, then, would seem to acknowledge two simultaneous complementary and antagonistic aspects of one and the same *pueblo*: multinationality (to go a step further than multiculturality) in its rural or provincial and less acculturated form versus multinationality in its urban and more acculturated and *mestizo-criollo* form. If the "unity of the *pueblo*" always depends on the recognition of internal socio-cultural difference, that is to say on the incommensurability and very contradictions within the *pueblo* itself, then, as Beverley suggests, instead of the "many becoming one," a new concept of the nation could be based on the idea that the "one becomes many." We go from utopia to heterotopia. In this more differentiated concept of the nation, the unity of the state would derive from the recognition of internal differences at both levels, within the indigenous nations in their more rural and provincial milieu, and within the more mixed *mestizo-criollo*-indigenous aspects of metropolitan relations in urban centers. The question then is, how could these criteria be used to remold the present state apparatus?

The present state apparatus simply does not have the capacity to generate the new spaces of governability necessary for a country that is in fact a conglomeration of nationalities in which each minor nation has its own language (or languages) and ways of life. The challenge then is to transform the former *mestizo-criollo* model of a monocultural, monolingual, and monoconstitutional state into a multinational, multilingual, and multiconstitutional form of democracy, capable of engaging with what Boaventura de Sousa Santos (2004) calls "high intensity democracy," rather than its previous representative form.

Certain clues to the design of an alternative state already emerge from the dysfunctional structures of the present state. For example, the organization of the nation into unequal territories, populations, and electoral districts, each one with a profoundly unequal access to democratic representation, or to national resources or tributary co-participation, implies rethinking the organization of the National Electoral Court. At present, the neo-dual organization of the chambers of Congress and other instances of the state apparatus simply tends to imitate the dual structures of countries such as the United States, England, and France but without a real element of duality in their operative level.

Political duality is an attractive option for several reasons. Historically, there is much evidence to suggest that Andean political systems were based on dual organizations of moieties, with rotation of office. For example, the Inka state was characterized by duality in political, ritual, and military spheres, and possibly even in a gendered parallelism, where the Coya oversaw women's organizations while the Inka oversaw the men's (see, for example, Rostworowski de Díez Canseco 1983). In the colonial period, as we have seen, elements of this dual organization continued in the parallel organization of the two semi-autonomous republics (the Hispanic and the Indian), both under the protection of the Spanish crown. Dual forms have also characterized many proposals for alternative state organizations. In the 1920s, Nina Quispe's "República de Collasuyo" proposed a dual division into two republics, but within the one nation of Bolivia. In the 1950s, as a result of the Bolivian Revolution, the co-government between the ruling MNR party and the principal workers' union, the COB, operated according to a model of "dual power" in Zavaleta's terminology (1974). A decade later, Fausto Reinaga's complaint about the problematic present-day "two Bolivias," reiterated in the year 2000 by Felipe Quispe, also acknowledges how deeply this sense of dual structures, now thwarted and confronted antagonistically, penetrates Bolivian society.

This duality could emerge from a reworked parity between the predominantly *mestizo-criollo* republic and the presently excluded indigenous populations. Perhaps elements of such an operative duality existed historically under a two-party system: the Republicans and the Liberals. Nevertheless, in the last fifty years, despite the proliferation of political parties, state structures have permitted the same elites to manage all levels of the political system while counting on the absence of any real political opposition. Even the constant alliances, pacts, and coalitions between the traditional political parties were concerned with the institutional reproduction of these same elites and not with generating real government and a shadow government of opposition as elsewhere.

The problem is that this dual alternative to the current state apparatus has already been skewed in different ways by distinct interest groups, mainly toward a more corporate variant, toward an autonomist variant, and toward a communitarian and indigenist variant. Let us trace the characteristics of each of these in turn.

One variant of the dual model is the corporative solution that challenges the dominant political culture of Bolivian democracy. In several works preceding the election of MAS in 2005, García Linera (2003b) identified the need to provide for this alternative corporative solution in what he sees as *two* existing fissures in the present state apparatus. The first is the existing conflict between a multinational and multilingual society and the monocultural and monolingual *mestizo-criollo* state. The second conflict involves *two* political tendencies: the present monocultural and monopolitical state as opposed to that of a wide corporate political field. In practice, this corporate field is composed of labor unions (*sindicatos*), *ayllus* and communities, and federations and trade associations (*gremios*), each with their own working rules, their rotative systems of office, politics, and ethics, their normative systems of traditional authorities, and their consensual forms of decision making, for example in communal assemblies. As García Linera pointed out, this alternative political field was in force before the Bolivian Republic was founded, has continued down to the present, and in addition has renewed its strength in the period 2000–2003 (2005).

For García Linera, the results of the first fissure (the split between society and the state) also impinge on an ethnically stratified labor market in which there are constant linguistic barriers to social ascendancy on the part of the indigenous populations. Moreover, as the state does not acknowledge the systems of social significance or the political practices of the majority indigenous world, then the problem *cannot* be resolved simply by introducing more indigenous members of Congress into Parliament, as was attempted in the election of 2001. On this occasion, the indigenous members of Congress were forced to form their own separate organization, as their voices and demands were not recognized in the existing parliamentary setting. To resolve this particular fissure, García Linera proposed a kind of decolonized nationalism as a way toward a multinational state, or even independent states in an autonomous model.

To resolve the second fissure, between the political fields in conflict and, as a result, the unequal access to the practical management of the political, cultural, and economic resources of society, García Linera proposed the introduction of a multi-institutional or multicivilizational dimension into the political system, as well as the need for endogenous institutional designs and not exogenous ones. Here, too, García Linera opted for an autonomous solution based on the antecedents of political theory and reality of other multicultural states (for example Switzerland, Belgium. and Great Britain). His solution was to have both autonomous multicultural cities and autonomous predominantly indigenous territories.

Overall, García Linera's proposal opted for a general pattern of government that unified and synthesized the cultural diversity of the country, accompanied by a vertical segmentation of the state power structure with differentiated levels of political competences. In this vertical segmentation, there would be a nonindigenous government and a parallel indigenous government. Then, at *meso* and subnational levels, including the municipalities, there would be autonomous regimes based on identity, for example in the Aymara and Quechua cases. At the same time, each autonomous region was to have its own normative constitutional regime, considered as the basic standard for the autonomous region, albeit below the national Constitution of the political community of the whole Bolivian state. Each region would also have its own legislative chamber, whose members would be elected to the executive level of the autonomous regime. Finally, there would be the constitutional recognition of regional autonomies, by cultural or linguistic community, so as to assure the equality of cultures within the state (see fig. 6.5).

This model is favored by many in the Constituent Assembly, particularly as García Linera is now MAS's vice president, and appeals to the middle-class vote. It is also not so different from a proposal formulated by the so-

A state with regional autonomies

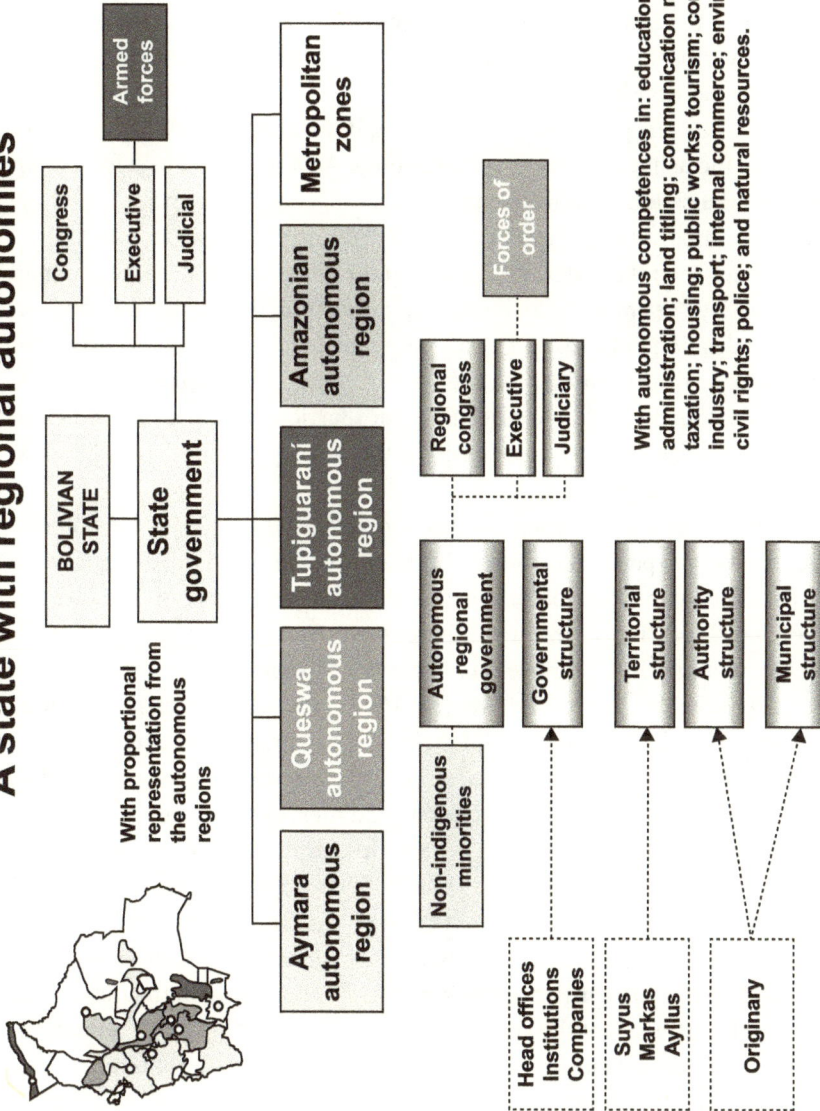

BOLIVIAN STATE

Congress

Executive

Judicial

Armed forces

State government

With proportional representation from the autonomous regions

Aymara autonomous region

Queswa autonomous region

Tupiguaraní autonomous region

Amazonian autonomous region

Metropolitan zones

Non-indigenous minorities

Autonomous regional government

Regional congress

Executive

Judiciary

Forces of order

Governmental structure

Territorial structure

Authority structure

Municipal structure

Head offices Institutions Companies

Suyus Markas Ayllus

Originary

With autonomous competences in: education; public administration; land titling; communication media; taxation; housing; public works; tourism; commerce; industry; transport; internal commerce; environment; civil rights; police; and natural resources.

Figure 6.5. García Linera's autonomous model of the Bolivian state (García Linera 2003b).

called Indigenous Block of some ten indigenous organizations, including CONAMAQ and strongly supported by MAS, in a conference held in Santa Cruz in September 2004. This indigenous proposal (which was originally for the election of members of the Constituent Assembly rather than for resolving the country's territorial organization) identified four indigenous electoral districts in the lowlands and, more interestingly, sixteen indigenous nations as the basis of electoral districts in the highlands, where the voting was to be according to indigenous "usage and customs" rather than the conventional individual secret vote of representative democracy (see fig. 6.6).{Fig. 6.6 near here}

Given this real possibility of rethinking Bolivian territorial organization through the deliberations of the Constituent Assembly, the craze for a total reterritorialization of Bolivia came to its peak, and the maps developed by different indigenous groups to reinstate Tawantinsuyu (or at least Collasuyu) have been the order of the day. On the government side, the original proposal by the Indigenous Block was developed by the vice ministry of decentralization in the MAS government into a mapping of some forty "indigenous territorial entities" in the country, both in the highlands and the lowlands. (See fig. 6.7, and also Albó and Barrios Suvelza 2006, 146–52.) This was the favored territorial basis for the development of García Linera's corporativist model.

Another important variant of a dual model is that for regional *autonomies*, this time at a departmental level. This has also dominated the deliberations of the Constituent Assembly, this time from the perspective of the elites on the Santa Cruz Civic Committee. This option, centered around the so-called Camba Nation, aims to divide the country into two huge blocks, which have come to be known as the "Half Moon" (*Media Luna*) of the eastern lowlands and the "Half Sun" (*Medio Sol*) of the western highlands, which clearly exaggerates the racial division between Cambas (mainly whites) and Collas (mainly Aymara and Quechua speakers and their descendants). While this debate is expressed in terms of a general decentralization of the country, in reality the Half Moon is made up of the Bolivian departments with the most immediate access to petrol and gas (Santa Cruz, Tarija, and Beni) and has the economic aim of taking advantage of the income from these sources, rather than seeking a just distribution of such funds between the richer and poorer departments of the country. The irony is that the Camba Nation, in its original Internet site, cites García Linera's indigenous autonomic model as the inspiration for its own autonomous demand (see fig. 6.8a and b).

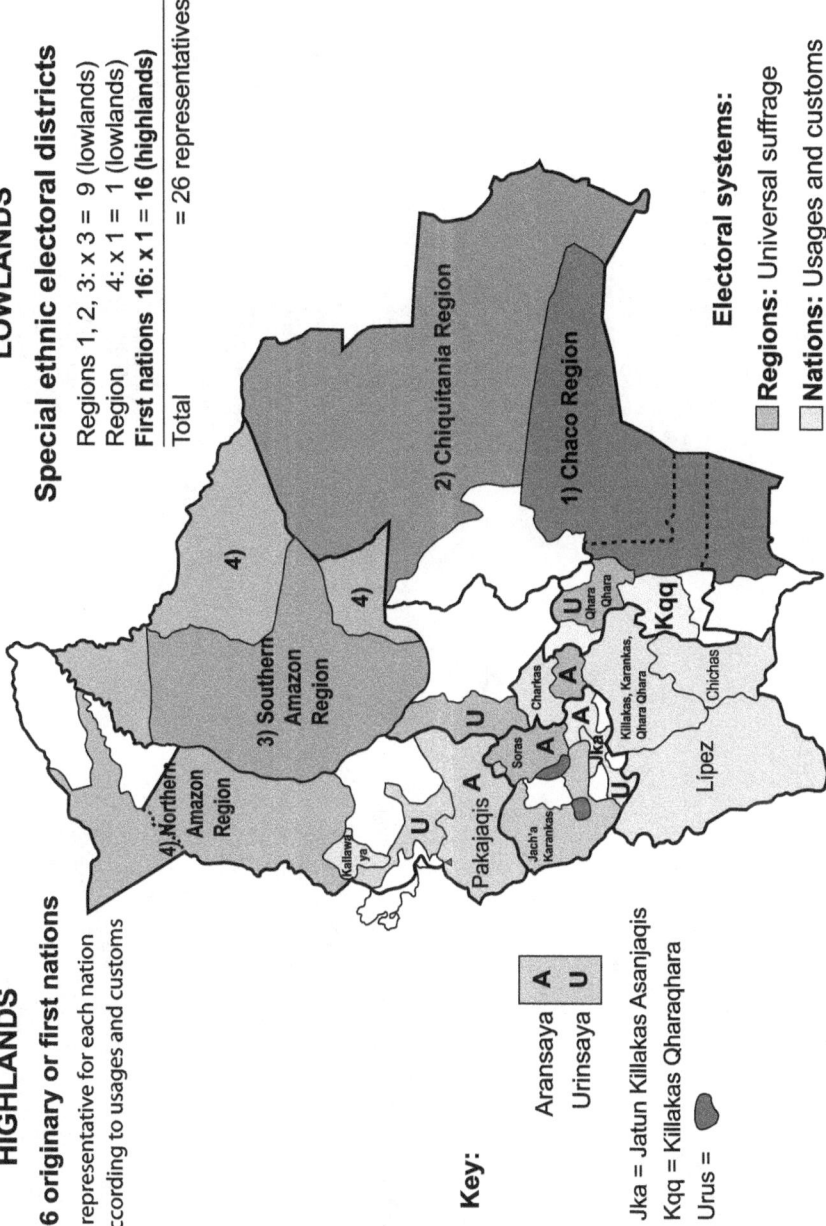

HIGHLANDS

16 originary or first nations

1 representative for each nation according to usages and customs

4) Northern Amazon Region

3) Southern Amazon Region

4)

4)

Kallawaya

Pakajaqis **A**

U

Jach'a Karankas

Soras

A

Charkas

Jka

A

U

Killakas, Karenkas, Qhara Qhara

A

U

Qhara

Qhara

Kqq

Lipez

Chichas

LOWLANDS

Special ethnic electoral districts

Regions 1, 2, 3: x 3 = 9 (lowlands)
Region 4: x 1 = 1 (lowlands)
First nations 16: x 1 = 16 (highlands)

Total = 26 representatives

2) Chiquitania Region

1) Chaco Region

Electoral systems:

◼ **Regions:** Universal suffrage
◻ **Nations:** Usages and customs

Key:

Aransaya **A**
Urinsaya **U**

Jka = Jatun Killakas Asanjaqis
Kqq = Killakas Qharaqhara
Urus = ●

Figure 6.6. The proposal by the Indigenous Block (2004).

MINISTRY OF THE PRESIDENCY
VICEMINISTRY OF DECENTRALIZATION
REGIONALIZED DECENTRALIZATION

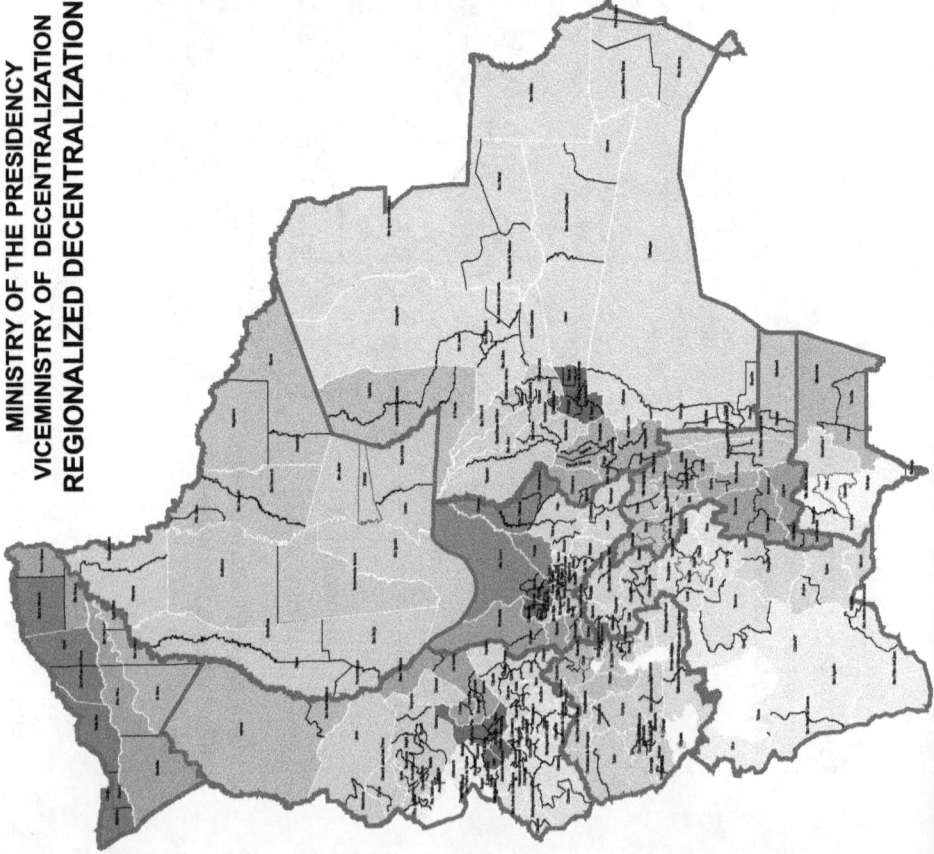

DEPARTMENTS OF
REGIONALIZED DECENTRALIZATION
BE-ITENEZ MAMORE
BE-MOJENA
BE-AMAZON
BE-YACUMA
CH-NORTH CHUQUISACA
CH-CENTRAL CHUQUISACA
CH-LOS CINTIS
CO- DEL CHACO REGION
CO-COCHABAMBA
CO-SOUTH CONO
CO-ANDEAN REGION
CO-TROPIC OF COCHABAMBA
CO-HIGH VALLEY
CO-LOW VALLEY
LP-METROPOLITAIN AREA
LP-NORTHERN PLATEAU CIRCUNLACUSTRE
LP-SOUTHERN PLATEAU
LP-VALLEYS OF NORTHERN LA PAZ
LP-SOUTHERN VALLEYS
LP-YUNGAS
LP-AMAZON
OR-JAKISA
OR-KARANGAS
OR-SORA
OR-URUCHIPAYA
PA-AMAZON-TAHUAMANU
PA-AMAZON-MANURIPI
PA-AMAZON-MOTHER OF GOD
PT-AYLLUS CENTRAL POTOSI
PT-AYLLUS NORTH POTOSI
PT-LIPEZ SALAR
PT-LOS CHICHAS
SC-METROPOLITAIN AREA
SC-CHIQUITANIA
SC-NORTH CRUCEÑO
SC-NORTH GUARAYOS
SC-CRUCEÑOS VALLEYS
SC-DEL CHACO REGION
TR-ANDEAN REGION
TR-SUB-ANDEAN REGION
TR-TARIJA VALLEYS
TR-DEL CHACO REGION

Figure 6.7. The reterritorialization proposed by the vice ministry of decentralization in the MAS government.

The Camba Nation:
A state associated with Bolivia
(Source: Antelo SCZ)

State model: autonomous, with a federal platform, multiple and asymmetrical

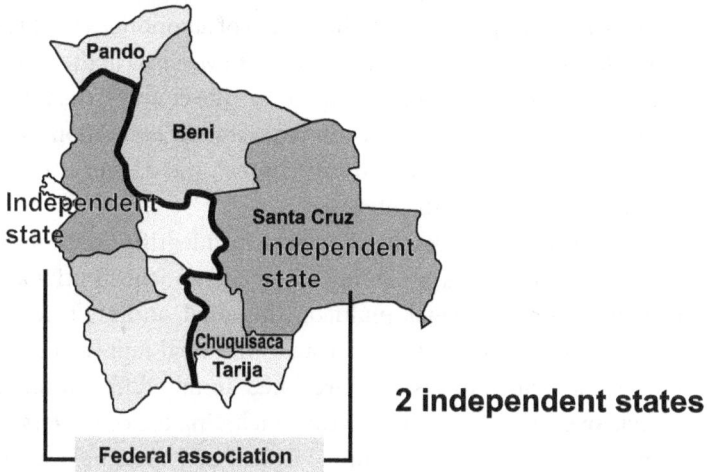

2 independent states

The separate Camba Nation:
making the "Half Moon" and the "Half Sun"

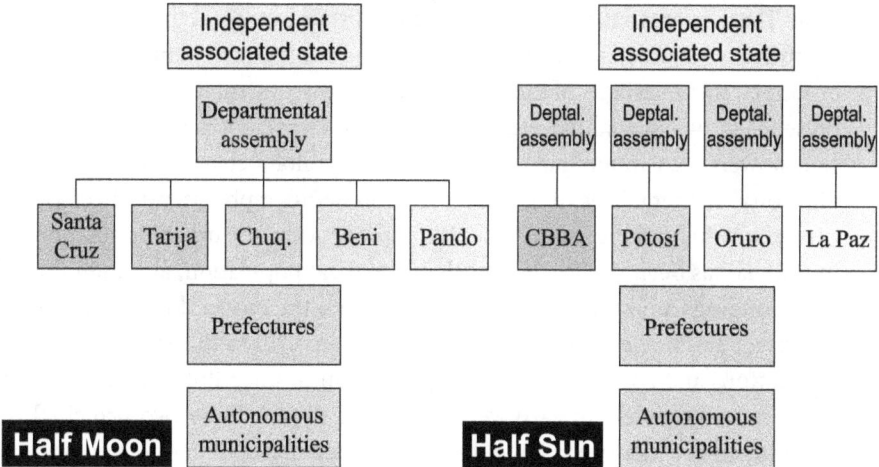

Competences: defined by their organization and territorial development.
Objectives: control of natural resources.
The union of independent states is associated federally into one single state.

Source: (Antelo SCZ)

Figures 6.8 a and b. The proposal by the Camba Nation of Santa Cruz (2004).

However, the problem with García Linera's autonomous proposal and others is that the present situation in Bolivia is not really conducive to political models of this type. It could possibly work in the poorer regions of the country, for example in the Andean Aymara- and Quechua-speaking regions of the altiplano, where the system of autonomies might allow a fairer redistribution of funds from the center. However, as in the case of the richer regions of Spain, of Cataluña and the Basque country, the richer regions of Santa Cruz and Tarija would soon request their separation from the model to form independent units. In this context, the danger is that Bolivia as a country would simply disintegrate.

A third attempt to resolve the problems identified until now, and transform a monocultural, monolingual, and monoconstitutional state into a new kind of multilingual, multiconstitutional, and multi-institutional democracy, would be by creating a state with dual representation. This solution, is its various forms, has circulated among different organizations in Bolivia over the past couple of years, including the colonizers' syndicate, as an option for organizing the initial Constituent Assembly, as well as for reorganizing the Bolivian state. This dual model would function around what is called in Aymara *taypi*, in the sense of a mediating center. This model proposes immediate changes to the political system, while allowing for a gradual and wider change (a *kuti*) in the political conduct of the Bolivian state. These relate to the organic structures of state power (at the legislative, executive, and judicial levels) that form the basis of government.

One of these variants of this dual model of government derives from the presence of *two* substantive elements of the whole society in the conduct of state power: a "cosmopolitan" and more "metropolitan" element, and an "indigenous" element. This division is based on demographic trends, because since the 1980s and the economic crisis of those years, the urban population in Bolivia has been slightly higher than the rural population, although the two groupings are more or less equal. However, the model does not make the direct and facile comparison between urban areas with *mestizo-criollo* populations and rural areas with indigenous ones, since Bolivian reality is much more complex. In early versions of the model, these two principal groupings were like two parallel but interrelated states, differentiated and yet intercalated at all levels (see figs. 6.9a and b).

On the one hand, the "cosmopolitan" element would be conformed by the white and *mestizo-criollo* metropolitan society, together with the high percentage of indigenous populations that also live in this setting.[7] This category would also have to take into account that the number of indigenous

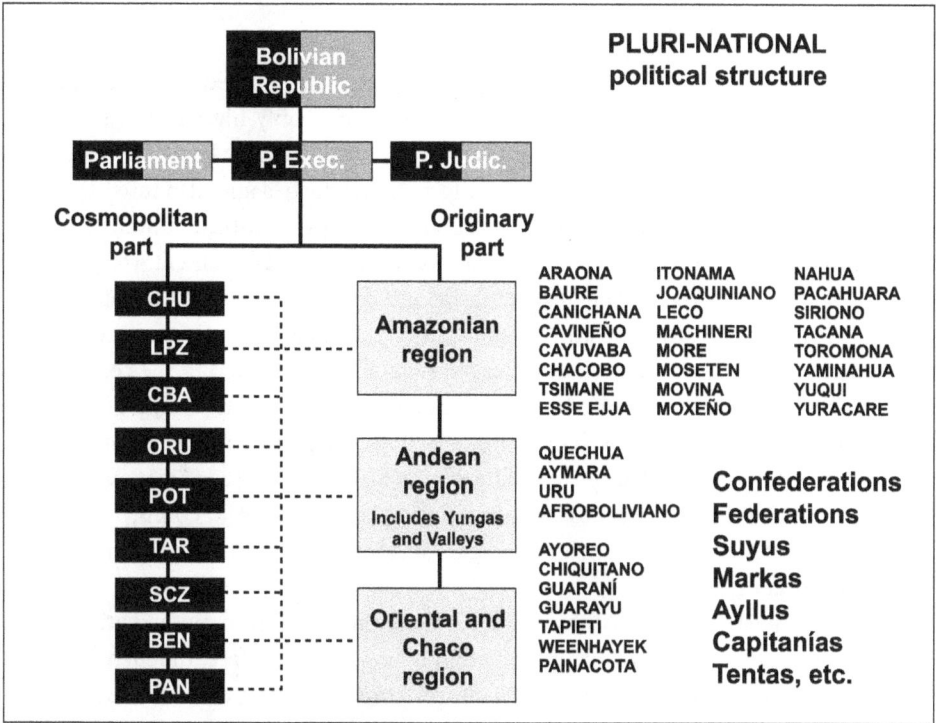

PLURI-NATIONAL political structure

Bolivian Republic

Parliament — P. Exec. — P. Judic.

Cosmopolitan part

CHU
LPZ
CBA
ORU
POT
TAR
SCZ
BEN
PAN

Originary part

Amazonian region

ARAONA	ITONAMA	NAHUA
BAURE	JOAQUINIANO	PACAHUARA
CANICHANA	LECO	SIRIONO
CAVINEÑO	MACHINERI	TACANA
CAYUVABA	MORE	TOROMONA
CHACOBO	MOSETEN	YAMINAHUA
TSIMANE	MOVINA	YUQUI
ESSE EJJA	MOXEÑO	YURACARE

Andean region
Includes Yungas and Valleys

QUECHUA
AYMARA
URU
AFROBOLIVIANO

Oriental and Chaco region

AYOREO
CHIQUITANO
GUARANÍ
GUARAYU
TAPIETI
WEENHAYEK
PAINACOTA

Confederations
Federations
Suyus
Markas
Ayllus
Capitanías
Tentas, etc.

Political structure and organization of a dual state

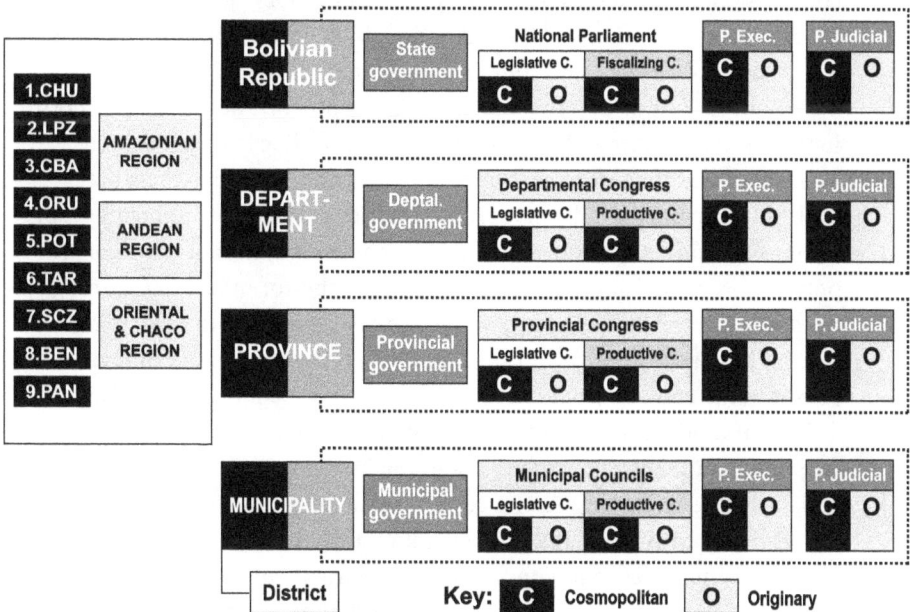

1.CHU
2.LPZ — AMAZONIAN REGION
3.CBA
4.ORU — ANDEAN REGION
5.POT
6.TAR
7.SCZ — ORIENTAL & CHACO REGION
8.BEN
9.PAN

		National Parliament		P. Exec.	P. Judicial
Bolivian Republic	State government	Legislative C.	Fiscalizing C.	C O	C O
		C O	C O		

		Departmental Congress		P. Exec.	P. Judicial
DEPART-MENT	Deptal. government	Legislative C.	Productive C.	C O	C O
		C O	C O		

		Provincial Congress		P. Exec.	P. Judicial
PROVINCE	Provincial government	Legislative C.	Productive C.	C O	C O
		C O	C O		

		Municipal Councils		P. Exec.	P. Judicial
MUNICIPALITY	Municipal government	Legislative C.	Productive C.	C O	C O
		C O	C O		

District

Key: C Cosmopolitan   O Originary

Figures 6.9 a and b. An early proposal for a dual state.

people living in both urban and rural settings simultaneously (through complex patterns of temporary migration) is probably higher than those living in either urban or rural settings (Calla Ortega 2003). This category of "cosmopolitan" society is grouped into political parties and also into other independent and corporate organizations (civic groups, trade unions and guilds, and so forth). On the other hand, the "indigenous" element would be constituted by the principal geocultural and economic areas of the country (the Andean region, the Yungas and valleys, the Amazonian region, and the Orient and Chaco, as well as other areas yet to be identified in the coming assembly) and represented by the indigenous nations (and ethnic group-ings) that form some 62 percent of the Bolivian population according to the census of 2001 (Ramírez Huarcacho et al. 2003). These indigenous na-tions have their own political systems of representation and conformation of authorities (in *ayllus*, neighborhoods, unions, and so forth) and their own electoral practices.

The basic concepts of this model are already recognized by the national Constitution in its first article, wherein it says, "Bolivia, free, independent, sovereign, multiethnic and pluri-cultural, constituted in a unitary Republic adopted for its government the representative democratic form. . . ." For the first time, this article would serve as the basis for the conformation of a new multinational state instead of disguising a state that is essentially mono-constitutional. Besides, as Kymlicka points out (2002), acknowledging the collective rights of the *pueblos* and nationalities of the country is the best way of defending the social culture of each *pueblo*.

In this variant of the dual system of government, the election of both members of Congress and senators would be according to these basic group-ings: the cosmopolitan or metropolitan areas and the indigenous nations. In the indigenous part, the numerical presence of senators and members of Congress could be according to their nationalities, perhaps in a form of pro-portional representation according to the number of inhabitants through the data gathered in the last census. In this case, there would be an overrep-resentation of the minority groups, since as a principle of government each nation in the country would have at least one representative in Parliament.

The proceedings for electing the representatives of each element, the cos-mopolitan and metropolitan areas and the indigenous nations, would be a variant of the following. At the cosmopolitan level, election would be by departments, provinces, and municipalities, through newly recognized po-litical constituencies, but with members of Parliament and through politi-cal parties, as before. At the level of areas with indigenous majorities (both urban and rural), election would be by nations and ethnic groups and their representatives and forms of election.

In one of the detailed variants of this model currently in play, the actual management of government, the senators and their technical teams would be responsible for the legislative part of government while the members of Congress with their technical teams would be responsible for fiscalization measures. This system has historical memories of Inkaic administration, with its rigorous fiscalization procedures (managed in those times by the *kipukamayuq* or *kipu*-holders), while also reflecting, for example, the way that the Chilean government works on a contemporary basis. In another variant, that of the National Assembly of Indigenous, Originary, and Farming Organizations and of Colonizers of Bolivia (2006),[8] the fiscalization measures would be carried out by a new independent power of state, called the Pluri-national Social Power, made up of representatives of social movements and so on.

In the preliminary versions of the dual model, the elected representatives in both axes of power (in the cosmopolitan and metropolitan areas, and those of the indigenous nations) would have conformed the basis of the dual system. Their sphere of action would have extended from the maximal levels of the executive to the most minimal levels of district powers in new forms of governmental and socio-political equilibrium. This form of government would also supposedly have improved the various mechanisms of social control at the different levels of the state apparatus.

In more recent versions, a separated dual system as such is superceded, and the two societal axes combined into one chamber of the Parliament, while the other chamber also consists of both kinds of society but at a regional level. This happens, for example, in the proposal by MAS's "political instrument for the sovereignty of the peoples" (MAS-IPSP), as expressed in its document "Refounding Bolivia to Live Well: Proposal for the Constituent Assembly, 2006," as the synthesis of the debates that have taken place in the most representative social organizations of the country. In other variants, the dual model takes on a more outright communitarian guise at all levels. In both of these proposals, MAS would seem to act as a one-party state, but with different positionings (more corporate, more indigenous) within its membership.

In most of these models, all public offices of the state would become institutionalized, in the sense of being voted in directly, not just the president, vice president, senators and members of Congress, and departmental prefects as at present. For example, the designations of judicial power corresponding to the Supreme Court would also be institutionalized, in terms of its president and ministers, as well as the president and speakers of the district courts. In the executive power of government, the dual presence of both cosmopolitan and metropolitan areas, and indigenous nations, would constitute the basis of both the internal and external levels of representation. Likewise, departmental and provincial governments would be institutionalized, and their representatives elected by a popular vote, or directly.

These proposals are not only very different from that of the former *mestizo-criollo* state, but also take their point of departure and difference from this very baseline. The problem now is how to forge a sense of nationhood from the diverse elements at play in Bolivia's interior.

Conclusion

The present structure of the Bolivian state is in a crisis, at times verging on cries for civil war. The immediate danger to the state is the emergence of regionalisms (whether of the Cambas in Santa Cruz or of Aymara nationalism) on the one hand, and fundamentalisms (whether criolloism or Andeanism) on the other, as centrifugal forces, while international pressures in the wider framework of regional geopolitics also vie for the external disarticulation of the state, as a centripetal force. In this context, any proposal for change should give priority to national unity, at least in the short term.

The new proposals for a pluri-national state give priority to respecting this unity, while respecting the diversity of the different nations that constitute the country. In the short term, these models could resolve some of the immediate problems the country is facing, such as the disjuncture between society and the state, and the rising need for the multi-institutionality of the constituent nations. In the long term, a governmental structure that includes *mestizo-criollo* society as well as the indigenous nations of the country could also allow the mediation (*el tinku*) of or in many cases the resolution of conflicts of very long standing. For example, it could provide in the near future a political atmosphere that could generate greater willingness to rethink the fundamental questions concerning territories and populations. A necessary part of this rethinking would be the greater harmonization of the former political categories of the state with those of traditional indigenous territories. Only this greater interweaving of the social capital of the country, in all its diversity, with its political capital, equally diverse, might solve some aspects of the present crisis.

Notes

1. Thanks to Juan de Dios Yapita, Víctor Villarroel, and Alonso Barros for helping me clarify many of the ideas discussed in this essay. Thanks too to Ian Marr for help with the translation of the paper into English.

2. Thanks to Víctor Villarroel for clarifying this point for me.

3. The Law of Popular Participation sought to rearticulate state political and administrative divisions with those of peasant communities and indigenous nations, but only at the municipal level. This attempt was not entirely new. Latin American municipalities had their antecedents in the colonial *cabildos* (dating to 1494 in the Dominican Republic), while modern municipal policies on the continent date to the 1980s, when various international organizations, such as PNUD, BM, BID ,and USAID, pushed for the institutionalization of the municipalities as local governments in which the new "model of development" was to be popular participation (Orellana 2000, 239).

4. According to the terms of the Popular Participation Law, these sums are divided into *two* amounts: 15 percent to be invested in running costs (for the salaries of authorities and so forth); and 85 percent to be used for public investment in what the law stipulates as municipal "development," interpreted as systems of micro-irrigation, roads, education, health, and electrification.

5. Various proposals as to how to do this were collected together in the book *La descentralización que se viene* (The coming decentralization) edited by Franz Barrios (2003), the main proponent of the *meso* idea. But again, with the exception of the essay by García Linera, the book presents a *mestizo-criollo* vision of the Bolivian state, in which indigenous populations do not figure at all. This point was reiterated in a meeting to discuss the book, when indigenous leaders themselves confirmed how little the decentralization process over the last twenty years, backed by the Germans, had actually benefited indigenous populations.

6. See, for example, the comments in Spedding 2003.

7. For example, the number of speakers of Aymara who live in the cities of El Alto and La Paz together is approximately 47 percent, while that of El Alto alone is much higher (74 percent by some estimates).

8. Asamblea Nacional de Organizaciones Indígenas, Originarias, Campesinas y de Colonizadores de Bolivia (2006).

Works Cited

Albó Xavier C., and Franz X. Barrios Suvelza. 2006. "Por una Bolivia plurinacional e intercultural con autonomías." In *Informe Nacional sobre Desarrollo Humano 2006, Documento de Trabajo 1/2006*. La Paz: PNUD, Informe de Desarrollo Humano.

Arnold, Denise Y. 2000. "La participación de la mujer en el proceso de reivindicación de los derechos indígenas en los Andes." Paper presented at the workshop "El *ayllu* y sus autoridades: Perspectivas de las demandas y el proceso organizativo indígena en los Andes de Bolivia," La Paz, June 19–21.

Arnold, Denise Y., and Juan de Dios Yapita. 2003a. "Las pugnas por un ordenamiento territorial indígena: Una cartografía comparada de los límites Laymi-Puraka, Qaqachaka y Jukumani en la guerra de los *ayllus* 2000." Paper presented at the 51st International Congress of Americanists, Santiago de Chile, July 14–18.

———. 2003b. "Reforma educativa y pueblos indígenas en Bolivia: Retórica y práctica." *Guarayo: Revista de cultura latinoamericana* 7.17: 49–70.

———. 2005. "Strands of indigenism in the Bolivian Andes: Competing juridical claims for the ownership and management of indigenous heritage sites in an emerging context of legal pluralism." *Public Archeology* 4: 141–49.

Asamblea Nacional de Organizaciones Indígenas, Originarias, Campesinas y de Colonizadores de Bolivia. 2006. *Propuesta para la Nueva Constitución Política del Estado*. http://constituyentesoberana.org/3/propuestas/osio/pactodeunidad.pdf.

Barrios Suvelza, Franz Xavier. 2003. "Entre lo federal y lo unitario." In *La descentralización que se viene: Propuestas para la (re)constitución del nivel estatal intermedio*, ed. FES-ILDIS, 33–53. La Paz: Plural, FES-ILDIS.

Barros, Alonso. 2003. "Notas sobre la antropología jurídica." Unpublished manuscript.

Baumann, G. 2001. *El enigma multicultural: Un replantamiento de las identidades nacionales, étnicas y religiosas*. Barcelona: Paidós.

Beasley-Murray, Jon. 2001. "Review of John Beverley, *Subalternity and Representation: Arguments in Cultural Theory*." *Bulletin of Latin American Research* 20.1: 142–44.

Beverley, John. 1999. *Subalternity and Representation: Arguments in Cultural Theory*. Durham, N.C.: Duke University Press.

Bouysse-Cassagne, Thérèse. 1987. *La identidad aymara: Aproximación histórica (Siglo XV, Siglo XVI)*. La Paz: Hisbol.

Calla Ortega, Ricardo. 2000. "Avizorando los retos para los pueblos indígenas de América Latina en el nuevo milenio: Territorio, economía, política e identidad." In *Un tapiz tejido a partir de las vicisitudes de la historia, el lugar y la vida cotidiana*, ed. Richard Chase Smith. CD-ROM. Boston: Oxfam América.

———. 2003. *Indígenas, políticas y reformas en Bolivia: Hacia una etnología del Estado en América Latina*. Guatemala City: Ediciones ICAPI.

Costas Arduz, Rolando. 2003. "Qué hacer con el meso en Bolivia." In *La descentralización que se viene: Propuestas para la (re)constitución del nivel estatal intermedio*, ed. FES-ILDIS, 91–129. La Paz: Plural, FES-ILDIS.

Daes, Erica-Irene A. 1999. "Indigenous Peoples and Their Relationship to Land." Final Working Paper, UN Doc: E/CN.4/Sub.2/1999/18, June 3.

Diaz Polanco, Hector. 1996. *Autonomía regional: La autodeterminación de los pueblos indios*. Mexico City: Siglo XXI Editores.

Dory, Daniel, Nelson Manzano, Cecilia Ríos, Luz Mery Quitón, and Moisés Bellota. 2000. *Lógicas territoriales y políticas públicas: Las condiciones de governabilidad democrática en Cochabamba*. La Paz: PIEB.

Fernández, Sonia. 2000. "Naciones indígenas: Análisis histórico y constitucional de los casos de Argentina y Chile." *Alertanet: Portal de derecho y sociedad (Forum II)*. http://www.alertanet.org/F2b-SFernandez.htm.

García, Y., Fernando Luis, Luis Alberto García O., and Luz Mery Quitón Herbas. 2002.

"Democracia y política en Bolivia: Rediscutiendo la construcción conceptual." *T'inkasos* 13: 69–92.

García Linera, Álvaro. 2001. "Sindicato, multitud y comunidad: Movimientos sociales y formas de autonomía política en Bolivia." In *Tiempos de rebelión*, ed. Raquel Álvaro García, Raúl Prada, Felipe Quispe, and Luis Tapia, 9–79. La Paz: Muela del Diablo.

———. 2003a. "Autonomías regionales indígenas y Estado Multicultural." *La descentralización que se viene: Propuestas para la (re)constitución del nivel estatal intermedio*, ed. FES-ILDIS, 169–201. La Paz: Plural, FES-ILDIS.

———. 2003b. "Democracia multinacional y multi-institutional." Debate against Jorge Lazarte in Pulso. http://www.pulsobolivia.com/analistas.html.

———. 2005. *Estado multinacional y multicivilizatoria: Una propuesta democrática y pluralista para la extinción de la exclusión indígena*. La Paz: Editorial Malatesta.

Hall, Stuart. 1996. "Cultural Identity and Diaspora." In *Contemporary Postcolonial Theory: A Reader*. London: Arnold: 110–21.

Hardt, Michael, and Antonio Negri. 2000. *Imperio*. Buenos Aires: Paidos.

Instituto Nacional de Estadística. 1999. *Bolivia: Un mundo de potencialidades; Atlas estadístico de municipios*. La Paz: CID.

Kymlicka, Will. 1996. *Multicultural Citizenship*: A Liberal Theory of Minority Rights. Oxford: Oxford University Press.

———. 2002. "El nuevo debate sobre el derecho de las minorías." In *Democracia y pluralismo nacional*, ed. Ferran Requejo, 25–48. Barcelona: Ariel.

Martínez Cobo, Miguel Alfonso. 1999. "Study on Treaties, Agreements, and Other Constructive Arrangements between States and Indigenous Populations." Final Working Paper, UN Doc: E/CN.4/Sub.2/1999/20, June 22.

Mendoza, Fernando, and Felix Patzi G. 1997. *Atlas de los ayllus del Norte de Potosí, territorio de los antiguos charka*. Potosí, Bolivia: Comisión Europea, Delegación en Bolivia (Programa de Autodesarrollo Campesino).

Movimiento al Socialismo, Instrumento Político por la Soberanía de los Pueblos. 2006. "Refundar Bolivia para vivir bien: Propuesta para la Asamblea Constituyente." *Constituyente Soberana*. http://constituyentesoberana.org /info/files/REFUNDAR%20 BOLIVIA%20PARA%20VIVIR%20BIEN.pdf.

Orellana H., René. 2000. "Municipios y territorios indígenas." In *Atlas: Territorios indígenas en Bolivia; Situación de las Tierras Comunitarias de Origen (TCOs) y Proceso de Titulación*, ed. José A. Martínez. La Paz: Plural Editores: 239–40.

Patzi Paco, Félix. 1999. *Insurgencia y sumisión. Movimiento indígeno-campesinos (1983-1998)*. La Paz: Comuna.

———. 2002. "Movimiento aymara, una utopía razonada contra el fatalismo de la democracia liberal." *Temas sociales* 23: 69–84.

———. 2003. "Rebelión indígena contra la colonialidad y la transnacionalización de la economía: Triunfos y vicisitudes del movimiento indígena desde 2000 a 2003." In *Ya es otro tiempo el presente: Cuatro momentos de insurgencia indígena*, with Forrest Hylton, Sergio Serulnikov, and Sinclair Thomson, 199–279. La Paz: Muela del Diablo.

———. 2004. *Sistema comunal: Una propuesta alternativa al cistema liberal*. La Paz: Comunidades de Estudios Alternativos.

Platt, Tristan. 1987. "Entre ch'axwa y muxsa: Para una historia del pensamiento político aymara." In *Tres reflexiones sobre el pensamiento aymara*, with Thérèse Bouysse-Cassagne, Olivia Harris, Tristan Platt, and Verónica Cereceda. La Paz: Hisbol.

Prada A., Raúl. 1997. *Análisis sociodemográfico: Poblaciones nativas*. La Paz: INE and UNFPA.

Ramírez Huarcacho, Isidro, with Instituto Nacional de Estadística (INE), and UNFPA. 2003. *Bolivia: Características sociodemográficas de la población indígena*. La Paz: INE, Censo 2001, UNFPA, and MACIA.

Rostworowski de Díez Canseco, María. 1983. *Estructuras andinas del poder: Ideología religiosa y política*. Lima: Instituto de Estudios Peruanos.

Santos, Boaventura de Sousa. 2004. *Democracia de alta intensidad: Apuntes para democratizar la democracia*. Cuaderno de Diálogo y Deliberación 5. La Paz: Corte Nacional Electoral.

Silverstein, Michael. 1998. "Contemporary Transformations of Local Linguistic Communities." *Annual Review of Anthropology* 27: 401–26.

Spedding P., Alison. 2003. "Movimientos campesinos en Bolivia: Una mirada a la producción intelectual de los últimos cinco años (1998–2002)." *Fe y pueblo*: 96–121.

Spivak, Gayatri. 1990. *The Post-Colonial Critic: Interviews, Strategies, Dialogues*, New York: Routledge

Tapia, Luis. 2001. "Subsuelo político." In *Pluriverso: Teoría Política Boliviana*, ed. A. García Linera, R. Gutiérrez, R. Prada, and L. Tapia, 111–46. La Paz: Muela del Diablo.

Taylor, Charles. 1992. *Multiculturalism and the "Politics of Recognition." An Essay by Charles Taylor with commentary by Amy Gutmann (editor), Steven C.Rockefeller, Michael Walzer, and Susan Wolf*. Princeton: University of Princeton Press.

Ticona A., Esteban. 2000. *Organización y liderazgo aymara: 1979–1996*. La Paz: Universidad de la Cordillera y AGRUCO.

———. 2003. "Pueblos indígenas y Estado boliviano: La larga historia de conflictos." *Revista gazeta de antropología* 19: Texto 19–10. http://www.ugr.es/~pwlac/G19_10Esteban_Ticona_Alejo.html.

Young, Iris Marion. 1999. *Justice and the Politics of Difference*. Princeton: University of Princeton Press.

Zavaleta, René. 1974. *El poder dual en América Latina: Estudio de los casos de Bolivia y Chile*. Mexico City: Editorial Siglo XXI.

3

Signifying Subalterns

7

Savage Emergence

Toward a Decolonial Aymara Methodology
for Cultural Survival

MARCIA STEPHENSON

In November 2003, following the terrible violence that took place in Bolivia, the *Latin American Weekly Report* published a headline article with the title "Is 'Indigenous Fundamentalism' the New Hemispheric Threat?"[1] This piece referenced an earlier article by Andrés Oppenheimer that was posted on the Internet on November 6, 2003, in which Oppenheimer expressed the following concerns: "The latest nightmare scenario in the Washington, D.C. quarters that follow Latin American affairs: Last month's bloody Indian-led uprising that toppled a constitutional government in Bolivia will spread to the vast indigenous populations of Peru, Ecuador, Guatemala, and southern Mexico. Are we witnessing the start of a region-wide uprising by leftist Indian groups?" (Oppenheimer 2003, n.p.). Such articles appearing in the media call attention to one fallout from "9/11," which is that epithets such as "fundamentalist" and "terrorist" have been increasingly applied to *any* group that rejects the latest efforts on the part of the United States and transnational corporations to assert their hegemony in a region. Depicted as the "new fundamentalists" of Latin America, indigenous peoples and movements once again seem to constitute a threat coming from outside of the modern, civilized world. In his response to Oppenheimer's article, published in the Quito newspaper *Hoy*, Carlos Arcos Cabrera expressed his concern over the growing presence of "anti-Indian fundamentalism" while pointing to some of the contradictions in Oppenheimer's line of thought: "If democracy has allowed the emergence of powerful indigenous movements, . . . what should we do? Limit democratic participation, promote dictatorships, or eliminate Indians?" (cited in "Is 'Indigenous Fundamentalism' the New Hemispheric Threat?" 2003, 1).[2] Given the violent encounters that took place in Bolivia during 2002–4, it would appear that the answer to Arcos Cabrera's rhetorical question was provided. Indeed, in a document that circulated via the Internet during the crisis of October 2003, the Aymara journalist Marina Ari editorialized that far from being a *golpe de estado*, what the world was witnessing was a massacre of indigenous peoples: the government brought out and used bullets, artillery, tanks, and tear gas against an unarmed people who believed they had the right to express an opinion regarding the use of the country's natural resources. According to Ari, the problems went even deeper than the political events of the moment: "Detrás existe una reivindicación mayor, es que cese el proceso de exclusión y racismo contra indígenas y afrodescendientes en Bolivia. Esto merece un cambio muy profundo en las instituciones bolivianas. Y pensamos que es hora de darse ese cambio" (There exists an even greater vindication behind all this, and that is to put a stop to the the process of exclusion and racism against indigenous people and people of African descent in Bolivia. That requires a very profound change in Bolivian institutions, and we believe that the time for that change has come) (Ari 2003, n.p.).

The aftermath of 2003 reminds us how certain discourses that we thought were overworked, and perhaps even behind us and thus irrelevant, must be revisited because they keep coming back to us. The sustained use of terminology such as fundamentalist, extremist, criminal, primitive, or savage, among others, to characterize and thus repudiate indigenous movements is a prominent example of how ongoing colonialist discourses still today position indigenous peoples outside modern, nationalist projects.[3] In his book *Disrupting Savagism: Intersecting Chicana/o, Mexican Immigrant, and Native American Struggles for Self-Representation* (2001), Arturo Aldama raises the provocative issue of how to contest dominant histories, ethnographies, and narratives that relegate indigenous peoples and other marginalized groups to subordinate roles and to the reified status of savages, or that strive to eliminate them altogether (3). Aldama takes as the point of departure critical theories of subjectivity and the making of meaning to call attention to the politics of representation and the problems of voice and agency in colonial and neocolonial discourse. He asks, "How does one disrupt how one is spoken of by a dominant or hegemonic discourse? and, second, how does one translate one's subjectivity into narrative terrain guided by rules of language-play that emerge from culturally different epistemologies?" (24). Although Aldama is asking questions within a cultural and political context different from the one that this essay analyzes, the issues he raises are nonetheless equally relevant in a country such as Bolivia, where colonial discourses continue to interpellate and codify bodies according to a racialized identity continuum (cf. Alarcón 1990; Stephenson 1999; Rivera Cusicanqui 2003).

This chapter will examine efforts in Bolivia by writers and activists who deliberately invoked and reappropriated "savagery" as a means of disrupting dominant forms of representation that naturalize the continuing violence of colonial social relations. In particular, it focuses on two specific moments during the second half of the twentieth century when Aymara intellectuals asserted themselves in the public sphere as activist reading and writing subjects dedicated to articulating alternative histories and identities. Fausto Reinaga was one of the first to claim a space in the Bolivian public sphere as an Indian writer. His controversial books on Indian power published in the 1960s and 1970s shocked the lettered public and outraged many due to the confrontational nature of their style and content (Reinaga 1964, 1967, 1969, 1970, 1971). Many from the Bolivian intelligentsia considered his work to be a form of lettered savagery. They called particular attention to his insubordinate rejection of nationalist discourses promoting racial assimilation for the country's majority peoples and to his call for Indians to rise up and recreate the Tawantinsuyu nation. Undaunted by this criticism, Reinaga countered these attacks by deliberately writing from the standpoint of the "savage" who was poised to devour colonial institutions that continue to marginalize or exterminate Bolivia's indigenous peoples.

Among those who read Reinaga's works was a group of young, first-generation Aymara university students who, in 1983, formed the nongovernmental organization known as the Taller de Historia Oral Andina (THOA). During the 1980s and 1990s, THOA took Reinaga's project one step further when its members engaged in the struggle to reclaim native history, memory, and territory. One member of THOA described the organization's decolonial project as a form of savagery because its activist-intellectual work fundamentally challenged prevailing discourses of modernity and civilization by engaging in indigenous projects dedicated to cultural survival. The group defined savagery as a strategy of decolonization that consisted of reading dominant discourses such as history, archaeology, and colonial and republican law against the grain, from the standpoint of Indians, in order to recover native epistemological foundations and territorial boundaries as they were delineated in the colonial land titles.[4] The physical reclamation of land was not separate from this enterprise, and as a consequence, THOA considered that its work in the reconstitution of native communities was its most "savage" undertaking of all.

Indigenous Peoples, Writing Subjects, and the Lettered Public Sphere

In order to understand the significance of savagery when it is reclaimed as a methodology of intellectual decolonization in the works of Reinaga and THOA, it is necessary to consider briefly the close relationship between savagery, alphabetical writing, and the public sphere in a colonial context. It is now a commonplace to observe that writing has been one of colonialism's most important handmaidens. In his discussion of writing and the invention of America, Tristan Platt refers to "ethno-graphy" as "the colonial inscription of the oral other, founded in the act of trans-Atlantic encounter" (1992, 135). The Indian is reified as a savage through writing and so can claim neither authority nor authorship. Outlining the precepts of Renaissance historiography and their relevance for understanding colonial Spanish American writings in general, and, in particular, the significance of a figure such as the Inca Garcilaso de la Vega, José Rabasa has noted that "in principle, there is no place for an Indian author (i.e. one who writes from the standpoint of an Indian) within a colonial discourse that claims universality for its subjectivity and its history" (1995, 80). Rarer still, Rabasa continues, is "he or she who has aspired to become an Indian author" (81). In a country such as Bolivia, it is traditionally held that to be an Indian means *not* to write, and therefore the Indian is condemned to inhabit the shadowy space of prehistory, as either a museum curiosity or an inert ruin. Writing is key to modernity's teleological narrative of progress because it differentiates itself from the "magical world" of indigenous orality and tradition (de Certeau 1984, 134). In Ajay Skaria's words, "The savage is not only without writing, but *before* writing. . . . Speech and writing stand in for savagery and civilization; the defeat of the former is inevitable but passionately regretted" (1999, 52; emphasis added). Both de Certeau and Skaria suggest that western modernity's linear narrative of progress renders virtually impossible what Rabasa calls "plural-world dwelling" (cf. Rabasa's essay in this volume).

During the nineteenth century, writing continued to play a prominent role in the formation of Latin American national identities. In his important analysis of the discursive formation of the nation, Fernando Unzueta examines the ways in which the national community was imagined in a variety of printed forms, including periodicals, literary texts, and administrative publications written by intellectuals and bureaucrats. Liberalism, as the primary ideologeme subtending nationalist discourses, was projected through historical fiction or national romances that delimited the racial boundaries of the nation (Unzueta 1996, 19). Liberalism's savage Other, *la barbarie*, was composed of indigenous peoples and other subaltern groups whose very presence challenged the assumed coherence of the prevailing ideology (23).

Unzueta's investigation points to the deeply embedded spatial and temporal structures of lettered culture and the deliberate ways in which a political, social, and economic hegemony is inscribed. Historically, such a cultural and political hegemony has had clear implications for indigenous peoples who even today continue to be disenfranchised from the nation-state. Thus, for example, Indians who attempted to form schools and teach community members to read and write Spanish were criminalized for their activities. Recently published indigenous historiographies document the life stories of several Aymara teachers from the late nineteenth century and the early twentieth, who, almost without exception, were persecuted, jailed, or murdered. Both Humberto Mamani Capchiri and Tomás Huanca have noted how undertakings to teach Indians to read and write in Spanish were met with strong opposition from the large landholders and *mestizo-criollo* townspeople. Teachers and students alike were pursued by local authorities who threatened to savage them by cutting out their tongues, hands, and eyes (Mamani Capchiri 1992, 81; Huanca 1993, 42). Roberto González Echevarría's observations on the relationship between writing and punishment during the colonial period ironically still held true for early twentieth-century Bolivia: "Writing, like the whipping post, involved a relationship with a code of interdictions set up by the State; that is to say, the relationship was not merely legal but more specifically penal" (1998, 49–50).

During the first decades of the twentieth century, reformists began to view education as a vital instrument of the state, and as a more efficient way of incorporating the primitive other into the nation. According to Brooke Larson, "Confronted with an entrenched colonial heritage of ethnic division reinforced by a nineteenth century legacy of political *caudillismo*, liberal reformers seized pedagogic reform as the panacea of 'racial degeneration,' cultural fragmentation, political instability, and economic backwardness" (2000, 1). Larson argues that during the first decades of the twentieth century, rural school reform, organized around the predominant liberal-positivist doctrines of the times, "emerged from intense intra-class power struggles and broader disagreements over the content and boundaries of race, class, and nationhood" until liberal and conservative pedagogic ideals finally came together around a "tutelary project of racial separatism, manual labor-training, and moral uplift" (18). Education would be the means of incorporating indigenous peoples into the nation, it was argued, even as it kept them separate and distinct from the *criollo-mestizo* citizen-subjects. For indigenous peoples, however, pedagogic reform served alternate agendas. They supported the establishment of rural schools for pragmatic reasons, seeing them as a vehicle for learning to use and manipulate the *criollo* language and legal system for the purposes of protecting indigenous communities. Schools were a key component of a larger strategy indigenous leaders and communities developed to retain their territory from the encroachments of the *hacienda* system; similarly, education helped empower local and regional authorities to take a more visible stance in the national political arena of the time (19). The momentum that indigenous mobilization had been gaining during the 1910s and 1920s, however, was brought to a halt with the onset of the Chaco War in 1932. As René Arze Aguirre (1987) and Carlos Mamani Condori (1991) have shown, the war provided *hacendados* and *mestizo* townspeople with yet another opportunity to seize indigenous lands. Many indigenous leaders were forcibly recruited and sent off to the frontlines, from where few returned, while others were jailed on the pretext of being communist agitators.

Following the Revolution of 1952 and the revisions to the Bolivian Educational Code in 1955, which stated that primary education should be "universal, free and obligatory" (cited in *Ley de Reforma Educativa* 1996, 21–22), Indian children entered the school system in greater numbers than ever before, but as a result they were more systematically subjected to a pedagogy of assimilation (see also Salmón 1997; Luykx 1999; Stephenson 1999). The Aymara historian Carlos Mamani Condori argues that the 1950s and 1960s were marked by the clear indoctrination of indigenous children who had no alternative to the dominant pedagogy of the school, the barracks, and the labor unions (2000, 6). He has referred to this alienating process as one that emphasizes the "de-Indianization" of Bolivia's majority peoples (2001, 50). In other words, learning to read and write in Spanish was understood to be the most expedient method of transforming the savage Indian into an acculturated, *mestizo* citizen-subject so that she or he could be brought into the space of the nation. This process is clearly illustrated in a case history much acclaimed by the educator Elssa Paredes de Salazar.[5] Paredes de Salazar tells the story of a man who, during his student years, officially "progressed" through three different racial categories. When he first migrated to La Paz as a child, he enrolled in a school that registered him as an Indian because of his perceived unkempt appearance and the clothing that he wore. After years of struggle and perseverance, he obtained his high school diploma, which listed him as a "*mestizo.*" Later on, when he finished a university degree in engineering, his documents described him as being of the "white race" (1976, 31). This illustration clearly reflects the prevailing faith in education's transformative powers. As Guillermo Mariaca Iturri so insightfully observes, "[Es] como si la alfabetización fuese la nueva extirpadora de idolatrías" ([it's] as if literacy had become the new eradicator of idolatry) (11). Mariaca's trope suggests that modernity's pedagogical project positions indigenous peoples in much the same way as did the campaigns of extirpation during the colonial period. Marked as "heretics" or "savages," indigenous peoples are defined in opposition to orthodoxy, civilization, and modernity, and, as such, they constitute a heresy that must be uprooted or extirpated with literacy (cf. White 1978, 151).

This was the predominant state of affairs until the work of Fausto Reinaga (1906–94) erupted onto the public sphere. Heralded as one of the most influential and controversial theorists of *indianista* discourse, Reinaga, with his unprecedented writings, delineated a theory of social revolution rooted in the historical and material circumstances of the Andes.[6] To place Reinaga's work in context, it was only in 1969 with the publication of his startling, incendiary book *La revolución india* that Aymara school teachers, first-generation Aymara university students, and young people found a text that articulated *and* affirmed a contestatory indigenous identity. Carlos Mamani Condori notes that indigenous university students, who constantly confronted discrimination in the classroom and hallways, desperately searched for information that would explain the causes of the prevailing logic of hierarchized identities (2000). Reinaga's books and works by other authors, such as Frantz Fanon's *The Wretched of the Earth*, that underscored native resistance to colonialism, fostered the development of the first nuclei of activist Aymara students during the late 1960s and early 1970s (Mamani Condori 2000, 6; 1998, 44).

Although Reinaga's work from these years is not without contradictions and tensions, it is important for the way it foregrounds alternative epistemologies in the public sphere. In his numerous books, Reinaga strategically positioned himself in relation to the dominant public sphere as an "Indian writer." Because of his outspoken style and the public nature of his critique, Reinaga was arrested several times, and on at least one occasion his library was confiscated by the police. Reinaga underscored the risks entailed in such an unprecedented writerly stance in the first pages of his book *La "intelligentsia" del cholaje boliviano* (1967). Reinaga opened the work with a copy of the letter that he wrote to U Thant, then the secretary general to the United Nations, requesting protection from the persecution and abuse he had received due to an earlier publication, *El indio y el cholaje boliviano* (1964).[7] In this publication, Reinaga fiercely, some would say savagely, critiqued one of Bolivia's leading intellectuals, Fernando Diez de Medina. According to Reinaga's niece and longtime assistant, Hilda Reinaga, Diez de Medina was so incensed by the book that he went around to La Paz's bookstores, buying all available copies in order to burn them, and in this way disposing of approximately one half of the books that had been printed.[8] In his letter to the secretary general, Reinaga protested that the state and the elite literati were attempting to eliminate him. There had been threats on his life, his books had been condemned by a conspiracy of silence, and his critics had damned him to hell: "Si no es la conflagración del silencio, es el puntapié del oligarca cerril o del 'comunista' irresponsable y bastardo que ha caído sobre las páginas de mis libros o sobre mis espaldas de indio. Es que en Bolivia nadie admite que un indio escriba . . ." (If it is not the conflagration of silence, it is the kick of the boorish oligarch or the irresponsible bastard 'communist' that has fallen on my Indian back or the pages of my book. In Bolivia no one admits that an Indian might be a writer) (1967, 8). Loudly and forcefully declaring himself to be an "Indian writer," Reinaga refused to be silenced and thus he gave voice to that aspect of Bolivia that had been excluded or repressed from the lettered public sphere.[9]

Reinaga's many publications indicate that for him language was a critical site of struggle. His "savagery" was expressed through the unharnessed rage that permeated his writings. According to Jean-Louis Hebert, Reinaga was a volcano in a state of permanent eruption (cited in Bonfil Batalla 1981, 58). From the standpoint of the Indian writer, of the savage, he continually engaged the dominant public sphere, disrupting it with "howls" through the repetition of verbs such as "rugir," screams with the strategic use of capitalization and exclamation points, and the use of harsh neologisms. Humberto Mata, Reinaga's biographer, described Reinaga's "puterías verbales," his "'tremendas' palabras, putigrafías y putilogías derivadas del cervantino vocablo . . ." (verbal grossness, "tremendous" words, whoriographics, and whoriology derived from Cervantine punning) (Mata 1968, 44). Mata claimed that Reinaga's violent language games were designed to drive home his right to use any word he wanted from the dictionary, "good or bad," and that he had the linguistic skills to talk back to the oligarchy, turning Spanish grammar on its head "conforme a las necesidades de indio hablando en jerga de mestizos, de sangre y alma cruzadas de vileza" (in accordance with the needs of an Indian talking the jargon of the *mestizos*, and whose blood and soul were cut across by vileness) (43). The work of bell hooks enables us to see that Reinaga spoke to the oppressor and to the oppressed in the same language (1989, 28–29). He addressed the oppressor by demanding a place in the dominant public sphere, and the oppressed by aggressively reclaiming an Indian identity.

For Reinaga, race was essential to the understanding of Bolivia. He rejected the ploy on the part of the dominant political party, the Movimiento Nacionalista Revolucionario, to assimilate indigenous peoples into *criollo-mestizo* culture through the substitution of the word "campesino" for "Indian." Taking his cue from the black power movement in the United States, he wrote: "Sería una aberración que los negros no quisieren llamarse negros, sino campesinos" (It would be an aberration for blacks to not want to call themselves blacks and instead call themselves peasants) (1969, 136). Reinaga argued that, in fact, "whites" in Bolivia, and in that category he included *mestizos* and those who "act white," are terrified of Indians self-identifying as Indians: "Los blancos . . . tienen hoy pavor y terror de llamar indio al indio. Diciéndoles 'hermano campesino' quieren y creen borrar de la memoria del indio lo que han hecho en cuatro siglos con el indio. . . . Pretenden presentar bajo el nombre 'campesino' a otro ser, no al indio" (Whites today are terrified and afraid of calling Indians Indians. By addressing them as "brother peasant" they want and believe that they are erasing from the memory of the Indian what they have done to him for four hundred years. . . . Using the word "peasant" they try to present another person, not the Indian (137). Reinaga embraced the name "Indian" precisely because this was the term that had been used to justify the oppression and extermination of indigenous peoples from the conquest to the present.[10]

For Reinaga, the indigenous struggle for power and knowledge must necessarily be tied to the recuperation of native historical memory and an Aymara genealogy. In both *La revolución india* (1969) and *Tesis india* (1971), he includes lengthy discussions that recover an oppositional indigenous history based primarily on resistance to colonial domination. For example, Reinaga was one of the first to call attention to the continued relevance of Aymara leaders such as Tupak Katari, Bartolina Sisa (eighteenth century) and Zárate Willka (nineteenth century), and to significant confrontations between indigenous peoples and *criollos* over land such as the uprising and massacre of Indians at Jesús de Machaca (twentieth century). He thus reclaims indigenous historical knowledge as a radical site of resistance where indigenous peoples can affirm and sustain their subjectivity. This knowledge will empower indigenous peoples and unleash a heretofore unknown force, one more dangerous than that of nuclear power: "la fuerza del odio y del hambre. Hambre y odio de cuatro siglos" (the force of hatred and hunger. Four hundred years of hunger and hatred) (1970, 12). The hatred and hunger are so great that when Indians rise up they devour their white-*mestizo* enemies (1971, 48).

Reinaga clearly gained agency and authority through his writing. In many of his books, he revisited elements of his personal history and genealogy, claiming that his mother's family could be traced directly back to Tupak Katari. Norma Klahn has persuasively argued that "life writing" enables marginalized peoples to claim authority and thus incorporate themselves as agents into a history that has locked them out, as well as their culture and their language: "Life writing is a tie to the past in relation to a contested present, and the ways authors situate themselves in historical and political terms becomes critical" (Klahn 2003, 118). By asserting a family bloodline that extended directly back to Tupak Katari, Reinaga was able to create an unprecedented space in the public sphere for the creation of an indigenous identity and imaginary (cf. Klahn 2003, 114). This personal genealogy had wider implications: it enabled him to imagine an alternative Indian nation.

In his writings, Reinaga called for the formation of an Indian nation based on the image and spirit of Tawantinsuyu, the Incan empire. For Reinaga, this discursive return to an alternative symbolic order was encapsulated in the visually striking square-shaped emblem made up of a rainbow-colored checkerboard pattern known as the *wiphala*. According to Reinaga, the *wiphala* and the *pututu* were signs of the emergence of a revolutionary indigenous subject: "¡INDIOS DE BOLIVIA!, la Wiphala y el Pututu, desde la cumbre del Illimani nos llaman a la lucha. Nos notifican que ha llegado la hora de nuestra LIBERACION. La Wiphala y el Pututu, la bandera y el clarín de los Inkas, de Tupaj Amaru y Tupaj Katari, de Micaela Bastidas y Bartolina Sisa, de Pablo Atusparia y Zárate Willka, nos premian imperativamente a la Revolución!" (INDIANS OF BOLIVIA, the Wiphala and the Pututu call to us from the top of the Illimani to come together in struggle. They tell us that our hour of LIBERATION has come. The Wiphala and the Pututu, banner and trumpet of the Inkas, of Tupaj Amaru and Tupaj Katari, of Micaela Bastidas and Bartolina Sisa, of Pablo Atusparia and Zárate Willka, are urging us on imperatively to Revolution) (1969, 447). For Reinaga, the *wiphala* served as a nationalist symbol that reclaimed a denigrated indigenous heritage, incited a political consciousness, and moved people to revolutionary action.[11] Thus its power to bring together peoples who were savaged by the violence of colonialism: "El español sembró de cabezas todo el territorio de América . . . en una palabra, a lo largo de todo el Continente, esto es, de Cuzco a La Paz y de La Paz a Chuquisaca se sembró de postes con cabezas de indios decapitados" (The Spaniard sowed heads over the entire territory of America . . . in a word, throughout the continent, that is, from Cuzco to La Paz and from La Paz to Chuquisaca they planted stakes with the heads of decapitated Indians) (1969, 266). Reinaga's evocation of the *wiphala* rather than the Bolivian national flag emphasized an Indian nationalism that demands the right to territorial, political, and cultural self-determination.

Reinaga's writings were some of the first to bring this insurgent history into the public sphere. In a discussion following a presentation I gave on Reinaga at the University of El Alto in 2001, Pablo Mamani suggested that Reinaga was seen to be a threat because prior to his publications predominant discourses positioned the Aymara Indian first and foremost as a Bolivian. Reinaga challenged this idea with his writings, and as a result he also questioned the prevailing notion of "Bolivianidad." In this way, Reinaga's work simultaneously reveals how colonialism works both implicitly and explicitly to eradicate any and all manifestations of indigenous identity, and it documents the painful battle to affirm indigenous subjectivity. It is an urgent project, one that is succinctly expressed in his emblematic phrase: "La Revolución India es Ser o no Ser" (The Indian revolution is about being or nonbeing) (1970, 77). Borrowing from the Chicana cultural critic Laura Pérez, I argue that Reinaga's writings have been deemed outrageous and extremist precisely because they "embody that which is meant to be disembodied within the dominant symbolic" (Pérez 1999, 19). For this reason, the process of decolonization requires the retrieval of Reinaga because his works provide a critical vocabulary and an epistemological framework with which to assess the violence of colonial domination in a country such as Bolivia.[12]

Reinaga's numerous publications resonated in the official public sphere and alarmed lettered elites from both sides of the political spectrum. Guillermo Lora, for example, described Reinaga as a "bellaco" (scoundrel) who, "pese a su inconducta—o acaso por esto mismo—ha planteado posiciones extremas" (in spite of his bad conduct—or perhaps because of it—has put forward extreme positions) (1987, 449). Some disparaged Reinaga by labeling him a racist because of his passionately expressed anti-white sentiments. Still others tried to discredit him by denying that he was really an Indian. The implication here clearly was that someone such as Reinaga, who was a lawyer, philosopher, and writer, simply could not also be an Indian.

With respect to the marginalization of indigenous intellectuals from this period, Guillermo Bonfil Batalla notes that

> la indianidad como conciencia militante cuya asunción conduce a la liberación del indio, aparece ante los sectores no indios de las sociedades nacionales, al menos en un primer momento, como discurso de intelectuales marginales cuya filiación india es dudosa, y de indios de origen pero con educación escolar y experiencia urbana que permite negar que sean ahora "verdaderos" indios. En otras palabras: el discurso de la indianidad se descalifica, con dispensa de trámite, por considerarlo ilegítimo de origen (Indianness as a militant consciousness whose assumption leads to Indian liberation appears to the non-Indian sectors of national societies, at least initially, as a discourse of marginal intellectuals whose Indian affiliation is doubtful, and as people who are of Indian origin but with urban schooling and experiences that allow for a denial of their "real" Indianness. In other words, the discourse of Indianness is disqualified out of hand because its origin is considered invalid). (1991, 76)

The question of legitimacy that Bonfil Batalla evokes here raises again the problem that, by definition, the Indian subject who writes either engages in an illegitimate act or else is not "truly" Indian. The combative, "savage" style in which Reinaga wrote provoked angry responses among the Bolivian intelligentsia, and members of the left and right attempted to silence the pen of "el manco del espanto" (the one-handed fright), as some called him.

Toward a Decolonial Methodology Called Savagery

Reinaga's work resonated throughout Latin America in the years following the publication of *Revolución india* and *Tesis india* due to its contestatory project that vociferously reclaimed the word "indio" and called for the recuperation of native history. In Bolivia, the subsequent generation of young Aymara activists and intellectuals drew from Reinaga's "savagism," valorizing his work as a spirited inspiration for making new kinds of connections that had otherwise been suppressed by colonialism. Now, what was most important was to formulate clearly articulated linkages between identity and memory and the material and symbolic space of the native *ayllu* community. In this second phase of rememorative work, savagism described a decolonial methodology that recovered indigenous agency through the reconstitution of native territory and traditional forms of authority.[13]

The figure whose seminal publications initiated this process linking memory and culture to the territory of the native Andean community was the Aymara historian Roberto Choque Canqui. Carlos Mamani Condori describes Choque Canqui's historiographic project as one that took as its point of departure "la duda respecto a una narrativa [histórica predominante], desde todo punto de vista extraña, incluso a nuestra fisonomía" (doubts regarding a mainstream historical narrative which was bizarre in all aspects, including our physiognomy) (2002, 4; cf. "Roberto Choque Canqui" 2002). Choque Canqui's internationally acclaimed publications constituted some of the first indigenous scholarship to argue that coming to know the past is key to a historiography committed to the decolonization of Andean spaces and identities.

The theoretical underpinnings of this decolonial historiographic project were elaborated during the late 1980s and 1990s in the work of the Aymara nongovernmental organization known as the Taller de Historia Oral Andina (THOA).[14] As a collective, THOA charted spaces that moved between written and oral memory as the members engaged in "savage" readings of archaeological, legal, and historical discourses from an Aymara standpoint. The Aymara historian Carlos Mamani Condori, a former member and director of THOA, explains how THOA's research interrogated nationalist discourses at the same time that it provided an alternative analytical method. This methodology recovered and revalorized indigenous oral history, passed down by community elders, and traditional ritual practices, many of which are enacted by women. He proposes that one way to understand this unorthodox methodology is as a form of savagery because savagery means recovery of that which was oppressed and denied by colonialism in the name of civilization and modernity (1992).[15] In this paradigm, "savagery" signifies the freedom to be agents of history, whereas "civilization" represents the submission of indigenous peoples through colonialism (1992, 10).

Crucial to this methodology is an important Aymara episteme expressed as "*qhip nayra*" or "past/present," and the phrase "Looking back [to the past] we will move forward [into the future]" was one that guided many of the group's endeavors. The theoretical implications of this episteme were developed in THOA's collective and individual projects, as well as by other Aymara activist-intellectuals in nongovernmental organizations such as the Centro Andino de Desarrollo Agropecuario (CADA) and the Centro de Desarrollo Integral de la Mujer Aymara (CDIMA), and more recently by independent scholars and new centers such as the Centro de Estudios Multidisciplinarios Aymara (CEM-Aymara).

A second, interrelated term for this decolonial methodology is *amuyiri* or "thinker," which, Mamani Condori explains, alludes to the action of thinking in one's own tradition in the space of the community (2000, 4). Memory is conveyed through the word "*amta*," which also means idea, a new plan; "*amtaña*" is the act of remembering the past: "Los ayllus a la cabeza de sus autoridades rememoran el pasado, valoran su tradición y guían su actuar de acuerdo a los referentes históricos, el pasado es futuro, *qhip nayra*" (The *ayllus* lead their [elected] authorities in commemorating the past and valuing tradition, while guiding their actions in accordance with historical accounts. The past is thus the future, *qhip nayra*) (Mamani Condori 2001, 48–49). Marcelo Fernández similarly defines *amuyu* as "pensamiento, darse cuenta de a paso" (knowledge and understanding acquired along the way) and *amuyt'aña* as "reflexionar y planear concertadamente" (reflection and planning in harmony) (2000, xxviii). Fernández expresses the relationship between *amuyu* and *qhip nayra* in the following manner: "Es decir que en el movimiento pendular entre el *qhip nayra* y el *amuyu* pudimos entender la simultaneidad del pasado y el presente, más allá de ver o constatar la simple yuxtaposición de datos o la notación de persistencias históricas" (In other words, through the pendular movement between *quip nayra* and *amuyu* we understood the simultaneity of past and present as something more than the mere juxtaposition of facts or the notation of historical continuities) (xxviii). Thinker, memory, idea, new plan, all converge in the territorial space of the *ayllu*, which is governed by its traditional authorities.

THOA's project of reconstituting native memory and territory contrasts starkly with civilizing narratives that have at their very core the erasure of indigenous identity. In a recent essay analyzing the fraught relationship of writing, history, and memory in the Andean region Mamani Condori asks:

> ¿Cuál es el peso de un pasado del que no se guarda memoria? Expresado de otro modo, ¿qué peso puede tener la memoria oral indígena frente a la memoria escrita? En un país como Bolivia, donde las relaciones coloniales se mantienen intactas, la memoria escrita autoidentificada ella misma como "historia" ha tenido un peso opresivo, cual es el de legitimar una realidad, un órden eminentemente colonial como normal, e incluso como nacional. Esta historia, a diferencia de su definición filosófica como sinónimo de libertad en un proceso continuo de cambios, es en verdad una narrativa perversa, cuyos objetivos son: el olvido de la identidad, los derechos y la libertad por los

pueblos indios (What is the weight of a past of which we conserve no memory? Put another way, what weight can indigenous oral memory have in the face of written memory? In a country like Bolivia, where colonial relations still obtain, written memory, which identifies itself as "history," has had an oppressive weight, which is that of legitimizing a reality, an eminently colonial order, as normal, and even as national. This history, unlike its philosophical definition as synonymous with freedom in a continuous process of change, is really a perverse narrative whose objectives are: the forgetting of Indian identity, rights, and freedom). (2002, 3)

In this passage, Mamani Condori reads terms such as writing, history, and memory against the grain, or "savagely," when he points out that prevailing historical (written) accounts of the nation are, quite literally, perverse because they turn away from a more inclusive, liberatory historiographic project; instead, they are complicit with nationalist discourses that promote the loss of identity, rights, and agency for indigenous peoples.[16]

Following Mamani Condori's argument, it is possible to read Alcides Arguedas's novel *Wuata Wuara* (1904) as a "nonsavage" or "civilizing" rendition of a nation-making narrative. The novel plots the loss of native identity when it equates the pervasive sense of death associated with archaeological ruins and the imminent demise of the nation's indigenous peoples. Arguedas's character, the poet Darío Fuenteclara functions as a spokesperson for this nonsavage version of national history when he makes this connection while nostalgically contemplating Aymara ruins: "Todo lo que ha sido y hoy no es, me causa una impresión honda. Parece que cerca de las ruinas, se respirara constantemente una atmósfera de muerte. No hay cosa más triste que contemplar una ruina" (All that has been in the past and now is no longer affects me deeply. It seems that close to the ruins one constantly inhales this atmosphere of death. There is nothing more sad than contemplating a ruin) (Arguedas 1988, 383). According to Edmundo Paz Soldán, Arguedas's depiction of ruins in the novel does not evoke a romantic archetype; instead, the image associates the Aymara with the idea of racial decadence, a decadence so extreme that their present condition appears to have lost all connection with the past (Paz Soldán 2003, 53). Key to this portrayal is the loss of memory or history through tropes of rupture, ruin, and degeneration. Again, Arguedas's character Fuenteclara continues:

Cuando yo vengo a contemplar estas ruinas que elocuentemente atestiguan del paso de la raza aymara, desecho de la idea de que alguna vez pudo haber existido, pues se me hace duro pensar que fue ella quien levantó tan soberbia edificación, y antes, por el contrario, me inclino a creer en la posibilidad de la existencia de dioses mitológicos. Una raza que por muchos siglos se ha impuesto, que ha sido inteligente y activa, no degenera hasta el extremo de perder su personalidad (Whenever I contemplate these ruins which eloquently evoke the past of the Aymara race, I reject the idea that it [these people] ever existed, because it is hard for me to think that they were the ones who built such magnificent structures. On the contrary, I'm inclined to believe in the possibility of mythological gods. A race that for centuries has been so imposing, intelligent, and active does not degenerate to the point of losing its personality). (Arguedas 1988, 383)

Loss of history and memory is created in two ways in these passages. Most obviously, Fuenteclara reflects directly on the seeming improbability that the "degenerated" indigenous people around him could have created such splendor. Also, however, in these passages the ruins are depicted in increasingly abstract terms, thereby progressively distancing them from the idea of a space that is lived and embodied. *Wuata Wuara* suggests that the racially degenerated condition of the indigenous population inhibits national regeneration and so the novel advocates for the elimination of otherness by means of racial assimilation and homogenization (Paz Soldán 2003, 55).[17]

In his essay "Historia y prehistoria: ¿Dónde nos encontramos los indios?" Mamani Condori argues that in Bolivia archaeological discourses have also been implicated in the exclusion and oppression of indigenous peoples. For example, mainstream archaeological studies use sites such as Tiwanaku as an important source of legitimation for the modern Bolivian nation. In this textbook version, Indians are external to history, figuring only as dead relics of a remote prehistorical past (1992, 1). Mamani Condori contends that the ties between archaeological discourse and the nation-state of 1952 were methodically articulated in the work of revolutionary ideologues such as the noted archaeologist Carlos Ponce Sanjinés and the two Portugals, Maks Emilio and Max (father and son). These men were pioneers insofar as they were the first to systematize the national study of archaeology. For them, important sites such as Tiwanaku were essential to providing the new nation with cultural roots dating back to before the arrival of the Spanish (Mamani Condori 1992, 2). In order to consolidate the idea of Bolivia as a modern nation, however, these archaeologists also emphasized in their publications a sense of loss or discontinuity between the past and the present. Mamani

Condori argues that they conducted an assault on native memory by using a number of rhetorical strategies in their writings. The first was to arbitrarily rename many of the sites, as if scientists had "discovered" them, thereby ignoring a long native tradition associated with these places, many of which were considered to be sacred. Second, when these sites were described, they were linked metaphorically to age-old ruins found in Europe and Asia. Thus the Portugals described Tiwanaku in the following manner: "Allí están la fortaleza de Nínive, los innegables muros de Babilonia, vencida por Ciro, rey del mundo; los célebres palacios de Percépolis y los fabulosos templos de Balbeck y Jerusalém" (One finds there the fortress of Niniveh, the undeniable walls of Babylon, conquered by Ciro, king of the world; the famous palaces of Percepolis and the fabulous temples of Balbeck and Jerusalem) (cited in Mamani Condori 1992, 3). By equating places such as Tiwanaku with Babylon, archaeologists implied that the nation's cultural roots were elsewhere after all, thereby eliding Tiwanaku's historical, geographic, and economic ties to the area and to other indigenous nations extending as far as the coast of the South American continent (2–3).

Mamani Condori recounts Aymara counternarratives to this normative view of history to show how alternative understandings of these places survive alongside hegemonic images. He argues that these ruins are key to a transformative, decolonial Andean historiography, and he calls our attention to these spaces as performative; in Mary Pat Brady's words he shifts "the grammar of the land from passive noun (object) to active verb (doing)" (Brady 2002, 5). For the Aymara, sites such as Tiwanaku function as a kind of bridge between the colonial present and the precolonial past. These ruins are *monumenta*, providing evidence of the past, thereby representing "an unbroken link with the past, a part of the past that is still available for direct, personal inspection" (Miles 1995, 17). For the Aymara, the ruins suture the past to the present, and so they are a dwelling place for memory, an archive. This view of space is one that is active and productive rather than "inert and transparent."[18]

Mamani Condori explains that because the Aymara have been condemned to inhabit "prehistory," they have access to their past only in clandestine, nocturnal ritual forms. The knowledge of this past comes through oral tradition passed down from generation to generation, and to the myths or narratives that provide explanatory power (1992, 7–8). Thus, Mamani Condori continues, the liberation movements of the Aymara center on the notion of a return to the past, *qhip nayra*, and the affirmation of a "savagery" that has been liberated from colonial oppression (12). He emphasizes that "return" in this context does not mean the romantic retrieval of a utopian past; instead, the past provides clues as to how indigenous peoples have managed to survive more than five hundred years of colonialism: "Si hemos de hablar de una filosofía aymara de la historia, no tenemos entonces una visión de progreso y avance como simple hecho de 'quemar etapas' y avanzar. El pasado no es inerte, no está muerto y no se lo deja atrás. Es a partir precisamente de ese pasado que se puede alimentar la esperanza de un futuro libre, para que el pasado pueda ser regenerado en el futuro" (If we were to speak of an Aymara philosophy of history, it would not be a vision of progress and advancement as mere forward movement through successive phases. The past is not inert, nor is it dead, and one does not leave it behind. It is precisely on the basis of this past that the hope for a liberated future is nourished, so that the past can be regenerated in the future) (14–15). The past thus provides a model for the future and the hope that the present circumstances of disenfranchisement and oppression can be reversed.

This interpretative framework was fundamental to THOA's historiographic enterprise, which centered on the investigation of the mobilization of the *caciques-apoderados* during the late nineteenth century and the early twentieth. These leaders and the movements they represented were dedicated to the struggle to retain communal territories in the face of increasingly violent incursions by large landholders or *hacendados*. The *caciques-apoderados* were Aymara authorities who went in search of their communities' land titles that had been purchased from the Spanish crown during colonial rule. One of the most renowned of the *caciques*, Santos Marka T'ula, was known as the *jacha t'ula* or "líder caminante" (walking leader), because he walked to archives located in Bolivia, Peru, and Argentina to find titles for communities throughout the altiplano region. Read "savagely," these documents functioned as important symbols of native identity because they could be used to recover the territorial boundaries of communities as they had been surveyed and paid for during the colonial period.[19] They also traced the bloodlines of regional *caciques*. For example, Santos Marka T'ula only recovered his last name when he read the colonial titles (Taller de Historia Oral Andina 1988, 19). It is not surprising to learn, therefore, that most of these men were perceived to be agitators and rebels, and so many were jailed or killed for their endeavors. Silvia Rivera Cusicanqui explains that in the case of one *cacique* who was arrested in 1918, accused of going around "stirring up the Indians," authorities seized various "subversive" documents, including copies of ordinances by Viceroy Toledo, deeds from the sixteenth and seventeenth centuries, cases regarding boundary disputes, and copies of republican decrees and laws that recognized communally held property and the authority of the *cacique*. All of these documents were incorporated into the case brought against the men who had been arrested (2003, 84).

Through archival research and oral interviews with community elders from *ayllus* located in the Ingavi Province, THOA learned of another compelling example of the "savage" use of colonial documents: that of the Aymara educator Eduardo L. Nina Qhispi, a contemporary of Santos Marka T'ula. In his study of the life and thought of the influential leader, Mamani Condori tells how Nina Qhispi wrote to President Salamanca in 1931, on the eve of the Chaco War, requesting that the president conduct a boundary survey of indigenous lands based on the colonial titles. This new land survey was legitimate, Nina Qhispi argued, because the titles had been rightfully paid for with gold and labor. This survey would provide evidence, moreover, that most of the indigenous communities' lands were currently held illegally in the possession of *hacendados*. On the basis of this argument, Nina Qhispi would ultimately go so far as to call for the official recognition of an autonomous Indian republic. Indeed, his request was sent to the president on letterhead stationary that read Sociedad República del Qullasuyu (Mamani Condori 1991, 145). Mamani Condori argues that Nina Qhispi was deliberate in bringing up the question of the colonial land titles just as the Chaco War loomed on the national horizon because the Bolivian claim to the Chaco land rested precisely on the same kinds of colonial documentation, some of which dated back to the sixteenth century (145–46). Headed by Humberto Vásquez Machicado, a Bolivian high commission traveled to Seville to consult the archives for the documents that would support the Bolivian stance. What further proof was necessary, then, to show that indigenous territory had similarly been under assault:

> ¿No era acaso su situación de república invadida, idéntica a la de la república boliviana, cuyos territorios heredados de las jurisdicciones de la Charcas colonial habían sido, y continuaban siendo arrebatados por la fuerza de las armas, violando jurisdicciones reconocidas y derechos de posesión centenarios? Porque, al igual que los comunarios indios despojados, Bolivia tampoco perdió la esperanza de recuperar sus territorios usurpados, ni renunció al justo título (colonial) que tenía sobre ellos" (Was not its situation as an invaded republic similar to that of Bolivia, whose territory, inherited from the juristidiction of colonial Charcas, was still being stolen by force of arms, in violation of its [internationally] recognized boundaries and centuries-old

rights of ownership? Because, just like the dispossessed peoples, Bolivia did not lose hope of recuperating its usurped territories nor did it
renounce the legitimate colonial title that it held over them). (146)

Nina Qhispi's "savage" audacity was eventually rewarded with a lengthy jail
sentence, and he died due to poor health shortly after his release in 1936.

Commenting on the historical significance of indigenous mobilization
during the first decades of the twentieth century, Rivera Cusicanqui observes
how the search for colonial documents broadened the horizon of collective
memory, legitimizing the communities' legal and violent actions at the same
time it provided an ethical sense of justice to the indigenous struggle: "Los
elementos de un pasado remoto, que yacían en papeles antiguos y se repro-
ducían a través de la tradición oral, de los mitos y cuentos populares, fueron
así puestos al servicio de una serie de demandas concretas de reforma social
propuestas por los rebeldes a la cerrada sociedad oligárquica que les negaba
el derecho a la existencia" (The elements of a remote past, which lay in old
papers and were reproduced through oral tradition, through popular myths
and folktales, were thus placed at the service of concrete demands of social
reform proposed by the rebels against the closed oligarchic society that denied them the right to exist) (2003, 86). Carlos Mamani Condori punctuates
Rivera's analysis when he observes how in this turn-of-the-century struggle
for territory and self-determination, the past and the present came together,
allowing the Aymara, albeit briefly, to reclaim their subjectivity as they attempted to reorder the course of history (1992, 10).[20]

The research by THOA on the movement of the *caciques-apoderados* is
exemplary for many reasons. It stands out not just because the group un-
covered information on an activist network of people that had been ignored
or suppressed by the predominant historical accounts, but also because it
brought to light important continuities between the struggles of the *caciques-apoderados* and THOA's own historiographic and activist projects that
were committed to the decolonization and safeguarding of Andean spaces
and identities. This work clearly suggests, moreover, that the colonial and
neocolonial nationalist projects in Bolivia were and are incomplete because
precolonial memory was never fully subjugated. By reading the present day
circumstances through the past, in oral and written sources of all different kinds, the *caciques-apoderados*, THOA, and other Aymara intellectuals
have attempted to shift the national debate from one emphasizing the question of ontology and all that that implies (racial hierarchies and positivist
discourses of racial degeneration and savagery), to one emphasizing the

question of territorial rights and alternative epistemologies and practices (cf. Brady 2002, 151). Aymara intellectuals argue that only by looking to the past and reclaiming and revitalizing "savage" histories and ways of knowing as they are expressed in the territory of the community will indigenous peoples be able to move beyond the dehumanizing circumstances of the colonial present. The fact that indigenous mobilization has been increasingly demonized in the public sphere only underscores the urgency of this decolonial work.

Notes

1. See *Bolivian Studies Journal/Revista E* 4.1 (February 2004), which is entirely devoted to analysis the events of 2003. I would like to thank Nancy Peterson, Aparajita Sagar, Estelle Tarica, and an anonymous reader for the press for their helpful comments on earlier drafts of this essay.

2. My thanks to Marc Becker for helping me locate this information.

3. For example, see Forrest Hylton's analysis of how dominant discourses made use of terms such as "criminal" and "communist" to depict indigenous rebels of Chayanta in 1927 (Hylton 2003).

4. Linda Tuhiwai Smith has similarly defined decolonization as a "recovery of our language and epistemological foundations. It is also about reconciling and reprioritizing what is really important about the past with what is important about the present. These issues raise significant questions for indigenous communities who are not only beginning to fight back against the invasion of their communities by academic, corporate and populist researchers, but to think about, and carry out research, on their own concerns" (1999, 39).

5. Although I have recounted this anecdote elsewhere (Stephenson 1999), its repetition here is useful.

6. Guillermo Bonfil Batalla argues that Reinaga was the intellectual to have the greatest impact on contemporary *indianista* thought throughout Latin America, and his work was the most radical of Indian ideology: "La influencia de su pensamiento y de su acción (es fundador del Partido Indio de Bolivia) es reconocida por las más importantes organizaciones indias, particularmente en la región andina" (The influence of his thought and of his action [he is the founder of the Indian Party of Bolivia)] is recognized by the most important Indian organizations, particularly in the region of the Andes) (1981, 58).

7. I gratefully acknowledge Estelle Tarica, who called my attention to this letter. I would also like to thank Charles Arnade, who generously provided me with copies of some of his personal correspondence with Reinaga.

8. From then on, Hilda Reinaga explained, Fausto Reinaga sold his books independently so as to avoid this disappearance of his work (personal interview, November 8, 2001).

9. The reader discovers in a postscript 247 pages later that Reinaga's request for protection fell on deaf ears, as the only response he ever received simply informed him that his letter had been filed according to protocol.

10. For Reinaga, the treatment of indigenous soldiers in the Chaco War (1932–35) was the quintessential example of this racial divide. He argues that the reason why Bolivians never see disabled Indian soldiers is because the Indian who went to the war was not injured, he was killed: "El indio es llevado al Chaco a bala. Los jefes militares mestizo-blancos le meten a bala en primera línea. Si muere nadie se acuerda de él; si cae herido, lo rematan a culatazos o lo dejan abandonado. Al indio le balean los 'bolis' por la espalda y los 'pilas' de frente. El indio muere a dos fuegos. He ahí por qué no hay inválidos, por eso no se ven ni cojos, ni mancos, ni ciegos entre los ex-combatientes indios" (The Indian is taken to the Chaco at gunpoint. The white-mestizo military commanders send him to the frontlines at gunpoint. If he dies there, no one thinks of him again; if he is wounded, they either finish him off with the butts of their guns or they simply abandon him. The Indian comes under fire from behind by the Bolivian soldiers and from the front by the Paraguayan soldiers. He is killed by this crossfire. This is why there are no invalids, why we don't see cripples, or men missing limbs, or soldiers gone blind among the Indian veterans) (1970, 44). Reinaga's claims about the ill treatment of indigenous soldiers in the Chaco War have been corroborated by historians of the conflict. Mamani Condori (1991) and Arze Aguirre (1987) document the fact that the Chaco War was both an international and national conflict over territory:

> Por ser una guerra no declarada, la magnitud de la violencia que significó la guerra interna para pueblos oprimidos y privados de sus fueros y derechos, sólo puede apreciarse si analizamos las diversas formas de agresión y enfrentamiento entre indios y criollos, entre 1932 y 1935. En este orden, hemos de ver: el reclutamiento forzado a que fueron sometidos los indios; las colectas igualmente forzadas que tuvieron que sufrir mujeres, ancianos y niños comunarios; el recrudecimiento de la usurpación de tierras y el establecimiento de una fuerza represora llamada "Legión Cívica." Todos estos hechos podemos considerarlos como aspectos, o frentes de la conflagración que hemos llamado guerra interna (Because this was an undeclared war, it is only possible to evaluate the magnitude of the violence and the toll that it took on oppressed peoples, who were robbed of the law and their rights, if we analyze the diverse forms of aggression and confrontation that took place between Indians and Criollos during the years 1932–35. In this regard, we find: the forced recruitment of Indians; the equally forced taxation of indigenous women, elders, and children, increased usurpation of lands and the establishment of a repressive force called the "Civic Legion." All of the above can be considered as elements or fronts of the conflagration known as the internal war). (Mamani Condori 1991, 102)

11. One important sign missing from Reinaga's alternative symbolic order is the *pollera*. This critical absence calls attention to the masculinist underpinnings of his discourse. For a reading of Reinaga's gendered discourse, see Stephenson 2003. Mary Pat Brady's discussion of the emergence of Aztlán as a cultural symbol in the Chicano move-

ment helped to shape my reading of the role of the *wiphala* in Reinaga's work (cf. Brady 2002, 141–42).

12. Diana Fuss notes that for Fanon "psychoanalysis's interest in the problem of identification" gives him "a vocabulary and an intellectual framework in which to diagnose and to treat not only the psychological disorders produced in individuals by the violence of colonial domination but also the neurotic structure of colonialism itself" (1995, 141).

13. For example, in 1993 THOA published the important *Estructura orgánica*, written by the Federación de Ayllus from the Ingavi Province. This booklet laid out the statutes for the governance of indigenous communities and groups of communities throughout the province. In addition to describing leadership positions and the ways in which the responsibilities of governance are distributed among men and women, it also underscored the relationship between the community and the distribution of territory. Similarly, Marcelo Fernández's *La ley del ayllu* (2000) examines indigenous forms of justice and its administration as they draw from the Aymara notion of *qhip nayra*. As discussed further on in the essay, *qhip nayra* emphasizes the interconnectedness between the past and the present, what José Rabasa calls a "multi-temporal present" in his chapter in this volume.

14. For histories of THOA, see Rivera Cusicanqui 1986; Choque and Mamani 2001; and Stephenson 2002.

15. Mamani Condori notes, "Es por eso que nuestros movimientos de liberación giran sobre el tema del retorno, y sobre la afirmación de un 'salvajismo' liberado de la opresión colonial. Los encargados de conducir tales movimientos reniegan de sus nombres civilizados y cristianos y adoptan los que a ojos occidentales evocan lo demoníaco: se vuelven serpientes como Katari o Amaru (aymara y qhichwa, serpiente), para arrancar de raíz esta civilización perniciosa y caótica" (This is why our liberation movements revolve around the theme of return and the affirmation of a 'savagery' liberated from colonial oppression. The leaders responsible for these movements renounce their civilized, Christian names and adopt those which to Western eyes evoke the demonic: they turn into serpents like Katari or Amaru (serpent in Aymara and Qhichwa), in order to tear this pernicious and chaotic civilization out by the roots) (1992, 12).

16. See Fernández 2000 for an important discussion of *ayllu* justice, transmitted through oral history and ritual, written from the perspective of the Aymara.

17. See Mary Pat Brady (2002, 5) for a similar analysis of the relationship between spatial transformation and racial homogenization in the work of Livia Leon Montiel.

18. Mary Pat Brady writes, "Claiming that space is 'produced,' of course, upends the assumption that space is simply the grand manifestation of the natural terrain. Viewing space as produced, productive, and producing means viewing it as interanimating and dependent in part on narrative for its productive effects—as 'active and generative,' in Kristin Ross's words—rather than as inert and transparent" (2002, 7).

19. For more on the symbolic currency of the colonial documents, see Platt 1992; Ticona Alejo 2002; and Huanca 1993.

20. Prevailing accounts treat these rebellions as irrational, violent outbursts. From there it is not difficult to trace the implicit, and sometimes explicit, references to native savagery.

Works Cited

Alarcón, Norma. 1990. "Chicana Feminism: In the Tracks of 'the' Native Woman." *Cultural Studies* 4.3: 248–56.

Aldama, Arturo J. 2001. *Disrupting Savagism: Intersecting Chicana/o, Mexican Immigrant, and Native American Struggles for Self-Representation.* Durham, N.C.: Duke University Press.

Arguedas, Alcides. 1988. *Wuata Wuara: In Raza de Bronce; Wuata Wuara.* Ed. Antonio Lorente Medina. Nanterre: ALLCA XX.

Ari, Marina. 2003. "La 'guerra del gas': Unidad de pobres, de indígenas, de excluidos y de obreros para diseñar una nueva Bolivia sin exclusion ni racismo." Oct. 14. http://dvlprod.free.fr/dvlprod.bolivia/textos/bolivia.doc.

Arze Aguirre, René Danilo. 1987. *Guerra y conflictos sociales: El caso rural boliviano durante la campaña del Chaco.* La Paz: CERES.

Bonfil Batalla, Guillermo. 1981. *Utopía y revolución: El pensamiento político contemporáneo de los indios en América Latina.* Mexico City: Editorial Nueva Imagen.

———. 1991. *Pensar nuestra cultura: Ensayos.* Mexico City: Alianza Editorial.

Brady, Mary Pat. 2002. *Extinct Lands, Temporal Geographies: Chicana Literature and the Urgency of Space.* Durham, N.C.: Duke University Press.

Choque, María Eugenia, and Carlos Mamani. 2001. "Reconstitución del *ayllu* y derechos de los pueblos indígenas: El movimiento indio en los Andes de Bolivia." *Journal of Latin American Anthropology* 6.1: 202–24.

de Certeau, Michel. 1984. *The Practice of Everyday Life.* Trans. Steven Rendall. Berkeley: University of California Press.

Fanon, Frantz. 1968. *The Wretched of the Earth.* Trans. Constance Farrington. New York: Grove Press.

Federación de Ayllus-Provincia Ingavi. 1993. *Estructura orgánica.* Qullasuyu: THOA.

Fernández O., Marcelo. 2000. *La ley del ayllu: Práctica de jach'a justicia y jisk'a justicia (justicia mayor y justicia menor) en comunidades aymaras.* La Paz: PIEB.

Fuss, Diana. 1995. *Identification Papers.* New York: Routledge.

González Echevarría, Roberto. 1998. *Myth and Archive: A Theory of Latin American Narrative.* Durham, N.C.: Duke University Press.

hooks, bell. 1989. *Talking Back: Thinking Feminist, Thinking Black.* Boston: South End Press.

Huanca L., Tomás. 1993. "Movimiento indígena desde la perspectiva de las comunidades andinas (1910–1950)." In *Naciones autóctona originarias: Vivir-convivir en tolerancia y diferencia,* ed. Simón Yampara Huarachi, 27–56. La Paz: Ediciones CADA; Inti-Andina.

Hylton, Forrest. 2003. "Tierra común: Caciques, artesanos e intelectuales radicales y la rebelión de Chayanta." In *Ya es otro tiempo el presente: Cuatro momentos de insurgencia indígena,* ed. Forrest Hylton, Felix Patzi, Sergio Serulnikov, and Sinclair Thomson, 134–98. La Paz: Muela del Diablo Editores.

"Is 'Indigenous Fundamentalism' the New Hemispheric Threat?" 2003. *Latin American Weekly Report,* November 18, 1.

Klahn, Norma. 2003. "Literary (Re)Mappings: Autobiographical (Dis)Placements by Chicana Writers." In *Chicana Feminisms: A Critical Reader*, ed. Gabriela F. Arredondo, Aída Hurtado, Norma Klahn, Olga Nájera-Ramírez, and Patricia Zavella, 114–45. Durham, N.C.: Duke University Press.

Larson, Brooke. 2000. "National Pedagogy, Andean Resurgence, and the Struggle for Public Culture, Bolivia, 1900–1930." Paper read at the Latin American Studies Association Conference, Miami, March.

Ley de Reforma Educativa. 1996. Law # 1565, July 7, 1994. Ed. Servando Serrano Torrico. La Paz: República de Bolivia.

Lora, Guillermo. 1987. *Historia de los partidos políticos de Bolivia*. La Paz: Ediciones La Colmena.

Luykx, Aurolyn. 1999. *The Citizen Factory: Schooling and Cultural Production in Bolivia*. Albany: State University of New York Press.

Mamani Capchiri, Humberto. 1992. "La educación india en la visión de la sociedad criolla: 1920–1943." In *Educación indígena: ¿Ciudadanía o colonización?*, 79–98. La Paz: Ediciones Aruwiyiri.

Mamani Condori, Carlos. 1991. *Taraqu 1866–1935: Masacre, guerra y "Renovación" en la biografía de Eduardo L. Nina Qhispi*. La Paz: Aruwiyiri.

———. 1992. *Los aymaras frente a la historia: Dos ensayos metodológicos*. Chukiyawu: Aruwiyiri.

———. 1998. "Colonialismo boliviano: Mito e invención." *Retornos: Boletín bio-bibliográfico* 1: 41–49.

———. 1999. "History and Prehistory in Bolivia: What about the Indians?" Trans. Olivia Harris. In *Contemporary Archaeology in Theory*, ed. Robert Preucel and Ian Hodder, 632–45. Oxford: Blackwell Publishers.

———. 2000. "El intelectual indígena hacia un pensamiento propio." Paper presented at the Latin American Studies Association Conference, Miami.

———. 2001. "Memoria y política aymara." In *ARUSKIPASIPXANASATAKI: El siglo XXI y el futuro del pueblo aymara*, ed. Waskar Ari Chachaki, 47–65. La Paz: Editorial Amuyañataki.

———. 2002. "Qullasuyu por siempre." Unpublished manuscript.

Mariaca Iturri, Guillermo. 2001. "Las huellas de la memoria: Rastros y rostros de la crítica literaria boliviana." *Revista de crítica literaria latinoamericana* 27.53: 7–25.

Mata, G. Humberto. 1968. *Fausto Reinaga: Akapi Jacha'j*. La Paz: Ediciones PIB.

Miles, Gary B. 1995. *Livy: Reconstructing Early Rome*. Ithaca, N.Y.: Cornell University Press.

Oppenheimer, Andrés. 2003. "The Oppenheimer Report: What Would Latin America Be without Western Influence?" November 6. http://www.cubaliberal.org/english/031106-Oppenheimer.htm.

Paredes de Salazar, Elssa. 1976. *Presencia de nuestro pueblo*. La Paz: Universo.

Paz Soldán, Edmundo. 2003. *Alcides Arguedas y la narrativa de la nación enferma*. La Paz: Plural Editores.

Pérez, Laura Elisa. 1999. "El desorden, Nationalism, and Chicana/o Aesthetics." In *Between Woman and Nation: Nationalisms, Transnational Feminisms, and the State*, ed.

Caren Kaplan, Norma Alarcón, and Minoo Moallem, 19–46. London: Duke University Press, 1999.

Platt, Tristan. 1992. "Writing, Shamanism, and Identity, or Voices from Abya-Yala." *History Workshop* 34: 132–47.

Rabasa, José. 1995. "'Porque soy Indio': Subjectivity in *La Florida del Inca*." *Poetics Today* 16.1: 79–108.

Reinaga, Fausto. 1964. *El indio y el cholaje boliviano: Proceso a Fernando Diez de Medina*. La Paz: PIAKK.

———. 1967. *La "intelligentsia" del cholaje boliviano*. La Paz: Ediciones Partido Indio de Bolivia.

———. 1969. *La revolución india*. La Paz: Ediciones Partido Indio de Bolivia.

———. 1970. *Manifiesto del partido indio de Bolivia*. La Paz: Ediciones Partido Indio de Bolivia.

———. 1971. *Tesis india*. La Paz: Ediciones Partido Indio de Bolivia.

Rivera Cusicanqui, Silvia. 1986. "Taller de Historia Oral Andina: Proyecto de investigación sobre el espacio ideológico de las rebeliones andinas a través de la historia oral (1900–1950)." In *Estados y naciones en los Andes: Hacia una historia comparativa, Bolivia, Colombia, Ecuador, Perú*, ed. J. P. Deler and Y. Saint-Geours, 1: 83–88. Lima: Instituto de Estudios Peruanos and Instituto Francés de Estudios Andinos.

———. 2003. *"Oprimidos pero no vencidos": Luchas del campesinado aymara y quechwa, 1900–1980*. La Paz: Aruwiyiri.

"Roberto Choque Canqui." 2002. http://www.aymaranet.org/RChoque.html, accessed on October 20, 2002.

Salmón, Josefa. 1997. *El espejo indígena: El discurso indigenista en Bolivia, 1900–1956*. La Paz: Plural Editores; Carrera de Literatura, Facultad de Humanidades, UMSA.

Skaria, Ajay. 1999. "Writing, Orality, and Power in the Dangs, Western India, 1800s–1920s." In *Subaltern Studies IX: Writings on South Asian History and Society*, ed. Shahid Amin and Dipesh Chakrabarty, 13–58. Oxford: Oxford University Press.

Smith, Linda Tuhiwai. 1999. *Decolonizing Methodologies: Research and Indigenous Peoples*. London: Zed Books; University of Otago Press.

Stephenson, Marcia. 1999. *Gender and Modernity in Andean Bolivia*. Austin: University of Texas Press.

———. 2002. "Forging an Indigenous Counterpublic Sphere: The Taller de Historia Oral Andina in Bolivia." *Latin American Research Review* 37.2: 99–115.

———. 2003. El uso de dualismos y género sexual en la formulación del discurso indianista de Fausto Reinaga." In *Identidad, cuidadanía y participación popular desde la colonia al siglo XX*, eds. Josepha Salmón and Guillermo Delgado. La Paz: Plural Editores, 153-161.

Taller de Historia Oral Andina (THOA). 1988. *El indio Santos Marka T'ula: Cacique principal de los ayllus de Qallapa y apoderado general de las comunidades originarias de la república*. La Paz: Ediciones del THOA.

Ticona Alejo, Esteban. 2002. *Memoria, política y antropología en los Andes bolivianos: Historia oral y saberes locales*. La Paz: AGRUCO; Plural Editores; Carreras de Antropología y Arqueología, UMSA.

Unzueta, Fernando. 1996. *La imaginación histórica y el romance nacional en Hispano-américa*. Lima: Latinoamericana Editores.

White, Hayden. 1978. "The Forms of Wildness: Archaeology of an Idea." In *Tropics of Discourse: Essays in Cultural Criticism*, 150–82. Baltimore: Johns Hopkins University Press.

8

Race, Ethnicity, and Nation in
Manuel Zapata Olivella's ¡Levántate, mulato!

Rethinking Identity in Latin America

LAURENCE PRESCOTT

> *. . . It is only by regaining the possibility of active conduct that individuals can dispel the state of emotional tension into which they are forced as a result of humiliation.*
>
> Alex Honneth (cited by Jorge Larraín)

Literature is one area of human endeavor that can be appreciated for its own sake as well as for the insights it offers on cultural production, knowledge, and power. In Latin America the essay is particularly valuable in this regard, perhaps also because, as Nicolas Shumway points out, of all the genres it "is the least defined and can include texts as diverse as letters, biographies, speeches, newspaper articles, political decrees, and philosophical treatises" (1996, 556). Traditionally, college and university courses, anthologies, and studies dealing with the Latin American versions of this flexible genre have focused primarily on those writers who are read and lauded as its founders and major representatives. These canonical authors have been predominantly male, white or *mestizo*, middle- and upper-class individuals whose gender, racial identity, class standing, educational and travel privileges, and other social and economic advantages afforded them opportunities not usually available to persons of different backgrounds. Consequently, awareness and study of texts by authors whose profiles do not match that of the privileged tend to be uncommon.

One writer who falls within this latter group is Manuel Zapata Olivella of Colombia. Born in 1920 in the Caribbean coastal town of Lorica and raised in Cartagena, Manuel Zapata Olivella, who died in 2004, has garnered much scholarly attention in recent years, largely because of his epic novel (or saga, as he preferred to call it), *Changó el gran putas*, which was published in 1983 and received Brazil's Premio Literario "Francisco Matarazzo Sobrinho" for Latin American Fiction in 1985. Zapata Olivella, however, was the author of numerous publications, which not only include novels, short stories, and plays, but also essays, travel narratives, scholarly studies, and hundreds of articles in newspapers, magazines, and books.[1]

A cursory examination of Zapata Olivella's literary production reveals that identity has been a constant concern of this prolific author.[2] His book *¡Levántate mulato! "Por mi raza hablará el espíritu,"* published originally in 1990, which, like Domingo F. Sarmiento's *Facundo: Civilización y barbarie* (1845), combines or partakes of different genres (for example, history, biography, sociology, memoir or autobiography) while simultaneously transcending them,[3] is also concerned with identity. Unlike Sarmiento (1811–88), however, Zapata Olivella belongs to and identifies with the historically disadvantaged masses of color (black, Indian, mulatto, *mestizo, zambo*) that Sarmiento and other privileged Creole writers, intellectuals, and leaders of the nineteenth and twentieth centuries too frequently disdained and dismissed as culturally backward, racially inferior, and politically unfit for full participation in the construction and development of Spanish American national life. The critic Richard L. Jackson has described *¡Levántate, mulato!* as the author's "most important statement on the Afro-Hispanic identity as well as a personal search for his own identity" (1994, 59). While this may be true, it is important also to note that Zapata Olivella has regarded all of his work as a search for identity (see Zapata Olivella, 1967).

Besides Jackson, other scholars—Marvin Lewis (1997) and Dina de Luca (2001), for example—have written illuminating studies on *¡Levántate, mulato!* as autobiography. Perhaps another useful way to understand the significance and writing of Zapata Olivella's multi-layered or pluri-discursive text and the implications it has not only for peoples of African descent in the Americas but for others as well is to read it as an essay within the context of writers and texts that have shaped both the Spanish American literary canon and the ways in which Latin Americans have thought about race, ethnicity, and nation. Zapata Olivella himself leads us toward this approach when he informs the reader in the introduction of *¡Levántate, mulato!* that several "intellectuals, poets, politicians, and philosophers" (1990, 17) influenced his thinking.

In addition to the already mentioned Sarmiento, whose program of national construction included education, European immigration, and annihilation of the indigenous population, Zapata Olivella cites four other major contributors to the Latin American essay of ideas. The first is the Mexican writer José Vasconcelos (1882–1959), whose provocative essay "La raza cósmica" (1925) offered a concept that, in the words of the critic Lourdes

Martínez Echazábal, "was taken up enthusiastically by many 'liberal' Latin American intellectuals and promoted as an example of the region's racial democracy" (Martínez Echazábal 1998, 35). The second essayist whom Zapata Olivella mentions is the noted Peruvian Marxist José Carlos Mariátegui (1894–1930), whose *Siete ensayos de interpretación de la realidad peruana* (1928), according to the critic José Miguel Oviedo, was among the first to frame "the problems of Spanish Americans . . . within the context of the struggles of the international proletariat" (1973, 377).[4]

"Less alienated" than Mariátegui and Sarmiento, according to Zapata Olivella (1990, 18) is the Argentine writer Ezequiel Martínez Estrada (1895–1964), the author of *Radiografía de la pampa* (1933) and other essays, whose "revisionism of national history and culture conferred upon him the role of teacher to younger generations" (Oviedo 1996, 388). The last of the four thinkers cited by Zapata Olivella is the Cuban poet, journalist, and independence leader José Martí (1853–95), whose many essays and other writings (for example, "Nuestra América" and "Mi raza") provided a mirror of identity and a blueprint for other independence-minded Cubans and citizens of the young Spanish American nations. Indeed, Martí, along with Sarmiento, laid much of the intellectual groundwork for Spanish American thinking about nation, race, and identity in the nineteenth century and in the early decades of the twentieth century. Later, Vasconcelos would also effect strongly the way Latin American peoples looked at themselves.

While these educated and privileged writers' approaches to overcoming the colonial heritage of Spanish America had continental implications, they failed to provide Zapata Olivella with a fully satisfactory representation of the ethno-racial history and reality that he, as a descendant of Africans, Indians, and Europeans, knew. Neither, it seems, did their evaluations and proposals always offer the kind of truly radical, uplifting, and comprehensive vision of Spanish America's peoples, cultures, and future that Zapata Olivella considered necessary to eradicate or overcome the colonialist mentality that still plagued the nations of the region. In this essay, therefore, I propose to examine *¡Levántate, mulato!* in relation to issues of race, ethnicity, and nation that the book raises, and in conjunction with key texts of three of the influential authors whom the author cites—namely, Sarmiento, Martí, and Vasconcelos. I contend that Zapata Olivella's text confronts and deconstructs established discourses of identity in Latin America and seeks to bring about a new consciousness that can lead, as he has stated elsewhere (1963, 3), to both individual and collective liberation.[5]

Thanks to stimulation in part by cultural studies, identity has been at the center of much current academic study, creative writing, and popular thought.[6] It has also been a preoccupation of Latin American intellectuals and peoples for decades, if not centuries, as Martin S. Stabb's early work suggests.[7] Whereas scholars once viewed identity as a given innate essence, today it is seen more as a social process of construction (see Wade 1999, 19). In his book *Identity and Modernity in Latin America*, the sociologist Jorge Larraín proposes that three elements participate in this construction. The first is that "individuals define themselves, or identify themselves with some qualities, in terms of some shared social categories" (2000, 24). The second is a material component that "includes the body and other possessions capable of providing the subject with vital elements of recognition" (25). The third, Larraín explains, "necessarily involves the existence of 'others' in a double sense." That is, these "others" are persons whose opinions about us we internalize; at the same time, "they are also those against whom the self acquires its distinctiveness and specificity. . . . Hence the subject defines himself or herself in terms of how the others see him or her" (26).

In the title of the introduction to *¡Levántate, mulato!*, Zapata Olivella asks rhetorically, "¿Cuál es mi cultura, mi raza, mi destino?" (What is my culture, my race, my destiny?). This question, evoking a concern for common heritage, lineage, and future that transcends the individual to establish or acknowledge identification with others, exemplifies and gets at the heart of the first two components of identity construction mentioned above: self-definition and material recognition. It also illustrates Larraín's assertion that "all personal identities are rooted in collective contexts culturally determined" (2000, 24). That is, an individual's identity usually involves or overlaps with various "group allegiances or characteristics—such as religion, profession, gender, class, ethnicity, sexuality, nationality—which are culturally determined and contribute to specifying the subject and its sense of identity" (24).

Zapata Olivella closes his introduction with several more queries that point directly to the third element of identity—namely, others' opinions of the self, which, in some cases, may entail negative assumptions or implications that cast doubt upon and destabilize the individual's sense of self and group identification. He asks, "¿Híbrido o nuevo hombre? ¿Soy realmente un traidor a mi raza? ¿Un zambo escurridizo? ¿Un mulato entreguista? O sencillamente un mestizo americano que busca defender la identidad de sus sangres oprimidas" (Hybrid or new man? Am I really a traitor to my race, a slippery *zambo*, a defeatist mulatto, or simply an American *mestizo* who seeks to defend the identity of his three oppressed blood strains?) (1990,

21). Although applied here self-referentially, the terms "traidor a mi raza," "zambo escurridizo" and "mulato entreguista" can be read as derogatory epithets used by other persons of different or same racial background to criticize and slander black and African-descended individuals of mixed race whose behavior and attitudes do not conform to expected norms; or who, succumbing to the prejudice and alienation that was the legacy of conquest, colonization, and slavery, sought to separate and distinguish themselves from less fortunate and less privileged group members so as to improve the chances for a better life for themselves or their progeny. Owing to personal choices and decisions that he made in his own life, and in light of the "crab antics" phenomenon displayed in certain postcolonial societies,[8] it would not be unusual if Zapata Olivella himself has been the target of such epithets.

In any case, it should also be noted that the final phrase of the cited queries is devoid of question marks, which makes it not so much an interrogation as an affirmation. That is, it constitutes a response to the immediately preceding questions and, implicitly, also serves as the author's personal statement of who he is: "un mestizo americano que busca defender la identidad de sus sangres oprimidas."[9] In ¡Levántate, mulato!, then, Zapata Olivella grapples simultaneously with understanding not only the process of construction of his own identity but also that of his family, his fellow costeños, other Colombians, and Latin Americans in general, who are a mixture of many peoples and whose history is marked by struggle against oppression and colonialism. Therefore, several aspects of identity, such as race, ethnicity, and nationality, all of which are intimately related, come under consideration in his book and will be examined here.

Although use of the term "race" may no longer be considered viable, acceptable, or politically correct,[10] Zapata Olivella recognizes that classification of people "by reference to physical attributes such as skin colour or other perceived bodily distinctions" (Hartley 2002, 192) has mattered historically and is still common today. As the anthropologist Peter Wade points out, "to deny a specific role to racial identifications . . . or to discriminations based on them . . . is to blur the *particular history* by which these identifications come to have the force they do" (1999, 20, original emphasis). In New Granada (that is, roughly the area encompassing Colombia, Ecuador, and Venezuela during the colonial period) and in other areas of colonial Latin America where parentage and physical features figured prominently in determining or assigning identity, individuals and groups were labeled not merely as white (*blanco*), black (*negro*), or Indian (*indio*)—a nomenclature that reflected the three principal groups comprising the populations—but also as *mestizo, mulato, zambo*, and other terms invented to explain, categorize, and denigrate the offspring resulting from the various combinations of the three stocks and their issue.[11]

Zapata Olivella alludes to this archaeology upon explaining the development of his own racial consciousness: "Los términos mestizo, bastardo, mulato, zambo, tan despreciados en la historia y sociedad americanas, me reclamaban una actitud consecuente conmigo mismo, con mi sangre, con mis ancestros" (Such terms as *mestizo*, bastard, mulatto, [and] zambo, so vilified in [Latin] American history and society, demanded a corresponding attitude from me, [considering] my blood, and my ancestry) (1990, 17). The inclusion of the word "bastardo" here is especially noteworthy. Presumption of illegitimate birth was associated with *mestizos* and mulattos and no doubt was partly responsible for the low regard in which they were held and the negative characteristics ascribed to them, which, in turn, may have further limited their opportunities for advancement.[12] The historian Jaime Jaramillo Uribe has shown that colonial documents generally described the *mestizo* as "vagabundo, inestable y hacedor de agravios, especialmente contra los indios" (vagabond, unstable and trouble maker, especially against Indians) (1965, 30), and as "buscarruidos, gente de vida irregular y malas costumbres" (low-lives, people of unruly lives and bad habits) (31). It should come as no surprise, then, that to be called a *mestizo*—or a mulatto, for that matter— was an insult. Jaramillo Uribe illustrates that fact by citing a number of cases and lawsuits brought against such calumny. For example, in a seventeenth-century criminal case against a black male slave, the defendant was accused, among other offenses, of having threatened and slandered a Spaniard by referring to him as "un perro mestizo y otras palabras feas" (a *mestizo* dog and other ugly words) (33). In a case in 1725 a man named Diego de Vargas sued a carpentry official for defamation because the latter had ridiculed "sus pergaminos y [había] propala[do] especies contra su honra y abolengos, diciendo que él y su familia eran unos zambos, mulatos y ensambenitados" (documents of pedigree and insulted his honor and ancestry, saying that he and his family were all *zambos*, mulattos, and a disgrace) (34).

It is evident, then, that although the variety of human types produced by *mestizaje* "tended to blur physical differences and create a color continuum that made difficult the enforcement of sharp distinctions based on racial origin and color" (Prescott 2000, 29), the privileging of whiteness in the society caused much jealousy and tension among the mixed-race persons (that is, *castas*) with regard to where they fell or stood on the socio-racial scale. Therefore, as Zapata Olivella observes in an earlier study on Colombia, "While whites claimed nobility, setting forth their 'purity of blood,' mixed-race persons claimed to be more [worthy] according to the lesser degree of black or Indian blood they possessed" (1974, 197; quoted in Prescott 2000, 30). His description of the behavior of some of his own relatives (1990, 59–62) offers convincing testimony of the persistence of alienation produced by such attitudes. In the case of one of his aunts, the Spanish heritage had erased all sense of black consciousness from her memory:

> Nada recordaba de sus antepasados remotos, ni reconocía ligazón con aquellos negros con quienes no tuviera un nexo familiar. La mayoría de los descendientes africanos, ansiosos de acomodarse en una sociedad discriminadora, arrastraban en Cartagena esta falta de identidad como un escudo (She remembered nothing of her remote ancestors, nor did she acknowledge any linkage with those blacks with whom she had no family ties. The majority of the people of African descent, anxious to find a place in a discriminatory society, dragged this lack of identity around in Cartagena like a coat of arms). (59)

> Sobran razones, pues, para que el ideal de dignidad y orgullo de los mulatos y mestizos de Cartagena no pueda alimentarse de su trágica ascendencia aborigen o africana. Sus aspiraciones e impulsos identificadores se han dirigido, al igual que los pocos desendientes de españoles sin mezcla, a mirarse a sí mismos como representantes de la cultura peninsular. Llevados por los ideales impuestos por el grupo dominante, los indios y negros frente a los espejos, apenas si tenían o tienen ojos para descubrir los rasgos étnicos de su verdadera raza (There is more than enough reason, then, for the ideal of mulatto and *mestizo* pride and dignity, to not find sustenance in its tragic indigenous and African ancestry. Their aspirations and identitarian impulses have been directed, just like those of the unmixed descendants of the Spanish, to seeing themselves as representatives of peninsular Spanish culture. Carried along by the ideals imposed by the dominant group, the Indians and blacks upon confronting themselves in the mirror barely had eyes to see the ethnic traces of their true race). (65)

In the decades immediately following independence and even later, disparagement of blackness and African ancestry remained entrenched in the societies and is evident in the writings of some of the distinguished authors whom Zapata Olivella mentions at the beginning of his book. For example, in *Facundo*, Sarmiento described *zambos* and mulattos as the "eslabón que liga al hombre civilizado con el palurdo" (the link between civilized man and the boor) ([1845] 1997, 63) and characterized the resulting mixture of the three principal races as "un todo homogéneo, que se distingue por su amor a la ociosidad e incapacidad industrial cuando la educación y las exigencias de una posición social no vienen a ponerle espuela y sacarlo de su paso habitual" (a homogenous whole, distinguished by its love of idleness and incapacity for industry when education and the exigencies of social position are not there to spur them on and take them out of their habitual rhythm) (63–64). In another section of his widely studied and influential work Sarmiento rejoices that the constant wars have exterminated the black male population (335). Considering also his campaign against the indigenous people, it is no wonder that Zapata Olivella labels him "el Búfalo Bill de las pampas argentinas" (the Buffalo Bill of the Argentine pampas) (1990, 18). Almost a century later, José Vasconcelos, commenting on the future effects of racial mixing, also implied that the extinction of black people was a beneficial result: "Los tipos bajos de la especie serán absorbidos por el tipo superior. De esta suerte podría redimirse, por ejemplo, el negro, y poco a poco, por extinción voluntaria, las estirpes más feas irán cediendo el paso a las más hermosas" (The low types of the species will be absorbed by the superior type. In this way, blacks might be redeemed gradually, through voluntary extinction; the more ugly strains will give way to the more handsome ones) ([1979] 1997, 72).[13]

In contrast, José Martí's rejection of the civilization versus barbarism binary, as well as his struggle against imperialism and his concern for all races and classes, no doubt led Zapata Olivella, like others, to admire and respect him.[14] Quoting Martí's celebrated essay "Nuestra América," Zapata Olivella writes: "Y Martí me atosigaba con el tizón encendido de la duda: 'Ni el libro europeo, ni el libro yanqui daban la clave del enigma hispanoamericano'" (And Martí's words, like burning embers of doubt, urged me on: Neither the book of the Europeans nor that of the Yankees provided the key to the Spanish American enigma) (1990, 18). That is to say, Martí's words gave him pause, perhaps inspiring him to question previously held ideas or to challenge the Euro–North American hegemonic discourse that weighed heavily on Latin American thought and institutions. In any case, *¡Levántate, mulato!* resonates with Martí's thought. For example, Martí's assessment in "Nuestra América" that the problem of independence was not a question of the change in forms but of the change in mentality (that is, *espíritu*) and his argument that the colony remained alive in the republic resound in Zapata

Olivella's description of contemporary Colombian society as "todavía ero-
sionada por los antagonismos de castas impuestos desde la Colonia . . ." (still
eroded by the antagonisms of caste imposed during colonial days) (1990,
177) and in his criticism of the nation's educational system:

> Los colegios y universidades creados en la República *perpetuarían el
> mismo espíritu selectivo* en la formación de los nuevos académicos y
> profesionales. Sin que hubiera un rigor exclusivista, la composición
> de las nuevas clases sociales en las que *persistió el criterio de castas—*
> criollos mandones y masas explotadas—determinó quiénes podían
> beneficiarse y quiénes no de una educación académica (The colleges
> and universities created in the republic *will perpetuate the same selec-
> tive spirit* in the formation of new academics and professionals. [Even]
> without a system of rigorous exclusion, the composition of the new
> social classes, in which *the criterion of caste still persisted—*of *criollos*
> giving orders and the masses being exploited—determined who could
> benefit from an academic education and who couldn't). (1990, 171;
> emphasis added)[15]

Other statements by Zapata Olivella show that he also agrees with Martí
on the necessity and importance of self-knowledge—both for the individual and the nation—in order to achieve and maintain true liberation, and
of recognizing and valuing the autochthonous, popular culture. Whereas
Martí declared, "Conocer es resolver. Conocer el país, y gobernarlo conforme al conocimiento, es el único modo de librarlo de tiranías" (To know
is to resolve. Knowing the country and governing it based on knowledge is
the only way to free it from tyranny) (1970, 89), Zapata Olivella observed in
his native Colombia that "en un país de mestizos y mulatos . . . el miedo a
conocerse a sí mismo" (in a country of *mestizos* and mulattos . . . the fear of
knowing one's self) (174) prevails, wherein "*ignorados* los temperamentos y
la psicología del indio, el blanco y el negro . . . siempre nos juzgamos con los
patrones extraños a nuestra idiosincrasia étnica" (*ignorant* of the temperament and the psychology of the Indian, the white and the black . . . we always judge ourselves by standards that are alien to our ethnic idiosyncrasy)
(1990, 174–75; emphasis added).

It would be erroneous to believe, however, that Zapata Olivella embraced
Martí's thinking unquestioningly. Where I perceive him taking issue with
Martí is on the question of race. Addressing the matter idealistically or
with much optimism, Martí declares in "Nuestra América": "No hay odio
de razas, porque no hay razas" (There is no race hate, because there are no

races) (1970, 92). And in "Mi raza," published two years later, Martí, emphasizing the oneness of humanity, asserts, " . . . peca por redundante el blanco
que dice 'mi raza'; peca por redundante el negro que dice 'mi raza.' Todo
lo que divide a los hombres, todo lo que los especifica, aparta o acorrala,
es un pecado contra la humanidad" (Whites who speak of "my race" are
being redundant, blacks who speak of "my race" are being redundant. Everything that divides men, everything that specifies, separates, or puts them
in a corner is a sin against humanity) (52). While Zapata Olivella may well
have appreciated Martí's need to foster unity among his compatriots in their
fight for independence from Spain and may have understood the circumstances that obliged him to deny or overlook the existence of or belief in race
(see Appelbaum, Macpherson, and Rosemblat, 2003, 7), even if the belief is
based on fallacious ideas or premises (Wade 1999, 14), Zapata Olivella realizes that the perpetuation of the problems of poverty, of the inequalities of
opportunity, and of the crisis of alienated identity in America are intimately
tied to race, class, and culture.[16] These problems, as he points out in the section on the Colombian university, are particularly evident in the failure of
students throughout the educational system to complete their studies:

> El alto índice de deserción estudiantil registrado en los establec-
> imientos de primaria y colegios de bachillerato, debido fundamen-
> talmente a su pobreza, también se hacía notoria en ella. Pronto ad-
> vertí que sólo un negro oriundo del Cauca, Marino Viveros Mancilla,
> sería mi compañero de banca en una facultad de medicina con más
> de cinco mil estudiantes. . . . Desde luego, la mayoría de mis condis-
> cípulos eran mulatos, mestizos y zambos asimilados psicológicamente
> al status de los "blancos." Después de un extenuante esfuerzo de sus
> padres campesinos u obreros, muchos de ellos se retiraban en los dos
> o tres primeros años de estudio. . . . Nadie, y menos los maestros, en-
> traba a analizar las verdaderas causas de su bajo rendimiento. Mejor
> enteradas estaban las dueñas de pensión y los propios condiscípulos
> que compartíamos su precaria supervivencia económica (The high
> dropout rate in our primary and secondary schools is due quite nota-
> bly to poverty. I realized quite early that only one black student, from
> the Cauca region, Marino Viveros Mancilla, would end up being my
> classmate in medical school, out of five thousand students. . . . Of
> course, the majority of my fellow students were mulattos, *mestizos,*
> and *zambos* assimilated to whiteness. After great effort on the part of
> their parents, peasants and workers, many of them withdrew in the

first two or three years of study. . . . No one, and even less their teachers, cared to study the true causes behind their low output. Those of us who were their classmates and the landlords of the places they lived were the ones who were most familiar with their precarious economic position). (1990, 172–73)

Thus for Zapata Olivella the realities of twentieth-century Colombia and Latin America require a more direct acknowledgment of the forces of racism—a frontal assault, if you will, on the bastions of racial and ethnic injustice. His initial questioning, "¿Cuál es mi raza, mi cultura, mi destino?" (What is my race, my culture, my destiny?) implies, then, a desire and a responsibility to seek and know fully his identity, to understand and express his cultural self without hatred or shame, and thus to become empowered to confront his history, which is also that of others, so as to forge a future grounded in truth and knowledge. For Zapata Olivella, achieving this goal requires that the nation discover its true identity as a multicultural and multiracial society, that it acknowledge and confront its history, and that it embrace all of its ancestral heritages. Such change implies a radical transformation of the educational system inasmuch as

los prejuicios raciales en Colombia se alimentan y sustentan en toda la sociedad mediante el eficaz instrumento de la escuela. En los textos de primaria y bachillerto se sostienen tesis que presentan a los negros como una raza tarada por la esclavitud, procedente de un continente desconocido, donde reyezuelos tiránicos cazaban y vendían a sus súbditos y hermanos. . . . Nada o poco de los verdaderos orígenes de la infamante trata de prisioneros humanos concebida y realizada por todos los imperios europeos, a sí mismos identificados como cristianos. La deformación cultural y social se extiende a los propios aborígenes americanos. En los grabados de textos de historia se presenta la imagen de un caribe alzando de los cabellos la cabeza de un europeo, macana en mano y dispuesto a devorarla (Racial prejudices in Colombia are fed and perpetuated throughout society by means of the school system. Primary and secondary school books present the thesis of blacks as a race deformed by slavery, coming from an unknown continent, in which tyrannical little kings hunted down and sold their subjects and brothers . . . [with] little or nothing [said] about the true origins of the infamous trade in human captives conceived and carried out by all the European empires who called themselves Christians. The cultural and social deformation is extended to the indigenous people of the Americas. The prints in the history books present the image of a Carib with a club in his hand and holding the head of a European by the hair, about to devour it). (184–85)

In another section of "Nuestra América," Martí, urging fellow Spanish Americans to recognize and embrace their own values and traditions, to join together, and to show charity to the less fortunate, exhorts, "¡Bajarse hasta los infelices y alzarlos en los brazos!" ([Let us] go down to the poor and raise them up in our arms) (1970, 91). The use of the verb *bajarse* implies that those who are to perform the action are in a position superior to that of the ones who are to be lifted up, as if these unfortunates were infants or children or physically handicapped. In contrast, Zapata Olivella's imperative *"Levántate"* speaks to the marginalized (masses) directly, instructing them to arise and, thereby, implying that they take the initiative, that they, using their own energies—not only physical but psychological, intellectual, cultural— raise *themselves* up, change their position, become the agents of their own liberation and destiny. In this respect, Zapata Olivella recalls Marcus Garvey's injunction to African American peoples: "Up you mighty race, do as you will."

José Vasconcelos, the author of the widely disseminated essay "La raza cósmica" of 1925, also occupies an important place in the development of Zapata Olivella's thinking on race, ethnicity, and nation. Like Martí, Vasconcelos acknowledged and spoke positively of the mixed-race character of Latin America.[17] Moving beyond the Cuban's stance, however, he discerned a steadily increasing tendency of human racial groups to intermingle, to the point that he believed that this synthetic process would lead eventually to a new, fifth, and final human type or cosmic race. Moreover, Vasconcelos posited that Latin America, because of its history of miscegenation and other reasons, was the precise place where the cosmic race would emerge. Understandably, his ideas stirred the hope, pride, and imagination of many a Latin American youth, including Zapata Olivella. Indeed, for Zapata Olivella, a young Colombian mulatto medical student who spent the latter years of World War II in Mexico, the optimism of Vasconcelos, a Mexican educator, politician, and philosopher, who gave to his nation's university its inspiring motto—"Por mi raza hablará el espíritu" (My spirit will speak for my race)—must have been encouraging. Vasconcelos's claim that the synthesis inherent in the fifth race "aspira a englobar y expresar todo lo humano en maneras de constante superación" (aspires to include and express all that is human in ways to improve itself constantly) ([1979] 1997, 59) and, concomitantly, "rompe los prejuicios antiguos" (break with old prejudices) no doubt appealed to Zapata Olivella, who was the first in his slave-descended family to study in the National University (1990, 176).

One paragraph of "La raza cósmica" in particular, echoing words of José Martí cited earlier, may have struck a familiar chord in Zapata Olivella. While it is clear that Zapata Olivella would later use Vasconcelos's famous motto as the subtitle of *¡Levántate, mulato!*, the title itself may well have been inspired by the first words of the paragraph in question, which begins:

> *Cada raza que se levanta* necesita construir su propia filosofía, el *deus ex machina* de su éxito. Nosotros nos hemos educado bajo la influencia humillante de una filosofía ideada por nuestros enemigos, si se quiere de una manera sincera; pero con el propósito de exaltar sus propios fines y anular los nuestros. De esta suerte nosotros mismos hemos llegado a creer en la inferioridad del mestizo, en la irredención del indio, en la condenación del negro, en la decadencia irreparable del oriental. . . . *Sacudimos un yugo para caer bajo otro nuevo . . .* pero ahora que se inicia una nueva fase de la Historia se hace necesario reconstruir nuestra ideología y organizar conforme a una nueva doctrina étnica toda nuestra vida continental. Comencemos, entonces, haciendo vida propia y ciencia propia. Si no *se liberta primero el espíritu*, jamás lograremos redimir la material (*Each race that lifts itself up* needs to construct its own philosophy, the deus ex machina of its success. To be frank, we have been educated under the philosophy of our enemies, whose intention was to achieve their own objectives and nullify ours. Because of this even we ourselves have come to believe in the inferiority of the *mestizo*, in the irredeemable nature of the Indian, the cursedness of the black man, the utter decadence of the Oriental. . . . *We shook off one yoke to fall under another one . . .* but now that a new phase of History approaches it is becoming necessary to reconstruct our ideology and organize life in our continent in accordance with a new ethnic doctrine. Let us begin, therefore, to make our own life and our own science. If our spiritual aspect is not first liberated, we will never be able to free the material aspect). ([1979] 1997, 74; emphasis added)

The intertextuality with Martí notwithstanding, in "La raza cósmica" Vasconcelos privileges the white, Anglo-Saxon race, minimizes the African blood in the Mexican or Latin American gene pool, and manifests an eagerness to eliminate the black race, all of which harked back to the Eurocentrism and racism of Sarmiento and others. Possibly composing his book in the Paris of the early 1920s and perhaps blinded or overwhelmed by the Negro vogue, Vasconcelos offered only an essentialist representation of the African American—"ávido de dicha sensual, ebrio de danzas y desenfrenadas lujurias" (greedy for sensual happiness, drunk with dances and uninhibited lechery) (61)—and thus a narrow assessment of black potential contributions not only to the cosmic race but also to the national cultures.

In contrast, Zapata Olivella, as if correcting Vasconcelos, enumerates other traits and values that he observed in fellow *costeños* and, especially, in his own family and which, in his opinion, defined the identity of Africans in the Americas, an identity informed by resistance: "El culto de los ancestros, el temperamento racial, los hábitos gremiales, el sentido del ritmo y la música, la alegría de vivir y procrear, el orgullo de la dignidad personal del negro nunca menoscabado pese al insulto y la opresión" (The cult of the ancestors, the racial temperament, the collective habits, the sense of rhythm and music, the joy of living and procreating, the pride of personal dignity in blacks that has never been diminished in spite of insults and oppression) (1990, 41). Although one could argue that Zapata Olivella simply replaces one set of essentialist ideas with another, it is evident that his text subverts the essentialist conceptions and traditional views of identity imposed on the voiceless, powerless masses of color by those who, because of physiognomy, wealth, education, and political status, were able to articulate and dominate the intellectual and literary discourses of their respective nations.

Perhaps the personal, autobiographical nature of *¡Levántate, mulato!*, combined with the author's vantage point of writing from within the community of which he speaks, allows for a certain flexibility or authority.[18] Moreover, it is worthwhile repeating that one must be careful "to avoid denying aspects of the African cultural background that are regarded by the people themselves as positive hallmarks of a rich and valued legacy" (Prescott 2000, 139). In any case, toward the end of his essay Zapata Olivella reclaims African peoples' transcendental contributions to America, asserting that they blackened (that is, enriched and transformed) the continent ". . . no por su piel negra, sino por su rebeldía, sus luchas antiesclavistas, su unión con el indio para combatir al opresor, por sus tambores y orichas guerreros, por sus pregones, por su músculo, por su inquebrantable optimismo de pueblo vencedor" (. . . not for their black skins, but for their rebelliousness, their antislavery struggle, their union with Indians to fight against the oppressor, for their drums and *orishas* of war, for their street sellers' cries, for their physical strength, for their unbreakable optimism as a people who overcome) (1990, 330).

Zapata Olivella's insistence on these traits and his evaluation of the absence and distortion of information about indigenous and African peoples in Colombia offer eloquent testimony to his understanding of the important role of education in legitimizing and naturalizing knowledge about dominant and marginalized groups, and their respective value or place in his nation's history and culture as well as in that of Latin America. That insistence and evaluation, however, also evinces Zapata Olivella's recognition of the power of such knowledge to shape the way a person (or group) sees him- or herself and is seen by others, and of the need—indeed, the obligation— of subordinated and marginalized peoples to determine their identity and their destiny. In sum, then, Zapata Olivella, comprehending and revealing the historical significance and interplay of discourses of race and ethnicity in shaping both individual and collective (for example, national) identities and being shaped by them, calls upon fellow *costeños*, Colombians, and Latin Americans to acknowledge and embrace their whole history and all of their heritages without privileging one over the other. If it is true, as Jorge Larraín observes, that "the subject's identity is built not just as an expression of the others' free recognition, but also as a result of the struggle to be recognized by the others" (2000, 28), *¡Levántate, mulato!*, with its personal and intrahistorical perspective, contributes significantly to educating the reader about the multidimensional nature and the manifold rewards of that struggle as it is waged daily by individuals, groups, and nations within Latin America.

Notes

1. For a listing of Zapata Olivella's principal works and some other publications, see the bibliography in Captain-Hidalgo 1994.

2. For examples, see the entry for Zapata Olivella in the works cited at the end of this article.

3. As Nicolas Shumway notes, *Facundo* is "an unusually complex text, part biography, part history, part sociology, part political commentary, and yet somehow more than these" (1996, 584). Zapata Olivella's book was first published in French as *Lève-toi, mulatre! L'esprit parlera à travers ma race* (Paris, 1987) and received the Prix des Nouveaux Droits de l'Homme. The title of the Spanish edition, unlike that of the French, lacks the comma that should follow the verb (*Levántate*) to set off the vocative (*mulato*). Although it is tempting to consider a possible postmodern interpretation of the title sans punctuation mark, the most likely explanation for the absence is typographical error of omission.

While most subsequent citations of the text in this essay will use a shortened form, future citations of the full title will include the comma.

4. Zapata Olivella states that in their eagerness to reclaim the Indian, both Mariátegui and Víctor Haya de la Torre (1895–1979), the dominant figures of modern Peru's political and ideological life (Oviedo 1996, 387), forgot about the Afro-Peruvian. Mariátegui, however, did not overlook Africans and their descendants in Peru but rather dismissed them as persons who could contribute little to Peruvian culture and society (1973, 334, 340–44).

5. Dina de Luca's remarks in this regard are worthy of note: "El plan de acción del autor consiste en comunicar y guiar al lector, a través de una pluralidad discursiva, por el sendero de la 'salvación' social. Esta 'salvación' sólo es posible por medio de la adquisición de una verdadera identidad cultural" (The author's plan of action consists of communicating with and guiding the reader, along the path of social "salvation," by way of a discursive plurality. This "salvation" is only possible by acquiring a true cultural identity) (2001, 51).

6. See, for example, Corbey and Leerson 1991; Winters and DeBose 2003; Bost 2003.

7. See Stabb 1967. Scholarship on Latin American identity has produced many studies in recent years and the already large list is still growing. Mention of a few works, however, is in order: Appelbaum, Macpherson, and Rosemblat 2003; Larraín 2000; Miller 1999; Wade 2001.

8. See Peter J. Wilson 1973. It is important to point out, however, that this phenomenon is not limited to African Americans or to the Caribbean, as the observations of the Chilean writer and traveler Tancredo Pinochet Le-Brun reveal: "Este espíritu [de ayuda] no lo tenemos en Chile. Si vemos levantarse á un chileno, creemos que eso nos humilla á nosotros y tratamos de sujetarlo, de dificultarle ó impedirle su ascenso. No comprendemos que su triunfo es triunfo de nosotros porque es nuestra sangre y nuestra raza la que se levanta" (We don't have this spirit [of mutual help] in Chile. If we see a Chilean improve himself, we believe that this puts us down so we try to hold him back, to make things difficult and to impede his progress. We don't understand that his success is our success because it is our blood and our race that is being uplifted) (Tancredo Pinochet Le-Brun 1914, 215).

9. The use of "*mestizo*" here is generic and does not suggest an attempt on the author's part to "improve" his identity. While the concept of *mestizo* refers in a limited, specific way to persons of indigenous or Amerindian and European mixture, it is also widely used throughout Spanish America as a general term for a person of mixed racial background and thus hegemonically conditions or makes for "an apparently natural and unarguable general interest, with a claim on everyone" (Hartley 2002, 99). This is not to imply, however, that Zapata Olivella accepted such claims uncritically. Indeed, his use of the term *mulato* seems to be a not so subtle effort to redress the imbalance and to revaluate and reclaim the identity. He changed the title of his proposed book from ¡*Levántate, mestizo!* to ¡*Levántate, mulato!*, which suggests a possible critique of the imposition and maintenance of ruling-class ideology on the subordinate classes and groups who are characterized, for the most part, as poor and of African and/or indigenous descent. See Zapata Olivella 1966 and also note 10 below.

10. See Wade 1999, 19; Appelbaum, Macpherson, and Rosemblat 2003: "'Ethnicity' became a more acceptable term for what had previously been referred to as race, but the term 'ethnic' was used mainly to describe groups—especially Indians—who did not conform to a racialized norm, generally coded as mestizo or white. The shift toward ethnicity did not displace the reifying equation of culture, place, and human biology" (8).

11. Zapata Olivella reproduces in his book (1990, 62–63) a familiar chart on various mixtures that includes many of these terms.

12. Without shame or boast, Zapata Olivella acknowledges "la condición de bastardo de mi padre" (that my father was a bastard) (1990, 176).

13. José Carlos Mariátegui, too, contributed to the denigration of black peoples and their mixtures (see 1973, 334, 340–44).

14. An early article by Zapata Olivella (1949) suggests that he shared Spanish American youth's respect for the Cuban hero.

15. Martí's text reads: "El problema de la independencia no era el cambio de formas, sino el cambio de espíritu. . . . La colonia siguió viviendo en la república . . ." (The problem of independence was not in the change of form, but in the change of spirit . . . the colonial mentality continued to live on in the republican period . . .) (1970, 90).

16. Nevertheless, Zapata Olivella's statement that "la oposición de razas se mantiene no solamente por prejuicios de los blancos sino de los propios negros" (Racial opposition is maintained not only by the prejudices of whites but by the blacks themselves) (1990, 183) recalls Martí's words.

17. In that respect, Appelbaum, Macpherson, and Rosemblat argue that he "challenged the prevalent coupling of whiteness with modernity and citizenship" (2003, 7).

18. Although the reference to procreation may suggest merely the sexual act, Zapata Olivella seems to have in mind the basic human drive of perpetuation of self, family, and species, the realization of which could not ordinarily be enjoyed or taken for granted by enslaved Africans and their descendants. José Martí, while denouncing the violence against African Americans in the United States, on at least two occasions saw fit to remark upon their reproductive habits and growth, which he attributed to the limitations imposed by poverty and a lack of education: "Y crecen: porque los ignorantes y los pobres, privados de los goces finos del espíritu, son padres fecundos"; "El negro crece, con la fecundidad de los matrimonios pobres, que en la casa tienen el único placer, y ponen en la esposa todo el amor y compañía que les niega el mundo. El hombre ha de crear: ideas o hijos" (And they multiply: because the uneducated and the poor, deprived of the finer pleasures of the spirit, are fertile parents; The black man multiplies, with the fertility of poor married couples, whose only pleasure is to be found at home, and who find in their wives all the love and companionship that the world denies them. Man must create: ideas or children) (1963–66, 11:238; 12:335; from articles titled "Lo que hay que aprender de los Estados Unidos" and "El problema negro," originally published in La Nación of Buenos Aires, April 15, 1887 and November 10, 1889).

Works Cited

Appelbaum, Nancy P., Anne S. Macpherson, and Karin Alejandra Rosemblat, eds. 2003. *Race and Nation in Modern Latin America*. Chapel Hill: University of North Carolina Press.

Bost, Suzanne Michelle. 2003. *Mulattas and Mestizas: Representing Mixed Identities in the Americas, 1850–2000*. Athens: University of Georgia Press.

Captain-Hidalgo, Yvonne. 1994. *The Culture of Fiction in the Works of Manuel Zapata Olivella*. Columbia: University of Missouri Press.

Corbey, Raymond, and Joep Leerson, eds. 1991. *Alterity, Identity, Image: Selves and Others in Society and Scholarship*. Amsterdam: Editions Rodopi.

de Luca, Dina. 2001. "La práctica autobiográfica de Manuel Zapata Olivella en ¡*Levántate mulato! 'Por mi raza hablará el espíritu*.'" *Afro-Hispanic Review* 20.1: 43–54.

González Echeverría, Roberto, and Enrique Pupo-Walker, eds. 1996. *The Cambridge History of Latin American Literature*. 3 vols. Cambridge: Cambridge University Press.

Hartley, John. 2002. *Communication, Cultural, and Media Studies: The Key Concepts*. 3rd ed. London: Routledge.

Jackson, Richard L. 1997. *Black Writers and the Hispanic Canon*. New York: Twayne.

Jaramillo Uribe, Jaime. 1965. "Mestizaje y diferenciación social en el Nuevo Reino de Nueva Granada en la Segunda mitad del siglo XVIII." *Anuario Colombiano de historia social y de la cultura* 3.2: 21–42.

Larraín, Jorge. 2000. *Identity and Modernity in Latin America*. Oxford: Polity; Malden, Mass.: Blackwell.

Lewis, Marvin A. 1997. "Manuel Zapata Olivella, and the Art of Autobiography." In *Memorias—IX Congreso de la Asociación de Colombianistas*, ed. Myriam Luque, Montserrat Ordóñez, and Betty Osorio, 279–91. Santafé de Bogotá: Universidad de los Andes/Pennsylvania State University.

Mariátegui, José Carlos. 1973. *Siete ensayos de interpretación de la realidad peruana*. Lima: Empresa Editora Amauta.

Martí, José. 1963–66. *Obras completas*. 27 vols. La Habana: Editorial Nacional de Cuba.

———. 1970. *Sus mejores páginas*. Ed. Raimundo Lazo. Mexico City: Editorial Porrúa.

Martínez Echazábal, Lourdes. 1998. "Mestizaje and the Discourse of National/Cultural Identity in Latin America, 1845–1959." *Latin American Perspectives* 25.3 (May): 21–42.

Miller, Nicola. 1999. *In the Shadow of the State: Intellectuals and the Quest for National Identity in Twentieth-Century Spanish America*. London: Verso.

Oviedo, José Miguel. 1996. "The Modern Essay in Spanish America." In *The Cambridge History of Latin American Literature*, ed. Roberto González Echeverría and Enrique Pupo-Walker, 2: 365–405. Cambridge: Cambridge University Press.

Pinochet Le-Brun, Tancredo. 1914. *Viaje de esfuerzo*. Santiago: Imprenta Universitaria.

Prescott, Laurence E. 2000. *Without Hatreds or Fears: Jorge Artel and the Struggle for Black Literary Expression in Colombia*. Detroit: Wayne State University Press.

Sarmiento, Domingo F. [1845] 1997. *Facundo: Civilización y barbarie*. Ed. Roberto Yahni. 3rd ed. Madrid: Cátedra.

Shumway, Nicolas. 1996. "The Essay in Spanish South America: 1800 to *Modernismo*." In *The Cambridge History of Latin American Literature*, ed. Roberto González Echeverría and Enrique Pupo-Walker, 1: 557–89. Cambridge: Cambridge University Press.

Stabb, Martin S. 1967. *In Quest of Identity: Patterns in the Spanish American Essay of Ideas*. Chapel Hill: University of North Carolina Press.

Vasconcelos, José. [1979] 1997. *The Cosmic Race: A Bilingual Edition*. Trans. Didier T. Jaén. Baltimore: Johns Hopkins University Press.

Wade, Peter. 1999. *Race and Ethnicity in Latin America*. London: Pluto Press.

———. 2001. "Racial Identity and Nationalism: A Theoretical View from Latin America." *Ethnic and Racial Studies* 24.5: 845–65.

Wilson, Peter J. 1973. *Crab Antics: The Social Psychology of English-speaking Negro Societies of the Caribbean*. New Haven, Conn.: Yale University Press.

Winters, Loretta I., and Herman L. DeBose, eds. 2003. *New Faces in a Changing America: Multiracial Identity in the 21st Century*. Thousand Oaks, Calif.: Sage Publications.

Zapata Olivella, Manuel. 1948. "Para conocernos a nosotros mismos. [¿]Cuál es el 'biotipo' colombiano?" *El Tiempo*, March 1, 4, 17.

———. 1949. "La sombra de Martí: Manuel Lorenzo." *El Universal*, September 6, 4, 8.

———. 1963. "América mestiza: Un gran tema de novela." *El Tiempo*, November 10, Lecturas Dominicales, 3.

———. 1966. "Medicina y conciencia mágica." *Páginas de cultura* 11 (January and February): 1, 7–8.

———. 1967. "Mis ajetreos en el novelar hispanoamericano." *Boletín cultural y bibliográfico* 10.1 (January): 69–73.

———. 1973. "Por una política educativa de identidad nacional." *Arco* 146 (March): 25–28.

———. 1974. *El hombre colombiano*. Bogotá: Canal Ramírez-Antares, Imprenta.

———. 1977. "Identidad del negro en América Latina." *El Pueblo*, August 28, Semanario Cultural, 6–7, 12.

———. 1987. *Lève-toi, mulatre! L'esprit parlera à travers ma race*. Trans. Claude Bourguignon and Claude Coffon. Paris: Payot.

———. 1990. *¡Levántate mulato! "Por mi raza hablará el espíritu."* Bogotá: Rei Andes Ltda.

9

Afro-centrism as an Intercultural Force in Ecuador

MICHAEL HANDELSMAN

De nosotros, los indios y los negros que en mi criterio, nos encontramos en procesos de definición
y re-afirmación de lo que hemos sido, de lo que somos y de lo que queremos ser. (As for us, the
Indians and Blacks, I believe we find ourselves in processs of definition and re-affirmation
of what we have been, what we are, and what we want to be.)

Airuruma Kowi, Kichwa writer

Preliminary Observations

It would be absurd to continue to hold on to the idea of a highly centralized and privileged Lettered City as the primordial source of thought and
knowledge at this stage of the history of social relations in Latin America;
in fact, the various indigenous and black movements throughout Latin
America, for example, render irrelevant the thought of the intellectual as
absolute defender and protector of marginal social groups. It would be just
as absurd, however, to think that intellectuals do not continue to play a
necessary and important role in the many struggles for democratization
and decolonization that have been so much a part of the world after the
fall of the Berlin Wall. Alain Touraine has pointed out in his book *Can We
Live Together? Equality and Difference* that intellectuals "must . . . provide us
with a representation of the world, of the changes occurring in it, and of the
actors who can transform the spontaneous tendency to defend and assert
the existence of the Subject into conscious actions and movements which
can, in their turn, make political action meaningful once more." Touraine
insists, "Our most urgent need is the need for ideas, rather than political or
economic programmes. Practices are always ahead of theories" (2000, 300).
George Yúdice in turn, has observed (quoting Mauricio Dias and Walter
Riedweg) that art, in general, is for raising questions: "Not to solve them
but to point them out, making them present and important as the resulting

end-products. Art can create space for doubts and fragilities that have more to do with real life than specific results do" (2003, 321).

These same affirmations regarding the still important contributions of intellectuals and art have also been made by Edouard Glissant, who suggested that "writing is a site of struggle."[1] This struggle, it is to be understood, acquires its true meaning when writing is deployed to counteract "the rhetoric of modernity" and "logic of coloniality," according to Walter Mignolo,[2] referring to the civilizing project that was born in Europe in the sixteenth and seventeenth centuries, and which for five hundred years has subjected Latin America's masses to untold policies and practices of exclusion and of exploitation. Mignolo's formulation is no different from Silvia Rivera Cusicanqui's observations to the effect that internal and internalized colonialism is explained more through its practices of domination than through exploitation.[3] The common thread in these proposals has to do with the need to take apart the power relations that constitute coloniality and colonial difference.

In declaring, "I write in the presence of all the languages of the world,"[4] and in defining Caribbean *creolité* in terms of identities that are relational instead of issuing from a single source (that is, according to the European tradition), Glissant created an international forum wherein the diverse voices among his audience began collectively to decipher the enigma articulated by Touraine: "How can we live together with our differences?" (2000, 51). With Touraine, we might therefore reiterate that "a society that can recognize the diversity of individuals, social groups and cultures will be a strong society, provided that it can also allow them to communicate with one another by stimulating their desire to see that both they and the Other are involved in the same constructive task" (181).

It might be felt that Gayatri Spivak's concept of strategic essentialism, articulated some years ago (1999), no longer serves as an effective tool in the struggle to resignify power relations, be they of race, class, or gender. The Afro-centrism, however, that has slowly emerged in Ecuador since 1990 forces us to take another look at Spivak's formulation in the intercultural context, to show thereby that certain supposedly essentialist movements, on the basis of their own specificities, still offer democratic alternatives. This is the case of Juan Montaño Escobar, a contemporary writer from Esmeraldas, whose work as an editor for the newspaper *Hoy* in Quito, on the one hand, and as a short story writer, on the other, allows us to see the degree to which the Afro-ideological element transcends isolated and isolating categories. As he himself states: "Expressing oneself from within the context of Negritude is not to limit nor to diminish oneself by seeking refuge in a limiting concept." It is, rather, "the concept of soul infused by worlds that may either be similar or contrasting" (2002g, 8).

In the following analysis, I propose a reading of Juan Montaño Escobar from the standpoint of "strategic essentialism." This might afford a decolonization of the official representations of Ecuador's people of African descent (and of all of the Afro-American disapora), since these representations continue to function as naturalizing and essentializing policies responsible for silencing and making the marginalized groups of Ecuadorian society invisible. To insist, therefore, on the Afro-diasporic concept in terms of a particular identity based on a common historical and cultural identity would thus constitute an act of confrontation and reappropriation that would subvert coloniality's power relations. If we look at the issue from the point of view of the conflicts and complexities that characterize a country such as Ecuador, where people of African descent, as well as indigenous people, question an entire history of exclusions, and propose a new Ecuador based on pluri-culturalism and pluri-nationalism, then we would understand how Afro-centrism constitutes an intercultural strategy. This strategy, instead of reproducing the binary of white-*mestizo*/Afro-indigenous, opens toward new social practices that, citing Catherine Walsh, "form part of a new . . . social, political and epistemological project of making Ecuador's diverse social actors *intercultural*" (2002a, 135).

Undoubtedly, Walsh's preference for a term such as "interculturality" highlights the fluid and evolutionary aspect of a still incomplete process, which conceives of identity beyond its traditionally static and homogenizing definitions on the one hand. On the other hand, it insists on the potential of the intercultural project for resignifying the power relations that characterize coloniality and colonial difference. It is important to bear in mind that the struggle to counteract and overcome the harmful effects of five centuries of deculturation, subalternization, and marginalization has to be effected from the multiple platforms of colonial difference. As Walsh observes, "Identity is an oppositional and strategically political term, a way to articulate historical and political difference . . . and of organizing a 'national conscience' in the decolonization struggles" (Walsh, Shiwy, Castro-Gómez 2002d, 183).

Although there are those who would wish to delegitimize the issue of identity as trite, anachronistic, and even separatist, especially with globalization and a world-system in which borders have disappeared, it is to be remembered that "the experience of globality is always that of historically situated individuals, with specific resources and limitations" (Trouillot 2002, 15). So that beyond a mere exercise in personal affirmation, identity is being articulated in many places the world over precisely as alternative propositions that promote thinking locally and acting globally. This is my understanding of Elisabeth Mudimbe-Boyi, who points out that "in this world order dominated by capitalism, nations, communities, and individuals are seeking ways of participating in a global culture, but without letting themselves be absorbed in it even when they interact with it and function within it" (2002, xi–xii).

This same contestatory spirit is behind the creation in Ecuador of the Fondo Documental Afro-Andino (Afro-Andean Fund), which is "an initiative of the Simón Bolivar Andean University in Quito and the Proceso de Comunidades Negras in collaboration with other black organizations in the country" to "address the invisibilization of African cultural premises in Ecuador and other Andean countries."[5] Obviously the problem of invisibility from which Afro-Ecuadorians suffer obtains all over the African diaspora in the Americas. Beyond the celebration, then, of remote ancestral roots in a continent far from America, the references to Africa are to be understood as an integral part of a broader strategy of combating coloniality as power and as knowledge. In other words, the above mentioned project of the Fondo Documental Afro-Andino, together with the organizing efforts of numerous grass-roots black organizations, is to be seen as part of a transnational process of recuperation and resignification of Afro-diasporic experience in the Americas.[6] Effectively, the themes of identity, of the ancestral past, of territory, of collective rights, and of ethno-education invoke an entire history of literal and cultural maroonage. In this they put in motion a process of reconstitution of new subjectivities capable of taking charge of their own representations inside and outside their respective communities.

The affirmation of an Afro-diasporic identity in Ecuador does not mean an enclosing of the black community in an isolating or essentialist category. The Afro-diasporic as a vindicatory project, according to Juan García, has the basic objective of making people of African descent visible, and of creating spaces from which they can take cognizance of their interests and needs. From this point they might generate their own political projects and policies thereby to realize the desired objective. Walsh, in turn, explains that "without social and political visibility in the national sphere, and without black institutions and nationally recognized leaders, Afro-Ecuadorian actors would remain invisible in society in general and also in the intellectual and academic world" (Walsh with García 2002c).

The true scope of the Afro-Ecuadorian movement is appreciated in Juan García's observation that "the life stories of the guardians of the *décima* tradition provide irrefutable proof that the populations of African descent who live along the Pacific coast possess a full cultural tradition whose real dimensions are known by few and which is today in danger of being lost for good as a consequence of the systematic loss of their ancestral lands" (García Salazar 2003a, 13). This brief sample of Juan García's thought situates the Afro-diaspora in several simultaneous and complementary contexts. First of all it refers to orality (the *décima* tradition) as a dynamic source of knowledge throughout history. In highlighting the fact of their ownership of the representation and dissemination of this same history, Juan García gives protagonism back to the people of African descent, and not as objects of study but as subjects of their own histories.[7] Juan García then reflects on Afro-diasporic communities and sees them in terms of their broader transnational commonality, since referring to them in terms of their coastal geography undermines the arbitrary nationalist cartographies that have tried to separate Afro-Colombians from Afro-Ecuadorians in particular. Finally, and quite apart from any intention of idealizing ancient Africa or freezing it folklorically as a lost and remote past, Juan García recognizes the dangers of acculturation and understands that cultural survival depends on the defense of territorial rights, rights that continue to be violated by mining interests, logging interests, and shrimping interests. Afro-diasporic identity as a cultural or ethnic expression (or that of any subalternized group) is thereby problematized and acquires a profoundly political dimension as well as one of self-defense.

Unfortunately, any social movement or discourse that is closely identified with a particular group, especially one defined in racial or ethnic terms, is likely to be taken to extremes or distorted in such a way as to undermine its credibility or legitimacy. This phenomenon is painfully evident in Ecuador in the case of the indigenous movement, for example, which still has not been able to convince the broader population that its interests are in the final analysis those of all Ecuadorians (for example, the defense of the environment, opposition to various neoliberal policies, protesting against corruption). Although the black movement in Ecuador is not as recognized as the indigenous one on account of its smaller population and certain organizational deficiencies, Afro-Ecuadorians also feel that their projects are ignored or misrepresented by the majority of Ecuadorians. The majority has been unwilling to think beyond the traditional racial and ethnic schemes; schemes that are infested with a racism born of five hundred years of coloniality. We are therefore forced once again to confront the problem of invisibility and, at the same time, the need to make visible what the majority refuses to see. It is from this that strategic essentialism as a reply and an act of self-defense emerges. In Juan García's words, "What Ecuador's black population now needs more than ever to be: different" (2003a, 13).

From "Strategic Essentialism" to an "In-house" Strategy

From the emergence in 1990 of an indigenous movement with a determinative role in Ecuador's contemporary history, together with the gradual and constant processes of vindication realized by Afro-Ecuadorian communities, a new discourse has emerged in the country. This discourse has appropriated Spivak's theory of strategic essentialism to defend itself in terms of interculturality. Undoubtedly, the most novel element of interculturality as a concept and as a social practice has to do with the fact that it was created by Ecuador's indigenous people (and by extension with an ever increasing number of black leaders) out of the very heart of their respective communities. In other words, the communities that were once excluded and silenced have now taken hold of the word to reinvent it and resignify it in describing democracy, the nation, and Ecuador itself. Unlike apparently similar concepts such as multiculturalism, hybridity, or even *mestizaje* itself, interculturality does not project itself merely as a celebration of diversity or in terms of the coexistence of racially or ethnically different communities. Interculturality refers to a process whose objective is social transformation.

Since interculturality implies a reconstitution of traditional modalities of representation of colonial difference, the symbolic field is an important component of the new process, which points toward the construction of new imaginaries of a pluri-cultural and pluri-national country in which communities of African descent and of indigenous people assume a protagonizing role in this process of decolonization and transformation. It should come as no surprise that from the very beginning of the indigenous movement, the importance of bilingual education has been stressed as a response to an educational system that has been exclusionary and homogenizing, in spite of being supposedly national. For their part, some Afro-Ecuadorian groups have concentrated on developing ethno-educational projects to combat their condition of invisibility. According to Juan García, "Ethnoeducation is what is now known as the process of in-house teaching and learning, aimed at strengthening that which our ancestors have taught us" (n.d., 14).

Rescuing or recuperating the collective memory has been conceived, in great measure, as an epistemological struggle since Afro-descendants—like other subalternized groups—have been folklorized and relegated to a preteritive a-modern position, bereft of knowledges that are assumed to be an integral part of the rest of the nation. Undoubtedly, while this collective memory remains lost, both for Ecuadorians in general and for Afro-Ecuadorians in particular, a relationship based on respect and equality cannot exist. Effectively, the project of ethno-education, aimed at "strengthening one's own," has as its objective the establishment of the foundations of an Afro-descendant identity based on dynamic practices of knowing on the one hand and of self-esteem on the other. This program of vindication and affirmation of blackness, therefore, has its raison d'être in the resignification and the subversion of programs of colonial differentiation. At the same time, while blackness as a racial category hails from colonial differentiation, the movements of Afro-descendants (such as the Regional Council of Palenques or Maroon Communities and the Proceso Black Communities of Esmeraldas) are not only reappropriating it on their own terms but also in full awareness of colonial power relations of the past and the present (Walsh 2002b, 68).

As an intercultural strategy, ethno-education proposes a paradigm of otherness whose historical point of departure is subalternization, and from this standpoint it turns protest into a proposal for a different society. It is instructive to recall here the words of Juan García: "There are many activists in the Afro-Ecuadorian community who oppose being identified only with music and marimba dance and who rightfully insist that Esmeralda's blacks are much more than merely marimba music" (2003b, 6). These are highly suggestive words, since they reflect the type of introspection that ethno-education provides as well as its struggle to reconstitute the black communities as agents of their own cultural representation, representation in socio-political, symbolic, and artistic terms. Effectively, the sense of being a community that is "culturally different, with all that that entails" reminds us of a process in which subaltern groups can "control and construct their own forms of otherness, acquiring thereby a dynamic form of cultural agency" (Young 2002, 160). At the same time it is clear that "ethno-education is a social process that is a product of the needs and expectations of the communities but always in the reflexive sense of projecting one's own elements as well as those of others, with the objective of promoting new forms of social and cultural interaction and new images of what it means to be black" (Walsh with García 2002c).

Juan Montaño Escobar and Afro-centrism as an Intercultural Strategy

Escribir desde la negritud es . . . el camino para llegar como cultura diversa a todas las culturas di-
versas (Writing from Negritude is the path to arrive as a diverse culture to all other diverse cultures).

Juan Montaño Escobar

So far I have tried to establish the social and historical context out of which I plan to analyze a representative sample of Juan Montaño Escobar's prose writing. In my book *Lo afro y la plurinacionalidad: El caso ecuatoriano visto desde su literatura* ([1999] 2001), I offered an analysis of some literary and cultural journals from Esmeraldas that were published during the course of the twentieth century, in order to establish the long and close relationship that existed among numerous provincial intellectuals and contemporary grass-roots activist groups such as, for example, the Proceso de Comunidades Negras del Norte de Esmeraldas (see chapter 7). Bearing in mind that the history of Afro-descendants of Ecuador is characterized by five centuries of maroonage and the creation of multiple maroon villages in that particular Pacific region of the country, I was interested in pointing out that that history, although absent from the official versions of the history of the country, forms the ideological bases of many works written by important Afro-Ecuadorian intellectuals. In effect, the basis of my argument came from Vincent Leitch's idea that "literary texts and non literary texts circulate inseparably" (1992, 164).

Adalberto Ortiz, Nelson Estupiñán Bass, and Antonio Preciado are three writers of renown in whose works one can find a dynamic intertextuality of oral traditions and written expressions. In the cases of Estupiñán and Preciado, perhaps more than with Ortiz, their literary production shows evidence of contacts and interactions that they have maintained with various local and regional communities. Juan Montaño Escobar is undoubtedly an important legatee of the best of this literary tradition, having distinguished himself as a reporter, short story writer, and political activist who defends the rights of people of African descent, both in his country and in the rest of the diaspora. As I hope to establish below, the literary output of this Esmeraldan constitutes a clear manifestation of his capacity for producing a literature that is integrally immersed in the processes of interculturality that I have commented on earlier.

Juan García's proposals on ethno-education and the need to recuperate and cultivate the collective memory of the ancestors are the very substance of Juan Montaño Escobar's work. The voices that were silenced and muzzled and desperate to be heard from their location within the struggle against coloniality and colonial differentiation make their presence felt through his work at all times. Their presence in Escobar's work is not limited to a superficial reproduction of linguistic expressions, colloquialisms, or local slang that might be easy to identify with certain Afro-Ecuadorian communities. Rather, Montaño Escobar's linkage to the diverse processes of identitarian affirmation is his awareness that the orality as well as the writing of the black communities of Ecuador suffer from the effects of being made invisible, hence his critique that "in Ecuador's official houses of culture there is no space for Afro-Ecuadorian creativity . . . it is not allowed in their publications, it is not included in their research projects, it is not included in their presses, nor does it form a part of their plans and projects" (2002g, 10).

Also, and in the same way in which ethno-education as an intercultural strategy would wish to reach beyond purely ethnic parameters limited by many to inoffensive multiculturalist discourses, Juan Montaño Escobar is elaborating a literary project with colonial difference and its power relations as its point of departure. That is to say that artistic representation through journalism or through fiction belongs to a collective process that is situated in a socio-historic context in which the ancestral register is conserved and cultivated because it feeds alternative experiences and strategies of making the invisible visible. According to Montaño Escobar, writing from the standpoint of negritude "is a way of recognizing ourselves in all of our faces and all of our souls. It is a way of making ourselves known in all the lives of the infinite polyhedron that we are. It is recognizing ourselves free from the prejudices, the schemes, and the murderous cultural syntheses of the rest of the society. To write from the standpoint of negritude is to defeat in its quotidian philosophy racism's ideological persistence" (2002g, 6–7).

Journalism as a Strategy for Afro-Ecuadorian Visibility

Juan Montaño Escobar is known primarily for his weekly column in the periodical *Hoy*, published in Quito and ranked as the third most widely read newspaper in the country. His opinion appears every Saturday under the pseudonym of Jazzman. Accordingly, his writing space is known as a jam session.[8] Bearing in mind that the Afro-centric writing of Juan Montaño Escobar ("writing from negritude") has as its fundamental objective to make the Afro-diasporic question visible within the national scenario, it is understandable that references to jazz invoke a collective that transcends cultural and geographic frontiers without abandoning its Africanist base.

Indeed, it is no accident that Montaño Escobar has compared his distinctly Africanist writing to an invitation directed at "other neighboring cultures to understand and appreciate us for that difference and within that difference" (2002g, 13.) As a musical idiom, therefore, jazz constitutes a diasporic expression par excellence, and owing to its origins in improvisation it points toward a creative process of open and spontaneous participation and a performativity that is without imposed and officialist limitations.

It is hardly surprising then that the language of this jazzman is eminently musical and percussive and full of alliteration, rhyme, and a general preference for oxytonical and proparoxytonical words. In fact, an Afro-Ecuadorian aura permeates the entire "jazzistic" discourse of this native of Esmeraldas who is willing to pick up and "swing" with any topic. As he himself has explained, "This jam session will make you hear some answer-finding drums." (January 26, 2002h, 4A); and on another occasion, "This jazzman loses restaint when he hears the drums." (May 4, 2002l, 4A). The constant references to Afro-diasporic musical instruments and to daily practices and religious traditions that evoke African origins are expressed by means of great agility in linguistic and cultural appropriation that not only recalls the poetic project of Nicolás Guillén's *Motivos de son* and *Sóngoro Cosongo*, but also reveals a long history of decolonization and resistance by way of "strategic translingualism ([1930-1931] 2002)." In other words, Montaño Escobar, without renouncing Spanish as his native language, makes it Afro-Ecuadorian by placing its Euro-Hispanic referents in such an uncommon juxtaposition as to render it difficult for one to decide whether it is the Afro-diasporic essence that is absorbing the Spanish or vice versa. Be that as it may, what is beyond a doubt is that Montaño Escobar's jam sessions open the possibility of resignifying the use and reception of the Spanish language in Ecuador as a "phenomenon of 'glocalization'" that disarticulates the rigid binary model of metropolis/periphery (at the international level) or of center/margins (at the national level).[9]

If we can indeed say that the Afro-centric proposition of Montaño Escobar seems to privilege expressions and cultural experiences that are foreign to the majority of Ecuadorians, his "in house" orientation does not propose an isolation of Afro-descendants from the rest of the country or a replacement of one exclusionary system by another. Making the Afro-diasporic visible within the national context is not the same thing as essentializing it, and he has, in fact, stressed with reference to the matter of "writing from negritude" that "it is not a question of upending Spanish by the use of colloquial forms created to close off areas of communication, or of creating hermetic communities of speech. No such thing. It has to do with cultivating our identity among other identities—cultivating interculturality. You have to write for a particular reading public, but by using what you have and having them understand you from the standpoint of what they have, what they identify, and value" (2002g, 12).

Although Montaño Escobar's journalistic topics vary greatly, each jam session overflows with satire and irony while the jazzman interprets a fragile Ecuador through the rhythms of a *son*, pure and defiant.[10] The eternal crisis to which Ecuadorians seem to have been condemned due to centrist governments that lose their way in the vagaries of politics from which the majority derives no benefit—while the elite benefit greatly, as always—produces, for example, an item titled "Tuesday 15th." On the eve of the presidential elections of 2002, Montaño Escobar exposes the contradictions of the current president, Gustavo Noboa, who was as distant from the urban ghettos as he ever was in his presidential palace at Carondelet. A general note of alarm is sounded from the first lines: "The slow beat of black music in the tropical pathways of my people, and the bewildering merriment of the national *caciques* irremediably stuck in prehistoric time. Nothing different from any given Tuesday" (2002j). Montaño Escobar makes his intentions clear immediately: "But that is not what this jam session is about. The president is making history way up there, but down here it's another story. The GNP's 54 percent growth does not trickle down here."

Following this invocation, Montaño Escobar turns his attention to the national crisis as experienced from the north in Esmeraldas and denounces, more specifically, the official policies that have resulted in the handing over of the province's natural resources to fishing, logging, and shrimping interests "whose price for the concession is 'ha ha.'" Not content with just critiquing the government, the jazzman makes reference to the state of confusion and doubt that besets the region's peasants, who "remember their maroon forefathers and still quietly, like a confession, seek solidarity from the Catholic Church at Esmeraldas before 'seeking help from the FARC.' Can anyone militarize the desperate hopes of the black communities?" With no hope in a system whose promises have gone unfulfilled for centuries, Montaño Escobar puts aside the subtleties of rhythm and makes a frontal declaration in defense of the Afro-Esmeraldan communities: "Let no one take pity on Esmerald's poor, any more, let them get mad and show their solidarity that way—as Malcolm X might say—this, of course, is politically more honest, and more correct."

Some months later, the jazzman returns to the topic of ecocide, which itself reflects much of Afro-diasporic history not only in Ecuador but also in the rest of the American continent. Inspired by a song called "Timbiré" by the Africa Homo Sapiens group, with a similar agenda, Montaño Escobar exclaims that "these brothers and sisters are right to sing about Northern Esmeraldas, which is being voraciously exploited and erased from the map" (2002l). At the same time the significance of the name of the group that has inspired this particular jam session should not be overlooked, nor can the readers and listeners ignore the call to popular resistance, one whose roots go back to their forefathers. First Montaño Escobar lets it be known that "there is enough sociology to stand as a record of the ethnic, political, and social violence; so this jazzman will take the route of the drums. Resentment has been refined over a long history of humiliation, [and] physical and spiritual suffering for some of us." Indeed, the collective memory does not lie, and after putting into context the injustices faced by the communities of Northern Esmeraldas Province, Montaño Escobar insists that "resistance can be born" out of the present predatory policies of the government.

Although it would be unfair to reduce Montaño Escobar's journalistic and literary contribution to strictly racial matters, or his concept of negritude to the particular interests of a sector of the national population that is merely 7 percent of the total, there is no denying the need to denounce the harm that racism continues to inflict on Ecuador's black communities. This is why I feel that it is important that he published one of his jam sessions on precisely this topic on August 10, 2002, on the very anniversary of the first call for national independence in Ecuador. In the midst of the festivities dedicated to the national heroes and their ideals, the jazzman's eulogies take a contrary rhythm and tone. His Ecuador is to be found in the neighborhoods in which "black people's lives are being made a mess of by those in power in our country: both central and local government, authorities of any stripe, metropolitan press and ugly paternalism. Beneath these entities," obviously, "lies a thinly disguised racism, as can be seen in the political neglect by the state and in the baseness of their rhetoric" (2002b). The celebrations of August 10, then, uphold a freedom that is still unattained, as he explains, "Afro-Ecuadorians continue the quest after this happiness through the ongoing secret desire that 'things will be better.'" And so as not to disengage himself completely from the nationalist celebration of the anniversary, the jam session closes on a patriotic note with the wish that things might indeed improve one day. "How can one doubt it, if black people's most powerful tool has been faith? Faith as a collective act of will that animated the humanity of Nelson Mandela, of Malcolm X, or of Jaime Hurtado."

August 10 as articulated by the jazzman is not lacking in patriotic spirit; rather, it celebrates the unbreakable resilience of the popular will that refuses to succumb and seeks inspiration in the glorious examples of its heroes. This same sense of struggle that unites Afro-Esmeraldans (and Afro-Ecuadorians in general) unites all liberation and human rights movements and has not dissipated into generalities.

In conclusion, the immediate imperative of black vindicatory movements continues to be that of making blackness visible, not as a folkloric project or by way of imagined essentialisms. In the words of the jazzman, there are eight reasons behind the idea of writing from negritude: "One: to throw stones at the system of ideas that exist about the Afro-Ecuadorian community. Two: as a means of cultural rebellion. Three: to reconstitute Ecuadorian and American life with us as primary actors. Four: for our art, to create a foundation for black pride. Five: so that no one else might speak for us or have a situation in which we are forgotten even though we are in plain sight. Six: because we have a lot to say from the abundance of our memories. Seven: as a means of cultural affirmation. Eight: because life is poliedric and requires other colors, sounds, and tastes" (2002g, 13). Maybe this last reason is the one that most clearly indicates the intercultural projection that defines blackness in the Ecuadorian context. In the final analysis, Afro-centrism, at least the way in which Juan Montaño Escobar, among others in the struggle, handles the concept, points toward a process of genuine democratization in a country that is still stuck between the power and knowledge of coloniality and the pluri-nationality conceived from the street corners of the neighborhoods invoked by the jazzman, where most of Ecuador's population lives.

Notes

Translated by Jerome Branche. This essay is a shorter version of a chapter published in my book *Leyendo la globalización desde la mitad del mundo: Identidad y resistencias en el Ecuador* (2005).

1. From an address at the Fourth International Conference in Latin American Cultural Studies, University of Pittsburgh, March 2004.

2. Ibid.

3. Ibid.

4. Ibid.

5. The fund consists of a collection of more than three thousand hours of recordings of recollections by elders from various black communities in Ecuador, done by Juan García, a historian and community activist leader, over the past thirty years. The fund has, besides, some eight thousand photographs of members of Ecuador's black popula-

tion, which, together with the tapes, preserve the memory of five centuries of history of Ecuador's citizens of African descent (information taken from a brochure from Simón Bolivar University).

6. The Fondo Documental Afro-Andino is not only a university or academic program dedicated only to the study of people of African descent. Effectively, the Simón Bolivar Andean University has transcended subject/object binary schemes with this project. Its presence is a clear expression of the intercultural potential to be realized when different groups are committed to working alongside each other.

7. Juan García conceives of the project of ethno-education in terms of the input of the elders in the Afro-Ecuadorian communities. The objective of this education is to enable them to reconcile the past with the future. As he has explained: " . . . Elders and guardians of tradition, in different communal spaces, have tried to instill in the younger generations of Ecuadorians the need that black Ecuadorians have of assuming responsibility for executing their own educational objectives." García adds, also, "The meanings and memory of slavery continue to be zealously retained in the voices of the ancestors through the collective consciousness of the communities as the most important reason for articulating processes of resistance to everything that is imposed by dominant society" (n.d., 11).

8. Juan Montaño Escobar has been writing for *Hoy* for more than ten years. Due to limitations of time and space, I have limited my analysis of his newspaper contributions to the year 2002. Although my choice of year has been arbitrary, I believe that the material under study is representative of his work and allows for relevant reflections regarding the Afro-diasporic question in the national context.

9. I am taking the idea of "strategic translingualism" from an essay of Emily Apter in which she analyzes the Martinican novelist Raphaël Confiant's *La Savane des petrifications* (see Apter 2002, 185–200).

10. The *son* is a traditional Afro-Cuban musical and dance form.

Works Cited

Albán-Achionte, Adolfo. 2003. "Lo afro: El problema de la identidad y el territorio." Paper for the Doctorado en Estudios Culturales Latinoamericanos seminar, Universidad Andina Simón Bolívar, August.

Apter, Emily. 2002. "Warped Speech: The Politics of Global Translation." In *Beyond Dichotomies*, ed. Elisabeth Mudimbe-Boyi, 185–200. Albany: State University of New York Press.

Castro-Gomez, Santiago. 2000. "Althusser, los estudios culturales y el concepto de ideología." *Revista Iberoamericana* 66.193: 737–51.

Corr, Rachel. 2003. "The Catholic Church, Ritual, and Power in Salasaca." In *Millennial Ecuador*, ed. Norman E. Whitten, 102–8. Iowa City: University of Iowa Press.

Dirlik, Arif. 2002. "Bringing History Back In: Of Diasporas, Hybridities, Places, and Histories." In *Beyond Dichotomies*, ed. Elisabeth Mudimbe-Boyi, 93–127. Albany: State University of New York Press.

Estupiñán Bass, Nelson. 2002. "Proceso de la literatura afroecuatoriana." In *Letras del Ecuador* 18 (August): 14–27.

García Salazar, Juan. N.d. *La tradición oral: Una herramienta para la etnoeducación; Una propuesta de las comunidades de origen afroamericano para aprender casa adentro.* Esmeraldas: FEDOCA.

———, comp. 2003a. *Los guardianes de la tradición: Compositores y decimeros.* Esmeraldas: PRODEPINE.

———, comp. 2003b. *Papá Roncón: Historia de vida.* Quito: Universidad Andina Simón Bolívar.

Guillén, Nicolás. [1930–31] 2002. *Donde nacen las aguas: Antología.* Compilación y nota preliminary de Nicolás Hernández Guillén y Norberto Codina, Mexico: Fondo de cultura económica.

Handelsman, Michael. 1999. *Lo afro y la plurinacionalidad: El caso ecuatoriano visto desde su literatura.* University of Mississippi: Romance Monographs.

———. 2001. *Lo afro y la plurinacionalidad: El caso ecuatoriano visto desde su literatura.* 2nd ed. Quito: Ediciones Abya-Yala.

———. 2005. *Leyendo la globalización desde la mitad del mundo: Identidad y resistencias en el Ecuador.* Quito: Editorial El Conejo.

Henry, Paget. 2000. *Caliban's Reason: Introducing Afro-Caribbean Philosophy.* New York: Routledge.

Kanneh, Kadiatu. 1998. *African Identities: Race, Nation, and Culture in Ethnography, Pan-Africanism, and Black Literatures.* London: Routledge.

Kowii, Ariruma. 2003. "Relaciones interétnicas e interculturales del pueblo afro en los Andes del Ecuador." Paper for the Doctorado en Estudios Culturales Latinoamericanos seminar, Universidad Andina Simón Bolívar, August.

Leitch, Vincent B. 1992. *Cultural Criticism, Literary Theory, Poststructuralism.* New York: Columbia University Press.

Montaño Escobar, Juan. 1999. *Así se compone un son.* Quito: Casa de la Cultura Ecuatoriana.

———. 2002a. "Andarele de 450 años." *Hoy*, September 21, 4A.

———. 2002b. "Así de Juan. . . ." *Hoy*, August 10, 4A.

———. 2002c. "Bao." *Hoy*, November 30, 4A.

———. 2002d. "Chigualo de color verdadero." *Hoy*, December 28, 4A.

———. 2002e. "Ecolipsis ahora." *Hoy*, May 11, 4A.

———. 2002f. "Encocao a lo Sun Tzu." *Hoy*, December 14, 4A.

———. 2002g. "Esencias de guaguancó." *Letras del Ecuador* 184 (August): 6–13.

———. 2002h. "Esnaqui." *Hoy*, January 26, 4A.

———. 2002i. "La Justicia 'mafiolitizada.'" *Hoy*, January 12, 4A.

———. 2002j. "Martes 15." *Hoy*, January 19, 4A.

———. 2002k. "Siembra." *Hoy*, October 19, 4A.

———. 2002l. "Timbiré, para memorizar." *Hoy*, May 4, 4A.

Mudimbe-Boyi, Elisabeth, ed. 2002. *Beyond Dichotomies: Histories, Identities, Cultures, and the Challenge of Globalization.* Albany: State University of New York Press.

Preciado Bedoya, Antonio. 2002. "Breves consideraciones acerca de la negritud en Esmeraldas." *Letras del Ecuador* 184 (August): 34–37.

Rahier, Jean Muteba. 2003. "Racist Stereotypes and the Embodiment of Blackness (Some Narratives of Female Sexuality in Quito)." In *Millennial Ecuador*, ed. Norman E. Whitten, 296–324. Iowa City: University of Iowa Press.

Spivak, Gayatri. 1999. *A Critique of Postcolonial Reason: Toward a History of the Vanishing Present*. Cambridge: Harvard University Press.

Touraine, Alain. 2000. *Can We Live Together? Equality and Difference*. Trans. David Macey. Stanford, Calif.: Stanford University Press.

Trouillot, Michel-Rolph. 2002. "The Perspective of the World: Globalization Then and Now." In *Beyond Dichotomies*, ed. Elisabeth Mudimbe-Boyi, 3-20. Albany: State University of New York Press.

Walsh, Catherine. N.d. "Interculturality and the Coloniality of Power: An 'Other' Thinking and Positioning from Colonial Difference." Unpublished manuscript.

———. N.d. "(Post)Coloniality in Ecuador: The Indigenous Movement's Practices and Politics of (Re)signification and Decolonization." Unpublished manuscript.

———. 2001. "The Ecuadorian Political Irruption Uprisings, Coups, Rebellions, and Democracy." *Nepantla* 2.1: 173–204.

———. 2002a. "(De)Construir la interculturalidad: Consideraciones críticas desde la política, la colonialidad y los movimientos indígenas y negros en el Ecuador." In *Interculturalidad y política: Desafíos y posibilidades*, ed. Norma Fuller, 115–42. Lima: Instituto de Estuidos Peruanos.

———. 2002b. "The Rearticulation of Political Subjectivities and Colonial Difference in Ecuador. (Reflections on Capitalism and the Geopolitics of Knowledge." *Nepantla* 3.1, 61–97.

Walsh, Catherine, with Juan García. 2002c. "El pensar del emergente movimiento afroecuatoriano: Reflexiones (des)de un proceso." In *Prácticas intelectuales en cultura y poder*, ed. Daniel Matos. Caracas: CLACSO: 317–26.

Walsh, Catherine, Freya Shiwy, and Santiago Castro-Gómez, eds. 2002d. *Indisciplinar las ciencias sociales*. Quito: Universidad Andina Simón Bolívar and Ediciones Abya-Yala.

Walsh, Catherine, ed. 2003. *Estudios culturales latinoamericanos: Retos desde y sobre la Región Andina*. Quito: Universidad Andina Simón Bolivar, Ediciones Abya-Yala.

Whitten, Norman E., ed. 2003. *Millennial Ecuador: Critical Essays on Cultural Transformations and Social Dynamics*. Iowa City: University of Iowa Press.

Young, Robert J. C. 2002. "Ethnicity as Otherness in British Identity Politics." In *Beyond Dichotomies*, ed. Elisabeth Mudimbe-Boyi, 153–67. Albany: State University of New York Press.

Yúdice, George. 2003. *The Expediency of Culture: Uses of Culture in the Global Era*. Durham, N.C.: Duke University Press.

Zúñiga, Luis. 2002. "El horizonte cultural de los pueblos Afrodescendientes." *Letras del Ecuador* 184: 28–33.

10

Creole Counterdiscourses and French Departmental Hegemony

Reclaiming "Here" from "There"

H. ADLAI MURDOCH

In a classic event that underscores the paradoxes of doubleness and ambiguity that continue to define the terrain of the departmental relationship, the fiftieth anniversary of the departmentalization law of 1946 that continues to bind Guadeloupe and Martinique to mainland France, across the reaches of history, culture, and the Atlantic Ocean, was feted twice, in both department and metropole. It was feted first in Paris through an exposition at the Palais de Chaillot from November 16 through December 15, 1996, under the title *Les départements d'outremer: Quatre siècles d'histoire commune.* The paradoxes, contradictions, and erasures implicit in the title of this event were made clear when it was then restaged in the Antilles in an installation in the Salle Osenat in Schoelcher, Martinique on April 9–26, 1997. This example of the double vision that plagues the *départements d'outremer* (DOMs), rendering them essentially and simultaneously both French and West Indian, sums up quite effectively the ironies, hierarchies, and inconsistencies of the now sixty-year-long overseas departmental relationship. Further, the key question of the doubleness of the DOMs—the divergences and differences arising from their complex ethnic, cultural, and historic intersections with France—sets the terms of their specific articulation of French Caribbeanness and points inalterably to central patterns of domination and exclusion, center and periphery that continue to shape this French Caribbean postcolonialism-that-is-not-postcolonialism and its corollaries of intellectual and cultural production.

The geopolitical status of the islands of Guadeloupe and Martinique symbolizes the ambiguities of political development for the French Caribbean region, for if the departmentalization law theoretically bestowed the same rights and privileges on Martinicans and Guadeloupeans as on

258 / H. Adlai Murdoch

French citizens from any other region—as those of the Bouches-du-Rhône, for example—then this relationship implied, in effect, ignoring or effacing continuing colonial dichotomies of race, history, and geography. Over time, then, the populace of the French Caribbean became the inheritors of a double perspective, marking a transatlantic duality of location that increasingly separated them both from their politically independent Anglophone Caribbean counterparts and from the social and cultural materialities of the metropole, to whom they remain inexplicably linked in a complex symbiosis of contentious subordination.

Such a perspective is reflective of a critical perspective articulated by Stuart Hall, who, as Mimi Sheller points out, "explains Caribbean identity in terms of a positioning which is not only dialogic, but also conflictual" (2001, 9). Indeed, this critical combination of geographical distance, economic domination, ethnic and cultural difference, and colonial history join with the political paradoxes of assimilation to render these territories more *colonies* of France rather than the equivalent political entities they theoretically are. Beverley Ormerod makes this point well: "The French Caribbean islands . . . are still owned and ruled by France. Their official status as Departments of France has not greatly altered the realities of political and cultural colonialism" (1985, 3). At the same time, ongoing patterns of capital repatriation, increasing unemployment, conspicuous consumption, and decreasing indigenous business ownership have tended to reinforce impressions of an across-the-board subservience to the metropole that appears to accompany French overseas departmentalization in the Caribbean. Meanwhile, metropolitan gestures toward a granting of increased autonomy are not always taken advantage of with the approbation or alacrity that might be imagined. For example, a recent double referendum, organized in the islands on December 7, 2003, asking the populace to decide on a proposed transformation of their two *régions monodépartementales* into a "new autonomous region" was roundly and soundly defeated, because (so the story goes) the residents feared that this nudge toward self-government would be but the first nail in a French-imposed coffin of enforced independence (with the concomitant loss of privileges and benefits). In other words, this episode provides a striking example of the pervasive paradoxes that have long plagued both axes of France's overseas departmental dyad, a Caribbean population divided from and dependent on its metropolitan center but unwilling, or unable, to assume the full mantle of its Caribbean identity in the political sphere. Alongside such ongoing paradoxes, however, and while bearing in mind the visibility gained by such self-affirming cultural phenomena as *zouk* and the Creole language in which it is sung, the material principles of *antillanité* and *créolité* that have been inscribed in theory and put into narrative practice by Edouard Glissant (1981) and Bernabé, Confiant, and Chamoiseau (1993) respectively clearly appear aimed at the assertion of departmental difference in the face of a metropolitan agenda that recognizes *francité* only as varied iterations of the same.

Given the complex and often conflictual nature of the relationship between the department and the metropole, these French Caribbean discourses should be understood primarily as counterdiscourses; that is, as discursive articulations of both difference and affirmation whose goal is to counter and contest previous hierarchical discourses of domination. In a seminal work, Richard Terdiman conceives and defines "counterdiscourses" through their function "of opposition to . . . modes of perception and assertion," culminating in a set of "principal discursive systems by which writers and artists sought to project an alternative, liberating *newness* against the absorptive capacity of those established discourses" (1985, 13; emphasis in the original). In this way, counterdiscourses are largely grounded in principles of contestation and assertion, using language as a primary tool to construct patterns of creative subversion aimed at "project[ing] the metalanguage on the basis of which a hegemonic discourse can be reconfigured as relative, as contingent, and thus as potentially transcendable" (57). Language is thus inscribed and encoded here as a key arbiter in the subversion of signs, and its capacity to counter hegemonic dominance in a specifically Caribbean context will call for elaborating a strategic relationship of resistance and subversion within a postcolonial framework, as Helen Tiffin points out: "These subversive manoeuvres . . . are what is characteristic of post-colonial texts, as the subversive is characteristic of post-colonial discourse in general. Post-colonial literatures/cultures are thus constituted in counter-discursive rather than homologous practices, and they offer 'fields' of counter-discursive strategies to the dominant discourse" (1995, 95–96). In a critical sense, then, these French Caribbean identitarian and cultural discourses are the product of the material realities that emerge from the DOMs' daily exchange and intersection with the metropole. In the final analysis, the work of Glissant and that of the *créolistes* would impel the radical restructuring of regional expression as a fulcrum for (post)colonial change and political redefinition. This revisioning is grounded in the recognition and realization of hybridity's role in formulating alternative discursive positions. Rather than the binary framework that typically drives the logic of the conceptual dyads—center and periphery, colonial and postcolonial, metropole and department—that have historically undergirded the socio-political structures of the region, principles of pluralism and fluidity begin to supplant the rigid polarities of colonial thought, and indeed such approaches become crucial to understanding the Caribbean process of creolization. For these thinkers, then, the ways in which we have viewed the Caribbean as a postcolonial society—as one dominated by *either* European *or* African socio-cultural traces—must be fundamentally transformed. Indeed, the ethnic, cultural, and linguistic pluralism that is at the center of Caribbean creoleness rewrites traditional notions of hybridity and, implicitly, identity. As Homi Bhabha puts it, "The importance of hybridity is not to be able to trace two original moments from which the third emerges, rather hybridity . . . is the 'third space' which enables other positions to emerge. This third space displaces the histories that constitute it, and sets up new structures of authority" (1994, 114). This process of borrowing and transformation is critical to the Caribbean practices of resistance and identitarian affirmation, as Manuel, Bilby, and Largey explain: "The entire Caribbean shares a history of European colonialism, slavery, ethnic and class conflict, nationalism, and, in the twentieth century, North American imperialist influence. Within this . . . complex process of creolization . . . Caribbean peoples have fashioned new, distinctly local genres out of elements taken from disparate traditions . . . and they often combine elements of cultural resistance as well as dominant ideology and . . . local traditions as well as those borrowed from international styles" (1995, 2). These strategies of transformation and recombination ultimately laid the groundwork for the distinctive multivalency of Caribbean performance culture.

Indeed, such varied but related regional theoretical concepts as Glissant's *antillanité*, Brathwaite's creolization, and Bernabé's, Chamoiseau's, and Confiant's *créolité* are proof positive of the dynamism of multicultural perspectives aimed at national or cultural self-affirmation. In an important way, these authors have extended the boundaries and limitations of previous discursive approaches to the regional geopolitical problematic, including the work of those critics and theorists who are perceived as writing from the margin. While Aimé Césaire's *négritude* was ultimately circumscribed by its implicit grounding in an alternative set of binaries to the colonial hierarchies it sought to contest, and Frantz Fanon's *Peau noire, masque blanc* and *Les damnés de la terre* successfully exposed the psychological dimensions, persistent hierarchies, and false assumptions upon which the practice of colonial domination and assimilation and its corollary of internalized inferiority were predicated, such analyses, as valuable as they were, never quite managed to deconstruct the specificities of the French Caribbean geo-political and socio-cultural experience. Edouard Glissant, in contrast, has long sought to construct a discursive framework for coming to terms with the myriad complexities produced by colonialism and, more importantly, departmentalization in the region, one that recognizes the extended impact of (neo)colonialism on the departmental subject. Indeed, as Celia Britton cogently points out, Glissant sees the departmental case as particularly se-vere in that "domination by the metropolis continues, but in a far more covert and mystifying form than previously, and . . . economic deprivation is not the main problem . . . but alienated identification with French culture is all the more pervasive" (1999, 4). Glissant's work stages the poetics and praxis of identity in the Caribbean context, his emphasis on the genesis and influence of regional pluralisms being of such far-reaching consequence that contemporary authors, such as Chamoiseau and Confiant, have long acknowledged his work as having provided the possibility for them to ar-ticulate their vision of a creolized Caribbean culture. For Glissant, the twin primary principles of *antillanité*, or Caribbeanness, and a *poétique de la rela-tion*, or a cross-cultural poetics, set the cornerstones of a discursive practice whose deliberate disjunctures of language and linearity and discontinuities of character and context reflect the specific tensions and teleologies of the (post)colonial encounter in the Caribbean.

Born in Martinique in 1928, Edouard Glissant has long been the pre-eminent practitioner of literature and theory in the region, beginning in the 1950s. *L'Intention poétique* was the first of his texts to lay out a theoretical framework for literary production; his first novel, *La Lézarde*, won the *Prix Renaudot* upon its publication in 1958 and has since been recognized as one of the seminal works in the Francophone Caribbean literary canon. In his subsequent novels, including such works as *Le quatrième siècle* (1964), *La case du commandeur* (1981), *Tout-Monde* (1995), *Sartorius: Le roman des Batoutos* (1999), and *Ormérod* (2003), as well as several works of criticism, Glissant has advocated an active cognizance of the multitude of factors—historical, political, cultural, and racial—that have worked together to pro-duce that compound cultural entity that is the Caribbean people. In these texts, Glissant outlines the form that this new identity should assume, the goals it should seek to attain, and the tenets of principle on which it should draw, and he charts the potential for subjective alienation and fragmenta-tion if the colonized do not consciously seek to come to terms with the insidious legacy of displacement and division imposed by the colonizer.

Glissant lays out the fundamental aspects of the paradoxes underlying and determining the Caribbean experience in literature and culture in a major theoretical work that appeared in 1981, entitled *Le discours antillais*. Here, Glissant elaborates his vision of the two cornerstones of identity in the Caribbean context: *antillanité*, or Caribbeanness, and a *poétique de la relation*, or a cross-cultural poetics. These two interrelated and interdependent concepts form the basis of Glissant's survey of the specificity of the Caribbean experience, with emphasis being placed on the pluralities that, as a result of social and historical interpolation, have become the principal signs of the Caribbean identity. *Antillanité* demands an awareness of and pride in Caribbean history and culture, a dramatic reversal and overturning of the more traditional devalorization by which the Caribbean has long been figured. In Glissantian terms, it is the specificity of this multiethnic and multilingual solidarity, forged within the region through and out of its cultural diversity, that provides *antillanité* with its character and context. But it is the particular significance of the departmental moment, the presumption of its capacity to divide the regional experience into a sort of ethereal "before" and "after" while simultaneously concealing its preservation of colonial realities that provides Glissant with a *point de repère*, or point of reference, for his exploration of the paradoxes and parameters of French Caribbean identity.

This recodification of the double vision generated by the various temporalities of the colonial encounter—strategically situated between uprooting and transformation—is the discursive terrain that Glissant specifically seeks to turn into hybrid possibilities of postcolonial presence in ways that will recognize the region's constant creative flux and its insistent patterns of transformation and exchange. The ruptures, discontinuities, and contradictions that may be traced through the historical trajectory of the region, from colonization and slavery through the arrival of subsequent settler groups such as the South Asian and Syro-Lebanese populations—with their own languages, religions, and music—to the metropolitan attachments of departmentalization, constitute new contingencies for rewriting the traditional peripheral localization of the Caribbean into a rhetorical reserve of resistance. Glissant insists on the integral relationship between language and subjectivity in the Caribbean region, on the materiality of departmentalization as an alienating structure of neocolonial reality, on the need to recognize the importance of cultural struggle and the pervasive presence and influence of the Other. Such patterns must be confronted and contested if the region is to articulate its subjectivity and recognize its cultural coherence, for it is in this recognition that identitarian affirmation effectively lies.

These complex boundaries of *antillanité* form the framework within which the fictional context of his work is situated; his novels explore and interrogate the fragmented trajectory and multiple subject positions of Martinican and Caribbean history, seeking to identify various points at which the disjunctures of the past can be assimilated into the complex cultural pluralisms of the present. In *Le discours antillais*, translated as *Caribbean Discourse*, he deliberately establishes connections and continuities between the transformative experience of slavery and the development of socio-cultural identity. He writes, "Il y a différence entre le déplacement (par exil ou dispersion) d'un people qui se continue ailleurs et le transbord (la traite) d'une population qui ailleurs *se change en autre chose*, en une nouvelle donnée du monde" (1981, 28) (There is a difference between the transplanting [by exile or dispersion] of a people who continue to survive elsewhere and the transfer [by the slave trade] of a population to another place where they change into something different, into a new set of possibilities) (1989, 14). Some years later, claiming Glissant as a spiritual and philosophical precursor, the architects of *créolité*, the Martinican authors Patrick Chamoiseau and Raphaël Confiant and the Guadeloupean linguist Jean Bernabé, sought to express the diversity of the Caribbean collective identity by articulating structurally similar concerns. Viewing Caribbean creolization as a plantation-driven phenomenon, they view the importance of the rupture, transmission, and transformation of tradition as coming into being in the hold of the slave ship: "Dans la cale, il y a plusieurs langues africaines, plusieurs dieux, plusieurs conceptions du monde. Le cri poussé vient d'où? De quel chiffre culturel, de quelle langue? Sa poétique relèverait-elle d'une totalité qui les préserverait toutes? Nous sommes forcés d'imaginer cela car ce cri contredisait l'intention coloniale" (In the ship's hold, there are several African languages, several gods, several ways of perceiving the world. Where does the cry come from? From which cultural basis, from which language? Will its poetics reveal itself as a whole which will save all? We must imagine this, for this outcry contradicted the colonial purpose) (1993, 33; translation mine). In this silence that marks "the first rupture" (33) there are already the traces of creolized patterns of doubling and transformation that would be further re-sited and fragmented in their subsequent encounter with the variety of cultural axes that ultimately came to determine the expression of Caribbean identity.

Identity, Relation, and Creoleness

Recent tendencies toward what Mimi Sheller has termed "the theorization of the cultural fluidity of 'postmodernity'" have engendered "the consumption of the metaphor of 'creolization' within sites of contemporary metropolitan self-theory, eras[ing] the specificity of Caribbean processes of creolization and of their historical, political, cultural, and economic roots" (2001, 1). But for Glissant, the aptness of *antillanité* as a definitive Caribbean creolizing discourse lies primarily in its capacity to embody and express the creative pluralities and discontinuities of the regional experience: "L'antillanité, revée par les intellectuels, en même temps que nos peuples la vivaient de manière souterraine, nous arrache de l'intolérable propre aux nationalismes nécessaires et nous introduit à la Relation qui aujourd'hui les tempère sans les aliéner. Qu'est-ce que les Antilles en effet? Une multi-relation" (1981, 249) (Caribbeanness, an intellectual dream, lived at the same time in an unconscious way by our peoples, tears us free from the intolerable alternative of the need for nationalism and introduces us to the cross-cultural process that modifies but does not undermine the latter. What is the Caribbean in fact? A multiple series of relationships) (1989, 139).

By inscribing and analyzing destructive regional tendencies toward what he terms Reversion—the misplaced obsession with a single origin—and Diversion—the neocolonial concealment of an ongoing domination—Glissant illuminates the disturbing facets of cultural and historical dispossession and economic hegemony that continue to plague the contemporary French Caribbean.[1] This groundbreaking vision frames the Caribbean condition in explicitly geopolitical terms, illuminating and interrogating the ongoing dilemmas of domination and development, even as it positions the French Caribbean squarely in the forefront of a developing field of discourse that draws upon the unfixed, relational nature of contemporary cultural identity in general and of its Caribbean paradigm in particular. At the same time, however, Glissant underlines the extent to which neocolonial realities continue to threaten the development of this discursive and cultural state of postcolonial awareness. It is in mediating the inscription of a creolized consciousness that helps to shape the articulation of a truly identitarian Caribbean vision that *antillanité* will find its true value:

> Il manque à l'antillanité: de passer du vécu commun à la conscience
> exprimée; de dépasser la postulation intellectuelle prise en compte par
> les élites du savoir et de s'ancrer dans l'affirmation collective appuyée
> sur l'acte des peuples. . . . Nous savons ce qui menace l'antillanité: la

balkanisation historique des îles, l'apprentissage de langues véhicu-
laires différentes et souvent "opposées" (la querelle du francais et de
l'anglo-américain), les cordons ombilicaux qui maintiennent ferme
ou souple beaucoup de ces îles dans la réserve d'une métropole donnée. . . . L'isolement diffère pour chaque île la prise de conscience de
l'antillanité, en même temps qu'il éloigne chaque communauté de sa
vérité proper. (1981, 422–23)

(What is missing from the nation of Caribbeanness is the transition
from the shared experience to conscious expression; the need to transcend the intellectual pretensions dominated by the learned elite and
to be grounded in collective affirmation, supported by the activism of
the people. . . . We know what threatens Caribbeanness: the historical balkanization of the islands, the inculcation of different and often
"opposed" major languages (the quarrel between French and Anglo-
American English), the umbilical cords that maintain, in a rigid or
flexible way, many of these islands within a sphere of influence of a
particular metropolitan power. . . . This isolation postpones in each
island the awareness of a Caribbean identity and at the same time it
separates each community from its own true identity.) (1989, 222)

Here the necessarily multifaceted scope of *antillanité*'s discursive praxis
becomes clear. Drawing on the relation between language, culture, and
identity to pinpoint the myriad forms and formulas of continuing metropolitan domination, the neocolonial tensions that the traces of the colonial
encounter perpetuate impede the Caribbean people from declaring their
multirelational identity. Glissant envisages a network of difference that inscribes a new articulative framework for identity through the latent openness and relational contact mapped by the regional experience. As we shall
see, the patterns prescribed by *créolité* certainly draw on its Glissantian
predecessor in that while *créolité* insists upon the transformative possibilities and pluralities inherent in cultural encounters and exchanges in the
(French) Caribbean context, it establishes its difference from *antillanité*'s
geopolitical concerns by concentrating on developing patterns of creative
expression that reflect and instantiate the multiplicity of the Creole mosaic.
Indeed, it is the Creole language that serves as a fundamental metaphor for
créolité's prise de position, particularly in its structural amalgamation and
transformation of various strands of both African and European lexical and
grammatical patterns. However, while Bernabé, Chamoiseau, and Confi-

ant insist that "*la pleine connaissance de la Créolité sera réservée à l'Art*, à l'Art absolument" (1993, 29) (full knowledge of Creoleness will be reserved for Art, for Art absolutely [90, emphasis in the original]), they are careful at the same time to point out that the Caribbean region has no inherent monopoly on creoleness. As they differentiate between a succession of geographical creolenesses generated out of the "historical maelstrom," they also differentiate this creoleness from the process of creolization: "Tout autre est le processus de créolisation, qui n'est pas propre au seul continent américain . . . et qui désigne la mise en contact brutale, sur des territoires soit insulaires, soit enclaves . . . de populations culturellement différentes" (30) (Altogether different is the process of Creolization, which is not limited to the American continent . . . and which refers to the brutal interaction, on either insular or landlocked territories . . . of culturally different populations) (92). Indeed, some care should be observed here with the attendant risk(s) of overgeneralization, for, as Stuart Hall has recently observed, creolization's "ubiquitous application has eroded its strategic conceptual value" (2003, 28). And it must be acknowledged that not only have the strictures of creoleness been overgeneralized and overapplied; much has been made of the programmatic, prescriptive nature of the formulas for cultural pluralism that can be located within the framework of this self-avowed manifesto. But ultimately, even the authors themselves have veered away from the formulaic implications of *créolité* as cultural construct. Rather than a framework for geopolitical identitarianism, creoleness seeks to mediate the expression of heterogeneous human experiences by valorizing culture itself as a composite construct. This compositeness, in its turn, serves as a marker both of Caribbean ethno-cultural pluralism and of the distinctness of experience that separates the French Caribbean paradigm from the metropolitan.

While acknowledging the groundbreaking work of Aimé Césaire and Edouard Glissant in defining and articulating Caribbeanness, Bernabé, Chamoiseau, and Confiant insistently inscribe a differential identitarian strategy. Since neither the European nor the African paradigm could contain the myriad ethnic influences and creative cultural exchange that had eventuated in the Caribbean, they sought to avoid the structural and philosophical trap of binarism, of exchanging one unitary model of culture for another. Indeed, as some critics have claimed, the paradoxes implicit in such a binary structure led ineluctably to the failure of the negritude movement.[2] Instead, the intrinsic ethnic and cultural pluralism of the islands would be valorized, and to accomplish this, the *créolistes* chose to base their approach on the hybrid, revolutionary character of the Caribbean cultural mosaic:

"Notre Histoire est une tresse d'histoires . . . Car le principe même de notre identité est la complexité. Explorer notre créolité doit s'effectuer dans une pensée aussi complexe que la Créolité elle-même" (1993, 26, 28, 33, emphasis in the original) (Our history is a braid of histories . . . For complexity is the very principle of our identity. Exploring our Creoleness must be done in a thought as complex as Creoleness itself . . . Creoleness . . . involves a double process: *the adaptation . . . to the New World; and the cultural confrontation of these peoples within the same space, resulting in a mixed culture called Creole*) (88, 90, 93, emphasis in the original). The Creole language serves as a fundamental metaphor for the complex exploration of this phenomenon of creolization; the product of the experience of colonization and slavery that was developed on the plantation, it was engendered by the attempts at communication by slaves deliberately separated by ethnic group to forestall the hatching of revolutionary plots. The Creole language and the cross-fertilization it symbolizes bring a new importance to the richness of regional cultural and ethnic admixture: ultimately, the language reinforces those key aspects of pluralism and transformation that undergird the heterogeneity of the Caribbean experience.

The authors are at pains to explain that their concept of Caribbean creoleness drew neither on Europe nor Africa exclusively, but rather sought to valorize the admixture of their influences with those of other cultures: "Le projet n'était pas seulement d'abandonner les hypnoses d'Europe et d'Afrique. Il fallait aussi garder en éveil la claire conscience des apports de l'une et de l'autre: en leurs spécificités, leurs dosages, leurs équilibres, sans rien oblitérer ni oublier des autres sources, à elles melées. . . . *Comprendre ce qu'est l'Antillais*" (21–22) (As a project it was not just aimed at abandoning the hypnoses of Europe and Africa. We had to keep a clear consciousness of our relations with one and the other: in their specificities, their right proportions, their balances, without obliterating or forgetting anything pertaining to the other sources conjugated with them. . . . *to understand what the Caribbean is*) (83, emphasis in the original).

If we extrapolate from these pluralisms of language and culture, then the Caribbean is implicitly inscribed as a geopolitical framework that mediates multiple forms of creative expression. Its intrinsic relationality functions as an overarching figure of innate complexity, conveying its intersubjective ground even as it effaces assumptions of unitary origin by effectively going beyond them: "La Créolité est une annihilation de la fausse universalité, du monolinguisme et de la pureté" (28) (Creoleness is an annihilation of false universality, of monolingualism, and of purity) (90). Plurality and transformation are thus firmly inscribed as the operating tenets of creoleness's discursive *schéma*.

Ultimately, this symbolic re-siting of the binaries and resonances of the colonial encounter functions by positioning the pluralisms of the regional cultural framework to simultaneously dislocate the cycle of metropolitan domination. By reshaping and redefining the borders of departmental identity through the intersecting, transformative patterns of artistic praxis, this creolized cultural vision allows Bernabé, Chamoiseau, and Confiant to turn assumptions of geopolitical marginalization into performative possibilities of discursive presence. What both *antillanité* and *créolité* share, however, lies in the fact that the discursive framework that they project marks both an independence from metropolitan hegemony and an affirmation of ethnocultural interdependence. The resulting discourses embody acts of discursive resistance that, in a critical paradigm shift, are also meant to displace and re-place the continuing binaries implicit in departmentalization's appropriation of (neo)colonial patterns of domination and submission, self and other, center and periphery.

If, in the final analysis, these discourses function as acts of resistance, this resistance is both enabled and contextualized by the arc of colonial history in the Caribbean. Chamoiseau, perhaps more so than his fellow *créolistes*, insists on history's impact on the imaginative process that undergirds artistic expression, a rubric he sets out clearly in his follow-up to the *Eloge de la Créolité/In Praise of Creoleness* entitled *Ecrire en pays dominé* (1997). Here, Chamoiseau sees the primary role of a regionally grounded imagination as the contestation of hegemony through an insistence on opacity. If opacity functions as a key component of a paradoxical Caribbean postcolonial discourse that is not one, it will frame writing in the Caribbean context through its difference from the constraints of linearity and causality, traits that can be linked to the binary system of domination and subordination undergirding colonial ideology and its concomitant praxis. In addition, inscribing the tensions and teleologies of Martinique's complex contemporary materiality combats such binarisms by eschewing traditional, inherited patterns of narrative order, such that the disjunctures and discontinuities of the historical or contemporary Martinican experience attain symbolic force. In this way, the integration of patterns and figures of creoleness will be "powerfully expressive of local conditions," as Stuart Hall puts it (2003, 28), and will constitute a discursive act of cultural resistance and affirmation grounded in *créolité* and functioning as "the existential and expressive basis for cultural production . . . an appendix to the project of national self-constitution"

(35). Thus, Chamoiseau's "sentiment d'un organisme polyrythmique, à voix multiples" (vision of a polyrhythmic organism, with multiple voices) (1997, 186) effectively becomes on this basis the fulcrum for a form of nationalist expression based on complex patterns of cultural syntheses, (re)constituting subjectivity from the material realities of Martinican marginalization.

Of key importance in this discursive *schéma* is the role of the *marqueur de paroles*, a constant fixture in Chamoiseau's fiction and probably just as often misunderstood. Simply put, the *marqueur* is a fictive, self-reflexive invention of Chamoiseau's, figuring in such texts as *Texaco* and *Solibo magnifique* as a contestatory foil for traditional, linear, causal patterns of representation and a subversion and interrogation of the traditional figure of the omniscient narrator. For Chamoiseau, the *marqueur* is the symbolic embodiment of a creative set of ongoing Martinican--as opposed to metropolitan—discontinuities, and more specifically of the Creole language's privileging of the oral over the written for an immediacy of form and expression not easily recuperable. Indeed, it is precisely the attempt to confront this discursive conundrum that grounds the discursive role of the *marqueur*. As the figural representation of the impossibility of representing the immediacy of play and pluralism intrinsic to Creole speech and creolized social structure, the *marqueur*'s goal is realism as well as resistance, a re-citing of discursive hierarchies that preserves their deliberate disjunctures rather than expose them to the procedural processes and discursive displacements that typically serve to mediate the functions of fiction. By thus skirting the authoritarianism and constructed omniscience of traditional narratives, Chamoiseau inscribes both a response and an alternative to a metropolitan discursive hegemony whose universalism seeks through its binary approach to claim indigenous patterns of community and difference. Rather, Chamoiseau's strategy is aimed, as Homi Bhabha puts it, at "elaborating strategies of selfhood . . . that initiate new signs of identity, and innovative sites of collaboration, and contestation, in the act of defining the idea of society itself" (1994, 1–2). In other words, Chamoiseau contests and interrogates key principles of hegemonic metropolitan discourses through a set of differential, transformative narrative acts, drawing on alternative articulations of style, form, and content to inscribe, palimpsest-like, a range of indigenous values and practices. These Creole counterdiscourses take their place alongside—and indeed work to supplant—an inherited metropolitan perspective whose first tendency is to transfer and engender a linear perspective of omniscience and authority in the periphery.

While Glissant's inaugural articulation of creolization as counterdiscourse has apparently adapted to the burgeoning globalization of hybridity between the publication of *Le discours antillais* in 1981 and the appearance of *Poétique de la relation* nine years later, Caribbean contestation for him appears grounded in his nationalistic inscription of the region as an intense, specific paradigm of a more global and variable phenomenon of creolization. Ultimately, Glissant posits, through a praxis of pluralism and polyvalence, disjuncture and discontinuity, a network of regional filiations that seeks to catalyze a nationalism seen as latent even within the departmental paradigm, one that acts as the geopolitical foundation of a flourishing Caribbean community. As Michael Dash explains, "Glissant's vision is different from earlier nationalisms and counter-discursive ideologies because it not only demystifies the imperialistic myth of universal civilization but also rejects the values of hegemonic systems" (1995, 148). By avoiding the linear teleologies of a *response* to metropolitan hegemony, he articulates *alternative* sites and strategies for this circulating, relational Caribbean identity whose fluidities elude the pitfalls of simple negation, of binary notions of origin and derivation that mark a regressive return to colonial thought. It is a moment that effectively constructs a creative framework of postcolonial difference for the French Caribbean, one that locates and adopts the binary framework of the relationship between metropole and department as its starting position, and then adapts and subverts it, transforming the nuanced, Caribbean-inflected sense of *francité* framed and furthered by departmentalism into a strategic site of multiplicity and slippage.

However, far from being read as palliative iterations of a cultural panacea, the Caribbean perspective produced by these voices has itself been subject to critique. The primary proponents of *créolité* have, within recent times, drawn fire for what some have seen as their gender-specific approach to cultural reconstitution. By basing their theory of *oraliture* on the historical figures of the *nègre marron* and the *conteur*, the resulting impression of an exclusionary masculinity grounded in slave-based forms of discursivity and resistance implicitly valorizes the male progenitor, in James Arnold's words, as "the gendered ancestor of all creole culture" (1995, 30). Indeed, Arnold's charge entails not simply the inscription of a penetrating phallocentrism at the heart of *créolité*, but also a challenge to the very validity of the Caribbean maroon as an historical paradigm of political and ethno-cultural independence: "We should note, however, that in the French West Indies these are imaginary, rather than historical, heroes. Moreover, within this model of a nascent creole culture, the maroons could not . . . be the effective vehicle for transmission of the syncretic new culture that would come down to the present day" (29). Yet the history of resistance in Caribbean culture clearly shows that along with widespread maroon forms of guerilla warfare on many islands, the *conteur* or *paroleur* functioned on the plantation as the discursive avatar of such subversive tactics. Indeed, his deriding and disparaging of his colonial master while giving the appearance of articulating another subject entirely is without doubt the immediate harbinger of contemporary musical forms such as calypso, zouk, and reggae, whose satiric and subversive double-entendres speak forcefully to power in the name of the people.

But while contemporary critiques may pinpoint the subtle paradoxes of positionality that can inhabit discourses of difference, ultimately the conjunctural ethno-cultural and discursive framework articulated by *créolité* acts as a viable discursive alternative to the long-standing pattern of metropolitan discursive domination in the French Caribbean. In an extended interview with Lucien Taylor marking the tenth anniversary of the publication of the *Eloge de la Créolité/In Praise of Creoleness*, a certain evolution in perspective and positionality on the part of its creators becomes clear. Raphaël Confiant insists that "the movement of Créolité isn't monolithic" (Bernabé, Chamoiseau, and Confiant 1998, 138), acknowledging that there are indeed a variety of ways and places in which creoleness took shape in the Americas. Patrick Chamoiseau, for his part, clarifies the ways in which his own strategies of discursive resistance have evolved over time: "The modes of resistance have changed. Which is why in *Ecrire en pays dominé* I transform myself from a word scratcher into a warrior. When I called myself a word scratcher, I meant to show how I found myself in an effervescent zone between Creole and French, between the oral and the written, facing the diversity of the world. I've had to transform myself into a warrior who can recognize that the battle against oppression and domination has moved into the realm of the imaginary" (140). In other words, it is the protean nature of regional resistance and its attendant discourses that is being emphasized here, such that the shifting ground of the materialities of domination necessitates a response in the terms and teleologies of regional identitarian affirmation. At the same time, the realities of diasporic dispersion now mediate not just an acknowledgment of critical pluralities, but an assertion that even as creolization has evolved, it continues into the present and extends well beyond the region. Chamoiseau continues, "So yes, the Antilles represent an archetype of creolization. But in general, creolization occurs when a number of peoples and worldviews are precipitated together and forced to get along. And in this sense, all the Americas are places of creolization—as, increasingly, are all the big Western megapoles. In any case, our position is that there are several Créolités. . . . There isn't some Creole essence. There's a state of being-Creole. . . . But this remains permanently in motion, pushing us headlong in a movement of diversity, of change and exchange" (142).

Here, the implicit essentialism perceived in some quarters as residing within the Creole *schéma* has given way to a recognition and, indeed, a praxis of pluralism, movement, and exchange, reflecting and embodying shifting definitions of Caribbeanness and creoleness in contemporary representations of the material conditions of such subjects. Ultimately the place and role of the many are valorized over that of the one, as the *créolistes* put it in their interview: "*Créolité* is all about understanding mosaic, multiple identities" (153). Importantly, this inherited either/or binary is also subverted by the recent observations made on the subject of creoleness by Maryse Condé, the *doyenne* of Guadeloupean letters. As an author and a critic, while acknowledging the differences in perspective and technique that separate her own vision of a Creole community from the specific discursive praxis of *créolité* as defined by Chamoiseau and Confiant, Condé insists that the region has also long been marked by intrinsic, incessant patterns of movement and migration whose myriad socio-cultural and geopolitical influences continue to effect a climate of change in both metropole and department, center and periphery, articulating a punctuality of openness and exchange where nomadic, transhistoric peregrinations transform long-held assumptions regarding French identity. As Glissant points out, such patterns are grounded in resistance and engage and mediate increasingly important contemporary markers of *métissage*:

> La rigidité du système des Plantations a entrainé des formes de résistance dont deux sont constitutives de nos cultures: la fuite ruisée dans le Carnaval, dont il semble qu'elle constitue avant tout une course éperdue hors des limites de la Plantation, et la fuite combattante du marronnage, qui est l'acte de contestation absolument generalisé dans toute la zone de civilisation qui nous concerne . . . cette pratique de métissage . . . met en Relation, sur un mode égalitaire et pour une des premières fois connues, des histories dont nous savons aujourd'hui dans la Caraibe qu'elles sont convergentes. (Glissant 1981, 461–62)

> (The rigid nature of the plantation encouraged forms of resistance, two of which have a shaping force on our cultures: the camouflaged escape of the carnival, which I feel constitutes a desperate way out of

the confining world of the plantation, and the armed flight of mar-
ronnage, which is the most widespread act of defiance in that area of
civilization that concerns us. . . . This practice of cultural Creolization
. . . establishes a cross-cultural relationship, in an egalitarian and unprecedented way, between histories that we know today in the Caribbean are interrelated.) (1989, 248–49)

It is here, at this intersection of history, culture, discourse, and geopolitics whose contemporary emblem is the mediating fluidity of the Caribbean
Sea, that these counterdiscursive intricacies and implications drawn on the
regional experience of marginality increasingly contest the persistent patterns of the disjunctive relationship with the dominant metropolitan center. Rewriting and re-placing the outmoded hierarchies of departmental
integration valorizes this re-siting of regional re-presentation, generating a
poetics of cultural affirmation that interrogates the colonial logic of binary
metropolitan thought as it simultaneously constructs an alternative signifying space for new sites and communities of cultural exchange.

Separately and together, these concurrent maneuvers challenge dominant
hexagonal norms, appropriating discourses to forge new textual patterns of
identitarian transformation. But the terms and conditions of this differential postcoloniality, in which the trace of multiplicity is recuperated and
reflected through discursive structures, themselves raise crucial questions
of scope and referentiality within the postcolonial condition. Indeed, the
region's geopolitical inconsistencies effect our attempts to define the Caribbean postcolonial condition even as they embody and underscore the difficulties implicit in abandoning the circular confines of the colonial experience. Further, the tensions and paradoxes at work within any articulation of
"postcoloniality" will tend to destabilize the possibility of inscribing recent
regional initiatives within the ambit of a discursive space that is itself unfet-
tered by the complications of neocolonialism, migration, colonial asymme-
try, or the acceptance of an implicit teleology of social progress raised by the
(dis)continuities of narrative or (post)colonial history. For while an articulative postcolonial discourse will scrupulously seek to avoid the reductive
gambit of simply responding to colonial stereotypes, the Caribbean experience also shows that the disparate patterns that tend to inform the colonial
experience sometimes seem to persist beyond a political transition to the
postcolonial condition. Questioning the temporalities of the relationship to
the imperial center or the impact of modern metropolitan domination and
the phenomenon of migration tends to recirculate rather than resolve these

ambiguities of geopolitical practice. On the one hand, then, while postcoloniality may been defined as comprising "a concern only with the national
culture after the departure of the imperial power," such a definition appears
to address the cardinal issues of nationalism and self-definition that lie at
the heart of any construction of a postcolonial identity based on notions of
cultural difference and political autonomy. On the other hand, alternative
formulations of postcolonialism seek to "cover all the culture affected by
the imperial process from the moment of colonization to the present day"
(Ashcroft, Griffiths, and Tiffin 1989, 1). While both definitions acknowledge
the importance of addressing the "continuity of preoccupations throughout
the historical process initiated by European imperial aggression" (2), it is
whether substantive change can be located in any transition from a colonial
to a postcolonial positionality, but particularly within the persistently cap-
tious context of departmentalization, that must be interrogated in order to
open up new discursive possibilities for re-siting and resolving the complex
tensions of the colonial encounter. Contesting such exclusionary strategies
without reinscribing their innate, inherited hierarchies poses perhaps the
most cogent challenge to the establishment of an ideologically integrated
postcolonialist position. Still, working to disrupt precarious patterns of discursive authority can articulate difference through the interstices, exploiting
the disparate disjunctures of the relational mosaic.

Counterdiscourse and Caribbean Poetics

The practical articulation of the postmodern, postcolonial paradigm elaborated above amounts to a new discursive approach, an alternative to colonial
binaries whose principal tenets have been described by Benita Parry as incorporating "complex transformations and transgressions of existing con-
ventions, whether realist or avant-garde . . . disrupt(ing)/invigorat(ing) prior
modes by integrating the narrative forms, such as performed storytelling
and public recitation, the aesthetic languages and the perceptual resources
from non-Western literary heritages and cognitive traditions" (2002, 71).
At the crux of this key transformative moment, in which specificities of
cultural form and its corollary of performance join to shape representations
of national identity, the capacity of fiction to "reinvent, defamiliarize, or
undermine authorized versions" as it plays itself out in and through ideology, as Parry claims (76), makes it central to the nascent inscription and
representation of a truly regional and composite Caribbean identity.

If metropolitan hegemony has historically encompassed a range of discourses—literary, economic, political, ethno-cultural—then contesting and subverting such discourses implicitly also entails the articulation of alternative approaches that differentiate themselves from the metropole's dominant agendas while simultaneously appropriating and relocating them. Indeed, as Simon Gikandi and a number of others have argued, our coming to terms with such complex conundrums is critically and intimately linked to understanding "what it means for [such] subjects to be agents in the discursive economy of modernity" (Gikandi 1996, 3). Critically, for the Franco-Caribbean subject, recognizing the importance of an ongoing inscription in the transformative, interrelational framework embodied in the contemporary Caribbean serves to catalyze this penchant for plurality through, in Edouard Glissant's words, "poétique latente, ouverte, multilingue d'intention, en prise avec tout le possible" (1990, 44) (a poetics that is latent, open, multilingual in intention, directly in contact with everything possible) (1997, 32). As discursive contestation comes increasingly to characterize and define Caribbean creoleness, the praxis of counterpoetics that Glissant proposes is intimately linked to specificities of language and community.

These categories are at the forefront of Glissant's vision of discursive difference. As Celia Britton explains, "The value of Glissant's concept of counterpoetics . . . is that it is not restricted to literary language, but is a collective response to the impossibility of a natural autonomous 'own' language. As such, it is a strategy of both resistance and accommodation. It forges its own *language* out of the tension of its relationship to the dominant language, which it simultaneously subverts and restructures" (1999, 34). Indeed, as Glissant insists with regard to Creole, its "génie est de toujours s'ouvrir, c'est-à-dire peut-être de ne se fixer que selon des systèmes de variables que nous aurons à imaginer autant qu'à définir" (1990, 46) (genius consists in always being open, that is, perhaps, never becoming fixed except according to systems of variables that we have to imagine as much as define) (1997, 34). In this *schéma* of openness and exchange, form also plays a critical role. When Glissant points out in *Le discours antillais* that realism is not a "natural" literary practice among colonized peoples, he contextualizes the narrative experimentation that is an integral element in this literature's quest for alternative modes of expression and representation. Tropes of difference and division increasingly overdetermine major aspects of this writing, especially in terms of character, narrative structure, and narrative voice, and with the historical landscape coming to play an unusually significant role in the development of both character and plot:

J'ai propose ailleurs que la langue nationale est la langue dans laquelle un people produit. . . . Or le réalisme, théorie et technique de la réproduction littéraire ou "totale", n'est pas inscrit dans le reflexe culturel des peuples africains ou americains. . . . La misère de nos pays n'est pas seulement présente, patente. Elle comporte une dimension d'histoire (d'histoire non évidente) dont le seul réalisme ne rend pas compte. . . . Il arrive que l'oeuvre ne soit pas écrite *pour quelqu'un*, mais pour démonter les mécanismes complexes de la frustration et des variétés infinies de l'oppression. (Glissant 1981, 198, 200, emphasis in the original)

(I have argued elsewhere that a national language is the one in which a people produces. . . . Now realism, the theory and technique of literal or "total" representation, is not inscribed in the cultural reflex of African or American peoples. . . . The misery of our lands is not only present, obvious. It contains a historical dimension (of not obvious history) that realism alone cannot account for. . . . It can happen that the work is not written *for someone*, but to dismantle the complex mechanism of frustration and the infinite forms of oppression.) (1989, 102, 105, 107, emphasis in the original)

The poetics of cultural specificity will thus assume a variety of forms in these authors' works, with shifts in temporality and point of view, narrative fragmentation and ethno-cultural intersection coming to signify the multivalent, discontinuous character of Caribbean creoleness both at home and in the diasporic "megapoles," in Chamoiseau's phrase. In the quest for identitarian subjectivity through discourse, narrative form embodies strategies of resistance predicated on new paths of cultural pluralism.

Further, as Glissant goes on to insist in his more recent *Introduction à une poétique du divers*, given the lexical and linguistic complexity of Creole languages, as well as the transformative fluidities stemming both from their originary plantation setting and from their bridging of colonial and metropolitan universalisms, the centrality of Creole languages to this identitarian *schéma* of openness and exchange—one that deliberately contests colonial notions of the singular—should be neither underestimated nor misjudged: "Confrontés au désordre implacable du colon, ils connurent ce génie . . . de fertiliser ces traces. . . . Les langues créoles sont des traces frayées dans la baille de la Caraïbe et de l'Océan Indien" (Confronting the colonizer's implacable disorder, they possessed the genius . . . to cultivate these traces.... The Creole languages are traces carved out of the Caribbean Sea and the Indian Ocean) (1996, 70). Despite the signal differences in form and function between *antillanité* and *créolité*, then, we can perhaps finally discern a certain discursive and philosophical commonality in their mutual quest to contest the ongoing metropolitan hegemonies to which *domtomisme* (the principle of departmental parity with the hexagon) is made subject through the judicious appropriation of local traces of historical, geopolitical, and ethno-cultural discontinuity to inscribe new formalities of pluralism and performance. For if, in Hall's words, creolization "is what defines the distinctiveness of Caribbean cultures: their 'mixed' character, their creative vibrancy, their complex, troubled, unfinished relation to history" (2003, 31), then he speaks here not only to the compound and varied patterns of the Caribbean mosaic, but also to key questions of historical subjection and, indeed, of whose history is inscribed and in what terms. Ultimately, it is in recognizing the overwhelming importance of discursive power, and by creatively appropriating the disjunctures emerging from the intersections of literature and culture that these indigenous patterns may be successfully turned into the fertile ground of in(ter)vention. Born of the intrinsic pluralism of plantation encounters, and refined over time as practical tools of communication and resistance, the disruptive non-linearities of the creolized horizon of Caribbean counterdiscourse consciously averts the universalizing continuities of the past even as they forge alternative foundations for Caribbean self-expression.

Notes

1. See Glissant 1981 for his presentation and discussion of these critical and interrelated historico-cultural phenomena.

2. See, for example, Taylor, *The Narrative of Liberation*, especially chapter 5.

Works Cited

Arnold, A. James. 1995. "The Gendering of *Créolité*." In *Penser la créolité*, ed. Maryse Condé and Madeleine Cottenet-Hage, 21–40. Paris: Karthala.

Ashcroft, Bill, Gareth Griffiths, and Helen Tiffin. 1989. *The Empire Writes Back: Theory and Practice in Post-Colonial Literatures.* New York: Methuen.

Bernabé, Jean, Patrick Chamoiseau, and Raphaël Confiant. 1993. *Eloge de la Créolité/In Praise of Creoleness.* Trans. M. B. Taleb-Khyar. Bilingual edition. Paris: Gallimard.

———. 1998. "Créolité Bites, an Interview with Lucien Taylor." *Transition* 74: 124–61.

Bhabha, Homi K. 1990. "Introduction: Narrating the Nation." In *Nation and Narration*, ed. Homi K. Bhabha, 1–7. New York: Routledge.

———. 1994. *The Location of Culture*. New York: Routledge.

Britton, Celia. 1999. *Edouard Glissant and Postcolonial Theory: Strategies of Language and Resistance*. Charlottesville: University of Virginia Press.

Chamoiseau, Patrick. 1997. *Ecrire en pays dominé*. Paris: Gallimard.

Chamoiseau, Patrick, and Raphaël Confiant. 1991. *Lettres creoles: Tracées antillaises et continentales de la littérature, 1635–1975*. Paris: Hatier.

Condé, Maryse. 1995. "Chercher nos vérités." In *Penser la créolité*, ed. Maryse Condé and Madeleine Cottenet-Hage, 305–10. Paris: Karthala. Translations from the French are my own.

Dash, J. Michael. 1995. *Edouard Glissant*. New York: Cambridge University Press.

Gikandi, Simon. 1996. "Introduction: Africa, Diaspora, and the Discourse of Modernity." *RAL* 27.4: 1–6.

Glissant, Edouard. 1981. *Le discours antillais*. Paris: Seuil.

———. 1989. *Caribbean Discourse*. Trans. J. Michael Dash Charlottesville: University of Virginia Press.

———. 1990. *Poétique de la relation*. Paris: Gallimard.

———. 1996. *Introduction à une poétique du divers*. Paris: Gallimard. Translations from this text are my own.

———. 1997. *Poetics of Relation*. Trans. Betsy Wing. Ann Arbor: University of Michigan Press.

Hall, Stuart. 2003. "Créolité and the Process of Creolization." In *Créolité and Creolization: Documenta 11 Platform 3*, ed. Okwui Enwezor, Carlos Basualdo, Susanne Ghez, Sarat Maharaj, Mark Nash, Octavio Zaya, 27–41. Ostfildern-Ruit, Germany: Hatje Cantz.

Manuel, Peter, Kenneth Bilby, and Michael Largey. 1995. *Caribbean Currents: Caribbean Music from Rumba to Reggae*. Philadelphia: Temple University Press.

Ormerod, Beverley. 1985. *An Introduction to the French Caribbean Novel*. London: Heinemann.

Parry, Benita. 2002. "Directions and Dead Ends in Postcolonial Studies." In *Relocating Postcolonialism*, ed. David Theo Goldberg and Ato Quayson, 66–81. London: Blackwell.

Sheller, Mimi. 2001. "Theoretical Piracy on the High Seas of Global Culture: Appropriations of 'Creolization' in the Discourses of Globalization." Paper presented at the conference (Re)Thinking Caribbean Culture, University of the West Indies, Cave Hill, Barbados, June 4–8.

Taylor, Patrick. 1985. *The Narrative of Liberation*. Ithaca, N.Y.: Cornell University Press.

Terdiman, Richard. 1985. *Discourse/Counter-Discourse: The Theory and Practice of Symbolic Resistance in Nineteenth-Century France*. Ithaca, N.Y.: Cornell University Press.

Tiffin, Helen. 1995. "Post-Colonial Literatures and Counter-Discourse." In *Post-Colonial Studies Reader*, ed. Bill Ashcroft, Gareth Griffiths, and Helen Tiffin, 95–99. New York: Routledge.

Contributors

Gislene Aparecida dos Santos of São Paulo, Brazil, is a member of the Graduate Board on Human Rights of the Faculty of Law at the University of São Paulo and is an assistant professor in the university's Department of Public Policy. She was recently nominated to the Universidade de São Paulo's Public Policy Commission on Blacks and has also carried out postdoctoral research on race and society at King's College, London. Her published books include *Universidade, formação, cidadania* (2000), *A invenção do ser negro* (2001; 2006), *Estudos sobre Ética* (2002), and *Mulher negra, homem branco: Um breve estudo do feminino negro* (2004). She has a forthcoming book, *Percepções da diferença*, and is engaged in research on the politics of recognition and on affirmative action in Brazil.

Denise Y. Arnold is an Anglo-Bolivian anthropologist. Her interests include kinship and gender, Andean literatures, textual practices and visual languages, and methodologies and data interpretation. She has been a Leverhulme Research Fellow and an ERSC Senior Research Fellow in England, and she is currently teaching at the Universidad Mayor de San Andrés (UMSA) and Universidad para la Investigación Estratégica en Bolivia (UPIEB) in La Paz, Bolivia, and the Universidad de Tarapacá in Chile. She is a visiting research professor at Birbeck College in London and the director of the Instituto de Lengua y Cultura Aymara in Bolivia. Among her recent publications are *River of Fleece, River of Song* (2001); "The Nature of Indigenous Literatures in the Andes: Aymara, Quechua and Others," in *Literary Cultures of Latin America: A Comparative History* (2004); *The Metamorphosis of Heads: Textual Struggles, Education and Land in the Andes* (2006); and *Hilos sueltos: Los Andes desde el textil* (2007).

Jerome Branche is professor of Latin American literature and cultural studies and chair of the Department of Hispanic Languages and Literatures at the University of Pittsburgh. He is the author of *Colonialism and Race in Luso-Hispanic Literature* (2006), the editor of and a contributor to *Lo que teníamos que tener: Raza y revolución en Nicolás Guillén* (2003), and the coeditor (with Ellen Cohn and John Mullennix) of and a contributor to *Diversity across the Curriculum: A Practical Guide for Faculty* (2007). His articles have appeared in *Revista Iberoamericana, The Afro-Hispanic Review, The Bulletin of Latin American Research,* and the *Latin American Research Review,* among others. He is currently working on a book on transatlantic black poetics.

Carolle Charles is an associate professor of sociology at Baruch College. Her research and teaching concentrate on processes and agencies both in Haitian society and within the Haitian immigrant communities of North America, especially three interconnected areas of research: labor migration and transnational patterns of migrants' identities; the dynamic of race, culture, and history; and gender and empowerment. She received a Fulbright award for study in Haiti in 2000–2001. She has been on the editorial boards of the journals *Gender and Society, Identity,* a journal of transnationalism, and *Wadabaguei,* a journal of Caribbean studies. She is also a member of many scholarly organizations, among others, the American Sociological Association, the Latin American Studies Association, and the Haitian Studies Association. She currently serves on the executive boards of the Caribbean Studies Association and the Haitian Studies Association. Her essays have appeared in many scholarly journals and as book chapters.

Michael Handelsman's principal teaching interests are Latin American narrative, Ecuadorian literature and culture, concepts of national identity, women writers, literary journals, Afro-Hispanic literature, and globalization. He has been the recipient of a research grant from the Organization of American States and of six Fulbright fellowships. His most recent book, *Leyendo la globalización desde la mitad del mundo: Identidad y resistencias en el Ecuador* received the Isabel Tobar Guarderas Award for outstanding book published in the social sciences in Ecuador in 2005 and the A. B. Thomas Book Award from the Southeastern Council of Latin American Studies (2006). Among his other published books are *Amazonas y artistas: Un estudio de la prosa de la mujer ecuatoriana* (1978), *El modernismo en las revistas literarias del Ecuador: 1895–1930* (1981), *Incursiones en el mundo literario del Ecuador* (1987), *En torno al verdadero Benjamín Carrión* (1989), *El ideario de Benjamín Carrión* (1992), *Lo afro y la plurinacionalidad: El caso ecuatoriano visto desde su literatura* (1999; 2001), and *Culture and Customs of Ecuador*

(2000). Professor Handelsman has been a visiting graduate professor at the University of Kentucky, the Universidad Católica Santiago de Guayaquil, and the Universidad Andina Simón Bolívar in Quito.

H. Adlai Murdoch is an associate professor of French and Francophone literature and African-American studies at the University of Illinois at Urbana–Champaign. His articles have appeared in *Callaloo, Yale French Studies, Research in African Literatures, Sites, College Literature,* and the *Journal of Commonwealth and Postcolonial Studies*. He is the author of *Creole Identity in the French Caribbean Novel* (2001) and the coeditor of the essay collection *Postcolonial Theory and Francophone Literary Studies* (2005), of a special double issue of the *International Journal of Francophone Studies* titled "Oceanic Dialogues: From the Black Atlantic to the Indo-Pacific" (2005)," and of a special issue of the *Journal of Caribbean Literatures* entitled "Migrations and Métissages" (2006).

Laurence Prescott is an associate professor of Spanish and African American studies in the Department of Spanish, Italian, and Portuguese at the Pennsylvania State University at University Park, where he teaches a variety of graduate and undergraduate courses, including Spanish American literature, Latin American civilization, and Afro–Latin American literature and civilization. He is the author of *Candelario Obeso y la iniciación de la poesía negra en Colombia* (1985) and *Without Hatreds or Fears: Jorge Artel and the Struggle for Black Literary Expression in Colombia* (2000), which was recognized as a Choice 2001 Outstanding Academic Title. He has also been published in *Latin American Research Review, Revista de Estudios Colombianos, The Langston Hughes Review, Afro-Hispanic Review, Revista Iberoamericana, Crítica Hispánica,* and other journals, and he has contributed chapters to several books. He is currently working on a study of African American life and culture in Spanish American travel literature and a critical bibliography of Afro-Colombian writers while also serving as the president of the Afro–Latin American Research Association.

José Rabasa teaches in the Department of Spanish and Portuguese at the University of California at Berkeley. He is the author of *Inventing America: Spanish Historiography and the Formation of Eurocentrism* (1993) and *Writing Violence on the Northern Frontier: The Historiography of New Mexico and Florida and the Legacy of Conquest* (2000).

Kelvin Santiago-Valles is an associate professor in the Sociology Department at the State University of New York at Binghamton. His research and teaching focus on the African diaspora, the Hispanic Caribbean, and the Americas. He is the author of *Subject Peoples and Colonial Discourses: Economic Transformation and Social Disorder in Puerto Rico, 1898–1947* (1994). He is currently finishing a book manuscript titled *Global Racial Regimes in the Historical Long-Term: Social Regulation in the Spanish Atlantic, 1720–1870* and has published several articles and book chapters in his areas of expertise.

Marcia Stephenson is an associate professor of Spanish and women's studies at Purdue University at West Lafayette. Her book *Gender and Modernity in Andean Bolivia* (1999) received the A. B. Thomas Award for excellence. She has also published articles in the *Latin American Research Review, Escarmenear: Revista boliviana de estudios culturales, Debate feminista, Chasqui*, and *MLN*. She is working on a book project on the history of the exportation of Andean camelids to Europe and the United States.

Gustavo Verdesio is an associate professor in the Department of Romance Languages and Literatures and the Program in American Culture at the University of Michigan. He teaches courses on colonial Latin America, indigenous cultures, and popular culture. A revised English edition of his book *La invención del Uruguay* (1996) has been published as *Forgotten Conquests* (2001). He is the coeditor (with Alvaro F. Bolaños) of the collection *Colonialism Past and Present* (2002). He has also edited an issue of the journal *Dispositio/n* (2005) dedicated to the assessment of the legacy of the Latin American Subaltern Studies group. His articles have appeared in *Texto crítico, Bulletin of Hispanic Studies, Revista de crítica literaria latinoamericana*, and *Revista Iberoamericana*, among other journals.

Index

Figures are indicated by an italicized f after the page number.

www.ingramcontent.com/pod-product-compliance
Lightning Source LLC
Chambersburg PA
CBHW020525270326
41927CB00006B/453